Time, Energy and the Psychology of Healing

Helen Graham

Jessica Kingsley Publishers
London

First published in the United Kingdom in 1990 by
Jessica Kingsley Publishers Ltd
118 Pentonville Road
London N1 9JN

Copyright © 1990 Helen Graham

British Library Cataloguing in Publication Data
Graham, Helen
　Time, energy and the psychology of healing.
　1. Alternative medicine
　I. Title
　615.5

ISBN 1-85302-066-4

Printed and bound in Great Britain by
Biddles Ltd, Guildford and King's Lynn

Contents

The Case for Complementary Medicine

A man came across the Mulla Nasrudin searching for something on the ground. 'What have you lost Mulla?' he asked. 'My key' replied Nasrudin. So they both went down on their knees and looked for it. After some time the man asked Nasrudin 'Where exactly did you drop it?', to which Nasrudin replied 'In my house'.

'Then why are we looking here?'

'Because there is more light here than inside my house' replied Nasrudin.

(Idries Shah, 1973, p.26)

Although Nasrudin's behaviour seems absurd, it is precisely what most of us do when we have a problem. Rather than search within ourselves we look outside, often recruiting the services of others, in the hope that we will find the key to a solution. This is nowhere more apparent than in the field of healing, or medicine (from the Latin *medicina*: the art of healing) which, perhaps more than any other discipline is expected to shed light on the human condition. In its attempts to do so, the medical profession has tended, like Nasrudin, to look where the light is good, the systematic investigation and apparent clarity of medical research and practice being greatly preferred in our culture to the mysterious fumblings of self-cure.

Certainly medical science has made some startling and significant discoveries and yielded important keys to understanding numerous conditions. Therefore, the possibility that, like Nasrudin, medicine is looking in the wrong place has rarely been considered - that is, until fairly recently when, despite its many advances, it has become clear that throughout the Western world there is a profound crisis in medicine and a growing disillusionment and dissatisfaction with health care, especially among those who provide it. As American physician Larry Dossey has observed 'in many ways medicine has never been weaker... medicine isn't right and we know it' (1982, p.ii). Moreover, as Illich (1975, p.35) indicates, 'the evidence needed for the indictment of our current medical system is not secret; it can be gleaned from prestigious medical journals and research reports.' What these reveal is that there is no evidence of any direct relation between change in disease patterns and the so-called progress of medicine, but rather that the environment is the primary determinant of the state of general health of any population. Thus, despite widespread belief to the contrary, the increased life expectancy of modern times is less a triumph for medicine than for improved sanitation, nutrition, housing, working conditions and standards of living, smaller families and other social improvements.

Analysis of disease trends reveals that the incidence of most bacterial diseases began to fall long before the introduction of sulfonamide drugs and antibiotics, ninety percent of the total decline in the combined death rate from scarlet fever, diphtheria, whooping cough and measles after 1860 having occurred before the advent of these drugs or mass immunization (Illich 1975). Similarly by the advent of Streptomycin in 1947, ninety-five per cent of the total decline in mortality from tuberculosis since 1800 had been achieved, and decline in mortality from streptococcal infections and pneumonia followed much the same pattern (LeShan 1984). The decline of cholera, dysentery and typhoid was also largely outside medical control. Advances in agriculture led to more varied and nutritious foods, giving rise to better diet and greater resistance to infection, assisted by developments in the purification of water, the pasteurization of milk, better food hygiene and improved sewage disposal. Thus, as Ornstein and Sobel (1988) point out, the farmer, food handler and sewage engineer deserve credit for improved health rather than doctors: 'Medicine has had some contribution to health but its interventions in disease has been greatly over-emphasized as to their real effectiveness and worth to society'. They conclude that 'People are healthier today not because they receive all this well-publicised better treatment when ill but simply because they tend not to become ill in the first place' (p.24). Accordingly, the effectiveness of doctors is largely illusory.

Stanway (1982) has suggested that the impact of drugs on infection is also an illusion. While this is not a position most doctors would support, drugs having played an unquestionable role in the control of pneumonia, gonorrhea, syphilis, malaria and many other conditions, it is nevertheless true to say that they account for only a small proportion of the increase in life expectancy, and have a very high price in terms of drug-induced illness and dependence. Certainly claims made for drugs have to be carefully evaluated and the benefits weighed against their dangers, drawbacks and disadvantages, which Weitz in his alarming book *Health Shock* (1980) shows to be considerable.

The possible dangers of drugs have been highlighted in recent years by scandals surrounding the anti-arthritic drug Opren, chemical contraceptives such as the Dalcon Shield and Depoprovera, tranquillisers such as Ativan; and their overprescription by many physicians (Fitzsimons 1988). Increasingly, attention is being drawn to the unwanted side-effects of medicines, or combinations which counteract each other (Dusquesne and Reeves 1982); addictive, mutilating and mutagenic drugs, and those which induce superinfection or contribute to drug resistant strains (Illich 1975; Weitz 1980). Fulder (1987) indicates that two-fifths of patients receiving drugs in treatment suffer side effects in many cases more serious than the problem being treated. Furthermore, the Boston Collaborative Drug Survey which monitored 1900 hospital patients, found that one in three suffered adverse drug effects, and that one in two hundred die from these, which is more than the number killed annually on U.S. roads. Fulder also draws attention to a recent World Health Congress report which indicates that 25 million people have sustained some permanent damage from drugs used in psychiatric treatment. It is therefore perhaps not surprising if 'the first movement away from what Western medicine has to offer starts with a disenchantment or even frank horror of what drugs do to people, mainly because going to the doctor has become synonymous with drugtaking' (Stanway 1982 p.19).

If going to the doctor has come to mean taking drugs, then going into hospital has become synonymous with undergoing surgery. Although life-threatening conditions such as appendicitis and peritonitis respond to surgery, Stanway observes that the actual amount of lifesaving surgery is minimal - a tiny fraction of the total - which is mostly for preventable conditions such as hernias, haemorrhoids or gallstones; and much is avoidable and unnecessary. Indeed, Illich (1975) claims that unnecessary surgery has become a standard procedure. This is certainly the case in obstetrics, where, as LeShan (1984) observes, in practice pregnancy is treated as 'a nine-month self-limiting illness often requiring surgery at the end'. Twenty-five per cent of births in the USA and 20 per cent in Canada are achieved by Caesarian section, and the number is rising (Hodgkinson 1988). Moreover, this trend is being followed in Europe. Concern has been expressed within the medical profession (*Lancet* Editorial Sept. 1988) about the growing trend towards Caesarian births in Britain. During 1988 this reached an all-time high of 11.3 per cent - that is, some 75,000 births annually. At some hospitals the rate is one in seven births, at others as high as one in five, and few of these are justified on health grounds, invariably being performed, as Hodgkinson indicates, for administrative convenience. Furthermore, Britain is following the American trend whereby up to 65 per cent of hospital deliveries employ forceps or vacuum extraction (Weitz 1980). As a result of these procedures, there is twice the chance of a baby being born brain damaged or dying during birth in the USA, where almost all births occur in hospital, than in Holland, where more than half the births take place within the home. Moreover, despite modern surgical techniques and drugs, infection and fever still occur in one in five mothers who undergo Caesarian section, and psychological disturbance is not uncommon.

It is not only babies and their mothers who are at risk from surgery. Illich draws attention to US Department of Health statistics which reveal that seven per cent of all patients suffer compensatable injuries while hospitalised; and to the fact that an estimated one in five patients admitted to a typical university teaching hospital acquires an iatrogenic or doctor-created disease (from the Greek *iatros*: doctor and *genesis*: origin), which would not have occurred without medical intervention. Indeed, of 815 consecutive patients studied at the Boston University Medical Centre, 36 per cent were being treated because of health problems created directly or indirectly by medicine itself (Fulder 1987). Sometimes this is a relatively trivial matter, although usually requiring special treatment, but as Illich indicates, one case in thirty leads to the patient's death.

Half of these incidents result from the complications of drug therapy, and an alarming one in ten from diagnostic procedures. Cousins (1981, p.29) points to other shortcomings in the practices of modern hospitals:

> The surprising lack of respect for basic sanitation; the rapidity with which staphylocci and other pathogenic organisms can run through an entire hospital; the extensive and sometimes promiscuous use of X-ray equipment; the seemingly indiscriminate administration of tranquillisers and powerful painkillers, sometimes more for the convenience of hospital staff in managing patients than for therapeutic needs; and the regularity with which hospital routine takes precedence over the rest requirements of the patient.

On the basis of these and similar observations Illich suggests that the medical establishment has itself become a major threat to health, with dysfunction, disability and anguish resulting from technical medical intervention now rivalling the morbidity due to traffic, work and even war-related activity. He concludes that 'It is only a matter of time before the majority of patients find out what epidemiological research discovers: most of the time they would be better off suffering without recourse to medicine' (1975, p.52).

It would appear, as LeShan (1984, p.1) suggests, that everyone has their own horror story about those who have suffered desperately from treatment methods, wrong diagnosis, incorrect treatment; those whose records have been lost, or have been told 'ten different truths by ten different experts'. Such experiences have led many people to lose confidence in medicine, to question its progress and its emphasis, which is predominantly on what Stanway terms 'plumbing'.

> This leaves a vast area that is badly taught, poorly understood and indeed almost ignored by modern Western medicine - the mind the soul and the spirit. So badly have most doctors been trained in these areas that they can't even recognise the malfunction of the mind, soul or spirit when it stares them in the face and even if they did most of them wouldn't be adequately trained to cope with it. And all of this in the face of studies that have shown that up to 40% of all patients seen by doctors in the West have nothing physically wrong with them at all (1982, p.23).

Indeed, as he observes, many patients simply don't need Western medicine *per se*, some eighty per cent of all conditions currently treated by doctors being self-limiting or chronic psychological and social problems. LeShan (1984) endorses this view, indicating that there is very little relationship between the physician's training and the tasks they are expected to perform. This, he suggests, has led to confusion, disappointment and anger in both the general public and members of the medical profession itself.

Recent research on the treatment of pain, reported by Gillie (1989) highlights the difficulty. A study conducted at the University of Southampton to investigate how much doctors knew about pain relief revealed that there was teaching on this subject in only 4 out of 21 medical schools in Britain and, even where taught, it was given only an average of 3.5 hours over a 5 year medical course, yet pain is one of the most common symptoms that doctors are required to deal with.

Viewing people solely in terms of 'plumbing' - by organ or disease only, as 'heart' or 'kidney' cases to the neglect of their other features - has other important consequences, which contribute in no small measure to the uncaring and inhumane character of much modern medicine. As LeShan observes, 'the more we learn about the technical craft of saving physical life, the less we seem to keep in touch with the *human art* of caring about the person' (1984, p.2). This is nowhere more evident than within hospitals. Although the word hospital derives from the Latin for 'guest', seldom are such institutions truly hospitable, as Siegel (1986, p.17) observes, with 'little attention ... given to caring and healing as opposed to medicating.' As a result hospitals are, according to Cousins (1981, p.29) 'no place for a person who is seriously ill'. Many of those needing contact with hospitals feel lost, alone, confused, anonymous and alienated, and this has led many people to turn to alternative therapies which are holistic and humanistic, having full regard for all aspects of the person, - physical, psychological, emotional, social and spiritual, - rather than viewing them merely as a collection of functioning or non-functioning parts. Ornstein and Sobel (1988, p.30) liken the general disregard of social and mental factors in health to the attitude prevalent in the 1800s when surgeons ridiculed the concept of sepsis and the germ theory of disease: 'Surgeons persisted in operating in unclean surroundings, sometimes defiantly sharpening their scalpels on the soles of their shoes to show their contempt for the putative power of invisible germs.' Similarly, they argue, the current ignorance and insensitivity to the 'invisible' symbolic messages in human interactions, including those between doctor and patient, limits the effectiveness of contemporary medicine.

The failure of many doctors to respond to patients as human beings - to neither listen to them nor give them information about their condition and treatment - accounts for much of the drift towards alternative approaches which recognise the person's role in maintaining health and overcoming disease, and encourage active participation in treatments which are non-invasive and non-iatrogenic. 'Advice like "its your age" or "you'll have to learn to put up with it" is beginning to wear thin and many people are seeking desperately for alternatives which will hold the promise of improved health' (Gibson and Gibson 1987). Indeed, as Patel (1987) observes, an increasingly well-informed public is becoming progressively disappointed with the failure of scientific medicine to live up to its promise and fulfil popular expectations, and demanding alternatives. Recognition of this fact prompted Glasgow University to announce in 1987 its intention to follow the universities of Manchester and Leicester in examining all future medical students in their ability to communicate with, and relate to patients.

Failure to do so not only loses patients, but also medical staff. Rankin-Box (1988) suggests that nurses are disillusioned with current approaches to health. While an holistic approach is the very cornerstone of nursing, nurses being trained to assess and respond to the person at every level, in practice this is denied within the existing system. A major cause of staff wastage in nursing is therefore the uncaring attitude within the medical profession; its authoritarian fixed attitudes, and treatment of people as machines (Lindop 1987,8).

Advocates of modern medicine argue that staff wastage and other shortcomings of medicine and health care services - shortage of hospital beds, ward closures, long waiting lists, lack of specialist nurses and trained personnel - are the direct result of underfunding and that, given more medical services, more people would be more healthy. However, as Ornstein and Sobel (1988, p.25) observe:

> In many respects people in developed Western societies have reached an age of diminishing returns whereby more and more medical care and more and more medical expenditures will probably contribute only marginally to better health because the increasing medical care and medical approaches were not responsible in the first place for much of it.

Illiffe (1988) supports such a view, indicating that life expectancy in Sweden has not increased over the last twenty years although its expenditure on health care has multiplied six times, and Scotland, which has a much higher per capita health expenditure than England, also has a much higher death rate for most of the common conditions. Moreover, despite vastly increased expenditure on its National Health Service, death rates in Britain from heart disease have not fallen as they have in other countries, infant mortality has increased, immunisation levels are low, and deaths from cervical cancer unnecessarily high. He claims that many of these failures stem not from underfunding *per se* but from government policies, widening economic division, mass unemployment and failure to tackle smoking, alcohol abuse and poor nutrition. Illiffe therefore identifies two crises in modern medicine - one a direct consequence of economic recession, and one a long-term structural crisis of medicine itself running over decades and common to the advanced industrial societies, which is the result of the system focusing on disease rather than health. Indeed, as Smith (1988) observes, the British Government's reaction to the growing impotence of the National Health Service is to urge greater attention to health, as opposed to disease.

It can be argued, however, that the current crisis in health care is rather more fundamental than Illiffe suggests, being conceptual in nature rather than either structural or economic. Increasingly, it is being recognised that Western medicine has built its notions of both health and disease around a conceptual model of the universe which is no longer tenable; a model which was fundamentally flawed from the outset, but is now outmoded and inappropriate to the world we live in. While the physical sciences have recognised this and have attempted since the early part of this century to revise their model, medicine has ignored these developments totally, with the result that it is left with a set of guiding beliefs 'as antiquated as are body humours, bloodletting and leeching' (Dossey 1982).

> Modern medicine has learned to look to the hard sciences as models, hoping to embody the precision and exactness demonstrated most notably by classical physics. Believing we have actually found that precision, we in medicine refuse to listen to the message that has come from physics for over half a century; that the exactness never existed. Today medicine is like a loser in a shell game - once we saw it, now we don't (Dossey 1982, p.xii).

Therefore the fundamental crisis in modern medicine, and one which urgently needs to be addressed, is not finance, politics or organisation, but that of perception - of the way in which the universe and man's place in it are viewed.

The world view which underpins contemporary Western medicine is generally unquestioned, it being assumed to be correct and the only view possible in the light of modern discoveries and knowledge. Accordingly, medicine grounded in the physical sciences is held to be the only way of mediating between people and disease. Alternative views, whether those of earlier epochs or other cultures, and medical approaches derived from them, where recognised at all, tend to be dismissed and even despised as 'primitive', defective, inadequate and inferior and, although untested, are disparaged in practice. It therefore comes as something of a shock to those who hold these views to realise that the world view which has emerged in the physical sciences of the West over the past half century is not only radically different to that on which contemporary medicine is based, but is also strikingly similar to those of ancient and oriental traditions. Such an awareness casts 'alternative' (ie non-scientific) approaches to healing in a very different light. Ironically therefore, if modern medicine is to be in the vanguard of scientific progress rather than consigned to its fringe, the medical profession, together with those striving to understand the growing appeal and acceptance of alternative approaches to healing, needs to recognise that many of these approaches are in fact complementary to any scientific medicine worthy of the name, and need to be given full and serious consideration. His Royal Highness, The Prince of Wales, in a written letter of 29th June 1983, urged the British Medical Association, of which he is president, to do precisely this:

> Sophistication is only skin deep, and when it comes to healing people, it seems to me that account has to be taken of sometimes long neglected complementary methods of healing which, in the right hands, can bring considerable relief, if not hope, to an increasing number of people.

What follows is an attempt to take account of various complementary methods of healing and the perspectives on which they are based, so as to highlight similarities and common themes which integrate these apparently disparate approaches within a common framework.

Part I

Perspectives:
Ancient, Modern, Eastern, Western

Chapter 1

Ancient Perspectives on Healing

The harmony of body and soul - how much that is! We in our madness have separated
the two and have invented a realism that is vulgar and an ideality that is void.

(Oscar Wilde: The Picture of Dorian Gray)

It might be supposed that the world view of early man was shrouded in mystery and that
without modern day understanding of mundane phenomena such as the weather or
seasonal and diurnal change the world was a magical and awesome place. However,
there are indications in the *Huang Ti Nei Ching* (The Yellow Emperor's Treatise on
Internal Medicine c. 770-467 BC) and elsewhere, that there existed an ancient wisdom
whereby man instinctively and collectively understood, and lived in accordance with,
the fundamental forces of nature. This wisdom was not a function of intellect or
reasoning about things but rather an intuitive grasping the truth of things; a seeing into
them. This instinctive aperception of reality, which Roszack (1970) describes as 'our
inherent attunement with the magical', is hinted at in various teachings which have been
passed down through history. However, as Butler (1982) observes, throughout the ages
magic has been so obscured by the 'lush growth of superstition' and uninformed thought,
that, in the Western world at least, its true appearance has been lost.

The magical tradition

Fundamentally magic affirms that the universe is one, with no part separate from any
other part. Thus all that exists in the universe or cosmos is the expression of an
underlying unity which subsists through all things. Nothing exists except as an integral
part of the universe which is timeless and eternal. The soul or essence of man is therefore
part of this greater universe, and man himself a replica of it; a microcosm of the
macrocosm.

Colegrave (1979) insists that this instinctive magical awareness of all things and
their relationship to each other has been lost by mankind and is unrecoverable. Others
such as Blavatsky (1888), Besant (1899), Freedom Long (1954), Gurdjieff (1978), Ashe
(1977), Drury (1978, 1987) and Butler (1982), argue that this wisdom, although

fragmented and obscured, has never fully disappeared, having been passed down the ages in various traditions, many of them secret. According to Butler the magical tradition 'runs like an underground river emerging now and then into the light of day, then disappearing again beneath the surface' (1982, p.11).

Within the West it has surfaced in a number of magical orders and fraternities including the Order of the Golden Dawn, The Order of Temple, The Albigensians, Brethren of the Golden and Rosy Cross, The Illuminati, Magnetists, Theosophists and Kabbalists, whose aim is self-transformation - the realisation of the truth of the world through the development of insight and intuition. It could be, therefore, that man's primitive awareness is not so much lost as overlaid by cultural influences, for as Watson (1985, p.100) observes, human beings appear to possess 'an awareness of and hunger for essential harmony; a need for relationship.'

Whatever the case, it would appear that man's perception of reality became blinkered with but a few individuals retaining true insight into the pattern and harmony of the universe. Such people who see clearly are termed visionaries, seers, clairvoyants, or mystics (from the Greek *muo*: to close or complete) because they have a complete view of reality, or cosmic vision. They are able to alter consciousness at will in order to penetrate the mysteries of the universe and man's own nature and destiny. Those able to work with universal forces to produce desired effects at will, often using spells, incantations, invocations and certain rituals in order to do so, are variously known as magicians, sorcerers, or shamans.

Shamanism

The term *shaman* was introduced to the West by Russians who first encountered Siberian tribes known as the Tungus. Among these people specialists known as *shaman, saman* or *haman* performed various practices directed at maintaining the psychic and ecological equilibrium of the people. Epes Brown (1985, p.397) observes that their powers were critical to communal life and human survival; helping people to maintain the necessary delicate balance 'between the world of pragmatic necessities and the more subtle world of spirits; acting as an intermediary between these worlds.' In addition to healing the sick, communicating with spirits, telepathy, divination of the future, dream interpretation, mastery of fire and rainmaking, the magico-spiritual powers attributed to them include levitation, flight, ascent into the heavens and descent into the underworld; flights of fantasy which occurred in the imagination or unconscious, and shamans, like other occultists, engage in various ceremonies to stimulate imagination and help them into a state of enlarged awareness. Shamanic techniques are therefore essentially a means of accessing, exploring and interpreting the landscapes of the mind.

> In these realms shamans enact rituals of discovery, propitiation, cure and salvation; they retrieve lost souls, guide the souls of those who have died, and directly communicate with the cosmic powers-that-be. These ancient mystic-healers serve to defend life, health and fertility - the world of 'light' - against death, disease and disaster - the world of 'darkness' (Baer and Baer, 1984, pp.1-2).

Archaeological evidence suggests that these techniques are at least 20,000 years old, very widespread, and remarkably similar throughout the world. This is confirmed by contemporary descriptions of such practices in Polynesia (Freedom Long, 1954), Japan (Reid, 1985), China (Saso, 1985), North America (Bergman, 1973; Epes Brown, 1985), Central America (Castaneda, 1973, 5, 6, 8; 1982, 1984), Africa and Australia (Taylor, 1987), Australasia and the South Pacific (Watson, 1976).

The universal feature of shamanism is ecstasy (the Greek for 'out of the body'), or trance. Peters and Price Williams (1980), on the basis of their analysis of shamanic practices in 42 cultures, have concluded that shamanic ecstasy is a specific type of altered state. Achterberg (1985) identifies it with what LeShan (1982) terms 'clairvoyant reality', a state he claims is experienced both by mystics and psychic healers, and which he describes as a timeless reality, a unified whole, where neither time nor space can prevent information exchange. According to Watson (1973, p.218), shamans

> All seem to be able to see through the filters of culture, language and sense systems to other aspects of the real world - to hidden non-ordinary reality. Australian aborigines call this using the strong eye.

Traditionally shamans use various methods to achieve the strong eye and thus intensify perception, intuition and imagination, including stimulant drugs, drum music, dancing, rhythmic movement and song. They also have the ability to generate and control internal heat. According to Eskimo tradition, cited by Achterberg (1985, p.34),

> Every real shaman has to feel an illumination in his body, in the inside of his head or in his brain, something that gleams like fire, that gives him the power to see with closed eyes into the darkness, into the hidden things or into the future, or into another man.

Healing in the shamanic tradition relies on insight and intuition, on the ability to create and interpret vivid images, and to induce in others altered states of consciousness conducive to self-healing. Avoiding death is not its primary purpose, and, as Achterberg (1985, p.17) suggests, 'Western mistrust of these systems often comes from the observation that shamanic healing may not have resulted in the extension of life.' However, for the shaman healing is a spiritual rather than a physical issue, disease being considered to originate and gain its meaning from the spirit. The purpose of life is therefore spiritual development and the maintenance of oneself in harmony or balance with all things. Losing one's soul is the gravest occurrence since it eliminates all meaning from life. Thus the aim of much shamanic healing is primarily to nurture and preserve the soul. Whereas in the modern sense illness is an external agent entering the body, something to be destroyed or protected against, in the shamanic system it is loss of personal power that allowed the intrusion in the first place. All shamanic treatment therefore emphasises augmenting the power of the sick person, and only secondarily in counteracting the power of the illness-producing agent, which is seen to constitute a threat to health only when a person's protective mantle develops a weakness. Accordingly, the shaman does not work exclusively in the context of disease. His aim is the restoration of balance, and as Achterberg observes, in tribal societies where shamanism has flourished the practice of healing overlaps with all of secular and sacred life, with prayer, farming, marriage, war, and taboo.

However, the magico-spiritual practices of the shaman have always existed alongside more mechanical and technological forms of medicine, so typically in shamanic cultures a healing hierarchy exists with specialists in physical manipulation and prescription succeeded by diagnostic specialists, then by those who use imagination to intervene with the supernatural.

The shamanic tradition in Western culture

Although the origins of Western medicine are shrouded in mythology, shamanic practices and hierarchical organisation of healers are nonetheless discernible.

Ancient Egypt

According to Homer, the Egyptians were more skilled in healing than any other people. Their medicine was rooted in the magical vision of a harmoniously interrelated universe suffused with the divine. Man was viewed as a microcosm of the macrocosm, and expected to reflect its order and harmony. This was achieved through a balancing of subtle energies, cosmic 'uranian' forces, and subterranean 'telluric' forces. The former were seen as an expression of God and symbolised as light radiating from the sun, or Ra, which is broken down into rays corresponding to the colour spectrum, each ray manifesting a different facet of the divine and influencing different qualities of life. The most important aim of life was for man to realise the light and thereby God; to become enlightened by opening up to the light, channeling and distributing it, and merging it with earth energy. The latter was characterised as spontaneous upward movement and symbolised by a rearing serpent. Those who had successfully raised this latent serpent energy to merge with the uranian forces are depicted in Egyptian paintings and sculpture with a snake emerging from their forehead, which was thought to be the seat of divine consciousness. Insofar that man achieved this union, he was the mediator of heaven and earth. Jacq (1985) points out that the aim of magic was to produce this connection, thereby 'bringing down the light', transferring and reflecting its power. The secrets of this ancient wisdom were passed on only to the highest order of priests for sole use in the service of man and his spiritual development. Magic and religion were thus inextricably linked with each other and with medicine, which was, as Pullar (1988) observes, sacerdotal, although essentially practical, catering for the whole person in mind, body and soul.

The vital energies were thought to be absorbed and regulated by a finer etheric or spiritual 'body' which enveloped the physical body, and the temple priests sought to direct these forces by passes over the body, and are often depicted thus in bas relief. They also recognised the therapeutic effects of colour and employed variously coloured sanctuaries in treatment. Moreover, they recognised the relationship of colour to other vibrational forms, and as Pullar observes, understood that rhythm - 'the expression of movement in life and the pulse of every existing thing' - carries with it the potential for creating harmony and healing or disintegration and destruction. The laws of rhythm were therefore among the most closely guarded secrets, passed from father to son, master to pupil by secret oral tradition. Rhythmical invocations and incantations, music and movement all played a substantial part in magic, religion and healing.

In addition to the temple priests there were healers of various grades. Those who could tap into and direct natural forces were at the highest level and bonesetters at the lowest. However, dream interpretation was of great importance in healing and those with the ability to provoke and interpret dreams in both diagnosis and treatment were highly prized.

The most renowned healer, Imhotep, born circa 3000 BC, clearly displays the shamanic origins of Egyptian medicine, being a master of magic, poetry, divination, herbal lore and rainmaking. On his death he was elevated first to the status of demi-god and then, circa 525 BC, to that of a full deity of medicine, being designated the son of Ptah, god of healing. In his name the traditions of healing were passed down and found their way into Classical Greek culture.

Ancient Greece

As Capra (1978) indicates the aim of the Greeks until the sixth century BC was *physis* - the attempt to perceive the essential nature of all things, and the word from which the term physics derives. It was therefore synonymous with mysticism and its practical applications consistent with magic. All knowledge concerned understanding the meaning and purpose of natural phenomena and living in accordance with the natural order. The concept of harmony was therefore of central importance to the Greeks, as was the related concept of measure. This was viewed not as an overt feature of phenomena but a deeper hidden harmony which was deemed to lie in the ratio of its inner proportions to one another and the whole. To understand this ratio and thereby have the measure of a thing was a form of insight into its essential nature and harmony. Maintaining a sense of proportion or right measure was vital because all things had measure, and it was of particular importance in human affairs because, as Protagorus observed, man - by virtue of his perception and insight - is the measure of all things. Indeed man was seen as the most significant subject of enquiry, and the main focus of study was his conscious or mental life. According to Plato, this could best be described in terms of pairs of opposites, the balance or harmony between which constituted the soul, essence or *psyche*, literally a moving or life force. Psychology, the study of the soul and its development, was therefore essential. Virtue or harmony consisted not in accentuating the positive but maintaining a dynamic balance between opposites. When the soul lost its right proportions or went beyond its proper measure it lost its overall balance, becoming fragmented (the literal meaning of ratio). It therefore cracked up, becoming irrational - the tragic consequences of which were dramatically depicted in Greek theatre.

Human problems were therefore seen as disharmony or dis-ease, as soul sickness - literally psycho pathology - and of a fundamentally spiritual nature. Physical disorders were largely regarded as symptomatic of this fundamental disharmony. Treatment was therefore directed to the cure of the soul, or psychotherapy, through the restoration of its balance and harmony. Accordingly, man had to be attuned to and in harmony with both spiritual and physical realities to be healthy, or whole.

The legacy of this idea is found in the terms health and healing which originate in the German *heilen*, meaning whole. This is closely related to the Old English words *hael* (whole), and *haelen* (heal), from which the English *hale* (as in the phrase 'hale and hearty') and the Welsh *hoil* derive. These terms are very similar to the German *heilig* and the Old English *halig* meaning holy. Etymologically speaking, therefore, to be healthy is to be whole or holy, which clearly embraces both the spiritual and physical aspects of man, and not merely the latter.

Such a distinction would have been meaningless to the early Greeks, who, as Capra (1978) observes, didn't even have a word for matter since they saw all forms of existence as manifestations of the physis, endowed with life and spirituality. All things were deemed to be comprised of gods and spirits and the universe to be a kind of organism sustained by *pneuma* or cosmic breath, in much the same way as the human body is sustained by air. As until about the 6th century BC gods and spirits were central to all thinking about the universe, healing was essentially a spiritual phenomena associated with these deities.

Three gods were seen as principally responsible for healing: Apollo, healer to the gods, who with his arrows, the rays of the sun, brought not only healing but also pestilence and death; his sister Artemis, on the one hand helper to women in childbirth and on the other the goddess of death; and Pallas, patron of eyesight. However, in the Homeric tradition this healing trinity is compounded by the myth of Asclepios, the son of Apollo and King of Thessally, who with his wife Epione, the soother of pain, created a dynasty of healers. His heroic sons Machaon and Podilirius were military surgeons, Telesporos brought about the completion of the healing process, and his daughters Hygeia and Panacea were respectively the dispenser of health and the friendly goddess of the sick; Panacea having knowledge of medicines to treat disease, and Hygeia advocating living in harmony with nature in order to avoid illness.

It is in the cult of Asclepios (known by the Romans as Aesculapius) that similarities with Egyptian medicine can most clearly be seen. Asclepios, like Imhotep, has uncertain origins. There appears to have been a mortal physician of that name revered as the founder of medicine who, on his death, becomes first a demi-god then a full deity. The followers of the latter, Asklepiads, or the sons of Asclepios, constituted the temple priests. They, like the Egyptians, worshipped the symbol of the rising sun. Moreover, Asclepios was typically depicted with the caduceus, or rustic staff around which is curled a serpent, representing earth energy. This was to become the emblem of the physicians of Kos where the Hippocratic school of medicine was founded, and later of Western medicine. Like the Egyptians Asclepiads made use of dreams in diagnosis and treatment, and therapeutic use of music and movement. Galen, the physician to Marcus Aurelius, who like Hippocrates and Aristotle was trained in the Asclepian tradition, used colour in treatment, and recognised the power of the imagination in sickness and health. He believed that dreams frequently provided clinically important diagnostic information.

By the fifth century BC the cult of Asclepios had spread widely, but among the healing deities the most revered was Hygiea. She was concerned with the promotion of health and personifying the wisdom that one can be healthy by understanding how to live in harmony with oneself and the environment, and can therefore be thought of as the deity of preventative medicine. The tradition which grew up in her name focused on special diets, baths, ablutions, exercise, dance and various methods such as listening to music, watching comedy, laughter being seen as of great therapeutic significance, or tragedy where evocations of pity and fear effected emotional purging, purification, or Katharsis. Theatre was, therefore instrumental in maintaining health and effecting cure.

In the sixth century BC Pythagoras of Samos employed the Hygiean concept of physiological and ecological harmony in his system of healing. He viewed disease as imbalance in the constituent elements of air, fire, water and earth which he associated with the qualities of coldness, dryness, heat and wetness, and with four humours, black bile, blood, yellow bile and phlegm which arose in four organs, the spleen, heart, liver and brain. Health involved the proper balance of humours, and illness their mixture in the wrong proportions. Accordingly healing involved restoring equilibrium within the fluid essences of man, and this view, subsequently systematised and codified by Galen in about 1 AD, was maintained throughout the Middle Ages.

The Hippocratic tradition

Subsequently, Hippocrates established a medical school on the island of Kos which flourished at the end of the 5th century BC. He integrated medicine into the universal laws of nature as they were then conceived, thereby joining medicine and philosophy into a unified way of life. The healthy state of man and nature was considered to consist of an equivalence of basic elements or harmony, which was an adaptation to context. Students of medicine were therefore advised to study the effects of natural cycles such as the seasons on health. The physician used all his senses to measure and define the environment, taking account of its geographic position in relation to the stars, sunrise and wind direction, the conditions of soil and water, and the weather. The physician, like the shaman, was a diviner of natural signs and an expert in natural lore. Moreover, like the shaman, he had a notion of the wholeness of things, and didn't look at disease as an isolated phenomenon. This holistic view is evident in the Hippocratic doctrine:

There is one common flow, one common breathing; all things are in sympathy.

Hippocrates also recognised nature's healing power - the *vix medicatrix naturae* - a life force inherent in all living organisms. He placed great emphasis on it, insisting that the healing process is only designed to assist the body's own self-healing, providing assistance to the natural forces by creating the most favourable conditions for the healing process. He viewed the physician as the servant of nature. Physicians trained in the Hippocratic tradition did not try to cure patients without educating them in the nature, origin and development of their illness. They clearly saw their role as that of helping nature heal herself, restoring the balance disturbed by disease but not interfering with nature. The role of the physician was therefore that of therapist - literally, an attendant (from the Greek *therapeia*: attendance) to the healing process.

There is little doubt that the Hippocratic philosophy, like that of Pythagoras, was inspired by mystical vision. It is therefore somewhat ironic that Hippocrates is regarded as the father of modern medicine, because in the main his views were diametrically opposed to much modern medical theory and practice. However, in the Hippocratic system there emerges for the first time the awareness that illness and health are natural biological phenomena rather than the work of gods and spirits; the reactions of the organism to its environment, life style and other factors. Hippocratic medicine therefore emphasised the fact that health and illness can be influenced by therapeutic procedures and by wise management of one's life, and in so doing it breaks with the magico-religious tradition of ancient medicine. Under its influence health became the ideal of culture - Plato writing that social, physical and emotional health are one.

However, the sixth century BC was something of a turning point in human history. It was, as Koestler (1984, p.27) observes, a period when 'rational thought was emerging from the mythological dream world' - a period when the mystic vision of the ancients became fragmented, obscured and virtually lost to Western civilisation. Ironically this was largely owing to the influence of Pythagoras 'whose influence on the human race was probably greater than that of any single man before or after him (Koestler, 1984, p.25).

The influence of Pythagoras

Pythagorean philosophy is the perfect embodiment of the mystic view of the universe. It integrates all science, religion, mathematics, music and medicine; body, mind and spirit, in what Koestler terms 'an inspired, luminous synthesis'. It is a philosophy in which all component parts interlock presenting 'a homogeneous surface like a sphere, so that it is difficult to decide which side to cut it.' However, his discovery that the pitch of a note depends on the length of the string that produces it, and that concordant intervals in the scale are produced by simple numerical ratios (2:1 octave; 3:2 fifth; 4:3 fourth, etc.) was epoch-making in that it reduced the ancient concept of harmony to mathematics:

> It was the first successful reduction of quality to quantity, the first step towards the mathematicization of human experience - and therefore the beginnings of science (Koestler, 1984, p.27).

Pythagorean mathematics were to prove the greatest single influence on Western thought for, as Russell (1948) indicates, mathematics are the chief source of belief in external and exact truth, as well as in a super-sensible and intelligible world. The exactness of geometry, which is not matched in the real world, suggests that all exact reasoning applies to ideal as opposed to sensible objects, and when taken further, to the belief that the objects of thought are more real than those of sense perception. It therefore raises the status of intellect and reduces that of the senses, intuition and feeling. Such a view is quite contrary to that of mysticism. However, as Koestler observes, the Pythagoreans were aware that the symbols of mythology and mathematics were different aspects of the same reality. They didn't live in 'a divided house of faith and reason', and this unitary awareness was reflected in their healing, but this was not to last for long.

Subsequently the concept of measure or ratio lost its mystical significance. Bohm (1980) surmises that it became routinised and habitual as it began to be learned by mechanical conformity to teaching rather than acquired intuitively through the development of insight. Ratio thus came to be conceptualised as that point on a line which divided it into segments such that the smaller is to the larger as the larger is to the whole. This measure or ratio, known as the Golden Mean or Section, came to be imposed by rule - that is, as an objective 'out there' fact about reality, or absolute truth, rather than some intuitive feeling about the inner essence of a thing. Thereafter measure came to denote mainly a process of comparison with some arbitrary external standard, and as such it was passed down by the Greeks to the Romans and to the rest of Western civilisation. The only sense in which its original meaning is retained is in the notion of 'getting the measure' of a person, thing or situation.

Consequently Western civilisation came to view knowledge as essentially linear - as meaning objective 'out there' fact or objective reality - and such facts as constituting the only valid knowledge of the world, an idea that was to have enormous implications for all subsequent thinking. From this same concept the West derives its notion of time - the idea of a linear sequence from the past, through the present to the future. Such a concept carries with it the idea of progress - that given enough time man will find out everything and discern all possible truth.

From the concepts of measure or ratio, Western science also derives its emphasis on measurement, standardisation, rationality and reason, all of which involve dissection and analysis. Western man thus came to believe in an orderly linear universe that he could in time explore rationally, i.e. through reason - the possession of which sets man above and apart from the rest of creation, - by reducing it to its constituent parts, a bit at a time. Dissection and analysis have since come to characterise Western civilisation and its science. As Toffler (1985, p.xi) says: 'We are good at it, so good we often forget to put the pieces back together again.'

The Greeks thus made a profound and lasting contribution to the development of Western thought. Capra (1978) indicates that the first evidence of dissection came with the Eleatic school in the 5th century BC. Parminides of Elea opposed Heraclitus who, consistent with the times, believed in a world of perpetual change or becoming; a continual flow, symbolised for him by fire. He regarded all static being as based on deception, all the changes in the world arising from the dynamic and cyclic interplay of opposites, any pair of which constitute a unity. Accordingly everything must ultimately flow into its opposite. Therefore any experience or values believed to be contrary and distinct are aspects of the same thing. Consistent with this law of opposition based on complementary factors - *enantiodromia* - he believed that man should 'have knowledge of the whole of things'.

Parminides challenged Heraclitus, claiming the basic universal principle as unique and invariable, and all apparent change as sensory illusion. Out of this came the notion of an indestructible substance as the subject of varying properties. This substance, matter, was made of several basic constituents - passive, dead particles moving in a void, the smallest individual units of which were termed atoms (atom being Greek for indivisible). The movement of atoms was unexplained but assumed to be spiritual in origin. Thus 'atomists' drew a clear distinction between spirit and matter and this eventually led to philosophy turning its attention away from the material to the spiritual and ethical.

Initially the Eleatic school assumed a divine unifying principle standing above all gods and men, but this devolved into a personal God, standing above and directing the world. God thus became external to, or other than man, and as such a fact or truth; indeed, the Ultimate Fact or Truth, and the very embodiment of Western thought. Russell (1959, p.56) has observed that were it not for the Greek concept of an external world revealed to the intellect but not the senses, the notion of God as it is known in the West might not have existed. However, the existence of this concept had important consequences insomuch that it led to the projection of man's personal powers onto God. Fromm (1951) argues that this resulted in man's alienation from himself, and separation from his most valuable force and potentials. This was the very antithesis of magic. Clearly, the magician's belief in his ability to alter consciousness at will and thus commune with and influence the forces of nature was an assault on the omnipotence of God. Therefore all practices which emphasised the development of human powers and potentials were systematically eradicated in Western culture. Sources of occult wisdom were eclipsed, and all bodies of knowledge framed within the dominant religious traditions. Hence by the end of the Classical period in Greek history several developments in thinking had occurred which were to have profound implications for subsequent Western thought - influences which overshadowed the instinctive wisdom of early man on which ancient systems of healing were based. Nevertheless, statues of the Asclepian family, the caduceus symbol, and the Hippocratic Oath have all persisted down through the ages and serve as a reminder of it.

Medicine in the Middle Ages

By the end of the classical period in Greece the scientific world view of antiquity had been systematised by Aristotle and in the Thirteenth Century Thomas Aquinas combined it with Christian ethics, thereby establishing the scientific framework that was to remain largely unquestioned and unaltered until the Middle Ages. Accordingly, science was rooted in a view of the universe which rested on the authority of the Church. Man was seen as the centre of God's creation, and earth as the centre of the heavens. The pursuit of reason was maintained and progress in knowledge was rapid.

The aim of science remained wisdom, understanding the natural order and living with it, which was tantamount to accepting man's powerlessness in the face of God. Ultimate knowledge was the preserve of God, and knowing too much constituted sin. All visionary movements were therefore suspect, and during the Middle Ages the Cathars, Albigenses, Bogomils, Freemasons, Rosicrucians, and Kabbalists were intensely persecuted by the Church. It was also largely because of the Church that there was no serious study or practice of medicine. Folk medicine prevailed, preserved by secret oral tradition, healing rites being regarded as mysteries to be shared only by initiates. Thus, as Achterberg (1985) observes, most healing practices can only be deduced from documents relating to witch trials, reflecting the fact that in the Anglo-Saxon world healing was largely the province of wise women or witches.

Witchcraft

In the ancient world women were generally believed to hold the secrets of life within their very being. During the Middle Ages those with superior knowledge were known as witches, and Achterberg suggests that they were in fact the most advanced scientists of the period. Thus although by the fifteenth century Greek thought, language and literature had been carried to every corner of Europe, Paracelsus (1493-1541), the distinguished physician and founder of modern chemistry, attributed his understanding of the laws and practices of medicine, particularly the role of the imagination in healing, to his conversations with the wise women, who were wholly shamanic in their regard for the unity of all things, in their attempts to use the forces of nature for healing, and in their understanding of the role of the healer. The latter is reflected in Paracelsus' observation, 'Man is his own doctor ... the physician is in ourselves and in our own nature are all the things that we need.' Many of their practices were clearly shamanic, most notably their imaginative 'flight' on broomsticks, and their use of spells. As purveyors of magic, they were regarded as heretics by the Church, and purged relentlessly during the Middle Ages.

> The advent of Christianity affected the practice of medicine in such a way that some scholars blame it for bringing about the darkest days in health care. The pagans (Greeks, Egyptians and Romans) had elevated the art of healing to a height it would not be see again for centuries. As Christianity spread its own gospel, all that was pagan, including the pagan practice of medicine, had to fall by the wayside. The theory advanced by the Church was that disease was caused by Satan, not by the pagan spirits, therefore pagan medicine could have no role in its exorcism. In other words, the Church expunged the exquisite surgical and herbal skills of the Greeks from the roster of available treatments and substituted instead frequently brutal practices such as mortifying the flesh. This brought the practice of physical medicine to an all time low (Achterberg, 1985, p.64).

Mind, matter and medicine

The orthodoxy of the Church came into question during the sixteenth century when Copernicus (1473-1543) challenged the biblical notion of the earth the centre of the universe by suggesting that the planets circled the sun, which effectively removed the earth from its geometrical pre-eminence and made it difficult to attribute to man the cosmic significance assigned to him in Christian theology.

The discovery of the laws of planetary motion by Kepler (1571-1630), which created a new astronomy, further challenged the validity of the old view of the universe, and Galileo (1564-1642) finally discredited it totally by demonstrating that the earth revolves around the sun.

Until this time the aim of science had been understanding and living in harmony with nature, but the emphasis of Francis Bacon (1596-1650) on using science to gain mastery over nature altered the entire concept of science and introduced the view that man was something apart from nature. This was essentially anti-theological in as much that it encouraged man to sequester powers formerly attributed to God. This brought science and religion into conflict and created a schism between the physical and spiritual realms. Descartes (1596-1650) advanced this fundamental separation by proposing two discrete realms in nature, mind and matter. This effectively created a split between mind and body which enabled scientists to treat matter as inert and completely distinct from themselves, and led to the belief that the world could be described objectively; that is, in terms of material objects which existed independently of human observers. As a result objectivity became the ideal of science. This material world of objects was considered to be assembled like a huge machine or cosmic clock, operated by impersonal mechanical laws that could be explained in terms of the arrangement and movement of its parts, and described using simple mathematics. Descartes' world view was thus mechanistic and materialistic but also analytic and reductionist in so far that he viewed complex wholes as understandable in terms of their constituent parts. He extended this mechanistic model to living organisms, likening animals to clocks composed of wheels, cogs and springs, and he later extended this analogy to man. He wrote:

> I wish you to consider finally that all the functions which I attribute to this machine ... occur naturally ... solely by the disposition of its organs not less than the movements of a clock.

To Descartes the human body was a machine, part of a perfect cosmic machine, governed in principle at least by mathematical laws, and this view of the body as a mindless machine has governed Western medicine ever since.

Isaac Newton (1643-1727) subsequently formulated the mathematical laws or mechanics which were thought to operate the cosmic machine and to give rise to all changes observable in the physical world. Capra (1978, p.56) observes that the stage of the Newtonian universe on which all physical phenomena took place was the three-dimensional space of classical Euclidian geometry. It was an absolute space, independent of the material objects it contains, always at rest, immovable, constant and unchangeable. All changes in the physical world were described in terms of a separate dimension called Time, which again was absolute, having no connection with the material world and flowing uniformly in linear sequence from the past, through the present to the future. These notions of time and space were to become so deep-rooted in the minds of Western philosophers and scientists that they were taken as unquestionable properties of nature.

Within this absolute space and absolute time moved material particles which Newton conceived as small solid indestructible objects out of which matter was made. Such a view was similar to that of the Greek atomists. The main difference was that Newton provided a precise description of the force acting between these particles, namely gravity. This was seen by Newton as rigidly connected with the bodies it acted on and as acting instantaneously over distance. Both particles and the forces between them were viewed as having been created by God and set in motion by Him at the beginning of time. All physical events were thus reduced in Newtonian mechanics to the motion of material points in space caused by their mutual attraction. In order to express the effect of this force on mass points in precise mathematical terms Newton developed differential calculus, and the resulting equations of motion form the basis of classical mechanics. The success of the latter in explaining the motion of the moon and planets encouraged the clockwork view of the universe and inspired the invention of mechanisms which imitated these regularities.

The divorce of psychology and medicine

Laplace (1748-1827) subsequently went further than either Descartes or Newton in assuming that similar laws governed everything else, including human beings. Thus by the nineteenth century the view of the universe was entirely mechanistic, reductionist and deterministic. Everything occurring in the cosmic machine was held to have a definite cause and to give rise to a definite effect, so that the future of any part could be predicted if its state at any time was known in sufficient detail.

The view of the universe inspired by Descartes and Newton subsequently guided all scientific endeavour in the West for over two hundred years, until the very existence of God, the creator of the cosmic machine, was brought into question as it became increasingly doubtful whether the universe had any beginning in time.

> So long as the universe had a beginning we could suppose it had a creator. But if the universe is really completely self-contained, having no boundary of edge, it would have neither beginning nor end; it would simply be. What place then for a creator? (Hawking, 1988 p. 140-1).

As science made belief in the creator increasingly difficult, so the Divine gradually disappeared from the scientific world view, with the result that in the Nineteenth century Nietzsche could justifiably declare God 'dead' in the sense that traditional meanings and values had been negated and physical science had become the ultimate authority in Western culture. This was to have profound implications, because, for the first time in the history of healing, psychology was distilled out from medicine.

During the seventeenth century *physis* with the addition of a 'c' had turned into a 'hard' science - physics - the science of physical matter, which, with its emphasis on rigor, clarity and objectivity became the standard for all sciences. This had major consequences for psychology. Descartes had not identified mind with matter, believing that it could be studied introspectively, by looking inwards. However, as all knowledge or science had, by his own dicta, to comprise that about which there could be no doubt, that is, agreed on as physical reality or fact by independent observers, this effectively ruled out the mind as a scientific area of study. This left psychology with something of a dilemma. By adopting scientific method and the total objectivity it implies, human experience, senses, feelings, consciousness, are all precluded from study.

Psychology was therefore left without its traditional subject matter - that is, if it wished to be seen as science, as a valid and respectable body of knowledge, - which it did. Therefore, with scant regard for the absurdity of the situation it jettisoned all its traditional concerns and began to focus solely on objective physical aspects of human functioning, ie. behaviour. Adopting a suitably clockwork metaphor it set itself the task of finding out how man 'ticks', without any reference to mind, much less soul or spirit, only to the brain, which as a physical entity was legitimately part of the cosmic machine. The resulting neglect of the mind-body link, when viewed against the history of healing is, as Siegel (1986, p.65) indicates, quite aberrant for 'in traditional tribal medicine and in Western practice from its beginning in the work of Hippocrates the need to operate through the patient's mind has always been recognised.'

The effect of this negation of mind on healing was devastating, as Achterberg (1985, p.69) observes: 'As humanity began its preparations for the new world view that would encompass the scientific method, all that was irrational, and all that was intuitive was subject to being purged. Women's science and women's medicine were prime targets.' Yet it was not, as she points out, purely femaleness that was so blatantly challenged, it was rather that the qualities traditionally associated with women posed a threat to the Newtonian world view. Intuition, feelings, non-rational thought, holism, nurturance and imagination simply had little place in the thought mode of a universe made of cogs and wheels. Thus 'the ebb and ultimate dissolution of women's influence on medicine and science were pivotal in directing healing away from the classic womanly virtues ... - all seen as threats and impediments to progress of the new scientific order' (1985, p.7). It was substituted with what Kaptehuk and Croucher (1986) term 'linear medicine' which focused on probing, detecting, isolating, controlling and usually destroying the 'problem' which was seen as an invasion, defect or aberration, quite separate from the person. The implications of this are outlined by Illich (1975, p.112):

> The hope of bringing to medicine the perfection Copernicus had given to astronomy dates from the time of Galileo. Descartes traced the coordinates for the implementation of the project. His description effectively turned the human body into a clockwork and placed a distance not only between body and soul but also between the patient's complaint and the physician's eye. Within this mechanical framework pain turned into a red light and sickness into mechanical trouble. A new

kind of taxonomy of diseases became possible. As minerals and plants could be classified, so disease could be isolated and put in their place by the doctor-taxonomist. The logical framework for a new purpose in medicine had been laid. Sickness was placed in the centre of the medical system, a sickness subjected to a) operational verification by measurement b) clinical study of measurement and c) evaluation according to engineering norms.

As Illich suggests, the use of physical measurement prepared for the belief in the real existence of diseases and their autonomy from the perception of doctor and patient. This led to a tendency to speak of disease as a thing, and not as part of the total life process. The person was therefore separated from the illness, and doctors' interest shifted from the sick to the sickness. Hospitals became laboratories for the study of disease processes, rather than institutions for the care of the sick, and nearly all talk about health actually became about disease; a focus, which is essentially negative.

Modern mechanistic medicine

Dossey (1982) claims that consistent with the reductionist, deterministic orientation of modern medicine, the thrust of medical scientists over the past century has been to understand disease processes at the molecular level, the assumption being that for any disease it will eventually be possible to locate the misbehaving molecule. In the meantime, consistent with it mechanistic orientation, medicine has settled for repairing, removing or replacing those parts it cannot as yet more successfully engineer, and as the century progresses the mechanics of medicine are increasingly evident in various developments in spare part surgery, the mechanisation of childbirth and engineering of every kind; genetic, biochemical, and structural.

Unfortunately, however, while during the twentieth century psychology and medicine have both been struggling to conform to the mechanistic model of nineteenth century physics, physics itself long ago abandoned this as outmoded and inappropriate, investigations of the sub-atomic realm at the turn of the century having completely undermined the Cartesian/Newtonian notion of a clockwork universe.

> Every basic tenet of the older Newtonian view of how the world behaves has been abandoned in our century in favour of a radically new model (Dossey, 1982, p.230).

Indeed, as physicist Paul Davies (1984, p.vii) observes:

> The New Physics soon revealed more than simply a better model of the physical world. Physicists began to realise that their discoveries demanded a radical reformulation of the most fundamental aspects of reality.

> They learned to approach their subject in totally unexpected and novel ways that seemed to turn common sense on its head and find closer accord with mysticism than materialism.

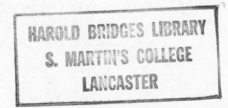

Chapter 2

Modern Perspectives on Healing

Crazy world. Or maybe its just the crazy view we have of it, looking through a crack in the door, never being able to see the whole room, the whole picture.

Judith Guest (Ordinary People).

Rosnow (1981, p.7) suggests that in an industrial age wedded to the machine the mechanistic model of classical Newtonian physics 'offered a deceivingly simple epistemology for addressing questions of great complexity that had puzzled philosophers since antiquity'. Its certainty promoted a sense of security about the universe and man's place within it.

However, this was completely undermined when, as a result of discoveries in the first three decades of this century, understanding of the universe shifted from the mechanistic, deterministic and certain, to the organic, relativistic and uncertain.

Two separate developments - that of relativity theory and atomic physics - shattered all the principle concepts of the Newtonian world view: the notion of absolute space and time, the elementary solid particles, the strictly causal nature of physical phenomena, and the ideal of an objective description of nature. None of these could be extended to the new domains into which physics was now penetrating. (Capra 1976 p.62-3).

The Special Theory of Relativity

The first major blow to the Newtonian world view was a series of papers published in 1905 by Albert Einstein, the third of which, the Special Theory of Relativity, radically altered traditional concepts of space and time, and thereby the very foundations of Newtonian physics.

In Relativity Theory space is not three dimensional and time not a separate entity. Both are intimately connected, forming a four dimensional continuum of 'space-time'. Therefore, one cannot speak of time without space, and vice-versa, and this has startling implications. In Newtonian physics it was always assumed that rods in motion and at rest are the same length. Relativity Theory has shown this not to be true. The length of an object depends on its motion relative to the observer and changes with the velocity of that motion. The change is such that the object contracts in the direction of its motion. A rod has its maximum length in a frame of reference when at rest, and becomes shorter with increasing velocity relative to the observer.

> It is important to realise that it makes no sense to ask which is the 'real' length of an object, just as it makes no sense in everyday life to ask for the real length of somebody's shadow. The shadow is a projection of points in three dimensional space on a two dimensional plane and its lengths will be different for different angles of projection. Similarly the length of a moving object is the projection of points in four dimensional space-time onto a three dimensional space and its length is different in different frames of reference (Capra 1976, p.177).

What is true for lengths is also true for time intervals. They also depend on the frame of reference of the observer, but contrary to spatial distances they become longer as the velocity relative to the observer increases. This means that clocks in motion, whether mechanical, atomic, or human (i.e. heartbeat), run slower; time slows down. This time-dislocation effect has the apparently bizarre implication enshrined in the celebrated 'twins effect', according to which one of two twin brothers on a round trip into outer space would, on his return to earth after ten years, be younger than his brother on earth, having experienced only one year of time in space because his heartbeat, bloodflow, and brainwaves would slow during the journey from the point of view of the man on the earth. The cosmonaut wouldn't notice anything unusual until his return to earth, when his brother would seem much older. This paradox, however unbelievable, is well tested in physics. Although these effects are normally not noticeable because they are too small at ordinary speeds, they are easily measurable and demonstrable using rapidly moving atomic clocks, capable of measuring billionths of a second precisely, or subatomic particles with known decay rates. In 1971 two physicists, Hafele and Keating, tested the time dilation effect by flying clocks around the earth in high speed jets, and found a shift of 59 billionths of a second. Greater accuracy is achieved by accelerating subatomic particles, and in 1978 at CERN accelerated muons were found to stretch their time scale by over twenty times. As Capra observes, these effects only seem strange because we cannot experience the four dimensional world with our senses, only its three dimensional images.

On a more mundane level, to a person travelling at speed on a train through a railway station, the station clock runs slightly slower from his frame of reference relative to that of a porter on a platform, although in compensation the platform appears slightly shorter. The mutual distortions of space and time can thus be regarded as a conversion of space, which shrinks, into time, which stretches. Therefore, in Relativity Theory all measurements involving space and time lose their absolute significance. Whereas previously time was regarded as absolute, fixed, universal, and independent of material bodies or observers, in Relativity Theory it is seen as dynamical, able to stretch, shrink, warp, and even stop altogether. Moreover, clock rates, rather than being absolute, are relative to the state of motion and gravitational situation of the observer. Space and time thus become merely elements of the language used by an observer to describe his environment, and they will be used by each observer in a different way.

Without direct sensory experience it is difficult to conceive of or describe four dimensional space-time. To do so requires a four dimensional picture or map covering the whole span of time, as well as the whole region of space. These space-time diagrams are four-dimensional patterns in space-time representing a network of interrelated events which have no definite direction of time attached to them. Consequently there is no 'before' or 'after' in the processes they picture and thus no linear relationship of cause and effect, unless the 'map' is read in a certain direction, say from bottom to top, and direction thereby imposed on the picture. All events are interconnected but the connections are not causal in the Newtonian sense. Depending on how a person accesses the 'map' or picture, ordering of events will be different. There is thus no universal flow of time as in the Newtonian model. Different observers will order events differently (i.e. take a different slice of the picture) if they move with different velocities relative to the observed events. Therefore, two events which are seen as occurring simultaneously by one observer may occur in different temporal sequence for other observers.

One casualty of this 'elastic' time is the division of time into past, present and future. Relativity Theory reveals that everyone carries around their own personal time, locked to his state of motion. The concept of the time - a universal and absolute standard of public time - is therefore an illusion, because what people mean by 'now' depends on how they are moving. Therefore, as Einstein observed, 'you have to accept the idea that subjective time, with its emphasis on the now, has no objective meaning'. Furthermore, if there is no universal now, then in some sense the past and future exist and are equally real in the present. Accordingly, events are simply *there* in space-time and do not *happen*. The apparent 'flow' of time therefore takes on a very dubious status, and is dismissed by some commentators as illusory. It would seem that what moves, is not time, but the human mind.

Mathematically, there are no problems with descriptions of this reality, but because in ordinary language words refer to conventional notions of time, descriptions which employ them are highly problematic. It is therefore difficult to deal with these concepts either intuitively or linguistically. As Capra (1982, p.80-1) observes, 'Relativity has taught us that our common notions of reality are limited to our ordinary experience of the physical world and have to be abandoned whenever we extend this experience'.

So basic are the concepts of space and time to the description of natural phenomena that a radical departure from the conventional view of them as demanded by Relativity Theory entails a modification of the whole framework used to *describe* the universe. Moreover, as the unification of space and time necessarily unifies other apparently unrelated features, it demands a fundamental modification of the way in which the universe is *perceived*.

The General Theory of Relativity

In 1915 Einstein extended the Special Theory of Relativity to include gravity. In the resulting General Theory of Relativity, which describes gravity and the large scale structure of the universe, he proposed that the effect of gravity is to make space-time curved. This curvature is caused by the gravitational fields of massive bodies. The degree of curvature depends on the mass of the object, and because in Relativity Theory space and time cannot be separated, the curvature caused by gravity cannot be limited to three dimensional space but must extend into four dimensional space-time. The distortions caused by gravity in curved space-time means that Euclidian geometry is no longer valid, as its two dimensional geometry cannot be applied on the surface of a sphere. Lengths of time intervals are also similarly distorted by the presence of matter. Therefore, time doesn't flow at the same rate in all parts of the universe as in flat space-time because as curvature varies from place to place according to the distribution of massive bodies, so does the flow of time.

> The idea that time effects matter is familiar to everyone who has ever seen a field in erosion or watched himself grow older, but the possibility that there may be reciprocal action, in which matter affects time is revolutionary. It means that nothing happens without effect and that whatever happens all of us are touched by it because we live in the continuum of spacetime (Watson 1973, p.297).

The General Theory of Relativity thus completely abolishes the concepts of absolute space and time. Not only are all measurements involving time and space relative, but also, as the whole structure of space-time depends on the distribution of matter in the universe, the concept of empty space loses its meaning. Moreover, the upheaval in our understanding of the universe demanded by Relativity Theory doesn't stop here. A fundamental postulate of Relativity Theory is that the laws of science should be the same for all freely moving observers, irrespective of their speed. Thus all observers should measure light as travelling at the same speed no matter how fast they are moving. The implications of this simple idea are dramatic. One of the best known is Einstein's equation $E=mc^2$, (where E is energy, m mass and c the speed of light) which initially concerned the properties of bodies moving at or close to the speed of light. It is the mathematical embodiment of the statement that mass and energy are equivalent - that mass has energy and energy mass, and that the energy which an object has owing to its motion will add to its mass. According to this formulation, any distinction between energy and mass has to be abandoned. Mass and energy are simply different manifestations of the same thing, mass being a bound form of energy. Therefore, mass is no longer associated with a material substance and is not seen as consisting of any basic 'stuff', but as bundles or 'quanta' of energy. Energy, however, is associated with activity, and with processes, and this implies that the nature of matter is intrinsically dynamic. Thus matter can no longer be pictured as in the Newtonian view as composed of units, whether tiny billiard balls or grains of sand. Such images are inappropriate because, not only do they represent the constituents of matter as separate, but they are also static three dimensional images. Subatomic particles must be conceived of as four dimensional entities in space-time. Their forces have to be understood dynamically as forms in space and time; as dynamic patterns of activity which have a spatial aspect and a temporal aspect, the former making them appear as objects with a certain mass, the latter as processes involving the equivalent energy. Thus the being of matter and its activity cannot be separated, they are but different aspects of the same space-time reality.

The laws of this subatomic realm were subsequently mapped out by a number of physicists in the early part of this century, and are known as Quantum Theory, and its mathematical formulation as Quantum Mechanics.

Quantum Theory

When Rutherford split the atom in 1909, it became clear that atoms are nothing like the solid objects conceived by Newton but are vast regions of empty space in which extremely small particles - electrons - moved around the nucleus, bound to it by electric forces.

The equivalence of mass and energy has since been verified innumerable times by physicists and has had a profound influence on our concept of matter, forcing a fundamental modification of existing notions. The mechanistic view of Newtonian physics was based on the notion of solid material bodies moving in empty space. This concept is so deeply ingrained in Western thought that it is extremely difficult to imagine a physical reality where it does not apply. Yet this is precisely what modern physics obliges us to do. Moreover, not only is the concept of matter drastically altered, but also the concept of force, which is now seen to have a common origin in dynamic energy patterns continually changing into one another, so that it unifies concepts formerly held to be distinct.

> The high energy scattering experiments of past decades have shown us the dynamic and ever changing nature of the particle world in the most striking way. Matter has appeared in these experiments as completely mutable. All particles can be transmuted into all other particles; they can be created from energy and can vanish into energy. In this world, classical concepts like 'elementary particle', 'material substance' or 'isolated object' have lost their meaning; the whole universe appears as a dynamic web of inseparable energy patterns (Capra 1976 pp. 83-5).

The distinction between matter and empty space finally had to be abandoned when it became evident that particles can come into being spontaneously out of the void, and vanish again into it: 'the vacuum is far from empty. On the contrary, it contains an unlimited number of particles which come into being and vanish without end' (Capra, p.234).

Investigations into the subatomic realm in the early part of the century produced astonishing results. It was found that subatomic particles make discontinuous jumps or quantum leaps from one orbit to another without leaving any trace of their path. Therefore, they have no meaningful trajectory but an abrupt and unpredictable motion. Thus, at the subatomic level, matter doesn't exist with certainty at definite places, nor do atomic events occur at definite times and in definite ways. Rather, matter shows 'tendencies to exist' and subatomic events show 'tendencies to occur'. These tendencies are expressed mathematically as probabilities which take the form of waves. These are not real three dimensional waves, like those of sound or water, but abstract probabilities. Hence particles can at the same time be waves depending on the way in which they are observed. Atomic events can therefore never be predicted with certainty, only the likelihood of their happening. Such a view completely overturns common sense, and Einstein preferred the common sense view that electrons really exist in a definite place and with a definite trajectory, maintaining that any ambiguity or uncertainty encountered in the observation of atoms is the result of imprecision in the measuring instruments used. However, the 'common sense' view was subsequently shown to be false.

The Uncertainty Principle

Heisenberg established that there are limits beyond which the processes of nature cannot be measured accurately at the time at which they are taking place; limits beyond which there can be no certainty, and which are not imposed by the inexactness of measuring devices or the extremely small size of the entities being measured, but by nature itself. All attempts to observe the electron alter it. Davies (1984, p.103) suggests that 'in the absence of an observation the atom is a ghost. It only materialises when you look at it'. Heisenberg's Uncertainty Principle thus suggests that reality is not only *not* independent of the observer but is shaped by him: the observer is not only necessary to observe the properties of an atomic phenomenon but to bring certain of these about:

> My conscious decision about how to observe say an electron will determine the electron's properties to some extent. If I ask it a particle question it will give me a particle answer; if I ask it a wave question it will give a wave answer. The electron does not *have* objective properties independent of mind (Capra 1982 p.7).

Therefore, 'we can never speak about nature without at the same time speaking about ourselves' (Capra, p.71-2).

The Uncertainty Principle, in dispensing entirely with the notion of a fixed, observable reality, signified the end of a model of the universe that could be completely predictable. As Hawking (1988, p.55) observes 'One certainly cannot predict future events exactly if one cannot even measure the present state of the universe precisely!' It follows, therefore, that the ideal of a measurable objectivity in science is totally unfounded.

Yet again, the implications of this seem bizarre, for as Pagels (1983, p.102) observes, 'The concrete matter of daily experience dissolves into a maelstrom of fleeting ghostly images'. Indeed, as Niels Bohr indicates, 'Those who aren't shocked by Quantum Theory have not understood it'.

Many people have failed to acknowledge the full implications of this quantum weirdness, regarding it merely as theoretical speculation, but as Davies (1984) and Hawking (1988) point out, despite its bizarre implications Quantum Theory is primarily a practical branch of physics which has yielded the laser, the electron microscope, the transistor, the superconductor, nuclear power, and the basis of modern chemistry and biology.

> At a stroke it explained chemical bonding, the structure of the atom and nucleus, the conduction of electricity, the mechanical and thermal properties of solids, the stiffness of collapsed stars and a host of other important physical phenomena ... In short the Quantum Theory is in its everyday application a very down to earth subject with a vast body of supporting evidence, not only from commercial gadgetry, but from careful and delicate scientific experiments (Davies 1984, p.601)

Moreover, as Berry (1987) observes, Quantum Theory must give the same predictions as classical Newtonian physics in spite of being on a very different conceptual basis. Bohr saw this relationship between the two as a deep truth, 'the correspondence principle'. Clearly Quantum Theory must agree with Newtonian physics when applied to large or heavy systems, that is in what is known as the 'classical limit' - the realm of daily experience. Newton's theory is therefore still used for practical purposes not merely because in the situations that we normally deal with the differences between its predictions and those of Quantum Theory are very small, but also because, as Hawking (1988) observes, it has the great advantage of being much simpler to work with. Nevertheless Quantum Theory

> No matter how formalised (it) projects the 'irrational' aspects of subatomic phenomena squarely into the macroscopic domain. It says not only do events in the realm of the very small behave in ways which are utterly different from our common sense view of the world at large, but also that events in the world at large, the world of freeways and sports cars, behave in ways which are utterly different from our common sense view of them (Zukav, 1980, p.30).

The New Physics and the concept of order

The New Physics, as it is now called, presents us with a totally different world view from that portrayed by Newton. It can be characterised as organic, holistic and ecological inasmuch as it suggests a basic oneness of the universe, the apparently separate parts of which are connected in an intimate and immediate way.

> Parts are seen in immediate connection in which their dynamical relationships depend in an irreducible way on the state of the whole system ... Thus, one is led to a new notion of unbroken wholeness which denies the classical idea of analyzability of the world into separately existing parts (Bohm 1980).

It highlights the inadequacy of mechanistic notions of order, or the way in which the universe is thought to be arranged. The mechanistic order of Newton may be described as explicate in that each of its elements lies only in its own regions of space and time and outside the regions appertaining to other things. It is in this sense that events are conceived as separate and independent, and understandable in terms of regular arrangements of objects as in rows or events in sequence. The undivided wholeness implied by the New Physics in which all parts of the universe, including the observer and his instruments, merge and unite in one interdependent totality demands a new concept or order. Physicist David Bohm has proposed a concept appropriate to this undivided separateness, by suggesting that the universe is holographic, or like a gigantic hologram.

A holographic universe

Each part of a hologram contains information about the whole and if the hologram is broken into pieces each piece will reconstruct the whole image. This means that the hologram cannot be understood in terms of mechanistic explicate order. It has to be understood in terms of a total order contained implicitly in each region of time and space. (Here 'implicit' - from the verb to implicate, meaning to fold inwards - is used in the sense that each region contains a total structure enfolded within it.) Examples of this implicate order are demonstrable in the laboratory, but the value of the hologram is that is focuses attention on this new concept of order in a clearly perceptible way. Nevertheless, the hologram is a static record of this order, whereas the order itself is conveyed in a complex movement of electromagnetic fields in the form of light waves, which is termed by Bohm, holomovement - or life energy; an unbroken and undivided totality from which particular aspects such as light and sound or electrons may be abstracted but which are essentially inseparable. This holomovement, which in its totality cannot be limited in any specifiable way, nor bound by any particular measure, is undefinable and immeasurable. Thus Bohm's theory is essentially that *what is* is movement, and that the explicate order - the world of manifest reality - is a secondary derivation from this primary order of the universe. Hard reality is therefore an abstraction from the 'blur' of basic reality, a notion long held by mystics and sages, and reflected in the teachings of Gibran's Prophet:

> Life and all that lives is conceived in the mist and not in the crystal. And who knows but a crystal is a mist in decay (Gibran 1978 edit. pp. 108-9)

Like the mystics of antiquity, Bohm in describing a holographic universe is depicting a world in which what appears to be stable, tangible and 'out there' is not really there at all, but an illusion, a magic show - what the Hindu traditionally describe as 'maya'. Such a view has also been advanced by neuroscientist Karl Pribram (1976) who, in attempting to account for the way in which memory appears to be distributed throughout the brain rather than localised in any one part, proposed that information is enfolded over the whole brain in much the same way as in a hologram. Then, having proposed this holographic model of the brain, he pursued the notion formerly advanced by psychologists of the Gestalt School that the world perceived 'out there' is isomorphic with brain processes; that is, they both exhibit the same form, and thereby arrived at the inescapable conclusion that the world is a hologram, apparently unaware that Bohm had done likewise. He went on to suggest that reality is not what is perceived by the eyes, but that the brain may act as a lens transforming mathematically the blur of primary reality into hard reality, and that without these mathematics we would possibly know a world organised in the frequency domain; a world without space and time, such as that described by mystics throughout history. Hence, in the words of St. Exupéry (1974), 'what is essential is invisible to the eye'.

Nevertheless, the problem for the physicist and neuroscientist is to account for 'normal' perception of mundane, 'explicate' reality, that which Hindu mystics and sages term *avidja* or a 'not-seeing'. Bohm suggests that we learn to see the world in certain ways. Therefore, we do not necessarily notice the primary order because we are habituated to the explicate order which is emphasised in thought and language, both of which are predominantly linear and sequential. Indeed, Western culture as a whole is habituated to the rational, the logical, the linear and sequential, and to a description of a manifest, explicate reality. As a result the ability to 'think straight' is highly valued and there is a tendency to feel that primary experience is of this order.

Another possible explanation, according to Bohm, is that the contents of memory, in the manner of a hologram, focus attention on what is static and fragmented, with the result that the more subtle and transitory features of the unbroken flow 'tend to pale into such seeing insignificance that one is at best only dimly conscious of them' (1980, p.206).

Mystical and magical traditions emphasize that true seeing or direct perception of reality can be achieved by developing insight, literally a looking inwards, which might be thought of as an enfoldment. This notion is consistent with the holographic notion that the world is enfolded within each of its parts. Accordingly, the truth of the universe, ultimate truth, resides within the person.

Just as the mystics of old held that this reality could be accessed by various means, so a number of modern scientists have suggested likewise. These include Lilly (1973) and Grof (1979) who propose that certain drugs, notably psychedelic drugs such as those traditionally used in shamanic ritual, prevent one from 'thinking straight', thereby circumventing what Huxley (1954) termed the 'reducing valve of ordinary conscious-ness', enabling direct perception of the holographic universe described by Bohm and Pribram.

Dissipative structures

Bohm's holographic theory finds support in the Transformation Theory of the chemist, Ilya Prigogine, for which he was awarded the Nobel Prize in 1977. This suggests the means of unfolding from the implicate order, and thus the way it is manifested in time and space. It also establishes the connectedness of living and non-living forms, and thereby bridges the critical gap between living systems and the apparently lifeless universe in which they arise.

Prigogine's theory concerns dissipative structures - that is, all living things and some non-living things such as certain chemical reactions which maintain their form by a continuing dissipation of energy. As such they constitute a flowing wholeness, which is highly complex and always in process. The greater its complexity the more energy the structure requires to maintain its coherence. This produces the paradoxical situation that the greater its coherence, the greater its instability. However, Prigogine suggests that this instability is the key to transformation because the dissipation of energy creates the potential for sudden reordering.

> The continuous movement of energy through the system results in fluctuations; if they are minor the system damps them and they do not alter its structural integrity. But if they reach a critical size they 'perturb' the system. They increase the number of novel interactions within it. They shake it up. The elements of the old pattern come into contact with each other in new ways and make new connections. The parts reorganize into a new whole (Ferguson 1982, p.178).

Accordingly, nature has the potential to create new forms by allowing a shake up of old forms, and it is this capacity which is the key to growth. Put another way, flexibility creates growth. Structures insulated from disturbance are protected from change and are therefore stagnant, never evolving toward a more complex form. This is as true for forms of knowledge or science as for any other system, and suggests that paradigm shifts are essential for the development of thought. Only through the chaos they introduce can order emerge. Such a view, is of course, fully consistent with that of the ancients, as is the central tenet of Prigogine's theory, which is that the meaning of the whole is traceable to the behaviour of its parts, which reverberate throughout the entire system. Here again there are parallels with the views of mysticism, which Prigogine has acknowledged and repeatedly drawn attention to.

Parallels between mysticism and modern thought

In the light of these speculations, mystical experience cannot be dismissed as trivial or as a mere anthropological curiosity. Rather, it has to be admitted into any scientific framework which purports to a complete understanding of reality. Indeed, it is now recognised that the New Physics, and to some extent modern chemistry, restates, albeit in the language of mathematics, the occult and mystical descriptions of reality common to ancient tradition throughout the world, and still emphasised within Eastern culture.

The striking parallels between the discoveries of modern physics and Easten mysticism have been identified by numerous commentators, and a thorough discussion of the correspondence between them provided by Capra (1976), Zukav (1980), LeShan (1982) and Graham (1986). These parallels have also been recognised by many of the most distinguished physicists of the century, including Heisenberg, Schrödinger and Bohr. Indeed when the latter was knighted for his achievements he chose as his coat of arms the T'ai Chi diagram, the symbol of traditional Chinese thought, because of the consistency of the Chinese world view with that of the most advanced physics.

This has forced acknowledgement, in some quarters at least, that in this respect the orientals may have got it right, and that if their basic world view is fundamentally correct, or at least consistent with the present state of scientific knowledge in the West, then maybe other aspects of their thinking which derive from this perspective such as that relating to healing are more appropriate than our own. Holbrook (1981) points out that for many people this idea is hard to accept, because we have all been conditioned to believe that modern Western science is qualitatively supreme among all other forms of knowing; and that 'all others are either primitive or false, or unsuccessful attempts to gain our level'.

For precisely this reason many physicists reared in the Western tradition were shocked by comparisons between the descriptions of physics and mysticism, but they have increasingly come to accept that mysticism provides a consistent and relevant philosophical background to Western science, which unifies and harmonises scientific discoveries and man's spiritual aims and beliefs.

In so doing they have come to appreciate that it is not so much a matter of choosing between alternative views, but of embracing what is complementary among them. As Jung (1978, pp. 8-9) observes:

> Science is the tool of the Western mind, and with it one can open more doors than with bare hands. It is part and parcel of our understanding, and obscures our insight only when it claims that the understanding it conveys is the only kind there is.

Medicine and modern thought

Unfortunately Western medical science has been less willing to accept this position, with the result that our notions of life, death, health and disease rest solidly on seventeenth century Newtonian principles. Medicine has resisted any redefinition of these notions and is still governed by mechanistic thinking, the body being viewed as a machine in good or bad repair, disease or disability as a thing or entity to be treated by elimination of symptoms, primarily with drugs and surgery, after diagnosis which relies on quantitative information. Psychological factors, where acknowledged at all, are regarded as of secondary importance, with psychosomatic illness treated by a separate specialism, psychiatry. All treatment, however, is viewed as a matter for professionals, who are emotionally neutral authority figures, responsible for patients who are passive and dependent.

However twentieth century descriptions of reality demand a radical re-examination of these principles and practices, and, as Dossey (1982) observes, to refuse to face its consequences is to favour dogma over evolving knowledge. The fundamental problem facing contemporary medicine is to reconcile ordinary descriptions of bodies, health and disease with the idea that the universe and everything in it is an inseparable entity. As Dossey (1982, p.111) observes 'separateness of bodies, and absolute distinctions between health and disease cannot be maintained in a context of quantum wholeness', and while this does not mean that these notions cannot be abstracted as apparently discrete features of reality, and spoken of as aspects of the world in just the way that physicists speak of the wave and particle features of electrons, it does mean that cognisance has to be taken of the underlying unbroken wholeness that envelopes all manifestations of the entire universe.

> If we cannot dissociate space and time in the modern universe, we cannot make separate distinctions between bodies, and health and disease. Just as electrons are not things, as Neils Bohr constantly insisted, so too are bodies not things. Just as

electrons do not 'have' particality or waveness, so too our bodies do not 'have' health or disease, they *are* these very qualities, which are more precisely described as unending, unbroken processes connected nonlocally and non-causally in both space and time.

Our habitual way of describing isolated healthy bodies as being recurrently besieged by spells of poor health from birth to the grave has to be reevaluated in any modern description of the world. If moments in time are inseparable then so are health and disease. If elements in space are inseparable, then so are our bodies. And if time and space are inseparable, then our bodies are one with the health and disease that we traditionally presume they 'possess' in some alternating sequence.

We arrive at a view which suggests that bodies, health and disease come together in much the same as the sky and its hues coalesce. Although we speak of different skies, the sky is a seamless inseparable entity. It is a whole. It does not 'have' blueness or redness or any coloration, for it is that blueness and redness. Temporally, as well as spatially, the sky does not end. It does not die. It is an unbroken whole in both space and time. So it is with human bodies, health and disease (Dossey 1982, p.111-112).

These new conceptions of reality thus draw attention to the principles of relatedness, oneness and unity, and away from fragmentation and isolation.

The 'new biology'

The so-called 'new biology' is consistent with this new understanding of reality. Rose et al (1984) insist upon the unitary ontological nature of a material world in which the biological and the social are 'neither separable, nor antithetical, nor alternatives; but complementary'. Awareness of this inter-relatedness and complementarity means that organisms or the environment can no longer be considered in isolation from each other.

> Just as there is no organism without an environment, there is no environment without an organism. Neither organism nor environment is a closed system, each is open to the other. There is a variety of ways in which the organism is the determinant of its own milieu (Rose et al, 1984, pp.273-4).

Hence there is no universal physical fact of nature whose effect on or even relevance to an organism is 'not in part a consequence of the nature of the organism itself' (p.276)

This new biology calls for a radical reappraisal of our thinking about 'being in the world' and has important implications for medical science. When translated into practice these new conceptions of reality require bodies, health and disease to be viewed as dynamic processes rather than discrete entities, which need to be understood in terms of patterns of relationships within the organism and its environment, rather than in terms of separate parts. Health and illness need to be viewed in relation to the wholeness or integration of these processes, rather than in terms of symptoms, or the lack of them.

Accordingly mind has to be regarded as a primary factor in health and illness and therefore so-called 'psychosomatic' illness becomes a matter for all health-care professionals, who are themselves therapeutic partners in the healing process, rather than 'external' to it. Essentially therefore the new description of reality demands, as did Hippocrates, that physicians understand the whole of things.

The physics of health

If Bohm's contention is correct and the entire universe can only be understood as an inseparable entity, the total order of which is contained implicitly in each of its parts, this means that information about the whole is everywhere at once. Therefore the organism has wisdom concerning all the body in each of its parts. This resolves some puzzling body-brain paradoxes such as 'phantom limb' sensations because as Achterberg (1985, p.133) observes, if the brain is a hologram it is unnecessary to have a leg in order for the brain to process leg information. It is sufficient to have once had a leg, or even thought about having a leg. Either way 'leg' storage patterns are established which give rise to sensation in an amputated limb, and some control over what the brain perceives as movement.

This has potentially important implications for diagnosis and treatment. Firstly, it suggests that qualitative information, including the patient's subjective experience and intuition, together with that of the medical practitioner, need to be considered as the primary data in diagnosis, with quantitative methods as an adjunct. Secondly, it suggests that the mind can, through generation of imagery, effect physical processes; and it also raises the possibility that both diagnosis and treatment can be effected by way of any given part. The latter has long been claimed by traditional and oriental systems of healing and those such as iridology which are currently accorded little validity or status. Indeed all of these principles are fundamental to ancient and oriental systems which traditionally employ intuition and imagination in healing, and regard healer and patient as equals in the healing process.

Transformation and health

Viewed within the framework of Transformation Theory disease, especially major illness, is clearly a perturbation. Accordingly it is a means whereby the system can, in Prigogine's terms, 'escape' to a higher level of organisation or integration, and thus to greater wholeness and health. Perturbation is therefore bound up in shifts towards physiological complexity. Dossey (1982) observes that the tenets of Transformation Theory are already invoked in many health-care methodologies including orthodox medical practice. Immunization, for example, involves inducing a mini-disease just sufficient to stimulate the body to produce protective antibodies, thereby 'producing an evolution toward biological complexity through intentionally perturbing the immune system' (p.89).

Dossey indicates that if perturbation of the body's integration never occurred it would be truly defenceless, because necessary mechanisms would not evolve, as is the case in children born with immune deficiency, who because they are unable to respond to perturbations from outside cannot escape to a higher degree of immune complexity and usually succumb to overwhelming infections in early life.

Clearly, therefore, processes of perturbation and health form a complementary whole. However as Dossey indicates, orthodox medicine frequently moves *against* perturbation rather than *with* it, 'battering the perceived threats with a constantly changing array of injections, pills and surgery', and trying 'to avoid encounters with external challenges to our health; failing that we struggle to resist them using any means at hand' (p.91).

Perhaps unsurprisingly, therefore, antibiotic, antibacterial, and anti-viral treatments often prove to be counterproductive - not only do they prevent development of the immune system by denying it the possibility of challenge, but by perturbing viruses and bacteria actually contribute to the development of super-resistant strains.

Clearly, therefore, general medical practice needs to be re-examined in the light of these factors. Dossey argues that health strategies need to incorporate flexibility as a primary goal - the ability to react effectively to challenges to the body-mind integration clearly being a fundamental requirement of health. Accordingly, he suggests, the interval between illness becomes crucial, because it is here that the person can sabotage the body's wisdom to resist perturbations, reducing its ability to react by negative habits, including smoking, overeating, fatigue, and attitudes

> Seen from this perspective the 'real' medicine is what we do between illness-events. All of the techniques which we relegate to the second-class status of preventative medicine are of critical importance, for they help determine the body's capacity to successfully reorder itself to a higher degree of complexity when actually challenged by disease processes.

> Conversely, the traditional approach of medicine and surgery should be viewed as a second-line of defense. These methods should be viewed as a last resort, as a supplement to the body's wisdom. Too often they are used as an effort to shield the body from physical onslaught - as in the condemnable practice of prescribing antibiotics for a common cold, or using tranquillisers for the commonplace anxieties of daily living. For most assaults to its integrity the body needs no shielding. In any event, our efforts of this type result less frequently in *protecting* the body than in *meddling* in its affairs and frustrating its wisdom' (p.91).

He concedes that sometimes a second line of defence is required, but points out that this is unusual, and that perturbation does not always end in reorganisation, but death. Nevertheless insufficient attention is given to approaches which complement the wisdom of the body, working with perturbations rather than against them - which is the fundamental principle of homeopathy, and contemporary 'humanistic' psychotherapies which, rather than opposing a problem, facilitate confrontation with it as the solution.

Yet Prigogine's theory that order and organization can arise spontaneously out of disorder and chaos through a process of self-organization helps to account for the effects claimed for psychotherapy.

> An individual reliving a traumatic incident in a state of highly focused inward attention perturbs the pattern of that specific old memory. This triggers a reorganization - a new dissipative structure (Ferguson 1982, p.183).

It also lends support to the view advanced by Laing (1959) that mental illness or 'dis-order' frequently enables reintegration of the personal self, rather than merely disintegration.

Ferguson (1982) observes that long before Transformation Theory had been confirmed Israeli research chemist Aharon Katchalsky had identified the brain as a perfect example of a dissipative structure. Unfortunately his untimely death prevented further research on how this might apply to investigations of the human brain and consciousness - research which might explain the transformative power of altered states of consciousness, imaginative processes, psychological therapies and the ancient and oriental healing systems which seem fully consistent with new descriptions of reality, and to enshrine its principles.

It would seem therefore that there is nothing to be lost, and a great deal to be gained from examination of the fundamental assumptions on which these systems are based. Indeed, as Lazlo (cited by Purvis, 1989) observes:

> The universe has been known by exceptional, deeply conscious human beings for thousands of years. It is the duty of science to acknowledge this.

Chapter 3

Eastern Perspectives on Healing

We are not victims of the world we see; We are victims of the way we see the world.

Shirley MacLaine

The astigmatism in Western medical science would appear to conform with what Scott (1983) terms 'Fort's Theorem', after the philosopher Charles Fort, which holds that if you encounter data which lie outside an area which you have defined for yourself as containing the only possible data, you will either fail to see it altogether or else will plausibly discredit it in terms of your own prior assumptions. This is particularly evident in Western attitudes towards Eastern ideas. Jung (1978, p.12) observes that when looked at from 'the incurably externalistic standpoint' of the Western intellect the practical importance which Eastern ideas might have for us is difficult to comprehend, with the result that they have been classified merely as philosophical and ethnological curiosities, and nothing more. Yet,

> As it now begins to appear, data for resolving the West's scientific impasse was available in the East all along but the East's culture and philosophy, both ancient and modern, was consistently assumed to be either puerile or defective, or both.
>
> The knowledge of the East was not tried and found wanting. It was assumed to be inferior and not tried (Scott 1983, p.19).

Eastern philosophy

Eastern perspectives on the universe are based on a philosophical tradition quite different from that of the West. The distortions introduced into the mystic tradition of ancient times by Classical Greek civilisation are not present, at least to the same extent, in cultures which largely lack its influence. Consequently the thinking in most Eastern cultures remains close to its mystical origins, being circular or cyclic rather than linear. Therefore in most of their traditions there is a strong intuition of the space-time nature of reality, and a different rhythm to life.

The awareness that space and time are inseparably linked, with each other and all other aspects of the universe, is stressed again and again, as are the concepts of change and movement, or energy, which may be one of the reasons why Eastern thought corresponds in general much better with modern scientific thought than does that of most Greek philosophy.

The interpenetration of space and time is most clearly expressed in Indian thought. As Needleman (1972, p.25) observes,

> The Indian mind is imbued with the sense of the relativity of all things and enterprises in the world and rigorously resists the yes or no, black or white tendency of much modern Western thought. Greek natural philosophy was on the whole essentially static and largely based on geometrical considerations. Its influence on Western thought may well be one reason why in the West we have great conceptual difficulties with the relativistic models of modern physics.

Indian thought

Whereas in Western culture the universe is seen as composed of parts distinctly separate from one another - nature, man, animals, birds, trees, plants, minerals and so on having been created by God in the beginning of time, the thinkers of ancient India regarded the idea of such separateness as erroneous. They considered there to be a connection among all these phenomena, a unity which pervades the whole universe including God. This one great, impersonal absolute power known as Brahman - an immutable, ultimate and essentially indescribable reality which pervades and transcends all things, unifying all the apparent differences of the phenomenal world, is the first principle from which all things derive, by which all are supported, and into which they eventually disappear. Indeed, all phenomenal existence was viewed as transitory, impermanent and in the process of change; a ceaseless cycle of beginning and ending which in Sanskrit, the ancient sacred writing of India, was termed *samsara*, literally 'a going around in circles'. Just as man is subject to cycles of birth and rebirth, the universe itself was thought to go through cycles of dissolution and recreation spanning vast periods of time. Such a process was held to be indivisible and irreducible. Therefore all reduction into objective facts and forms constitutes illusion, or *maya*. Stutley (1985) indicates that a frequent metaphor for Brahman is 'ocean', denoting inexhaustible potentiality. Like Brahman the greater part of the ocean is never visible or known, while the rising and disappearing waves represent the ephemeral lives of myriads of living creatures who come into existence for a while and then are reabsorbed into it.

Nikhilananda (1968, p.29) observes that etymologically the word 'Brahman' denotes an entity whose greatness, powers and expansion cannot be measured. Thus the realms of reason, rationality, objectivity, analysis and dissection with their implicit notions of measurement, which are so esteemed in the West, are seen as *avidja*, or ignorance, which is not so much a not-knowing as a not-seeing the reality of the world. As such it is the very antithesis of knowledge or philosophy, the Sanskrit word for which is *darsana*, or seeing, and the aim of which is held to be understanding the unity of all things, or Natural Law.

Vedanta, the philosophy expounded in the earliest scriptures of the Hindu - originally the Persian word for Indian - comprises all the various sects that exist in India. It derives from the Vedas, ancient teachings, or knowledge, (from the Sanskrit *vid*: to know) and is a practical philosophy rather than mere intellectual understanding, in which reality must be directly known and this knowledge applied in daily life. Vedanta therefore teaches that life has no other purpose than learning to know ourselves for what we really are - a manifestation of the Ultimate Reality. Essentially therefore its teaching is that a man can by personal effort and use of inner knowledge attain union with the divine while on earth. Its aim is to harmonise all. This is possible because Ultimate Reality or Brahman and the individual soul (atman), though seemingly apart, are in actuality one, as is conveyed in the teaching: 'The real is one. It is the mind which makes it appear as many'. This illusion, maya, disappears when one attains direct knowledge of Brahman. Understanding maya - the illusory nature of reality - is therefore of key importance. The 'three strands which constitute the rope of maya with which men become bound to the phenomenal world' (Nikhilananda, 1968, p.42) are termed gunas, and symbolised in the Indian 'trick' in which a rope appears to observers to be a snake. The gunas, known as Sattva, Rajas and Tamas, are held to be present in various degrees in all phenomena, including mind, intellect and ego.

Rajas is characterised by energy, and manifests in ceaseless activity. It creates attachment and suffering, whereas Tamas, which manifests in inactivity, dullness, inadvertence and stupidity, is the mother of illusion and represents the veiling power of maya. Sattva, which manifests as spiritual qualities, strikes a balance between the opposing characteristics of Rajas and Tamas.

Although these gunas are present in all things sometimes one preponderates and sometimes another. According to Vedanta when these three gunas are in balance the universe remains in a state of non-manifestation, or dissolution; and when this equilibrium is disturbed through a preponderance of one or other guna, the creation of the material universe occurs.

The first element to evolve at the beginning of a cycle is *akasha*, often incorrectly translated as ether, space or sky. It is the intangible material substance that pervades the whole universe - that which fills all space between worlds and molecules. It is the substance from which all else is formed, and, often referred to as prana or breath, it is seen as the primal life-giving force, and thought of as a subtle biological conductor in the body. Gradually four other elements become manifest; air, fire, water and earth, although these are not the elements perceived by the sense organs. Initially subtle, they become more gross through a process of combination, and from the gross and subtle elements emerge physical objects, the body, mind, intellect, mind-stuff and ego. Vedanta speaks of five elements only because from the standpoint of sense perception there are only five elemental features in the universe, namely sound, touch, form, taste and smell.

After these material forms are projected through maya, the material cause of the universe, Brahman, the pure intelligence or efficient cause of the universe, enters into them as life and consciousness and animates them. Divinity thereby pervades all things and this belief forms the basis of Indian morality. Prana is thus material and immaterial, endowed with intelligence and likened to the spirit. The flow of this psychic energy is therefore the totality of the entire self, and the equivalent of vitality.

According to the Hindu tradition, as in that of Ancient Egypt, cosmic energy is distributed down through the body to the base of the spine, where it mixes with dense, dormant Earth energy represented by the coiled serpent, Kundalini, which symbolises the stored energy, or potential of the organism. It is seen as the task of the individual to mix, balance and refine these energies, and direct them upwards. The ascent occurs along two major pathways or *nadis*, the Ida on the left, and Pingala on the right, which criss-cross around the central Shushumna. This is represented symbolically as twin serpents coiling upwards around a central staff (cf: the caduceus). As the ascent occurs the various energies are blended and transmuted creating a variety of experiences and profound changes in awareness, which have been documented by Gopi Krishna (1971). The ultimate goal is not only to raise the vertical energy but to appropriately open and balance the energy in each centre in flowing harmony through the total mind/body/soul system. It is therefore directed to achieving a state of harmony, wholeness or holiness, oneness with the Ultimate Reality, which is synonymous with health. The whole culture is therefore concerned with health or healing, which is essentially spiritual in nature.

Belief in the Self

Vedanta recognises that the human mind is incapable of imagining the Ultimate Reality with which it seeks union, and that it therefore turns towards the highest it can conceive, either a God or gods with attributes which are projections of human virtues, or the God-like men or exemplars such as Ramakrishnan who strengthen and purify by example. The dynamic unity of the universe is personified in the god Shiva, the cosmic dancer, who sustains the manifold phenomena of the universe, unifying by immersing them in his rhythm and making them partake in the cosmic dance. Such deities are worshipped in the hope that through devotion the worshipper can become like them. Vedanta doesn't condemn cults of this kind but reminds the worshipper that the god or exemplar must not come between them and the knowledge that they are both essential projections of the same Ultimate Reality, and that in worshipping those in whom eternal nature is revealed, they are revering their own divine nature which is more or less obscured. Vedanta has thus sustained and interrelated many cults of gods and divine incarnations, which as Isherwood (1972) observes, has led many commentators to conclude that Hinduism is polytheistic. However, this is not the case, rather that there is but one truth, called by many names. Essentially, 'Vedanta teaches men to have faith in themselves first' (Vivekenanda, 1974, p.6) and this is reflected in traditional Indian medicine - Ayurveda.

Ayurvedic medicine

The tradition of Ayurveda, which is claimed as the grandfather of all holistic health systems, is some 3000 years old, and until the formation of the British Empire when Western medicine overtook India, it was dominant on the Indian sub-continent. Since 1945, when India gained her independence, there has been a remarkable resurgence of interest in this system and many colleges and universities now offer training in this discipline.

Ayurveda, and its offshoot Unami, which is dominant in Pakistan, have become known in the West only relatively recently through its practice within immigrant Asian communities, but in 1980 the World Health Organisation suggested that its principles should be widely known as they could help to integrate complementary and modern medicine. Ayurveda is Sanskrit for the 'science of life' and it is a section in the last four Vedas, the Atharva Veda, written about 1200 BC. Although its early history is obscure it contains magical spells and charms to cope with a wide range of natural and supernatural conditions, suggesting origins in early magic. Moreover, as Ancient India had no writing, all its teachings were memorised and handed down by the highest caste, the Brahmins, in characteristic occult tradition.

The first school of medicine as such was established at Banaras in 500 BC, and here in 5 and 6 BC respectively the main texts *Susruta Samhita* and *Charaka Samhita* were written. Together they constitute a comprehensive system of medicine which is essentially cosmological, for, as in all traditional systems, health is considered as a balance between constituent qualities and energies of man and the universe. Fundamental to it is the idea that man must be regarded as a whole, with no separation of his mind, body or soul.

Only one third of the system is concerned with disease, it being mostly concerned with health and providing a guide to living. As such it is an excellent system of preventative medicine and balanced living.

Healing is based on the premise that balance can be achieved through the tridosha or tridhatu, which differentiates into three elements, kapha, pitta, vatu or vayu. Kaphic energy which is associated with air is concerned with growth and nutrition (anabolism), pitta (associated with fire) with digestion (catabolism), and vata or vayu (or water) with the nervous system, mind and the distribution of psychic energy. It also controls and regulates the other two elements which come under the general heading of metabolism. Vata thus has a central role and reflects the psychosomatic component of Ayurveda.

All areas of human functioning are located in one or other of these doshas or cosmic forces, each of which has two aspects, *purusha* - the material side of man and his conscious state - and his essence, *prakriti*, the unmanifest self, subconscious or spirit. The former is composed, as are all things, of gunas, and people are thought to be constitutionally of one type or another. The aim is therefore to identify the predominance of any guna by observing the person's attitudes and behaviour. Part of the physician's role is thus to maintain the balance of gunas in the body. Since they are identifiable in foods, minerals and natural remedies, choosing the correct one is a logical process. So, for example, Sharma (1985) observes that the condition commonly known as asthma is one in which the Ayurvedic physician would note a dominance of air (kapha). He would therefore prescribe a diet which excludes vayu food such as rice and spices and would use a remedy that would stimulate the other two elements. (Fulder (1987) indicates that the complexity of Indian curries owes partly to the necessity of balancing various components such as water generating coriander with heat producing chilli.) Neverthe- less diagnosis and prescription is no simple matter, given that Siddha, the Tamil language version of Ayurveda, recognises 4492 different sicknesses, and all remedies need to be prepared with regard to the patient's individual susceptibilities, seasonal and climatic variations, and the like. Here again one can see close similarities between the Ayurvedic and Hippocratic traditions, which have prompted some commentators to suggest that at some point Pythagoras was influenced by Indian philosophy. It is more likely, however, that these similarities arise from their common origin in the mystical, shamanic traditions of the ancient world.

Access to prakriti or the spirit is by way of five doshas or essence types. The energy system and the five fundamental powers of nature, space, air, fire, water and earth are seen fundamentally related, and all bodies as different combinations of these natural elements, all of which arise out of the absolute substance prakriti. In human bodies these elements combine in special ways to become transformed into seven tissue types of dhatus. Abuse of any of these through excess, underuse or misuse is considered to be an important cause of unmeasured being, and eventually of ill health.

Jacobs (1987) observes that the alienation of man from his natural environment can be seen as the loss of the natural relationship between the senses and the elemental powers of nature at both the individual and social levels. In this way, modern man has 'taken leave of his senses'. He therefore needs to return not only to his senses but to right measures, knowledge of which according to Jacobs is present in the human heart.

> They come most readily to mind when it is still and quiet, in the full awareness of the senses working in the moment. Then discrimination is seen to act by itself and the right measures become clear and the right actions needed can be undertaken with confidence (p.126).

In this concept of measure one finds, yet again, close similarities with the early Greek tradition, and also in the view of the physician-patient relationship. Sharma (1971) observes that unlike Western medicine Ayurveda has always been based on positive interaction between physician and patient.

> An understanding of the need to strive for spiritual self development is taken for granted and in this respect the physician combines the role of spiritual guide. The patient understands that his obligation is to direct himself towards purity ... This is in marked contrast to the relationship between a Western doctor and his patient, who is the passive recipient of the practitioner's treatment, often ignoring his obligation to strive for his own physical well-being (p.21).

Self-help is therefore fundamental to Ayurveda.

A great deal of research in Ayurveda is carried out and published in the *Journal of Research in Indian Medicine*, although this is little known in the West. Fulder (1987) indicates that when he was investigating Ayurveda in India he was shown remedies which would induce muscles to regenerate, which is not held to be possible by Western medicine. However, some Ayurvedic practices are becoming more widespread in the West with the increase of immigrant Asian communities, among whom practitioners of Ayurvedic medicine are commonly known as hakims or vaids. Some of their traditional practices, such as vaccination, anaesthesia by inhalation and dietetics have only been practised in the West for the last hundred years or so.

Yoga

One of the practices of Ayurveda already well-known in the West - albeit only during this century - is yoga, which as Day (1951, p.34) observes, is not, as some Westerners suppose, merely a system of physical exercise 'that requires a pupil to contort his limbs into the weirdest and most intricate positions which only ballet dancers, acrobats and the limbless can achieve'. This belief has gained currency because of certain practices highlighted by the media which are concerned with the promotion of physical fitness. However, yoga is more than a combination of exercises and breathing. It is a complete philosophy and self-help system which embraces the whole person in their physical, mental and spiritual aspects.

The term itself derives from the Sanskrit *yuj* meaning to join or yoke, and it signifies the yoking or union of the individual with the Ultimate Reality. It is thus essentially a spiritual discipline; a means of attaining the highest aim of Vedanta and the Hindu tradition. It is 'the most eloquent expression of the Indian mind and at the same time the instrument continually used to produce this peculiar attitude of mind' (Jung 1978, p.160). In pointing out that its training of the parts of the body unifies them with the whole of the mind and spirit, Jung observes that yoga practice is unthinkable and ineffectual without the ideas on which it is based, and that the Western mind makes it impossible at the outset for the intentions of yoga to be realised in any adequate way; 'The Indian can forget neither the body nor the mind, while the European is always forgetting either one or the other' (1978, p.80).

There are many different forms of yoga: *Hatha*, which is concerned with integration through strength, the body and vital energies being brought to the peak of health and efficiency through physical exercises and breathing; *Jnana*, which involves deep study of and meditation on sacred texts; *Bhakti*, intense devotion to a chosen deity, or isvara; *Karma*, or integration through right action and good works; *Raja*, which aims the control the subconscious mind; and also Mantra, Kundalini, Laya and Tantric yoga.

Mantra yoga is based on the inherent power of sound and vibration as revealed by ancient seers. Its aim is to alter ordinary consciousness by rhythmical repetition of divine names or phrases known as mantras.

Kundalini, which is synonymous with *shakti*, the divine cosmic energy thought to exist in every living being, signifies unlimited potential. It is symbolised as the female serpent curled half-asleep at the base of the spine. The aim of Kundalini yoga is to raise this energy upwards through the body, generating intense heat, and various psychic effects, documented by Gopi Krishna, (1971), which are achieved primarily through meditation and imagery. As such Kundalini is consistent with the shamanic practice of generating heat; the raising of the serpent being a metaphor to enable description of energy movement which cannot be expressed clearly in any other way. *Laya* yoga, like Kundalini, is concerned with arousing cosmic energies enabling the individual to merge with Universal Being. It helps the adept gain mastery over his senses, rather than remain enslaved by them. *Tantra* according to Eliade (1970) is also a refinement of ancient shamanistic practices which uses nature to transcend nature and discipline body and mind. It endeavours to overcome and thereby dominate the distractions of the world which stand between the individual and the Absolute, by using them to destroy the desire for new experience. Erotic practices are intended to enable the adept to utilize the immense power of sexuality to overcome every vestige of desire, and to be efficacious they have to be conducted in a strictly ritual manner. The tantric aim is a kind of 'eternal orgasm', a union with Ultimate Reality which transcends the duality of self and other. In the West, and to a lesser extent in India, its methods are frequently misunderstood as giving rise to unbridled sexuality and libertinism.

All forms of yoga are developments of the Upanishads, that portion of the Vedas dating from 1500 BC devoted to philosophy. Its original formulation is obscure, but Patanjali is held by most authorities to have been responsible for collecting and correlating the early teachings just prior to the time of Christ, although virtually nothing is known of him, and his true identity has not been ascertained. Nevertheless, the *Yogasutra* in which the metaphysical and doctrinal aspects of yoga are expounded is attributed to him. Patanjali's *Aratamsahasutra* clearly suggests a holographic understanding of the universe:

> It is said that in sky of Indra as a net of pearls so arranged that when you look at one pearl, you see all the other pearls reflected in it. Whenever you enter one part of the net you set a bell ringing which reverberates from every part of the net, from every part of reality (Vollmar, 1987).

The yoga of Patanjali consists of eight parts and is known as ashtanga yoga, or yoga with eight limbs. These are *yama*: abstention from evil thought and deed; *niyama*: daily observances such as purity, austerity, contentment, study of the scriptures and devotion; *asana*: posture; *pranamaya*: regulation and control of breathing; *pratyahara*: subjugation of the senses to bring them under the control of the mind; *dharana*: concentration of the mind; *dhyana*: steady, unbroken concentration, or deep contemplation; and *samadhi*: ecstatic union or integration with Ultimate Reality. Thus, as Gopi Krishna (1988) observes, it is technically quite incorrect to describe anyone performing several postures or asanas efficiently as practising yoga, just as it is inaccurate to describe mere concentration as yoga.

When Westerners speak of yoga they are usually referring only to Hatha yoga, yet this was never intended to be pursued in isolation from the other forms. Its function is to prepare for concentrating the powers of the mind, or meditation, which is held to be the only way to know Ultimate Reality, because only by overcoming physical obstacles can the yogin commence the inner journey towards integration or union, which is the aim of yoga.

Furthermore, Westerners typically regard Hatha yoga as merely a system of physical exercises and breathing techniques. However, Hatha yoga includes practices of internal and external hygiene largely unknown in the West and, a branch of Hatha yoga, Anna yoga or the yoga of food, governs diet and nutrition (Santa Maria, 1978). These practices, and many more, are all intended as a preparation for meditation.

Meditation

All Eastern traditions share a common emphasis on meditation, which is said to be a state in which the true self is known. From a psychological point of view it can be thought of as a modification of the process of attention, an introversion or drawing inwards away from the ephemera of the external manifest world to that of the inner self. The thoughts, images and experiences with which the mind normally identifies fade away so that one ceases to think 'I am this or that' but simply 'I am'. When the sense of self is relinquished the person is said to be in a state of pure being in which he feels unified with the whole of life and creation. This state, which in the Hindu tradition is known as samadhi or still mind, can be likened to a state of inner mental silence, a void or no-thingness, in which experience as it is usually known ceases.

Buddhism

Westerners appear to take the view that Buddhism is a characteristic Indian tradition, and while it is true that Buddhism emerged from Hinduism as a dominant philosophy of the Indian sub-continent, there are nevertheless relatively few Buddhists in India. Wilson-Ross (1973) indicates that although in time Buddhism was reabsorbed into the all-embracing Hinduism from which it sprang, it was destined to become and remain the dominant influence in vast regions of Asia, Ceylon, Burma, Cambodia, Thailand, Vietnam, Laos, Tibet, Mongolia, China, Korea and Japan, 'where it has had an almost incalculable effect on art, literature and ways of life'.

It is an evolving tradition extending over two and a half millennia. Indeed no other philosophical tradition has existed in such disparate cultures as a major influence for so long. Over fifty per cent of the world's population live in areas where Buddhism has at some time been the dominant philosophical force.

Buddhism originated circa 6th century BC in the teachings of the Indian sage Siddhartha Gautama, the so-called Buddha or Awakened One who has 'woken up' to the true nature of reality; one who knows the basic truth of the universe.

The cardinal principles expounded by the Buddha are held by his followers to be fundamental truths which explain the human condition. He asserted that the individual lives in process, or continuous motion (samsara) and it is thus that life is experienced as change or flux. The impersonal law operating within this process and governing growth and development is termed karma, the law of causation, or cause and effect. The doctrine of karma holds that everything performed during life has a moral significance and will influence the fate of the individual in subsequent incarnations. Consequently all living beings live under conditions they have inherited by their deeds. This Cosmic Law shapes all deeds on earth, but without eliminating human free will, as man can decide his actions and therefore his karma. To Westerners karma often appears to suggest a deterministic view of man as activated by uncontrollable, external forces, and to justify a resigned attitude to life. However, Patel (1980) indicates that such a view is a misrepresentation of karma, for in the teachings of Buddha the human mind has a dual aspect. One aspect creates its own bondage and suffering by its attachment to and apparent inability to grow beyond the appearance of things. This is viewed by Buddha to be a form of ignorance, or not-seeing, which reflects the human tendency to obscure and veil the true nature of the universe. The other aspect of the mind has the potential to transform karma into the pursuit of wisdom and enlightenment, implicit in which is the ability for transcendence which frees the individual from all desires and needs. Therefore when the mind is turned inwards it is the cause of release and freedom, but when turned outward it is the cause of bondage. The outer aspect of mind is identified with ego or rational mind, and its attachment to power and possessions is likened to a monkey which plays tricks on man by creating illusion or *maya*, while the inner aspect of mind is identified with essence or authentic being. For the individual freedom from the endless cycle of existence, symbolised by a circle or wheel, lies in looking inwards. Thus Buddhism focuses on the self-liberating power of the introverted mind.

This self-awareness or self-perception is literally insight, and emphasis is placed upon its development through meditation, and the abandonment of ego, for in Buddhism the perfect man has no self or ego, but fuses with the Ultimate Oneness or unity of the universe which is indivisible, timeless and formless. Its aim is the attainment of one's centre, a point of balance or harmony, a still point from which the infinite in all things is perceived. Achievement of this state constitutes perfect health or holiness. Buddhism thus fundamentally addresses itself to healing the human condition.

The Buddhist concept of suffering

Indeed the essence of the whole teaching is deliverance from suffering through maximal development of consciousness. One of the Buddha's most penetrating insights was the understanding of the role of sorrow, suffering or *dukkha* in human experience. This is intimately connected with the concept of impermanence or anicca which is a consequence of living in process. Buddha observed that sorrow is experienced because of the impermanence of things, or change, whether physical, psychological or emotional, and man's awareness of it, and its consequences - illness, ageing, disease, death, loss, changing relationships and separation. Buddha recognised that change is stressful and produces anxiety and fear, and that man's hunger for security and permanence, represented as resistance to change, are manifestations of suffering, as is clinging to the ego, and our deep-seated fear of losing our identity or sense of self. Nevertheless, irrespective of man's intolerance of it, change is intrinsic to the human condition. Indeed the human condition is the cause of sorrow. Man therefore defends himself against change by clinging to the familiar and the habitual, which gives a false sense of security.

Buddha, however, saw the possibility for transformation through acceptance of change, which requires attention to and confrontation with the very anxieties it generates. This is achieved primarily by meditation, which in 'switching off' ordinary consciousness allows unconscious contents to present themselves, and also by adherence to a code of conduct - a way of achieving balance between the extremes of self-indulgence and asceticism. Nancy Wilson-Ross (1973) renders the basic formula for deliverance from suffering as:

1. First you must see clearly what is wrong;

2. Next decide to be cured;

3. You must act;

4. You speak to aim at being cured;

5. Your livelihood must not conflict with your therapy;

6. Therapy must go forward at the 'staying speed', the critical velocity that can be sustained;

7. You must think about it incessantly;

8. Learn how to contemplate with the deep mind.

The same procedure for cure can also be stated more succinctly in a simple list of steps;

- Right seeing (or understanding)
- Right purpose
- Right conduct
- Right speech
- Right means of livelihood and vocation
- Right effort
- Right kind of awareness or mind control
- Right concentration or meditation.

Buddhism however does not encourage a solemn view of life. On the contrary, Buddha recognised that laughter is a great healing force, a view shared by Hindu sages and reflected in Rajneesh's statement that 'humour will glue your fragments into one whole'. Hence traditionally, the Buddha, who sees beyond the illusion of life, and thus 'sees the joke', as it were, laughs.

Buddhist meditation

As in the Hindu tradition, all forms of mental and physical hygiene are a preparation for meditation, which is the means through which the individual realises his true nature. The techniques of what is known as the Theravada School of Buddhism has two stages: *satipatthana*, in which the mind is controlled, or trained to see things as they are, without emotion or thought of the self; and *satpatthana*, transcendence of mind, which involves concentration, and commences with the practice of attention and the attempt to bring the mind under the owner's will. Humphreys (1962) likens this to training a dog to come to heel and stay there. Only when this is achieved is a person thought to be in a fit state to start meditation. For exercises in self-control the person may focus on external features such as a rose or door-knob, or internal ones such as breathing or the emotions. Potential subjects are endless. The third stage, known variously as *vipassana*, *satori* or *samahdi*, is an utterly impersonal awareness of the essence of the subject under observation such that 'the observer becomes the essence of the thing observed'. This is a state of no-mind, void of all particulars. Only when the truths of the Theravada School have been assimilated can the individual grasp the expanded and deepened truths of the Mahayana School. These different schools have arisen because as Buddhism spread from India it found different forms of expression. So, the schools of Buddhism in various cultures differ from each other.

Almost from the beginning there have been two schools of Buddhist teaching. The Theravada or School of Elders, is the Buddhism of Burma, Thailand, Kampuchea, Laos, Sri Lanka, Vietnam, Bangladesh and India; the Mahayana or Large Vehicle - the majority sect - spread north and east, to Tibet, Mongolia, the Himalayas, parts of China and the Soviet Union, Japan and Korea. In general the former is more strict and austere, the latter more flexible and permissive. Consequently in countries where Mahayana has flourished a far wider diversity of practice has arisen. Within the latter it is therefore possible to distinguish broadly between Northern and Eastern Buddhism. Nevertheless, as Wilson-Ross (1973, p.84) observes, this diversity rests on a basic unity that exists in spite of many denominational differences in interpretation and practice.

Tibetan Buddhism and Medicine

This is part of the Mahayana school and includes a third force, that of Vajrayana or Tantric Buddhism, which is known as the Diamond Vehicle, because it is many faceted.

In Tibetan Buddhism ego is viewed as a limitation of human reality and as such is a physical as well as a mental and spiritual problem, because as Anderson (1982) indicates, holding on to a rigid self-image, struggling to censor and manipulate experience to meet its demands, is hard work involving physical tension and pain. Tibetan Buddhism therefore promotes a series of exercises in relaxation to deal with life's anxieties. The Tibetan approach to healing thus reflects the belief that optimum well-being is a relaxed, balanced open state.

Human illness, however minor, is seen as a cosmic event.

As a body man is a microcosmic but faithful reflection of the macroscopic reality in which he is embedded and which preserves and nourishes him every second of his life; as a mind, he is a ripple on the surface of a great ocean of consciousness. Health is the proper relationship between the microcosm which is man and the macrocosm which is the universe. Disease is a disruption of this relationship (Yetsehe Dhonden, personal physician to the Dalai Lama cited in Anderson, 1982, p.219).

The aim of medicine is to restore harmony and balance. Healing is therefore essentially spiritual and the leading physicians are lamas or monks. As Anderson observes, although Tibet developed a complex system of medicine with elaborate techniques, a long period of training for physicians, and a sophisticated system of pharmacology, it has never resembled its Western counterpart.

There are three levels of medical practice in the Tibetan system: the 'gentle' methods which include simple practices such as giving medicines or applying salves to the skin; the 'stronger' methods, such as bloodletting and lancing abscesses; and the 'violent' methods including removal of foreign objects and cauterization of wounds. Wherever possible the gentler methods are used. Surgery, although developed to a fairly high level and practised for several centuries, was abandoned for reasons unknown but thought to be because permanent nerve and vein damage may make meditation difficult and therefore physical self-control and self-healing impossible.

Diagnosis and care in traditional Tibetan medicine operate on several levels. Emotional, physical, spiritual and ecological aspects of the disorder are considered. The physician always looks into the life situation of the patient and may determine disease to be some expression of disturbance in the psycho-social environment such as a bereavement, personal misfortune or sudden change in routine. Tibetan medicine thus anticipates contemporary work on stress and life change by several thousands of years.

Emotional nourishment may be the prescribed remedy for such conditions. In most cases extensive physiological diagnosis is also conducted, the doctor examining the body, and taking the pulse, analysing urine, faeces, sleep and eating patterns. Where medicines are called for, herbs, flowers, fruits, roots, honey, and minerals are used as infusions, poultices and vapours.

The patient is an active participant in cure rather than a passive participant:

> The feeling tone of the healing experience is extremely important, perhaps more important than the specifics of medical practice. A certain caring and trust has to be present and mutually experienced (Anderson, 1982, p.98).

Compassion is the supreme virtue of the medical practitioner, but the state of mind of the patient is equally important. The optimum emotional state for healing includes such qualities as compassion for the self, awareness or mindfulness, a realistic understanding of karma in illness, cheerfulness and optimism and a basic confidence in the naturalness of the healing process.

Zen Buddhism

Buddhism reached China in, or some time before the first century AD and from its introduction one form was unique in purpose and method, focussing on meditation - called *Djana* in Sanskrit, the Chinese version of which Chu'an was subsequently rendered as zen when passed on via Korea to Japan. The character of zen has largely been influenced by its cross-cultural evolution, it being, as Wilson-Ross (1973) observes a unique blend of Indian mysticism and Chinese naturalism seived through the rather special net of Japanese character. Its relationship to other forms of Buddhism is described by Humphreys (1962, p.81):

> If the foundations of the building called Buddhism are best seen in the Theravada school, and the Mahayana schools may be viewed as so many rooms on the first floor, then the zen school is the top storey, above which there are no more, nor any roof to the building which at this level is utterly open to the sky.

It is based on specific teachings of the Buddha, most notably 'Look within, thou art the Buddha'. It therefore emphasises the development of insight through meditation. Its aim is enlightenment, the realisation of the Ultimate Reality which is beyond words or reasoning.

Zen denies that understanding of the universe can be achieved by conceptual thought or ever fully communicated, but can best be accessed and expressed through wordless activities. Wisdom is derived from intuitive awareness or insightful understanding which is achieved by close attention to the performance of mundane activities. For the student of the Rinzai school of zen brought to Japan in 1191 by the Japanese monk Ersai, the path to enlightenment may involve archery, judo, kendo (fencing), ikebana (flower arrangement), the ceremonial preparation of tea, the building of a garden, haiku, the Japanese 17 syllable poem, and calligraphy. All are used as ways to the One.

However in the Soto school of zen, introduced by the monk Dogen, intuitive insight is achieved primarily by *zazen* or seated meditation which is directed to riddles or koans which defy reason and rational analysis, their aim being complete destruction of the rational intellect.

Although the aim of zen and its basic approach is stated in Buddhism, it and all Japanese culture were profoundly influenced by Chinese philosophy and thought. Indeed the priests who were the indigenous physicians in early Japan were completely displaced by Chinese medicine by the ninth century AD, and according to a Book of Laws published in 702 medicine and education were already regulated along Chinese lines.

Taoism

China has two classic philosophies, Taoism and Confucianism which are said to represent the two sides of Chinese character, the mystical and practical respectively. Both teach trust in human beings and in humanity; express belief in man's intuitive wisdom which only needs awakening to serve as his support and guide; maintain a strong case for being present-centred; and are concerned with the Tao, which in the pre-Confucian world had become implicitly and explicitly a symbol of the ideas of men.

The ancient concept of Tao is therefore implicit in every system of Chinese thought. Watson (1986, p.101) observes that 'the Chinese have always recognised a magical link between man and the landscape, viewing the world and themselves as part of a sacred metabolic system'. The cosmos in their view is an organic unit which spontaneously, out of itself, evolved the manifest and unimanifest worlds. The cosmic source, without beginning or end, is the Tao or Dao, which is roughly translated in English as 'the Way'.

Colegrave (1979, p.8) indicates that the 'concept of Tao is one of the oldest and certainly the most fundamental in all Chinese thought from its emergence out of prehistoric myths up until the Twentieth Century'. As she observes, the character for Tao composed of a foot and a head suggests the idea of walking and thinking, of knowing the correct path and following it. In combining the idea of a 'foot' and a 'head' it personifies personal wholeness, from 'head to foot' as it were, and since the head is often equated with Heaven and the foot with Earth, it also implies cosmic wholeness. The Tao is thus at once the primal principle of the universe and the way to achieve a personal realisation of it. According to Jung the most important secrets of the Tao relate to consciousness, which is expressed in analogies with light. Tao is therefore symbolised by white light. The *Hui Ming Ching* - the Book of Consciousness and Light - contains instructions as to the way of producing light within the self.

Taoism, or the Teachings of the Way, was formally expounded in the doctrines of Lao Tzu in about 600 BC and later expanded by Chuang Tsu. Other than the Tao Te Ching, or Book of Changes attributed to Lao Tzu and Chuang Tsu there is no other authentic text. The Tao Te Ching therefore forms the basis of classical Taoism.

At the centre of Taoist thinking is the concept of chi, ch'i or qi, known as ki in Japan, which is translated inaccurately as gas or ether, and refers to the vital energy or breath which animates the cosmos.

> Chi inflates the earth, moves wind and water (feng and shui), and breathes life into plants and animals. It pulses through the planet motivating each thing that moves and irrigating every landscape (Watson 1976).

It was first described by Emperor Fu Hsi circa 2900 BC, and is likened to dragon veins, running in invisible lines from sky to earth (Blofield, 1979), which is a similar notion to that found in Ancient Egypt. The movement of this energy between two poles or extremes known as yin and yang is the activating force of all phenomena. Everything has chi, but the rate and quality of this movement or vibration between the two poles of yin and yang vary in different phenomena, giving rise to their distinctive character. Yin and yang are therefore tendencies in the movement of energy.

Yin, which means literally 'dark side' (Waley 1942, p.110) is the term used for the tendency towards expansion, or centrifugality emanating from the planet earth, and is associated with sedation, passivity and negative force, and characterised as feminine. Earth energy is thus yin chi. Yang, or the 'sunny side', is the tendency towards contraction or centripetality or energy acting on the planet Earth from beyond. It is symbolised as the force of Heaven, and associated with activity and positive energy, and characterised as masculine. Yang chi is therefore cosmic energy. When the contracting force reaches its limit it changes direction and begins to expand, and vice versa. Thus at the extremes it changes into its opposite, and it is this constant flux between extremes that can be observed in all things from the smallest molecule to the pulsation of the galaxies. It can be perceived within the human body in the rhythm of the heart and lungs, and in the peristaltic waves of the intestines. Often the transition from yin to yang or vice versa takes place in a spirallic manner, which again is discernible in the spirallic formation of the embryo, and in the structure of muscle and bone. The movement is typically characterised as like two fishes (see diagram below) a symbol which implies the dynamic principle of constant movement, but also the unity of opposites.

As Watts (1976, p.26) observes:

> The yin-yang principle is not therefore what we would ordinarily call a dualism, but rather an explicit duality expressing an implicit unity.

Figure 1

Indeed, Taoism asserts that although man's experience of the world is characterised by continual movement or change, there is within this change a pattern which is non-random and has a kind of structural unity, constancy or fixity. This is the Ultimate Unity or background against which the two opposite but complementary yin-yang forces are reconciled, and as such it gives coherence, continuity and unity to all things. This unity or One was identified by Lao Tzu as the Tao, which is indivisible, inaudible and unfathomable. 'It is the same One, past and present; it embraces form and formless alike, being as well as non-being. The One is therefore a unification of duality and multiplicity' (Chuang-Yuan, 1975, p.31). It is eternally without action, yet there is nothing it does not do. By doing nothing (wu-wei) and saying nothing (puh-yeh) the condition of equilibrium or balance (hu-wu) is achieved. Wu-wei is therefore having effect without acting; a state of being rather than doing. The Tao is therefore similar to Ultimate Reality or Brahman in Indian thought, and its vehicle for subtle energies chi, similar to prana. Moreover there are clear parallels between the concept of chi and central concepts of modern physics. Colegrave (1979) observes that sinologists have considerable difficulty in translating it because they are largely prisoners of a dualistic conception of the world which divides reality into matter and spirit, space and form. Within the Newtonian tradition where matter is viewed as a concrete phenomenon which forms the building blocks of the material world, there is no place for a concept which describes both matter and space simultaneously. Yet this is precisely the case with chi and prana, which in some circumstances becomes form and in others remains space:

> If material force (chi) integrates, its visibility becomes effective and physical form appears. If material force does not integrate, its visibility is not effective, and there is no physical form (Chang Tsai, AD 1020-77, cited by Colegrave p.60.).

The concepts of chi and prana therefore appear to be an intuitive recognition of this reality long before there were scientific instruments with which to observe it.

According to Taoism, within any situation a particular balance may be discerned between the yin and yang energies which comprise this unity. In nature the balance is deemed to be correct, but in human affairs influenced by individual choice and volition. The person is therefore the mediator of these two great powers, the centre of his own universe, and is seen as needing to maintain a balance between its forces physically, mentally and emotionally.

Man is thus seen as infused with the powers of the universe - as a microcosmic image of the macrocosm, and like the cosmos as a whole, the body is seen as being in a state of continual, multiple and interdependent fluctuations whose patterns are described in terms of the flow of chi. This cosmological view is central to the Tao Te Ching which teaches that the task of the sage is to create a conscious harmony between himself and the cosmos. Being infused with all the powers of the universe, man necessarily must look to himself for wisdom rather than to some external source. The aim of finding one's centre and balancing these forces is therefore achieved by looking inwards, or insight. The more off-centre or unbalanced the individual, the more dangerous the opposing forces become because at the extremes they become antagonistic and destructive. However, complete awareness, wakefulness or mindfulness transcends and dissolves all extremes promoting wholeness or health. Inner development is thus a precondition of health, and when healthy a person resonates with the vibrations of their environment, so that their chi is in harmony with that of their surroundings. All physical and emotional illness is seen as resulting from imbalance in the flow of chi. Oriental medicine therefore aims at maximising the harmonious flow of chi in the body, balancing the yin and yang.

Chinese medicine

Chinese medicine was founded by the half-mythical Fu Hsi (circa 2900 BC) who first described chi and the two complementary principles of the universe, yin and yang. His successor Huang Ti (c. 2600 BC) introduced into medicine the principles of ancient natural philosophy which regarded the human body as an image of the cosmos. Conversations between Huang Ti and his minister Ch'i Po form the content of the *Nei Ching*, variously known as the Theory of Internal Diseases, or the Yellow Emperor's Classic (or Treatise) on Internal Medicine, written c. 2500 BC, and still in use today. According to the principles established in the Nei Ching, there are definite pathways of chi in the body, known as *ching mo* or meridians, associated with different bodily functions or organs. Chi flows along these in much the same way as blood and lymph circulate through the body, keeping the organism alive, and any obstruction of it gives rise to ill health. Illness is a breakdown of the process, and energy flow is consequently unbalanced. Treatment therefore focuses on normalising energy flow and restoring the balance of yin and yang.

Acupuncture

At various intervals along the meridians there occur sensitive points, known as acupuncture points in China and tsubo in Japan. Stimulation of these points is thought to exert an influence on the body organ related to the meridian on which the point lies. By giving treatment on one or more of these carefully selected sites the skilled practitioner re-establishes normal energy flow and health. Different forms of therapy employ these sites, the best known in the West being Zhen Jin or acupuncture in which fine golden needles are inserted into these points and stimulated manually or electrically.

Acupressure, the application of manual pressure to these points is also used; and also moxibustion, whereby *moxa*, the dried leaves of the plant *Artemis vulgaris* or mugwort, are formed into a small cone which is placed over the acupuncture point and ignited in order to supplement the energy available at the site. Remedial massage, respiration therapy and various herbal treatments are also employed in the redirection and normalisation of energy flow, and T'ai Chi Chu'an, a system of exercises designed to promote the flow of chi through the body, is also widely used, both in therapy and as a form of preventative medicine.

Diagnosis in the Chinese system is complex and subtle. According to the theory drafted by the famous physician Pien Ch'io (in the 6th or 5th century BC) the state of energy flow along the meridians can be assessed at two radial pulses felt on the forearm just above the wrist. Therefore the condition of yin and yang and the state of the various systems in the body can be estimated before any signs or symptoms are apparent.

According to this theory all the major meridians course through the limbs and have their respective terminals or 'well points' located next to the bottom corners of the finger and toe nails.

These are very important because it is here that chi is believed to enter and leave the meridians. The energy level at these points is therefore said to reflect accurately the condition of the entire meridian, and in the case of acute illness acupuncture at these sites is known to have an immediately beneficial effect. The condition of the spine is also important because in Chinese medicine the Governor Vessel meridian, which is one of the most influential, is said to flow along this path. (The all-important Sushumna nadi of the Hindu tradition through which the tremendously powerful Kundalini energy flows would appear to correspond with this meridian.)

There are, however, many more ways of diagnosing meridian functioning, one of which involves pressing the well points and noting skin colour. When on light pressure the skin appears white or cold, chi energy is held to be deficient, where warm and red, normal. When pressure results in pain, chi is excessive, whereas if pain only develops with deep pressure chi may be deficient. The half-moon of the finger and toe nails may also show the state of the associated meridian. If there is no moon apparent this is indicative of chronically deficient energy flow, and excessively small nails suggestive of a long-term deficiency of chi energy flow in corresponding meridians. A nail showing normal pink colour indicates a healthy meridian. Vertical wrinkles in certain nails indicate a deficiency in their blood supply, and consequently deficient meridian flow, whereas ridges or bumps reflect deficient blood supply through the entire body, as does nail colour which is excessively pale or white.

A further way of checking meridian function is by noting the way in which the fingers form when contracted into a fist and opened out again. Fingers which feel or appear weak show weakness in the associated meridians. Deficient energy is also reflected in peeling skin at the well points, and excessive flow in rashes (Motoyama 1987).

Japanese medicine

Japanese medicine corresponds very closely with that of the Chinese. Acupuncture is widely used, as is Shiatsu - the Japanese word for finger pressure, which is analogous to acupressure. This employs varying degrees of touch, from the laying on of hands to firm physical pressure. It was first developed as a special therapy by Toru Nami Koshi who established the Shiatsu Institute in 1925 (Gulliver 1988). Do-In is also a form of self-therapy widely practised in Japan. It involves self-stimulation of areas by pressure, friction, percussion, stretching and breathing techniques. Anma, the precursor of Shiatsu, is also found in Japan and the Far East. This is a form of healing which involves daily massage, pressure, kneading and stretching. There is also Akido, a system of exercise to promote ki flow in the body, which corresponds closely with T'ai Chi Ch'uan. A form of Japanese therapy becoming more widely known in the West is Reiki, the Japanese word for universal life energy. It was developed as a method of healing during the last century by Usui and it involves the channeling and balancing of this energy within oneself, and from person to person, through the laying on of hands and the use of visual symbols. It emphasises the importance of creating a trusting, loving environment in which healing can take place.

Similarities among Oriental healing traditions

Clear similarities can be seen between the healing traditions of China and Japan and those of India and Tibet. All recognise the subtle energy system within the universe and its reflection within the body. Motoyama (1987) concludes that they are, despite differences in terminology, essentially the same. The correspondence is not exact owing to the different cultural contexts in which they arose but it is nonetheless clear that they deal with the same fundamental reality. Nadi and meridians correspond quite closely with each other. Motoyama has charted this correspondence using descriptions given in the Upanishads, traditional Chinese medical texts, and his own clinical experience. He observes that the discovery of the energy pathways in both cultures seems to have resulted from the experience of masseurs who noted a series of flows while feeling for reactions in the body during massage, and also that of Taoists and yogins who recognised the channels of vital energy intuitively and extrasensorily during meditation. Similar energy systems were thus discovered and treatment systems developed accordingly. When these systems encountered each other communication and mutual supplementation appears to have occurred quite easily owing to their similarity. Indeed, Motoyama indicates that according to the historians Pierre Huard and Ming Wong, the nadi theory of yoga and the meridian theory of China were brought into contact with each other some 2,500 years ago in Nepal and Tibet.

At about this time two very significant theories of the meridians emerged in China. These differed from the traditional yin-yang dualism by dividing all aspects of the universe into five parts and the body into three regions, physical, emotional and spiritual, each controlled by a separate energy system. These ideas seem to be essentially the same as those found in the Indian concept of prana dividing into five winds or vayus, and the body into four regions. Although the number of divisions is different the basic concept appears to be much the same. A further similarity is that the person is seen as inextricably part of the environment. In the Chinese system disease is interpreted as originating in man or the environment. Internal causes are mostly viewed as emotional in nature, because normally a person's emotions dictate their response to a given situation. When this is too intense or too prolonged disease may ensue, discernible at first as a distortion of energy balance within the individual, and eventually in distortion of the organs themselves. Conversely if an organ becomes diseased there is corresponding imbalance in the emotion associated with that organ. It is considered therefore that emotional problems can be traced back to the physical and vice versa. Thus excess anger allows energy to rise up in stiff shoulders, headache, tinnitus and sinusitis, and according to ancient classics, shock and joy injure the heart, anger the liver, worry and overconcentration the spleen, grief the lungs, and fears the kidneys. External causes of disease are largely associated with climate but also trauma and poisoning.

The role of the Chinese physician, like their Indian counterpart, is to prevent disease and recognise pre-disease conditions, and to treat disease according to the patient's needs rather than their symptoms. Tradition has it that Chinese physicians were only paid while their patients remained in health, and this is reflected in the proverb 'the superior doctor prevents illness; the mediocre doctor imminent illness; the inferior doctor treats actual illness.' The physician takes into account all the features of the patient, his appearance, facial colour, the sound of his voice, body odour, quality and texture of the skin, appearance of the tongue, the iris and the pulses, and also his disposition.

One of the apparent differences between Chinese and Indian medicine is their application. In acupuncture, knowledge about the flow of chi energy is used to identify which points along the meridians should be stimulated. In Ayurveda, the flow of prana is regulated and the condition of the nadis affected by means of yoga postures, breathing exercises, meditation and other self-help remedies. However, Chinese culture has its own system of movement therapy in T'ai Chi Chu'an, which like Yoga seeks to regulate the flow of subtle energy by conditioning of the channels.

The condition of the meridians is important because they function as the intermediary between the three bodies of the human being, the physical, emotional and spiritual. When energy is prevented from flowing smoothly too much may accumulate in some parts of these bodies and too little in others. When such a condition persists illness on all three levels will follow. Therefore the proper stimulation of the meridians will harmonise the functions of the three bodies and produce a person who is healthy in the holistic sense of the word.

Common themes in Eastern traditions

Several common themes can be identified in all the traditions of the East. They are relativistic, focusing on the illusory nature of time and form; holistic in recognising the inter-relatedness of all things; and they all share an awareness of subtle energies within the universe. Man is viewed as imbued with these universal forces and as manifesting them on three levels; physical, spiritual and emotional. The traditions of the East all aim at achieving balance of these forces within man, and between man and the environment. This integration or wholeness is synonymous with holiness and health. Typically, therefore, Eastern traditions are characterised as religious or philosophical. However, as Watts (1961) observes 'the psychological window is the best one from which to view the traditional wisdom of the East'. Hence Ornstein (1973, 75) refers to 'the traditional esoteric psychologies of the East', and Tart (1975) to its 'spiritual psychologies'.

In the West psychology is generally thought to have little part in the promotion of health and disease. Mind and matter still occupy largely distinct realms, whereas in the East there is no separation into body and mind, nor indeed between the individual and the universe; they are all intimately related in a dynamic manner. Human beings are viewed essentially as dynamic processes rather than material entities and are not analysable into separate parts, and they are closely linked to the environment. Health is therefore characterised as the harmony of fluid movement, as balance, and all approaches to healing treat the whole person, not only the relation of body and mind, but of this whole to its entire context. They are thus organic and ecological.

All forms of healing are concerned with insightful awareness into universal energies and how they are being utilised for good or ill. They all involve the person in the entire healing process because they all emphasise the need for awareness, for greater attention on the part of the individual to the pattern of their life.

Emphasis is laid on direct immediate experience of the universe through breathing, postural adjustment, ritual movement, dance or meditation. The aims of the healer are to help the person towards a reordering of his world view, and the realisation that he is in process, rather than static, and part of a whole rather than an isolated entity; and to assist him in getting in touch with his being and his situation through awareness of internal and external relationships, thereby achieving balance, health and tranquility. Common to all Eastern traditions, therefore, is the notion that it is the capacity for being 'shaken up' or reordered which is the key to health. Prigogine's idea that new order is created by perturbation thus resonates with that of the Buddha, who, in recognizing the possibility for transformation through acceptance of change, saw man's clinging to the habitual as a defence against impermanence and a barrier to growth.

Similarly, the idea of creating new order by perturbation is paralleled in numerous ways in the traditional wisdom of the Orient, and reflected in certain practices such as the zen master striking his pupil, thereby enabling him to 'see' the truth of a paradoxical koan.

Indeed as Watts observes,

> if we look deeply into such ways of life, we do not find either philosophy or religion as these are understood in the West, we find something more nearly resembling psychotherapy (1961, p.19).

Chapter 4

Western Perspectives on Healing

'The things we see', said Pistorius gently, 'are the things which are already in us. There is no reality beyond what we have inside us. That is why most people lead such unreal lives; they take pictures outside themselves for the real ones and fail to express their own world.

Herman Hesse (Demian).

With the displacement of religion by science during the Nineteenth Century medicine became progressively secularized and the spiritual components of disease obscured, and then ignored. Emphasis within medicine shifted entirely onto the physical aspects of disease as medicine became exclusively concerned with the body. Disease whose origin could not be attributed to the physical body was incorporated into the framework of physical science by the simple expedient of converting the soul or psyche into mind, and then into brain function, or by dismissing it altogether.

The materialistic prejudice of medicine explains away the psyche as a merely epiphenomenal by-product of organic processes in the brain. Accordingly any psychic disturbance must be an organic or physical disorder which is undiscoverable only because of the insufficiency of our actual diagnostic means (Jung 1946, p.10).

Therefore, as Jung indicates, 'either the body is ill or there is nothing wrong with it'. Psychopathology, formerly sickness of the soul, came to be seen as mental illness - a concept which Szasz (1979) claims enables human problems to be treated as if part of medical science and in accordance with its principles. Similarly, psychotherapy came within the remit of the 'brain sciences'.

One implication for medicine of this shift was that doctors became heir to what Frankl (1969) terms a 'medical ministry' for which they had no specialized expertise. It fell to them to wrestle with the task of reconciling the spiritual or psychical with the material and medical - a venture doomed to failure, given, as Jung (1978, p.79) observes, that Western science paid no attention to these hopes and expectations, living its intellectual life unconcerned with spiritual and religious convictions. Indeed rather than effect a reconciliation it resulted in a schism between the pioneers of modern psychotherapy, Sigmund Freud and Carl Gustav Jung.

Sigmund Freud

Freud is generally credited as being the founder of modern psychotherapy. More properly he can be thought of as the pioneer of medical psychology in as much as everything embraced in his approach originated in medical science. As Jung (1966, p.34) observes, 'it bears the unmistakable imprint of the physician's consulting room - a fact which is evident not only in its terminology but also in its framework of theory.' It is also discernible in its most distinctive feature, the analyst's couch!

Indeed, in Freudian psychotherapy one constantly comes upon postulates which the physician has taken over from natural science. This is not surprising, because as Fromm (1980) points out Freud was very much a man of his time, and like other doctors of the period saw science as the great legitimiser. He also had a horror of the occult, by which, according to Jung (1972, p.173) he meant virtually everything that philosophy, religion and the emerging field of parapsychology had contributed to an understanding of the psyche. He therefore wished to establish psychotherapy as a scientific discipline, and in his attempt to do so he used the basic concepts of Newtonian physics in his descriptions of psychological phenomena.

He assumed a kind of psychic energy capable of increase, diminution, displacement and discharge, spread over the memory traces of ideas in much the same way as an electrical charge is distributed over the surface of the body. This circulated within a mental apparatus which he conceived as having structure. Initially he described this in two parts, the conscious and unconscious, but eventually he came to view it as having three components, id, ego and superego.

Ideas, impulses and emotions were regarded as located at specific parts of this apparatus, and changes thought to result from movements of energy from one region to another, while actions were thought to be accompanied by a discharge of energy. Freud held that this energy existed in two forms, mobile and bound, the former characteristic of unconscious mental processes, which he regarded as chaotic and unstructured, and the latter characteristic of conscious mental processes, conceived of as having structure and organisation. Freud saw both forms of energy originating in bodily processes which generally he equated with sexual energy and libido. He believed that the unconscious (id) impulses and ideas strive energetically to become conscious but are prevented from doing so by the action of various mechanisms which defend the conscious mind or ego from them. Accordingly the person's character may be a defence against these unconscious strivings, and manifest in habitual stereotyped responses to situations.

Mind, in Freud's terms, is thus a structure divided against itself, a concept not dissimilar to that found in Indian thought. Moreover, just as the latter advocates a turning inwards to gain freedom from the bondage of the conscious mind or ego, Freud also promulgated a cleansing of the mind, or catharsis, by looking inward, with the aim of achieving balance between the ego and id. The early stages of this process consisted in putting a person in touch with the hinterland of their mind, and thus into a state described in Eastern traditions as meditation or contemplation. In so doing, Freud's role as therapist was little different from that of the shaman. Moreover the methods he employed were remarkably similar, involving as they did evocations and interpretations of imagination through hypnosis, fantasy, word associations, and dreams, which were of central importance, Freud declaring them to be 'the royal road to the unconscious.' Freudian psychology thus 'aims at an artificial introversion for the purpose of making conscious the unconscious components of the subject' (Jung 1978, p.84) and in this respect can be likened to Yoga, tantra[1] and traditional magic.

Psychoanalysis as science

Freud, however, would not have welcomed any such comparison with occult practices. Acceptance of his approach by the medical profession crucially depended on its being consistent with the scientific thinking of the times - and he was determined to ensure that it was. Capra, in highlighting the parallels between Freudian theory and Newtonian physics (1978, p. 186), indicates that just as Newton established absolute Euclidian space as the frame of reference in which material objects are extended and located, so Freud established psychological space as a frame of reference for the structures of the 'mental apparatus' - the id, ego and superego, which were seen as some kind of internal objects, the interactions of which explained human nature.

Accordingly, spatial metaphors such as 'depth psychology', 'deep unconscious' and 'subconscious' are prominent throughout Freudian theory. Although Freud described these structures as abstractions, and resisted attempts to associate them with specific structures and functions of the brain, they nevertheless had all the properties of material objects, as Capra (1982, p.187) indicates:

> No two of them could occupy the same place, and thus any portion of the psychological apparatus could expand only by displacing other parts. As in Newtonian mechanics, the psychological objects were characterised by their extension, position and motion.

The dynamic aspects of psychotherapy, like that of Newtonian physics, consists in describing how the material objects interact with one another through forces that are essentially different from 'matter'. These forces have definite directions and can reinforce or inhibit one another, the most fundamental among them being instinctual drives, notably sexual drive or libido.

> Thus in the Freudian system the mechanisms and machineries of the mind are all driven by forces modeled after classical mechanics (Capra, p.187).

A characteristic aspect of Newtonian mechanics is the principle that forces come in pairs - that for every active force there is an equal reactive force of opposite direction. Freud also adopted this principle, calling the active and reactive forces drives and defences respectively. Hence *libido* is paired with *destrudo* and *eros* with *thanatos*, and as in

Newtonian mechanics they are described in terms of effects. However, the intrinsic nature of these forces is not investigated, and so, just as the nature of the force of gravity in Newton's theory is problematic and controversial, so is the nature of libido in that of Freud.

Moreover, as in Newtonian mechanics, the Freudian model is rigorously deterministic, with every psychological event giving rise to a definite effect, and the whole psychological state being uniquely determined by events in early childhood and biology.

Understanding the dynamics of the unconscious was essential for understanding the therapeutic process. The role of the therapist was therefore essentially reductionist and analytical, hence Freud's adoption of the term 'psychoanalysis' for the therapist's attempt to understand the workings of the mind-machine in terms of these elements. To Freud unfulfilled repressed desires, conflicts between the demands of the id and superego, and the preponderance of various ego 'defence mechanisms' give rise to pathological symptoms culminating in mental illness. The analyst concentrated on eliminating obstacles to the direct expression of primary forces. Psychoanalysis was therefore concerned with symptom alleviation, and as such clearly reflects the disease model of medicine wherein health is absence of disease or pathological symptoms. It was thus essentially negative and conservative in approach. As Jung observes (1966) Freud simply brings into action the civil war that is latent and leaves it at that; thus psychoanalysis is a method of diagnosis rather than treatment.

Moreover, the methods of psychoanalysis are cold and impersonal. Indeed, as Capra indicates, Freud advised his followers to cultivate the scientific ideal of objectivity, and to be as 'cold as surgeons' in their explorations of the mind. He assumed that observation of patients during analysis could take place without appreciable interaction between patients and analyst, and insisted that there should be no physical interventions at all. Freudian psychotherapy thus reflects the mind-body division characteristic of medicine, and neglects the body just as emphatically as medical treatment neglects the mind.

Carl Jung

During the early years of the twentieth century Freud attracted a substantial following within the medical profession throughout Europe. One of his most influential supporters was the Swiss psychiatrist Carl Gustav Jung, initially a close collaborator. However, although sharing many of Freud's views on the nature of the unconscious, the significance of dreams and other unconscious processes, Jung became increasingly critical of Freud's approach, which he came to see not as a psychology of the healthy mind, but as a one-sided generalisation from features relevant only to neurotic states of mind. He preferred to look at man in the light of what is healthy, sound, and positive, rather than in terms of the negativity which he believed coloured everything written by Freud.

However, it was Freud's determination to make psychoanalysis 'an unshakeable bulwark against the black tide of mud', which is how he described occultism, that struck irrevocably at the heart of their friendship. Freud's denial of all things spiritual or psychical was to Jung an absurdity, and an irony, given that in certain respects Freudian methods were very similar to those of 'occult' traditions. Jung insisted that 'man has, everywhere and always, spontaneously developed religious forms of expression, and the human psyche from time immemorial has been shot through with religious feelings and ideas. Whoever cannot see this aspect of the human psyche is blind, and whoever chooses to explain it away or to "enlighten it" away has no sense of reality' (1966, p.140). He considered that until the religious dimension of man is given proper consideration the problem of the psyche cannot be approached, and it is therefore essential to any system of psychology which purports to study man.

He therefore added to Freudian instincts the religious dimension or instinct as a counterpart to biological drives and an essential part of the constitution of man. He viewed repression of any of these instincts as unhealthy, all energies being necessary for man to achieve his full potential. He insisted that 'a religious attitude is an element in psychic life whose importance can hardly be overrated' (1966, p.77), claiming that he had not seen one patient over thirty five years of age

> whose problem in the last resort was not that of finding a religious outlook on life. It is safe to say that every one of them fell ill because he had lost that which living religions of every age have given their followers, and none of them has been really treated who did not regain his religious outlook - this of course has nothing whatever to do with a particular creed of membership of a church (1966, p.264).

For Jung therefore a truly religious attitude presupposes a healthy mind, and healing is essentially a spiritual problem. Thus, as Jacobi (1962) observes, Jungian therapy is a *heilsweg* in the two-fold sense of the German world: a way of healing, and a way of salvation. It has curative power and can release psychic disturbances, but also lead the individual to his 'salvation', to knowledge and fulfilment of his own personality. It is therefore both a method of medical treatment and of self-education, and of value to the sick and healthy alike. For Jung therefore the central thrust of psychotherapy was to be understood and described as modern man in search of a soul. His philosophy was, however, that the soul or pysche does not take much searching out:

> It is only not there where a nearsighted mind seeks it (1946, p.11).

His central concerns were to map out both the structure and dynamics of the psyche, and to understand its totality, as it relates to the wider environment. He conceived of the psyche as a self-regulating system comprising two antithetical but complementary spheres, the conscious and unconscious, which is not individual in nature but collective and common, not merely to the whole of humanity, but the whole cosmos. Thus, just as our physical bodies bear within their structure the marks of their evolutionary development from the lower kingdom of nature, so, in Jung's view, the mind shows a similar line of ascent. This being the case Jung may properly be regarded as the Darwin of psychology (Butler 1982, p.16). In his theory there is a personal subconscious beneath the conscious mind consisting of ideas, emotions and memories which have been pushed below the threshold of consciousness because of the individual's refusal to acknowledge them. These complexes tend to break away from the general unity and become independent or dissociated. Deeper within this level is the collective unconscious where reside primordial or archaic images, or archetypes, emotions and thoughts which are shared with all humanity, present and past, and according to Drury (1979) this is the terrain of the shaman's venture inwards.

Jung conceived of the psyche as a self-regulating system and like Hippocrates he recognised the regulative function of opposites. He conceived of psychic energy or the life force, for which he adopted Freud's term *libido*, as play between pairs of complementary features, each of which is opposite in content and energic intensity. However, in the total system the quality of energy is constant and only its distribution variable. Thus Jung's law of conservation of energy and the Platonic concept of soul as 'that which moves itself' are similar. From this law it follows that energy can also be displaced - it can flow from one member of a pair to its opposite, and can also be transferred from one to another by a directed act of will, in which case its mode of operation and manifestation are transformed.

Displacement of energy occurs only when there is a gradient of intensity; or difference in potential, expressed psychologically by the pairs of opposites. This explains why blocking of libido causes neurotic symptoms and complexes, and why when one side is emptied the pair of opposites disintegrates.

Energy lost by consciousness in this process passes into the unconscious and activates its contents which then embark on a life of their own and erupt into consciousness, often provoking disturbances, neuroses and psychoses. Thus Jung also sees neurosis as a state of being at war with oneself, but unlike Freud he did not see this as negative, maintaining that neuroses tend towards something positive, shaking people out of their apathy. Therefore, in spite of their own laziness they can touch off the struggle for whole personality and health. In so far as Jung sees order and organisation arising spontaneously out of disorder and chaos through a process of self-organization, his views are similar to those of Prigogine and Eastern thinkers. Indeed, regarding the 'self' as a dissipative structure helps to account for many of the effects he claimed for psychotherapy.

The flow of energy has direction - which is distinguishable as progressive or regressive movement in temporal succession. The former takes its direction from the conscious mind and the latter from the unconscious when the former fails. Progression is thus a conscious act of will, regression unconscious. Both are necessary, transitional flows of energy. One can therefore see in Jungian psychodynamics similarities with the Chinese concepts of yin and yang, and Serrano (1966) also suggests similarities between his concept of libido and Kundalini.

The second important quality of energy is that it moves not only forward and back but inward and outward. The specific form in which energy manifests in the psyche is the image, which is raised up by the formative power of *imaginato* or creative fantasy from the material of the collective unconscious. Creative action of the psyche transforms unconscious content into such images, and intuitions as appear in dreams, visions and fantasies. Thus when normal conscious energy is turned inwards it proceeds to work on material of the unconscious. Jung saw use of active imagination as a training for switching off conscious thought thereby giving a chance for unconscious contents to develop. This he regarded as important because as long as unconscious information is not understood it keeps intruding as symptoms into consciousness, therefore the overwhelming of the conscious by the unconscious is more likely if the latter is repressed.

From the Jungian perspective the aim of psychological development is integration or wholeness, and therefore the conscious and the unconscious have to be worked on simultaneously in order that parts of the self which are neglected or dissociated can be rediscovered and reintegrated. Accordingly Jung saw therapy as a journey along a path of personal development which he termed individuation, a process whereby all aspects of the conscious and unconscious are integrated, resulting in the experience of a new centre of personality or Self. Jung recognised this centre or Self as an unattainable ideal, as the maximum natural expression of individuality in a state of fulfilment of totality, synonymous with perfect health.

> Jung in describing the process of individuation, of the reconciling of opposites, was calling attention to a symbolic process of healing which is of great importance.

> He recognised that man, the symbolic animal, could resolve even the deepest divisions within him upon the symbolic plane; and he invented a technique of psychotherapy by which this could be accomplished (Jacobi, 1962).

Jungian therapy

Jungian therapy essentially comprises various techniques for deliberately mobilising creativity or active imagination. For Jung, therefore, 'What the doctor does is less a question of treatment than of developing the creative possibilities latent in the patient himself.' Techniques for encouraging active imagination include painting and drawing visions and dreams, poetry, modeling, sculpture and dance. Much emphasis is laid upon the interpretation of these imaginary products, not simply by the therapist, as in the Freudian tradition, but through the collaboration of both patient and therapist. Dreams are regarded as of central importance because for Jung 'the dream is specifically the utterance of the unconscious' (1972, p.13). Fantasy is also highly regarded, especially those which come to people when they are neither awake nor asleep but in a state of reverie in which judgement is suspended but consciousness not lost.

According to Storr (p.88) the conscious attitude which accompanies individuation or integration is essentially one of acceptance, of ceasing to do violence to one's own nature by repressing any side of it or overdeveloping any particular aspect.

Jung describes this attitude as 'waiting upon God', therapy being for Jung unquestionably a spiritual journey, and a religious experience. He saw the therapist as a fellow traveller on the journey of self-realisation.

> The doctor is effective only when he himself is affected ... When the doctor wears his personality like a coat of armour he has no effect (Jung 1972, p.155).

Jung thus broke with the authoritarian relationship between doctor and patient, redefining the doctor's role in such a way as to be more like that of a guru or master, and that of the patient as chela or disciple. He highlighted the interpersonal aspect of therapy, emphasising that 'the relationship between physician and patient remains personal within the frame of the impersonal professional treatment' (1966, p.56), and he drew particular attention to the importance of personality within this relationship:

> The meeting of two personalities is like the contact of two chemical substances: if there is any reaction both are transformed. Expect the doctor to have an influence on the patient in every effective treatment but this influence can only take place when he too is affected by the patient. It is futile for the doctor to shield himself from the influence of the patient and to surround himself with a smoke screen of fatherly and professional authority (1966, p.57).

In the Jungian approach the human quality of the doctor or therapist is crucial, not his medical diploma. His psychotherapy was therefore no longer bound to the consulting room. Jung also recommended a non-judgemental approach, indicating that a person is never in touch with the psychic life of another when he passes judgement. He insisted that the patient does not feel accepted unless the worst of him is also accepted and that no one can bring this about by mere words. It is conveyed through the therapist's sincerity and attitude. Whether the therapist judges in words or only into himself makes no difference, it estranges him from the patient. He must therefore have a deep respect for the circumstances and experiences of the person who suffers them. Jung thus advocated an attitude of unprejudiced objectivity which he claims as characteristic of the truly religious person; an attitude in which the person is not repelled by illness or corruption. As Jung observes, condemnation doesn't liberate, it oppresses. Therefore in his view if a doctor wishes to help a human being he has to accept him as he is - 'warts and all'. In reality he can only do this when he has already seen and accepted himself as he is. In Jung's terms, no one can enlighten his fellows while still in the dark about himself. Accordingly, the first stage in healing is for the doctor to first heal himself: applying to himself the system that he prescribes for others.

Jungian therapy as magic

Jung's therapeutic approach has many parallels with various Indian and Chinese traditions which attempt to lead man to self-realization and share the common aim of achieving one's centre or point of balance. It also has differences, as von Franz (1975) observes, inasmuch that active imagination is not programmed and is completely individualistic. The therapist does not take on the role of guide, as does the Eastern guru, but merely initiates the process after which the individual undertakes the inner work on his own, becoming independent of the therapist and standing on his own feet. His psychology also has parallels with the magical tradition, especially alchemy. To alchemists inorganic matter is not 'dead' but alive and must be investigated by establishing a relationship with it rather than by technical manipulation. They sought to establish this relationship through dreams, in meditation exercises, and a disciplined fantasizing - 'phantasia in vera et non phantastica' - a very similar process to Jung's active imagination. Indeed, Butler (1982) sees Jung as the greatest magician of the modern age, for as he points out, the aim of the genuine magician is realisation of the True Self, and thus the truth of the world, which is masked by the earthly personality. Central to Jungian psychology is the concept of the personality (from the Greek *persona*: mask) as a mask of the soul. Jungian therapy, like magic, operates on the non-verbal level of pictures and images, accessing the subconscious mind (known in magic as the Treasure House of Images) through the archaic images of its symbols and rituals, and thereby producing changes in consciousness as the psychic energy which evokes the unconscious is reinforced by this primordial force emanating from spaceless and timeless regions. The resurrection of the 'deeper Self' results in regeneration and reconstitution of the personal self.

Jung's system involves several methods whereby this resurgence can be effected, just as magic involves various forms of training directed towards this end. In magic symbolic images are chosen and used by the magician to build up the mental atmosphere which will evoke the deeper levels of the mind where archaic images and power reside. These tend to group around certain definite centres, which in the Jungian tradition are termed archetypes, and which recur throughout fairy tales, mythology, religious and mystery traditions.

Jungian therapy thus embodies two of the most central principles of magic expressed in the maxim *gnothi se auton*: know thyself - the inscription over the entrance to the Temple of the Oracle at Delphi in ancient times - and *solve et coagula*: dissolve and reform. It is in his aspousal of psychological and occult traditions that one encounters the major differences between Jung and Freud. Jung (1959) described the gulf between them as a difference in philosophical background, claiming that while he was steeped in philosophy, Freud had no philosophical training. However, the contrasts between them are discernible at many levels.

Jung's psychology is naturalistic, rather than mechanistic, as is reflected in his statement that 'if you think along the lines of nature them you think properly' (1959). Accordingly,

> In Jung's psychology everything is dynamic, subject to change; only the most important perspectives, only the basic principles are unalterable. The rest, like the psyche itself is subject to the Heraclitan principle that 'everything flows ...' The undogmatic character of Jung's ideas prevents them from forming a closed system and leaves the way open for continuous new development and differentiation (Jacobi 1962. p.xi).

Whereas the Freudian system is fixed, rigorously deterministic, causal and dogmatic, the Jungian system is fluid, relativistic, and finalistic in the sense that it is always concerned with the totality of the whole psyche. Hence many of the differences between Freudian and Jungian psychology parallel those between Newtonian and modern physics, and thus between mechanistic, reductionist paradigms on the one hand, and holistic, organic ones on the other. Certainly there are several clear parallels. Jung views all processes as energetic. Just as in modern physics there can be no direct perception of the sub-atomic realm, only inference of the existence of waves and particles from their effects, so the unconscious can only be known indirectly through images and symbols encountered in dreams, fantasies and visions, and in describing the psyche Jung used concepts which parallel those of modern physics. For Jung the psyche is not confined to space and time. He insisted that only ignorance denies this fact, and that when the psyche is not under obligation to live in time and space, as in dreams and fantasy, it is not subject to these laws. Jung's space-time awareness is also apparent in his concept of synchronicity, the acausal connecting principle, whereby all the experiences of humanity and all events are linked through coincidence in time rather than sequentially or causally. He therefore saw a web of relationships throughout the universe, implicit in which is the fundamental belief in the unity of all things. In developing his concept of synchronicity he worked in collaboration with the Nobel prize-winning physicist Wolfgang Pauli, and he recognised that sooner or later nuclear physics and psychology would have to draw together, because from different directions they mapped out the same reality, or transcendent territory.

He believed that eventually they would arrive at an agreement between psychological and physical concepts and achieve thereby a mind-body, spirit-matter synthesis. Therefore, if, as Watts (1961, p.19) observes 'there is no Einstein of the mind', clearly Jung comes very close to it. Yet his psychological theory was dismissed as 'mere' mysticism rather than science, by most psychologists of the time who were apparently unaware that physical scientists had already moved into precisely that realm.

The psychology of Wilhelm Reich

Another 'visionary' was Wilhelm Reich (1897-1957), whose attempt to synthesise psychology and physics led to derision and his social humiliation. As a young man Reich, an Austrian psychoanalyst and student of Freud, contributed significantly to the development of psychoanalysis. Subsequently he became increasingly interested in aspects of human nature which have traditionally been regarded as within the domain of mysticism, and his unorthodox interests and views eventually led to his severance from the psychoanalytic movement.

All Reich's ideas had their foundations in Freud's theory of psychic energy. His orgasm theory proposes that sexual energy is constantly built up in the body and needs release through orgasm and that if this natural reflex is inhibited for any reason stasis of the energy sets in, giving rise to all kinds of neurotic response. Release of the blocked bio-energy through re-establishment of the function of the orgasm is the therapeutic goal since this is held to establish the natural flow of energy and eliminate neurosis. Reich believed that a person's neurotic responses were indicated in his entire behaviour, including his characteristic muscular expressions and posture, which he termed 'muscular armouring', and his character analysis was directed towards identifying and eliminating this. In Reichian terms the neurotic is literally a rigid, tense and unrelaxed person, and this led him to the idea of attacking the character defence directly through the body. In Reich's view appropriate manipulation of the musculature rendered the patient incapable of sustaining his defences against spontaneous expression of emotion, and this emotion would be released. He termed this new therapeutic technique 'vegetotherapy' and in so doing made a clean break with psychoanalysis in which the analyst maintains physical and psychological distance from the patient. By contrast, vegetotherapy was a highly dramatic and direct encounter between the patient and Reich. His approach to therapy

> did away with the psychoanalytic taboo of never touching a patient, substituting physical attack by the therapist on the muscular attitudes (amouring) in the patient: thus the therapist treats the patient not only from the characterological point of view, but also physically by provoking in him a sharp contraction of the musculature in order to make the patient aware of those contractions which have become chronic. The relaxation of the bound-up energy in the musculature in whatever part of the body would often be accompanied by recall of the trauma which had led to the contraction or neurotic symptom in the first place. In this way neurotic symptoms could be attacked at the same time in their psychic and somatic manifestations (Ollendorff-Reich 1969, p.36).

Reich noticed that people under tension inhibit their intake of oxygen. Accordingly people with psychological problems tend to breath shallowly in order to create less vital energy, which in turn makes their impulses easier to master. Shallow breathing eventually becomes a habit. Therefore neurotics characteristically breath less deeply than others.

Reich insisted that the first step in overcoming nervous tensions is to learn to breath deeply using the stomach and solar plexus as well as the chest. He instituted breathing exercises as part of therapy, and found that many patients felt vital and alive, and experienced a oneness with nature, a mystical harmony which some personified as 'God'. Reich therefore came to believe that he had discovered a biological energy or bioenergy which pervades the universe and which is the active force responsible for man's longing for orgastic and mystical union with God. Thus in his search of the biological foundation of the Freudian concept of libido he claimed to have discovered the life force, which he called orgone energy and described as blue in colour.

However, orgone energy was not merely a biological energy but energy endowed with a spiritual quality, since an essential part of the subjective experience of orgasm is longing to reach beyond oneself to merge with that beyond. As such, he claimed, it is functionally equivalent with love. In Reich's view therefore the life force, love, which literally makes the world go round, permeating the universe and sustaining all life forms. It is therefore the basic principle of health in all living creatures, lack of which causes disease.

He tried to demonstrate the efficacy of orgone energy in the treatment of psychosomatic disease and cancer, which he believed to be caused by blockage of vitality. The devitalised tissues, he claimed, began to degenerate and form T-bacilli which produce cancer. He claimed that orgone energy could be collected in orgone accumulators and used in treatment of various disorders, and the sale of these boxes eventually led to his imprisonment for alleged fraud, and he died in prison in 1957.

Reich's claim that the life force or orgone energy is synonymous with breath is paralleled in both the Indian and Chinese traditions, where it is known as *prana* and *chi* respectively, and in the ancient traditions of many cultures, including those of the West. In Arabic *rih* or wind is etymologically similar to *ruh* meaning soul, and the Latin words *animus*: spirit and *anima*: soul are the same as the Greek *anemos*, or wind. The Greek word *pneuma* or wind also means breath and was used to refer to the cosmic life force. Moreover, the aims of vegetotherapy are very similar to those of many Oriental traditions, notably the Tantric which are concerned with raising Kundalini energy through ritualised sexual practices.

Indeed in his *The Function of the Orgasm* he admits to having been impressed by the principles of Buddhism. It is perhaps not surprising therefore that Reich's work also resembles in certain respects ideas about the body found in Tibetan Buddhism. Reich's character analysis led him to the view that character itself is a disorder, a hardening of the fluid human reality into a fixed and limiting pattern of behaviour, a view not dissimilar to that of Jung. However he regarded this as both a mental and physical problem, the body merely expressing the mind's rigidity, and developing character armour as a defence against the fearful uncertainties of life and inevitably against feeling. Reich became convinced that as emotional problems had physical manifestations they could be attacked through the use of physical techniques, including breathing exercises and massage.

It is also possible to discern in Reich's later work similarities with shamanic practices. Reich believed that orgone energy could be accumulated and directed to effect natural processes other than healing. He claimed to have demonstrated rainmaking in this way, which lent support to his opponents who viewed him as a 'quack' and as suffering from a paranoid delusional system. At best Reich was seen within the scientific community as a mystic, attempting to express in scientific terms what mystics such as Wordsworth and Blake had conveyed in poetry, and dismissed as fanciful and pathetic (Rycroft 1979). Nevertheless Reich attracted a number of enthusiastic supporters and his influence has proved to be considerable, and largely underestimated (see chapter ten).

Behaviourism

The hostility towards Reich, which eventually led to his incarceration and death in prison, needs to be understood in context. In trying to gain acceptance as a *bona fide* scientific discipline, psychology had been trying to distance itself from the 'irrational' aspects of its subject matter since the early part of the Twentieth Century. Accordingly Reich and his followers were a source of profound embarrassment. Psychology had reconciled the apparent incompatability of science and the psyche by denying the existence of the latter and conceiving of man solely in terms of his objective behaviour. This 'behaviourism', as developed by Watson, Hull and Skinner, viewed man as a complex machine responding to various environmental stimuli by way of conditioned reflexes. Its basic principle was that complex phenomena could be reduced to combinations of simple stimulus-response patterns, and these were seen as adequate explanations for all human endeavor including art, religion and science.

The attempt to understand man in terms of what Koestler (1975) terms 'slot-machine mechanics' implied a rigorous causal relationship which would allow psychology to predict the response for any given stimulus and conversely to specify the stimulus for a given response. The 'mindless' approach of behaviourism was seen as more consistent with the aims and methods of science and it overtook the psychologies of Freud and Jung. Subsequently it dominated the discipline for most of the first half of the century, reaching the peak of its ascendency during the 1950s at the very height of the machine age.

Ironically, at precisely the time that psychology was attempting to claim with certainty the predictability of human beings, physics was demonstrating the uncertainty and unpredictability of the electron. Moreover, psychology was denying the existence of mind just when physics was highlighting its importance. Nevertheless psychotherapy was substituted with behaviour therapy, which viewed psychological disorder as learned maladaptive behaviour patterns. The goal of behaviour therapy was to rectify deviant behaviour patterns and restore the individual to normal functioning. It was therefore essentially negative and conservative in approach, and both simplistic and demeaning in the image of man it projected, for irrespective of whether man is viewed literally as a machine, or metaphorically as if one, the net result is that he is reduced to something less than human.

In extinguishing man's essence, his psyche, behaviourism had obliterated his very humanity; it had, according to Heather (1976), effectively murdered the man it claimed to study, apparently without remorse, as is reflected in Skinner's statement (1973, p.196):

To man qua man we readily say good riddance.

Humanistic psychology

However, as Jung (1959) observes 'Man does not stand forever his nullification', and during the 1950s a growing number of psychologists, especially in the USA, refused to view man as a machine, enslaved by environmental contingencies and his past, and attempted a fully human alternative to the mechanistic view of man prevalent within Western thought. Their concerns, focusing as they did on the individual as a perceiver and interpreter of himself and his world and a determiner of his own behaviour, represented a return to the fundamental questions regarding the nature of the human self, soul or psyche and its development, and reinstated these as legitimate questions for psychology. What came to be known as 'Humanistic Psychology' addressed itself to spiritual human concerns, and with devising new methods with which to study the significant problems of man rather than insignificant problems which fitted the alleged scientific methods. These methods included a number of different therapies, all of which focused attention on subjective experience, feelings, impressions, dreams, fantasy, personal responsibility and choice, volition, personal powers and potentials.

All the therapies and spiritual trips that have been percolating through American society are part of paradigm shift, a still incomplete effort to move beyond Darwinism and Freudian and behaviourist perspectives into a newer and richer conceptualization of human life (Watts, 1961, p.195).

As Watts observes, there is no central figure around whom this effort was organized, but one voice usually acknowledged as of central importance was that of Abraham Maslow.

Abraham Maslow

Maslow, who was for many years Professor of Psychology at Brandeis University, took Western psychology to task for its emphasis on determinism and its concommitant neglect of the human. Like Jung he was opposed to generalisation from the 'mentally ill' to man as a whole, arguing that psychology should be concerned with the study of mental health, which he viewed as the fulfillment of a five-level hierarchy of need culminating in self-actualization.

He based his theory on the assumption of man's intrinsic good nature, which he viewed as an essentially biological feature, partly general to the species and in part individual and unique. He conceived of this inner nature or self as possessing a dynamic for growth and actualisation, but weak rather than strong, and easily frustrated, denied and suppressed. Like Freud and Jung he saw denial or suppression of self as the major cause of illness and distress, much of it arising out of man's fear of and consequent defence against his capacities, potentialities, creativeness and goodness. Maslow's view of man as engaged in a struggle against his own greatness is thus similar to Jung's notion of man at war with himself. According to Maslow, man effectively turns his back on himself out of fear of doing otherwise and is thereby constrained into outmoded and ineffectual action which generates a state of being which he termed 'the psychopathology of the average'. In contrast, Maslow viewed health as equivalent to self-actualisation, features of which include enhanced perception of reality; increased acceptance of self, others and nature; increased spontaneity, creativity, autonomy; and ability for mystical-spiritual experiences. He regarded the latter as evidence of man's ability to transcend personal experience to some ultimate experience or reality. Thus in Maslow's humanistic psychology there are echoes of Jungian psychology and the ancient and oriental traditions. His model of health is also strikingly similar to that which is central to homeopathic medicine.

The homeopathic model

Reibel (1984) points to numerous parallels between humanistic psychology and the homeopathic approach to healing pioneered in the Nineteenth Century by Dr. Samuel Hahnemann, a physician whose approach to treatment was closely allied to that of Hippocrates and Paracelsus. Hahnemann used the term 'vital force' to describe the balancing mechanism within each living organism which promotes, or at least protects health. He claimed that this vital force, comparable with Hippocrates' *vix medicatrix naturae*, is stimulated by internal and external disorders to build up a counteractive reaction. The result of the interaction between the vital force and the conditions which set it in motion produces various symptoms in the body revealing that an imbalance has occurred. Disease is thus a product of stress and failure of the body's own attempt to heal it, whereas health is the maintenance and development of the vital force of inner nature of the organism itself. Any treatment or healing must therefore deal with the whole organism in both its objective and subjective aspects, taking into account the individual's perception and interpretation of his or her symptoms and their individual features. Therapy consisted not in opposing a problem, as in conventional medicine, but in using the problem as its solution, ie by using a natural substance which in its raw state can produce similar effects to those of the illness, hence the homeopathic axiom: like cures like.

> The apparency of anything can be annulled by the creation of a perfect duplicate. The homeopathic physician seeks to create a perfect duplicate of the patients illness by selecting a medicine whose properties produce an artificial illness that exactly mimics the patient's illness (Hamlyn 1979 p.17).

The aim of treatment is therefore to establish a total pattern of symptoms that mirrors the whole patient, and is a reflection of their overall pattern of adjustment. However, according to Vithoulkas (1980, p.140) the therapeutic relationship is of particular importance in homeopathy:

> The encounter between a patient and a homeopath is an intimate interaction for both ... The prescriber ... is not merely a passive observer protected behind a wall of objectivity. Each patient engages the homeopath in a deep and meaningful way ... When homeopathy is practised with this degree of involvement it stimulates growth in the homeopath just as it does for the patient

In both theory and practice humanistic psychology parallels homeopathy, not only in sharing its view of the conditions in which the vital force flourishes, but also in recognising that solutions to problems can be facilitated by reflection of their symptoms. This insight is central to the therapeutic approach advocated by Carl Rogers.

The client-centred therapy of Carl Rogers

Carl Rogers, a distinguished professor of psychology and one-time President of the American Psychological Association, takes a broadly similar view to Maslow but draws particular attention to the dynamic features of the self - its tendency to expand, extend, grow and develop. He believed that this tendency exists in every individual and awaits only the proper conditions to be realised and expressed or actualized. For Rogers this self-actualization is synonymous with health, wholeness or integration. He considered therapy to be a process wherein the individual has the opportunity to integrate and actualize the self. Therefore, he viewed the central process of therapy as facilitation of the individual's experience of becoming a more autonomous, spontaneous person. Nevertheless, while insisting that the potential for self-actualization resides within the person, Rogers claims that the conditions for facilitating its development reside in the relationship between the person and the therapist, and comes about through a close, emotionally warm and understanding relationship in which the individual is free from threat and evaluation and has the freedom to be fully themself.

The type of therapeutic relationship Rogers seeks to provide has three particularly significant qualities, the first of which is the authenticity or genuineness of the therapist. For this to be achieved the therapist must be aware of his or her feelings in so far as is possible and rather than present any facade be able to express these where appropriate.

The second quality required in the therapist is their unconditional positive regard for the client - the ability to value, respect and care for him or her irrespective of his or her condition, behaviour, attitude or feelings. The third necessary quality is empathic understanding, or genuine listening; the continuing desire to understand the feelings and personal meanings which the other person is experiencing.

Rogers argues that within such a relationship there is an implicit freedom to explore oneself at both the conscious and unconscious levels, and that under such conditions the person moves from fear and defence of inner feelings to encouragement and acceptance of them; from being out of touch with feelings to greater awareness of them; from living life by the introjected values of others to those experienced by him or her self in the present; from distrust of spontaneous aspects of the self to trust in them; and towards greater freedom and more responsible choices. Essentially, Rogerian therapy ideally affords a situation in which the individual learns to be free, and as such is an educational process. It can be seen therefore that in its theory and practice it is largely a restatement of Jungian principles, and likewise it has close parallels with ancient and oriental traditions in its conceptions of health and the role of the therapist in its promotion.

Rogers' concept of therapy is close to original Greek word *therapeia* meaning service or attendance. Accordingly the therapist is an attendant, and Rogers emphasises that attending to a person is not about doing anything to or for them, but is simply about *being*. Simply being attentive, caring, open and genuine, in his view, is in itself therapeutic, bringing about positive changes which move a person in the direction of wholeness and health. In this aspect the Rogerian concept is very similar to that of Eastern traditions, and quite alien to the West with its obsessive concern for performance, and especially to Western men - the majority of therapists - who are especially conditioned to *doing*. Jourard (1971) observes that a considerable dread of passivity is discernible among therapists, for whom, he suggests, it constitutes a threat to masculine identity, and also, no doubt, to their work ethic. Therapists are therefore he suggests, frequently attracted to manly active therapeutic techniques which makes them feel that *they* are doing something to get the client well. This technical behaviour, as he points out, often impresses the client but insomuch that it is a manipulation of them by the therapist, rather than an open, spontaneous response, it may provoke vigorous defences. This is no less true of attempts to do things to put people at ease, such as offering cigarettes or coffee, or effecting certain postures and mannerisms, which are features of many would-be therapeutic approaches. Jourard observes that many people assume a 'professional manner' as soon as they are in the presence of clients or patients, which is an attempt to manipulate them to their own advantage. Thus despite appearances to the contrary these therapists are attending primarily to themselves rather than others.

If one is to attend or reach out to others (from the Latin *attendere*: to reach out) it is necessary to put aside any barriers which may be in the way. Professional roles and personal mannerisms are only one kind of barrier. Others include one's thoughts, problems, beliefs, prejudices, preconceptions, fantasies, concerns. In other words, the various aspects of one's self or ego. Unless these can be overcome, despite all attempts to listen to others one succeeds only in listening to oneself.

Implicit in the Rogerian approach therefore is the notion of the therapist putting aside ego, albeit temporarily. Here one finds clear parallels with Eastern and magical notions of the master as egoless, a condition often likened to that of a mirror which reflects but does not hold reality and therefore reveals it in a non-selective manner.

This notion is central to the Rogerian concept of reflection, whereby, to the extent that the therapist can put aside or suspend ego, the client is effectively talking to themself, much as if speaking into a mirror, and in so doing confronting features of themself possibly for the first time. Accordingly the client is able to use this new awareness or insight for personal growth and change.

The Rogerian therapist reflects back to the client the content and manner of the person's attempts to communicate as faithfully as possible without the distortions that arise from egoistic involvement, that is, from his own hunches, speculations, theories, experiences and ideas on life, and without being directed to any specific content.

Rogers claims that confronted with such sustained reflection persons attend more to themselves and come to see themselves more clearly. Their awareness progresses from the general to the specific, from the superficial to the deep, from thoughts to feelings, from the abstract to the concrete - in fact in exactly the same direction as in meditational practices of the East which aim at developing attention to the self and achieving insight.

However, the concept of reflection carries with it a limiting feature - the nature of the 'mirror' of which it is a property. A non-human mirror is non-selective in what it reflects in the sense that it is not directed to any particular feature of the reality it mirrors. Likewise the ideal of the mirror-like individual is non-selective, but most therapists have not, and never will attain such a state and tend to be highly selective in what features of the client they reflect. Thus rather than being non-directive as Rogers claims, his approach is in practice highly selective, relying mostly on reflection of the client's words. It ignores to a great extent paralinguistic features, posture, gestures, facial expressions, and thus the whole range of nonverbal expression and communication.

Arguably the approach is also somewhat superficial, accepting at 'face-value' the truth of what is said and facilitating a potentially misleading view of the person. Therefore the therapist needs to be rather more like a magnifying glass than a mirror, bringing certain features into sharp focus and thereby promoting insight into the various modes of a person's being and integration of formerly disowned or unrecognised parts

of the self. Such an approach was advocated by Frederick (Fritz) Perls, and in his Gestalt
Therapy one can yet again see striking similarities with ancient and Eastern traditions,
notably zen, not only in focusing on one-pointed awareness, which is the aim of many
meditational practices, but also in its emphasis on the importance of the total environment in determining health.

The Gestalt Therapy of Frederick Perls

Perls viewed the individual organism as existing within an environmental field in which
all parts are interdependent, so that change in any one part affects all other parts; 'The
individual is inevitably at every moment a part of some field which includes both him
and his environment' (Perls 1976, p.16). The nature of the relationship between the
individual and the environment is therefore of key importance, determining his 'being'
in the world. Perls' view, like that of Rogers, is therefore essentially holistic and
integrative, and lays emphasis on self-actualization - the 'becoming of what one is' -
which Perls viewed as an inborn goal in all living things. He argued that this fundamental
need for self-actualization can only occur through integration of the various parts of self
because it is in this way that the self emerges as a unified figure or gestalt against its
environmental field. Only then, when the self is clearly defined and located in relation
to others and the world does it become possible for the individual to fulfil his potential,
because this integrated self, like any unified field is more able to utilise its potential and
act. Such a process requires constant monitoring of the self and redefinition of its
boundaries, because the *gestalten* of the environmental field, rather than being static
and fixed are dynamic and ever changing as the demands of the self, others and the
environment alter.

The satisfaction of these needs, which is equivalent with psychological health, is
something of a balancing act, maintained by a kind of homeostasis or self-regulating
process, the fundamental requirement of which is awareness of the immediate situation.
Hence the aware individual is able to perceive changes in existing gestalten or configu-
rations and act accordingly to create new patterns, thereby restoring the equilibrium
between the self and its surroundings. In Perls' approach as in ancient and oriental
traditions balance and harmony are central features. Like Maslow, Perls attributes much
of the difficulty in achieving the figure/ground discrimination necessary for gestalt
formation to society. He saw the problem as residing largely in the prescription of one
central enduring role to the individual who is consequently obliged to suppress, disown
or project outside himself all those features which are inconsistent with the maintenance
of that role. This denial of self invariably results in a progressive fragmentation of the
person and a difficulty in establishing boundaries between self and others, and the
external world. The person cannot satisfy their needs because they are unaware of what
they are, and such confusion may ultimately lead to complete breakdown of a physical
or psychological nature, or both. Perls viewed neurosis as the inability to perceive
boundaries clearly, with the result that the individual experiences the world as encroach-
ing on them, and characteristically responds by fear, anxiety, avoidance tendencies and

elaborate defences all aimed at avoiding this intrusion. Moreover, being unable to define personal boundaries the neurotic typically manipulates the environment for support in various ways rather than utilizing his personal potential. The individual is thus able to satisfy his needs and remains in a state of disequilibrium that might justifiably be thought of as 'unbalanced'.

The emphasis in Gestalt Therapy, as in zen and other oriental traditions, is that all things are changing. It is not concerned with explanations or interpretations of past history, or speculations about and planning for the future. Like Buddhism it emphasises the living of life rather than the meaning and obliges followers to give up explanations and rationalisation and to concentrate on the business at hand. It is essentially anti-intellectual, as is revealed in Perls' directive to 'lose your mind and come to your senses'. Like Buddhism Gestalt Therapy is also present-centred. For Perls 'now' covers all that exists: 'The now is the present, is the phenomenon, is what you are aware of, is that moment in which you carry your so-called memories, and your so-called anticipations with you. Whether you remember or anticipate, you do it now' (1976, p.44). This statement implies that the past and future exist in the present. In this sense Perls' is speaking of a timeless reality, and in this respect his world view is similar to those of both ancient and oriental traditions, and modern physics. That he recognised this similarity is clear:

> our scientific attitude has changed. We don't look to the world anymore in terms of cause and effect: we look upon the world as a continual ongoing process. We are back to Heraclitus, to the pre-Socratic idea that everything is in flux. We have made in science the transit from linearity and causality to thinking of process, from the why to the how (1969, p.46).

Accordingly he described Gestalt Therapy as being 'like a koan - those zen questions which seem to be insoluble. The koan is: Nothing exists except the here and now ... These are the two legs upon which Gestalt Therapy walks: now and how' (1976, p.44).

By focusing on this koan, Gestalt therapy, like zen, aims to promote insight and integration, and thus transformation. However, as Jung (1978) observes, the major difference between psychotherapy and zen or other forms of Buddhism is that unlike the latter psychotherapy does not deal with people who, like zen monks, are ready to make any sacrifice for the sake of truth, but very often with the most stubborn of people. Thus the tasks of psychotherapy are much more varied and the phases of the process much more contradictory than is the case in zen. Perls recognised this and employed many different methods whereby integration might be achieved, and in this respect it is similar to Tibetan Buddhism which employs strategies such as bodywork and visualization. He believed that individuals can assimilate projected and disowned features of the self by role playing, and many of the methods he used with the aim of heightening perception, awareness and emotion were of an essentially theatrical nature. In this respect Gestalt Therapy is reminiscent of Greek theatre. Working with his clients 'centre-stage', as it were, in front of an audience, Perls required the client to play all the parts of the drama themselves, either by acting each role (including those of the props) in turn, or in the form of dialogues between these elements, whether animate or inanimate. For this latter purpose the famous 'empty chair' technique was developed whereby the client projects into a vacant chair any element of the drama in order to confront it. The 'occupant' of the chair might be an aspect of the self typically unexpressed in a given situation - the repressed self, which Perls labeled the 'underdog', or other aspects of the personality; real or imagined persons, creatures or objects - indeed anything that the client or therapist wishes it to be, the idea being that by bringing these into the open and confronting them the client might be able to identify and integrate the diffuse parts of himself, distinguishing them from other features of the environment, and thus achieve an individual gestalt and clear figure/ground discrimination. Perls worked on unresolved conflict situations, interpersonal relationships, thought and fantasies in this way, and also dreams, which he regarded as 'existential messengers' because of their potential importance to individual self-understanding.

In his emphasis on dreams, as well as in the other features of his approach, Perls reflects not only the practice of the Greeks but also shamanic practice in general. As in these healing traditions his is a system which relies heavily on the imagination and in which the therapist in true shaman-like fashion is the facilitator whereby its terrain is accessed and interpreted. His approach also encourages a sense of humour and fun, and typically there was much levity and laughter in Perls' therapeutic workshops.

It is perhaps in its emphasis on dreams, however, that Gestalt Therapy most clearly resembles earlier healing traditions. Perls, like Jung, recognised that dreams form a self-contained whole or dramatic action which can be broken down into elements like those of a Greek play, each of which can be developed through a process of amplification in which their content is broadened and enriched with the help of images or associations provided by both client and therapist. Whereas Perls restricted these images to those provided by the client, therapist and members of the audience, Jung amplified dream content with the symbolic imagery of fairy tales, mythology and the like, which he considered illuminated the universal aspect of human concerns. However, both recognised the dream as a statement, uninfluenced by consciousness, which expresses the dreamer's inner truth or reality, and that the manifest dream content is not, as Freud would have it, a facade.

Gestalt Therapy emerged as one of the most powerful therapies to be developed this century and it was to prove one of the most influential forces in the development of Humanistic Psychology and what became known as the Human Potential Movement (see Graham 1986).

The Human Potential Movement

During the 1960s Maslow, Rogers and Perls found a particularly receptive setting for their ideas on America's West Coast. They were invited to the Esalen Institute in California where the development of human potential and the promotion of qualitative changes in being were emphasised. Here too exponents of many disciplines from Eastern and Western cultures, including yoga, meditation, the martial arts, dance and body work, and various forms of healing; together with religious and spiritual leaders, philosophers, artists, physicists and psychologists, were invited to exchange and develop their views in seminars, workshops and residential programmes, the first of which were offered to the general public in 1966. This interchange yielded many different approaches to, and techniques for the development of human potential; those derived from oriental philosophies and religions, or esoteric traditions frequently being grafted onto the more familiar psychological approaches of the West, particularly those employed in psychotherapy.

Out of this curious synthesis numerous new-style therapies emerged and various ancient and esoteric traditions resurfaced. One therefore often finds striking parallels between these and humanistic psychology in relation to concepts such as awareness, self-actualization, peak experience, and also in practices of sensory awakening, awareness and relaxation.

Elsewhere within Western culture, as travel and other developments opened up the East, people made more contact with its traditions which often served to put them in touch with formerly hidden and obscure sources of similar wisdom within their own cultures. Awareness of its similarity prompted further examination of both, for as Jung (1966, p.48) observes;

> 'When an idea is the expression of psychic experience which bears fruit in regions as far separated and as free from historical relation as East and West, then we must look into these matters closely. For such ideas represent forces that are beyond logical justification and moral sanction.'

Footnote

1. A thorough discussion of the correspondences between Freudian psychology and the tantric tradition is provided by Kakar, 1982.

Towards an Holistic Approach

Ancient, modern, Eastern and Western perspectives on 'life, the universe and everything' appear to be one and the same - quite literally.

They are all holistic, all parts of the universe being seen as inter-related and inseparable, with no distinction between mind and matter; body, soul or spirit. They all recognise the pre-eminence of mind, consciousness and the subjective, and therefore emphasise the psychological and spiritual rather than the physical and material. They share a space-time intuition, an awareness of subtle universal energies and their role in health and disease. All reinforce the wisdom of Hippocrates who insisted that doctors should have 'knowledge of the whole of things'.

Increasing recognition of the 'whole of things' in the West has led to advocacy of holistic medicine - a term whose exact meaning remains elusive. It is an umbrella term which has come to embrace many different approaches and methods, ranging from dietetics and homeopathy to crystal therapy and spiritual healing. Properly, however, as LeShan (1982) observes, there is no such thing as an holistic technique or modality, only an holistic attitude - a concern to promote the understanding that all levels of a person's being, physical, psychological, emotional, spiritual, social and ecological, are of equal importance in the prevention of disease and the search for health; and that the potentials for promoting health and overcoming illness reside within the person.

He suggests that the remarkable and rapid rise in this new medical model, which appears to offer an alternative to conventional reductionist approaches, owes a great deal to the lack of concern for the whole person in conventional mainstream medicine, and the growing awareness that technology alone is not enough.

In fact many of the approaches now seizing the public imagination, such as homeopathy and osteopathy, have long existed alongside orthodox treatments, while new or unfamiliar ways of promoting health are constantly appearing or reappearing and gaining publicity. Cousins (1981) points to two dozen or more schools or approaches of varying validity, not all of them compatible and some of them competitive, crowding the centre of the holistic stage. As he observes, 'Some conferences on holistic health seem more like a congeries of exhibits and separate theories than the occasion for articulating a cohesive philosophy' (p.119). He thus highlights troubling contradictions within the holistic medicine - a movement based on the concept of wholeness becoming progressively fragmented and divisive, with many of its proponents dogmatically and narrowly advocating their approach as the 'only' one, and hostile to other holistic approaches or traditional medicine. He suggests that the parts seem to be at odds with a movement based on the need for an integrated approach to health, and that the movement has tended to take on the character of the least workable and reputable of the contending parts.

Certainly, many of the methods which attract paying customers to holistic medicine have not persuaded the medical establishment of their acceptability. LeShan (1982, p.129) indicates that while many are serious and complex methodologies 'Some of the specific techniques are the sheerest kookiness ... and may be dismissed without further investigation'. Cousins sees this as a continuing difficulty, suggesting that in any case, 'it is difficult to think of a unifying principle that can bring these together' (p.119).

However, the position adopted here is that there is such a principle, which not only brings together the many disparate approaches of holistic medicine, but also reveals no conflict between the apparently silly or irrational and the sensible or rational, enabling both to be seen as fully consistent with the principles of modern science and understandable in terms of the related principles of time and energy:

> Accordingly schools of thought that are currently based on seemingly incommensurate world views may well turn out to be closer than seems apparent at present (Patel 1987, p.174).

Part II

Timely Interventions

Chapter 5

On the Nature of Time

Time present and time past
Are both perhaps present in time future,
And time future contained in time past.
If all time is eternally present
All time is irredeemable.
What might have been is an abstraction,
Remaining a perpetual possibility
Only in a world of speculation.
What might have been and what has been
Points to one end, which is always present.

T.S. Eliot (Burnt Norton).

It is commonly said that 'time is of the essence'. The phrase is generally taken to mean that time is essential, vitally important, absolutely necessary, a matter of urgency, and a property of the external world of objective reality. This view, which pervades Western culture, is largely unquestioned. Yet the phrase has quite different connotations when viewed etymologically. From this perspective time is an intrinsic feature of being, a property of the soul, psyche or essence (from the Latin: *essentia*), and has very different implications for the way we live our lives.

Absolute linear time

A basic assumption of Western culture is that time is absolute; a fact; a feature of external out-there reality existing independently of human consciousness. Such a belief derives from the linear mode of thought that Western civilisation inherited from the Greeks. Accordingly, time, symbolised by a straight line, is seen as composed of a rigid, fixed succession proceeding in one direction from the past, through the present to the future, and irreversible. As such it is finite, limited and static, having a beginning and an end, making everything seem once and for all. It is also, as Ferguson (1983, p.111) observes, tangible: 'It is spoken of as being saved, spent, wasted, lost, made up, accelerated, slowed, crawling and running out'. Therefore, although imposed, learned and arbitrary it tends to be regarded as though it is built into the universe. Indeed such a view pervades Western culture to such an extent that it is difficult to conceive of any other concept of time. Yet quite different concepts of time exist, and have existed since antiquity.

Cyclic or cosmic time

Conceptions of time in the ancient world derived from the awareness of periodicities in nature. Cooper (1981, p.22) points out that the laws of nature are those of the curve, the circle and endless repetition. Observation of the cycles in nature, such as the succession of day and night and the seasons, the waxing and waning of the moon, the ebb and flow of tides, gave rise to the idea of time as a cyclic phenomenon. Accordingly primitive notions of time mirrored the cyclic aspect of the world. So, for example, the ancient Egyptians are thought to have derived their calendar from observations of the arrival of the Nile floods at Cairo. The Greeks also largely followed the cyclic tradition, Pythagoras and Plato both teaching the doctrine of the eternal return or *anakuklosis*, according to which time progresses in a circle or in an indefinite series of cycles, in the course of which the same reality is made, unmade and remade in succession. Therefore, not only is the same sum of existence preserved, with nothing being lost or created, but the same situations reproduced as they have been in previous cycles, and will be in subsequent cycles *ad infinitum*.

No event is unique, occurring once and for all, but occurred, occurs and recurs perpetually; the same entities appearing and reappearing at every turn of the cycle, for cyclic time is self-contained, making the transient subject to the law of recurrence. It therefore diminishes the power of death and places emphasis on the cosmic rather than the individual.

In ancient India this doctrine of cosmic cycles was elaborately developed into a philosophy of continual metamorphosis. A complete cycle was thought to comprise 12,000 years, each ending in dissolution from which creation proceeds. To the Hindu therefore, the universal world and social order are eternal and not temporal, and personal life but a sample of a succession of lives repeating themselves endlessly. Perpetual rebirth or reincarnation makes any quantitative view of a particular period of time meaningless: 'Life, infinitely cycled, makes history less significant and an individual's biography is merely a transient moment in the process' (Luce 1973, p.30). The Hindu thus live in a time domain characterised by a changeless sense of ever becoming. Consequently India has never produced a written history.

In early China naturalists and philosophers also observed the evolutionary transformations of living organisms, and some sixteen centuries before Darwin they expressed an evolutionary naturalism which embodied a succession of phylogenetic unfolding rather than a single linear train of evolution. These early concepts of time led to remarkably sophisticated theories that included accurate perception of astronomical change, views on the nature of fossils and explanations of the unity of vast time cycles in the development and history of each man.

The *Tao Te Ching* gives an estimate of phases in the evolution of life covering approximately 130,000 years. Similarly in Japan the concept of the transience of the physical world led to the intuitive awareness that time is not an absolute or objective feature but a process - the change of nature. These cultures all accepted the notion of biological rhythmicity connecting human life with natural or cosmic cycles, and held that these cosmic rhythms manifest order, harmony and balance.

This is reflected in their shared conception of time as a turning; as the principle of revolution, renewal, change and movement, variously symbolised as a sphere or wheel. This naturally implies the metaphysical concept of the centre, eye or heart found in most Eastern traditions; the point from which all force emanates and returns, the place where opposing forces come to rest in perfect equilibrium; where the pull and tension of opposites are finally resolved; from where the infinite in all things can be perceived.

In these early cultures man didn't have the irreversibility of time to contend with. He lived in an eternal present containing everything that ever happened or is likely to. Indeed, as Wittgenstein (1978) suggests 'if we take eternity to mean not infinite temporal durations but timelessness, then eternal life belongs to those who live in the present', a feature of primitive consciousness which Eliade (1959) claims is common to mystics, modern physicists who recognise the space-time nature of reality, and peoples such as the Hopi Indians whose language contains no words referring to time. Such a concept is largely incomprehensible to modern Western man for whom time 'presents itself as a precarious and evanescent duration, leading irremediably to death' (Eliade, p.113).

Time in the modern world

In the era when the Chinese were calculating astronomical periods in millions of years, Western notions were, by contrast, primitive. The linear concept of time dictated that time must have a beginning and an end and as late as the seventeenth century many Europeans believed in Archbishop Ussher's calculation of the date of the creation of the universe as 6th October 4004 BC. The idea that time had to begin with some significant event is still found in 'Big Bang' and other theories of the origin of the universe (Hawking 1988). This simple linearity dictated much of Western thought, custom and philosophy; 'It encouraged a self-centred concept of our place in the universe, our hustling individualities and our philosophy of cause and effect' (Luce 1973, p.29), notions which have been instrumental in the development of Western science.

However, linear time runs contrary to the laws of nature, cutting across them, and with the development of the pendulum clock in the seventeenth century man became less observant of cyclical processes in nature. As Dossey (1982, p.25) observes, 'He needed nature less in a world of clocks', and, he argues, some three hundred years later our lives are so dominated by clocks that we have not only become largely unconscious of the cycles in nature, but also inured to cycles within ourselves. As a result we no longer eat when hungry and sleep when tired but follow the dictates of the clock.

Clock watching is so important to the modern Western way of life that we hasten to teach children to do so. By the end of childhood most can tell the time and are also aware that time also tells on them. This curious reciprocity is highlighted in a recently advertised watch with a holographic eye on the face which appears to look back when the wearer looks at it - thereby reinforcing the idea that not only do we always have an eye on the time but that it always has its eye on us.

Indeed in Western culture the passage of time is inextricably linked with the awareness of ageing and death. Gottleib (1959) therefore points to the watch as a symbol of death. Accordingly, 'using a watch we watch. We watch time and are fixated by it, dominated by it' (Dossey 1982, p.21). Watching as we do we are acutely aware of time passing and with it those things we associate with our past, our youth, looks, unblemished complexions, hair. We are always looking over our shoulders to what we were or could have been and thus we inevitably tend to hold on to the past rather than the present, and we fear change. Buddha's insight into the human condition highlighted this reluctance to accept change, and by implication identified time as a major cause of suffering and distress.

Dossey (1982, p.21) reiterates this view, arguing that 'we can destroy ourselves through the creation of illness by perceiving time in a linear one-way flow'. He insists that many illnesses - perhaps most - may be caused, either wholly or in part, by our misperception of time. He therefore believes that it is possible to eradicate certain illnesses by adopting a non-linear view of time, wherein past, present and future merge into a timeless stillness, or cosmic time. Indeed, he claims that during his medical practice, through observing patients heal themselves by adopting such a time strategy, he came to recognise that patients can become healthier by gaining a new experiential meaning of time.

Understanding time

> Time is not a single concept. The time of the physicist is not that of the poet. The time of the calendar is no help in knowing when to cook potatoes, although it can tell us when to plant them. The 'time of my life' is not the same thing as the time to arrive at a party. The football official's 'time-out' is not the same as three-quarter waltz time. The time of the mystic is not that of the scientific investigator (Dossey 1982, p.23).

As Dossey observes, we wander through varied sorts of time each day, giving little thought to the matter, discarding one concept of time in favour of another whenever it is convenient to do so. Yet ordinarily we maintain the illusion that time is a single concept; a phenomenon needing no explanation.

Robert Ornstein, (1969) points out that most psychologists considering time have taken for granted the existence of a real time, external of our construction of it, which is linear. Such an assumption is at the root of the scientific model psychologists endeavored to adopt at the beginning of this century, and it has adversely influenced research, leading to a great deal of confusion. If correct, then human beings should possess a real sense of time identified with the clock, just as they have a visual sense which emanates from a special organ of perception. However,

> To perform an analysis of the experience of time, one can point neither to an organ of consciousness such as an eye, nor to a physical continuum such as the wavelength of light for study by objective methods. There is no immediate physical or physiological point of departure for a scientific analysis of time experience. There is no process in the external world which directly gives rise to time experience, nor is there anything immediately discernible outside ourselves which can apprehend any special 'time stimuli' (Ornstein, 1969).

Indeed, as Ornstein indicates, even a little reflection will reveal that the clock is not a receiver but a special definer of time. Yet some researchers continue to overlook this lack of a time organ and try to approach temporal experience as if there were a special time sense, which, although useful in ordinary conversation, seriously impedes understanding of the time experience.

Temporal experience

The most commonly held idea of how time is experienced is that it flows like a liquid. However even those who share this view are likely to disagree as to the rate of flow. For some time is sluggish and viscous, for others fast moving like rushing water. Moreover, within the individual the flow of time is not constant but a variable changing experience. This can be seen throughout the lifespan. A week has little meaning for a three year old and the interval between one Christmas and another is seemingly endless for children of eight or nine years of age. Piaget (1959) found that in young children a sense of 'vitesse-mouvement', or rhythmical frequency, appears before they develop a sense of time. Therefore, like early man, they live in an eternal present characterised by an awareness of rhythmic cycles.

Until the age of about eight time is generally experienced as being very expanded and as passing slowly. In very young children therefore, each day is its own universe, and they don't appear to have any sense of ordering events. However, as one ages and acquires a linear concept of time, years seem to pass more and more quickly or to shorten, even though some of their constituent hours, days, weeks may appear infinite.

This experience of hours, days, weeks or even years lengthening or shortening - of one interval passing more rapidly than others - constitutes our normal experience of time. It is affected by many variables other than age, including personality and social class (Ornstein 1969).

It is also related to memory. Ornstein found that subjects judge intervals as relatively longer when they recall the contents than when they do not, and the harder they have to 'work' at remembering this information the longer they believe their exposure to it to be. Thus, the more they have to code information in an abbreviated manner, or to 'chunk' it, the longer the intervals appear. This, he suggests, might be why children experience an expanded time sense before they have learned how to code or reduce information, and why a dull, disorganised speech which is difficult to code seems to last far longer than one which is well-structured and organised. He observes that coding seems to affect a person's experience of time even after the event. Summarized thus in the mind a holiday experienced as long and crowded with activities shrinks to a short interval in the long and familiar pattern of life.

The implications of this are significant because if the experience of time is related to memory, the way we remember is related to the way we think. In the West thinking is linear and reductionist, and lends itself to chunking or coding, with the result that the time sense is shorter and there is a sense of urgency lacking in the East where different cognitive, and therefore temporal attitudes prevail.

The content of time intervals is also a major determinant of how they are experienced. Most people recognise that when they have little interest in or liking for an activity the sense of time is constricted and the time sense enhanced. When engaged in a dull or unpleasant activity time drags, it lies heavily on us. By comparison, when engaged in pleasant activity, time flies.

Time and Relativity

... Or, at least it appears to. That it does so, however, is an illusion, as the following parable suggests:

> Two monks were arguing about a flapping banner. One insisted that the banner was moving, not the wind, the other that the wind was moving, not the banner. A third monk passing by pointed out that neither the wind nor the banner were moving, only their minds.

The awareness that it is the mind that moves is central to most Eastern thinking about time, and a similar awareness is at the very heart of modern physics. Relativity Theory reminds us that we do not know reality directly but must rely on sense impressions for our constructions of reality. Therefore there is no outward reality at all, only individualistic and relativistic constructions of it. As Einstein observed: 'If a man sits with a beautiful woman two hours seems like two minutes. Whereas if he sits on a hot stove for two minutes it seems like two hours. That's relativity'.

The implications of Relativity Theory, since confirmed empirically by the New Physics, is that our ordinary notions of time are incorrect. Rather than being dependent on some external reality independent of our senses, time is bound up with our senses; it is part of us, not 'out there'. There is no absolute reality, no external world to consult, so we must look inwards for our understanding of the universe, and for our understanding of time and its relationship to health and disease.

Time, health and disease

Our sense of time has a major effect on health and on the development and course of specific disease. In 1943 Flanders Dunbar found that male coronary patients had a compulsion to work long hours and meet deadlines, rarely took vacations and had excessive competitive drive. They also tended to be obsessive about numbers, to eat rapidly and excessively, smoke and drink too much, get insufficient sleep and to be anxious. Women with these traits were also found to be prone to coronary heart disease. Subsequently two cardiologists Friedman and Rosenman (1974) confirmed this pattern. 'One of the earlier clues indicating that a consistent pattern of behaviour might exist among coronary patients came to Friedman and Rosenman from an upholsterer who noted that their patients' chairs were worn only on the front edges, as if people had been sitting in tense expectation' (Pelletier 1978, p.124). This matched the cardiologists' observations of their patients, and subsequently, over years of study using question-naires and interviews they developed a detailed profile of two types of personality which they termed Type A and Type B, claiming that the former characterised coronary heart patients.

> Type A behaviour pattern is a particular action-emotion complex which is exhibited or possessed by an individual who is engaged in a relatively *chronic* and excessive struggle to obtain a usually unlimited number of things from his environment in the shortest period of time or against the opposing efforts of other persons or things in the same environment (Friedman and Rosenman 1974).

Type A personalities are characteristically ambitious and frequently highly successful. They are preoccupied with deadlines and have a continual sense of time urgency. They also display an easily aroused hostility, and a fierce impatience, features which are pronounced even when the person is at leisure.

Time is literally their enemy, and creates undue pressure on them, leaving them frustrated, nervous, hostile and even more firmly determined to step up their output. Unsurprisingly they generate tensions in others. Type A traits also manifest in Type B persons but basically people tend to fall into one or other category, and the traits are relatively enduring. Type A behaviour patterns have been demonstrated in children (Mathews and Volkin 1981) and in students (Musante et al, 1983).

Type B persons are not necessarily less effective nor less ambitious, and they are just as likely to be successful, but their 'drive' seems to steady them, giving them confidence and security. They are therefore largely free of the frantic sense of time urgency which characterises Type A individuals, except perhaps when it is warranted. Time is never an oppressive factor in their leisure activities, which they value, Type B persons being able to relax without guilt or the need to measure themselves in terms of achievement.

Type A behaviour may be attributable to the puritan work ethic and to an economic system which encourages competition, achievement and the acquisition of material wealth. Certainly contemporary Western society has instituted and glorified these traits, and so Type A behaviour is regarded with some reverence and promoted enthusiastically. Friedman and Rosenman (1974) suggest that at least fifty per cent of the male population of large urban complexes in the USA exhibit this behaviour pattern, and that their numbers are increasing significantly. However, while the lifestyle of these people may appear enviable to some, what is less so is its brevity, for as a group they are characterised by a very high susceptibility to mortality from coronary heart disease. Quite simply they tend to die earlier, and often suddenly, highlighting the wisdom of the matchbox caption which reads 'sudden death is Nature's way of telling you to slow down'.

Deadlines are just that - deadly, and this is not merely a whimsical notion. The time sense of Type A people is translated into physical behaviours such as brisk body movements, fist clenching during normal conversation, explosive and hurried speech patterns, upper chest breathing, and lack of total body relaxation; and into concommitant physiological effects. These include high blood pressure, elevation of certain blood hormones such as adrenalin, norepinephrine, insulin, growth hormone and hydrocortisone - which are only secreted in an exaggerated way during periods of urgency or stress - increased respiratory rate, activity of the sweat glands and muscle tension. Comparisons between Type A and Type B individuals have proved clear cut and startling. Friedman and Rosenman (1974) found that even when total carbohydrate and animal fat intake, and physical activity were substantially the same, the level of serum cholesterol of Type A persons is significantly higher than that of Type B individuals, average blood clotting time more rapid, with 28 per cent of them exhibiting clear cut signs of coronary heart disease compared with only 4 per cent of Type B persons. The majority of Type A individuals also have significantly elevated serum pre-beta protein.

These features - symptoms of what is termed 'time' or 'hurry sickness' - reflect the fact that the Type A person is always at full stretch, and constantly stressed.

Stress

According to Cox (1981) the word 'stress' may derive from the Latin *stringere*: to draw tight. As such it is similar in meaning to the word anxiety, which derives from the Latin *angoustia*: meaning narrowness. Both accurately describe the physical reactions known as 'fight or flight' responses set out by Cannon (1914) and Selye (1956), which indicate the approach or avoidance tendencies of the resulting action, and involve tension or tightening of the musculature throughout the body and narrowing of the organs in the throat and chest.

The specific changes of the body involve the slowing of the digestion so that blood may be directed to the muscles and the brain; more rapid breathing to supply oxygen to the muscles; speeding up of the heart and increase in blood pressure to force blood to parts of the body in need of it; increased perspiration to cool the body, tensing of muscles in preparation for action; and the release of chemicals to make the blood clot more rapidly in the event of injury. Sugar and fats also pour into the blood to provide energy for quick action, and the level of certain hormones is elevated, notably epinephrine which releases stored sugars, norepinephrine, which increases heart rate and blood pressure, and cortisol, which aids in the preparation for vigorous activity. These changes are typically experienced as 'butterflies in the stomach', heart pounding, sweating, and stiffness in various parts of the body, especially the back.

During human evolution these reactions have served important survival needs, as they still do when prompt action is required to avoid injury or death. However, these responses are often triggered by any situation which requires adjustment, and when employed inappropriately they become habitual. The body remains in a continuously reactive state, or state of dis-ease, which may become chronic, thereby taking a toll on body organs and health.

Stress-related disease

Seventy-five per cent of all medical complaints are estimated to be stress related (Charlesworth and Nathan 1987). Stress has been identified as a major factor in the causation of high blood pressure, coronary heart disease, migraine and tension headaches, ulcers and gastro-intestinal conditions, asthma, chronic backache, arthritis, allergies, hyperthyroidism, vertigo, multiple sclerosis, and diabetes (Benson 1975); pruritis, constipation, menstrual difficulties and tuberculosis (Cooper et al. 1988). Dermatologists have identified stress as a factor in skin disorders such as eczema, dermatitis and psoriasis, and it is also implicated in smoking, overeating, alcohol and drug abuse, which frequently have negative health consequences.

Stress-related conditions are not merely inconvenient, they can also be deadly. Sustained high blood pressure or hypertension is a very dangerous condition because it increases the rate of development of atherosclerosis, or hardening of the arteries. Cholesterol, fats, blood clots and calcium are all deposited within the walls of the arteries as a result of the high blood pressure causing the normally soft elastic open arteries to become hard, inelastic and partly or completely blocked, often with dire consequences. Sudden death or permanent damage to the heart or brain may occur after many symptom-free years.

When atherosclerosis does occur its target is usually one or more of three organs: the heart, brain or kidneys.

The heart must generate the high blood pressure by pumping more forcefully, and as a result muscle fibres in the heart increase in size, enlarging the heart. This requires more blood flow, but because of the inability of the arteries to enlarge owing to hardening, blood flow cannot be increased, which results in a heart attack.

The brain is affected directly through high blood pressure bursting blood vessels, resulting in a brain haemorrhage; or indirectly through atherosclerosis which leads to temporary or permanent brain damage, or stroke.

The kidneys usually control blood pressure but when diseased by high blood pressure they make blood pressure worse. Normally if blood pressure decreases to low levels the kidneys secrete hormones that increase it. They can therefore be thought of as sensors which monitor and maintain adequate blood pressure. However, if atherosclerosis develops in the kidney blood vessels it will increase the amount of blood flow to these organs and the kidneys will become shrunken. Blocked kidney vessels leads to low blood pressure in the kidneys and the organ responds by secreting hormones and raising the blood pressure in the body. A vicious cycle is therefore established because the raising of the blood pressure leads to more atherosclerosis which further blocks blood flow to the kidneys, which further increases blood pressure. Moreover, some of the excess hormones that the adrenal glands release can interfere with the body's immune reaction to infection.

The immune system

The immune system consists of more than a dozen different types of white blood cells concentrated in the spleen, thymus gland and lymph nodes, which circulate the entire body through the blood and lymphatic system. They are divided into two main types, the B-cells which produce chemicals that neutralise toxins made by disease organisms while helping the body mobilize its own defences, and the T-cells and their helpers which are killer cells that destroy invading bacteria and viruses. Both are controlled by the brain, either directly through hormones in the blood stream, or indirectly through the nerves and neuro-chemicals. When stress reactions are prolonged the primary action of the adrenal hormones is to suppress the work of the immune system. Thus what is in the short term an adaptive response can eventually become the cause of every conceivable disease that involves the immune system; cancers, infections, and auto-immune disorders such as rheumatoid arthritis and multiple sclerosis. Furthermore, as Achterberg (1985) indicates, the massive changes sustained during prolonged stress go far beyond immune activity to every gland targeted by the pituitary, including those involved in the reproduction, growth, integrity and well-being of the body at the cellular level.

The link between stress and cancer is well-established (Blumberg et al. 1954, LeShan 1966, Stoll 1979, Solomon 1969, Jacobs and Charles 1980, Rosch 1984, Greer and Watson 1985), as is the connection between stress and the endocrine and immune systems (Mason 1968, Curtis 1979, Rose 1980, Ader and Cohen 1975, Rogers et al. 1975, Editorial 1985,87)

Dr Arthur Samuels (1984 cited by Achterberg 1985), a haematology and cancer specialist, suggests a common group of causes for cancer, heart attack, stroke and related thrombotic diseases, which includes chronic stress, a predisposed personality type and chronic hyperactivation of neural, endocrine, immune, blood clotting and fibrinolytic systems. When stress is prolonged the clotting mechanism becomes hyperactive and the fibrinolytic mechanism, which normally inhibits excessive clotting fails. The resulting blood clots are implicated in both heart attack and stroke as well as other peripheral vascular conclusions.

Stress outcomes

Charlesworth and Nathan (1987) list the outcomes of stress under three headings: disorders, drugs and dollars; to which can be added death. They point out that 30 million Americans have some form of major heart or blood vessel disease and every year one million Americans have a heart attack. Twenty-five million Americans suffer from high blood pressure, eight million have ulcers and 12 million are alcoholics.

Five billion doses of tranquillisers are prescribed to Americans each year, three billion doses of amphetamine and five billion doses of barbiturates (sleeping tablets). 15.6 billion dollars is lost to US industry every year because of alcohol abuse, 15 billion dollars because of stress-related absenteeism, 700 million dollars is spent every year trying to recruit replacements for executives with heart disease, and 19.4 billions because of premature death of employees.

Time and illness

One of the insights of the Buddha was the human tendency to react to the passage of time with fear, and to defend against this anxiety by engaging in endless motion and activity. Nowhere is this more evident than in Type A people who are typically highly anxious and manifest this physically in narrowing of the chest and throat, resulting in upper chest breathing and acceleration of the heart rate, and psychologically in narrowing of the time sense. This heightened awareness of time can cause illness - 'time sickness' - and in some cases it can prove fatal. Dossey observes that time sickness is often part of the normal response to serious illness inasmuch as temporal factors begin to influence perceptions profoundly when a person becomes ill. The more severe the illness the greater is the likelihood that the sufferer will be reminded of death.

Serious diseases ... force us to confront the end, the final state, the forever (p.52).

- in other words, the possibility that one's 'time is up'.

When time appears to be running out the time sense is constricted and this may have a significant effect on the subsequent course of the illness. Dossey suggests that time sickness, expressed as fear of death, seems to present an increased risk in the acute phase following a heart attack.

He cites Cassem et al (1968) who found that those patients admitted to a coronary care unit following an acute heart attack who seemed intensely anxious survived in fewer numbers than those who appeared calm. The reasons for this are to be found in the physiological correlates of acute anxiety, primarily high blood pressure coupled with increased secretion of adrenalin. Moreover, because of its direct nerve connections with the heart, the hypothalamus of the brain when stimulated can produce electrical instability in the heart itself. Thus the fibrillatory threshold in the heart muscle is lowered and it is easier for the heart to fibrillate, or beat in a rapid, chaotic manner resulting in sudden death. The increase in heart rate and blood pressure require the heart to do more work, and requires more oxygen, which cannot be supplied because oxygen lack is what triggered the heart attack in the first place, through obstruction of one of the coronary arteries supplying the heart with blood. Therefore it would seem, as Dossey suggests, that time related anxiety can kill; time sickness can be fatal.

Time and terminal illness

Dossey also suggests that in terminal illness time sickness can hasten death. He claims that it is associated with panic, anxiety, depression and resignation, and that this 'coping style' is in itself malignant - a cancer which eats away at the person. He argues that it should be dealt with as promptly as the physical components of disease. Yet the medical profession persist in focusing exclusively on physical issues such as diet, blood cell count and clotting mechanisms, which although real and important, are only part of the total picture, which includes the time strategy being employed by the sick person.

The patient's relationship to time is invariably ignored, although the first question asked by patients or their relatives on receiving a diagnosis of serious illness is usually 'How much time do I have?' or 'How much longer has he got?'. However, Siegel (1986, p.39) observes that 'The physician's habitual prognosis of how much time a patient has left is a terrible mistake. It is a self-fulfilling prophecy'. Dossey takes a similar view, proposing that frequently 'people destroy themselves in response to an invitation originating from others to stop living' (p.93-4); so when a person has reached the time or age at which he is expected to die, he invariably obliges by dying, assisted in this project by the expectations of others that he will not be around too long. Cancer specialist Dr. Michael Wetzler condemns the practice of giving patients a specific survival time, as does Dr. Peter Maguire, director of the Cancer Research Campaign's psychological Medicine group at Christies' Hospital Manchester who advises doctors never to do so (McKee 1988).

Time and pain

Pain is often a feature of serious or chronic illness, and is generally experienced as unpleasant. Like other unpleasant experience it causes the time sense to constrict. Evidence suggests, however, that pain can be lessened by stretching the time sense. It is well established that certain drugs, including marijuana, LSD, DMT, and opiates effect what Huxley termed 'the reducing valve' of normal sensory awareness. The time experience is frequently reported as lengthened or suspended by those taking these drugs. Opiates have a particularly devastating effect on the perception of time. As Burroughs (1977) indicates heroin 'kills' time, and under its influence the person lives in a timeless, painless state. Indeed heroin is one of the most powerful analgesics or painkillers known to man, and is widely used in medicine, especially in the treatment of terminally ill cancer patients. Therefore, without actually realising it, stretching the time sense is something that orthodox Western physicians do all the time, for, as Dossey observes (1982, p.47) 'Almost all substances that we use to treat serve pain modify the sense of time'.

However, any device or technique that expands the sense of time - anything which helps to still the mind - can be used as an analgesic. He observes that it is not without coincidence that many people, on receiving the diagnosis of cancer, take up fishing. Many hobbies and pastimes share the capacity to 'kill' time, which is a fairly accurate description of the change in time flow experienced during repetitive activities which allow a person to step 'out of time' into complete absorption in a task. Many athletes describe an experience that resembles non-linear non-flowing space-time, or cyclic time, as a feature of their activities. They also commonly describe 'crossing the pain barrier' and experiencing a pain-free, tranquil state, or a 'high' (Colt et al. 1981). Indeed there is abundant evidence that certain activities, and concommitant mental states can evoke actual changes in brain physiology to alter pain perception. Endorphins and enkaphalins, natural opiate - like pain killing substances in the body can be triggered not only by various physical sports and exercise, but also by mental states which are characterised by absorption in a given process, such as music (Goldstein, 1980). According to Dossey (p. 168) such absorption annuls the psychological experience of time inasmuch that events which are sequentially changing do not happen in the usual linear sense; they simply *are*. He points to various activities, including all forms of meditation and relaxation techniques, biofeedback, hypnosis, autohypnosis and autogenic training, which, insofar that they invoke this psychological mode or shift in time perception, and enable an individual to develop a friendliness with time, can be regarded as 'time therapies', with numerous applications in the field of healing.

Chapter 6

Meditation and Biofeedback

> When the mind is disturbed the multiplicity of things is produced;
> When the mind is quieted, they disappear
>
> *(Hui-neng).*

Laurie and Tucker (1982, p.89) liken our constricted view of time to a man travelling on a train. From the window he cannot see very far ahead, and his view of a bridge the train is approaching is thereby limited. He can see part of the bridge as the train nears, get a better view during the crossing, and only a little of it again when it is behind him. However, if he were positioned a mile from the track he could see the whole bridge. From such a standpoint - looking in on the scene rather than out upon it - he can see the full picture. Similarly from the introverted perspective of meditation one can see the whole of things, and realise that the linearity of time is an illusion.

Shapiro (1982) defines meditation as 'a family of techniques which have in common a conscious attempt to focus attention in a non-analytical way and an attempt not to dwell on discursive ruminating thought'. This amounts to an attempt to still the mind; to shift from the active 'doing' mode to a passive 'letting things be' and is therefore a state in which experience as it is usually known ceases. In Buddhism this is described as a void; in Hinduism as samadhi or still mind; and in Taoism as tso wang, sitting with no thoughts.

It crucially involves an introversion; a shift of attention from the external world to the inner. Western culture is characteristically extrovert in attitude and preoccupied with action or doing, direction and control. Thus the passive, receptive, introverted attitude necessary for meditation - and non-doing, is generally regarded as foreign and alien.

The Western tradition of Meditation

In fact meditation has been practised in the West for many centuries. As early as 4000 BC it was part of Egyptian religious ceremony and in the Old Testament (Genesis: 24.63) we are told that 'Isaac went out to meditate in the field at eventide'. Early Christians were urged by Paul to meditate (Timothy I:4, 15), and meditative practices of early Christian monks were very similar to those of Hinduism and Buddhism. According to Goleman (1978) the 'Jesus Prayer' known as Hesychasm, after a fifth century teacher Hesychius of Jerusalem, fulfills Paul's injunction to pray always. The prayer, which is still observed in the Trappist Order, is rehearsed during every activity, the aim being quiet, a state of no-mindedness, rest or quiet. This constant remembrance of God, and verbal or silent repetition of prayer, or scriptural passages is similar to the practices of Bhakti yoga, while constant repetition of phrases such as *Kyrie Eleison* can be likened to the use of mantras.

Maupin (1969) observes that the Catholic Church has articulated a psychology of meditational experience or contemplation in which the conscious exercise of attention to specific content such as Christ, the Virgin Mary or the saints leads to a spontaneous flow of experience to which the person becomes a receptive onlooker, and in the extreme leads to loss of the feeling of separateness as the person attains union with the object of contemplation.

Within Christianity there is also the tradition of silent prayer which is close to that of contentless meditation, and is not directed to any specific content but to becoming more open to and aware of one's experience. The Brotherhood of Friends, or Quakers emphasise this 'waiting' and 'listening' to inner experience. The mystic tradition of Judaism, Kabbalism, seeks to train students to enter into a state of consciousness where they become more attuned with higher consciousness, and no longer enslaved by the body and conditioning. To achieve this the individual must observe the workings of the Yesod, ordinary mind, or ego, so as to see through self delusion and bring into awareness the unconscious forces that shape personal thoughts and actions. Central to this awareness is attainment of a state of clarity called tiferet, which involves one-pointed focus on a single subject or kavanah.

Despite these traditions, or perhaps through ignorance of their existence, most Westerners appear to regard meditation as a somewhat strange oriental practice, a view largely reinforced, and to some extent justified in the cults which have grown up in the West around certain Eastern Traditions in recent years.

Eastern traditions of meditation in the West

Hindu meditation

Although the aim of meditation is common to all Eastern traditions the means vary with different schools of thought. There are many forms of meditation within Hinduism but the most widely practised is *bhakti*, or spiritual devotion, the aim of which is one-pointed concentration on an *ishta* or devotional object, such as a deity or divine being. This is achieved by *kirtan*, chanting or singing, and *japa*, silent or spoken repetition of the ishta's name, which is frequently assisted by the telling of the beads of a *mala*, or rosary. This practice is central to the International Society for Krishna Consciousness founded by His Divine Grace A.C. Bhaktivedanta Swami Pradhupada, and since the 1960s

Westerners have become familiar with their *Hare Krishna* chant, popularised by former Beatle, George Harrison.

Tantric meditation

The tantric tradition, common to both Hinduism and Buddhism, aims at alteration of consciousness by arousing normally latent energies. It offers a wide variety of techniques for transcending sense consciousness, including *mantra*: repetition of sounds; *shabd*: concentration on supersubtle inner sounds; *yantra*: visualization of objects such as mandalas; *asanas*: postures; *pranayama*: concentration on the chakra energies; and *maithuna*: controlled sexual intercourse during which the person achieves detachment and thus converts sexual energy into higher forms through the repetition of mantras. In attempting to transcend earthly desires it breaks with various taboos and is widely misunderstood by those who adopt a superficial view of it.

A modern version of tantra which employs traditional practices is Siddha yoga taught by Swami Muktananda. Its aim, shaktipat, is distributing psychic energy, symbolised as a serpent. However, perhaps the best known proponent of tantra in the West is the controversial Bhagwan Shree Rajineesh, whose Orange Movement, so called because of the orange garments worn by devotees, gained a cult following in Europe and the USA during the 1970s, and equally forceful opposition which eventually resulted in his expulsion from the latter during the next decade.

Rajneesh first gained notoriety in his native India where his apparent encouragement of sexual practices attracted thousands of young Westerners to his ashram at Poona, and led to charges of libertinism and debauchery in the Western press. Hindu traditionalists were also opposed to his secularisation, modernisation and Westernisation of ancient practices.

The hallmark of Rajneesh' approach is its eclecticism. Nevertheless, while he draws on the wisdom of many ancient traditions and also the findings of contemporary psychology, closer scrutiny reveals that his teachings are firmly in the mainstream of the tantric tradition, and concerned primarily with transcending attachment to physical needs and the world. Rajneesh recognises that people differ in their needs and he addresses himself primarily to those of modern man. He therefore advocates many different meditation techniques, some of which derive from psychotherapeutic approaches such as Gestalt Therapy. He attempts to show that mundane activities such as cleaning the teeth or jogging can be meditative activities, and that heightened awareness can be achieved in everyday contexts. He acknowledges that the attitude of non-doing is largely alien to the Western mind and that as a result Westerners generally find it difficult to meditate. He therefore prescribes methods suited to the West which are active and dynamic, employing movement, dance, music and chaotic breathing, in addition to more passive forms.

Transcendental Meditation

Another traditional form of meditation packaged for a modern Western audience is Transcendental Meditation or TM. Brought to the West in 1958 by the Maharishi Mahesh Yogi it attracted public attention and a huge world-wide following during the 1960s when embraced by the Beatles. However, as Harding (1988) indicates, TM has outlasted the trappings of kaftans and beads and is currently practised by some 3 million people world-wide and by about 130,000 in the UK. Goleman (1978, p.68) describes it as a classic Hindu mantra meditation; a modern restatement of the basic teaching of Sankaracharya's eighth century Advait School of Vedanta. Thus, although not stated as such, the aim of TM is samadhi, or union with Brahman. Indeed, as Goleman indicates, the Maharishi downplays the orthodox nature of his approach, stripping much of the religious element and dogmas from his teachings, avoiding Sanskrit terminology, and using scientific findings to validate meditation in a sceptical culture.

Thus, although claimed as unique, TM is in the mainstream of Jnana practices which sees duality as the main cause of suffering and aims at one-pointedness or transcendent consciousness. This is achieved by control of attention, which involves turning the attention inwards towards subtle levels of thought until the source of the thought is reached. Maharishi (1969) depicts the finer levels of one-pointedness as increasingly blissful and sublime, and describes the increasing 'charm' as the mind enters progressively more subtle realms of thought.

The technique for achieving one-pointedness commences with repetition of a single word or mantra for twenty minutes twice daily while seated with eyes closed. Much emphasis is laid on the tailoring of the mantra to the individual. 'There is a mystique about the specialness of each person's mantra and teachers admonish newcomers never to reveal theirs to anyone or even speak it aloud. But meditators are sometimes chagrined to learn people who fall into general categories of age, education and so-on are given the same mantra' (Goleman 1978, p.70).

In TM meditators are taught effortless passive concentration, being told to bring the mind gently back to the mantra whenever it wanders. The next stage is the infusion of transcendent consciousness into waking, sleeping and dreaming states by alternating ordinary activities with periods of meditation. This achieves what is termed 'cosmic consciousness' and the means to these higher states are given to meditators over the course of several years practice and service to the TM movement and never divulged to others.

Zen

Little was known of zen in the West before 1927 when the first volume of Suzuki's *Essays in Zen Buddhism* was published. During the 1950s it was promoted by Kerouac, Ginsberg and other writers of the 'Beat' period, and during the 1960s by Suzuki, Watts, and Humphreys. Then during the 1970s it was popularised, notably by Pirsig (1974), after which a cult developed around it.

This 'pop zen' was, according to Roszack (1970) a 'distortion of the fundamental philosophy, flawed by crude simplifications and vulgarised by the young'. Nevertheless, despite these simplifications zen is difficult for Westerners to understand. As Humphreys (1962, p.138) explains, they are troubled with an itch to interfere in others' lives and the self-governance of the universe; to put right what they consider wrong, and find it hard to accept zen which is the universe and what makes it tick. Its methods of meditation, zazen or seated meditation, or ritual activities such as flower arranging, are also difficult for Westerners to comprehend and master. Zazen, although simpler in form than the Rinzai rituals, is in fact so subtle that according to Humphreys (1962, p.106) only a genuine mystical awareness will prevent the practice deteriorating into just sitting in which nothing happens at all, and which, over a number of hours or days, can be very stressful and painful.

Sufi

Sufi is the mystic tradition of Islam and its meditation practices became more widely know in the West as a result of the teachings of Gurdjieff who gained a considerable following in the West during the 1920s and subsequently.

The main form of Sufi meditation is *zikr* or *dhikr* the underlying principle of which is constant remembrance of God, most usually by way of repetitive chants. Perhaps the best-known is 'La ilaha illa' - there is no God but God - which is enhanced by circular dancing whereby ecstasy or out of the body consciousness is achieved. This 'whirling' meditation is characteristic of the ascetic Muslim monks or Dervishes. Drawing on this tradition, Gurdjieff prescribed repetitive movement, dancing and remembrance of actions as a means of transcending ordinary consciousness.

A similar tradition underlies the breathing and movement exercises known as *zhikr* which is a feature of Arica, a therapeutic system developed by Oscar Ichazo, which aims at achieving mind/body balance through a system of psychocalisthenics.

Contemporary meditation practices in the West

These forms of meditation are now widely practiced in the West. According to a Gallup Poll published in *Newsweek* magazine in September 1976, by the mid-70s there were no less than five million Americans practising yoga, six million meditating regularly, and some two million deeply involved in Oriental religions. However, these practices, which were widely and wrongly regarded as confined to the young also attracted 'much middle-aged and geriatric disfavour' (Editorial 1977, p.478). A major objection to meditation is that it produces introverted people, and in the West introversion is largely synonymous with shyness and frequently carries the connotation of weakness. It is therefore generally regarded as an undesirable trait which produces withdrawn and other-worldly people who gradually lose touch with reality. Not uncommonly it is associated with madness. Indeed, this confusion in both lay and medical circles between the characteristics common to mysticism and mental disorder prompted an attempt at clarification by the US Group for the Advancement of Psychiatry which was reported in the British medical journal, *The Practitioner* in 1977. This indicated that the resemblance between the mystic and the schizophrenic is only superficial, the retreat of the former to the inner world being deliberate rather than obligatory and partial rather than complete. They acknowledge that the 'comfort and satiation of the consumer society may create a need for non-material satisfaction, and the material advances of science and technology a desire for experience that transcends the rational' but finally confessed to doubts and difficulties about the absolute distinction between mysticism and mental disorder, concluding that 'from one point of view all mystical experiences may be regarded as symptoms of mental disturbance, and from another, they may be regarded as attempts at adaption'.

It is not necessary to have a mystical rationale in order to practice meditation. Nevertheless suspicion about meditation continues, often reinforced by misunderstanding of so-called altered states of consciousness which are suggestive of psychosis or disturbance, and frequently associated with the use of illicit drugs. However, LeShan (1978) argues that

> 'in an altered state of consciousness you view the world as if it were put together in a different fashion that the way you normally view it. This by no means implies that you are insane or are deluding yourself. Einsteinian physics is a statement that the world is put together and 'works' in a different way than is believed in a commonsense view or by the older 'classical' physics. No-one would call an Einsteinian physicist insane because of this views. The physicists would say he is using a 'different metaphysical system', a different explanation of reality. The mystic would say he is in 'an altered state of consciousness'. The only difference between the two is that the physicist is describing, analysing intellectually and examining the implications of this other view of reality, the mystic is perceiving and reacting to it. The first is talking about something; the second is living it.'

Nevertheless, Perls is critical of the catatonic-like withdrawal and interference with the spontaneous flow of life that can result from meditation. Similarly among spiritual leaders there is criticism that cross-legged posturing may be an investment in 'precious encapsulated practices' rather than directed towards whole being (Krishnamurti 1966), and Rajneesh insists that in attempting 'to practice' meditation it merely becomes another doing.

The same charges can be levelled against any spiritual practice, or psychotherapy, where what occurs in the therapists's office is somehow of a different order to the rest of the person's life. Nevertheless, as Maupin (1969, p.178) observes:

> These are serious objections. The primary problem seems to be that people who engage in practices designed to produce personal growth tend to split these practices off from the rest of life. True growth must take in ordinary living.

Similarly the cross-legged posture is not a necessary feature of meditation. Hirai (1975) observes that zazen or seated meditation is far from easy to achieve and may be counterproductive inasmuch that it can lead to drowsiness, so walking meditation (kinhin) is frequently employed, as is *fukanzazeng* or meditation in a reclining position.

Rajneesh indicates that in the Book of Tantra there are 112 meditations, many involving movement, and some, as in the Japanese tradition, focusing on mundane activities.

Most of the criticisms of meditation reflect misconceptions about what in involves. Nevertheless many people persist in their belief that meditation is very difficult, requiring intense concentration, which is not altogether surprising given that the *Visuddhimaggia*, the classical Buddhist text which describes the way in which the meditator trains his attention, begins with a description of an advanced altered state of consciousness which is quite rare and which most meditators never experience. In so doing it neglects the more prosaic stages and ordinary experiences in the initial stages of meditation such as mind wandering and the tension which results between concentration on the object of meditation and ordinary thought. It also prescribes the attainment of purity as a prerequisite of meditation.

TM has done much to reverse many of the ideas held in the West about meditation by demonstrating that anyone can meditate irrespective of life style or disposition; by emphasising that the 'good life' proceeds from meditation, rather than being a prerequisite of it; and that it involves no renunciation of worldly affairs and need only be practised for 20 minutes twice a day.

Much confusion arises because in the West the term concentration has connotations of focusing the rational mind or intellect, and is synonymous with study. However, absorption in a task is perhaps nearer to the Eastern concept of the term. Indeed, Rajneesh insists that meditation is not concentration which is antithetical to the aims of meditation inasmuch that it involves the self concentrating on an object which is concentrated on. This constitutes a duality of consciousness and results in tiredness and exhaustion because such a willed act is hard work. By contrast in meditation there is no duality, no observer and no observed, because the subject and object of concentration are one. Thus meditation involves a letting go of the individual self and an absorption in what one is, part of the totality. It is a state of no will, of inaction, or non-doing, which if forced or effortful is doomed. Inasmuch that it is letting go - of notions of self or ego and its limitations; of the illusion of separateness; of what one believes or would like oneself to be, into what one is - it is the equivalent of relaxation, a view reinforced by the Maharishi's (1969, p.287) claim that 'life in cosmic consciousness is tensionless'. Moreover in promoting wholeness or holiness it is synonymous with healing and medicine. Indeed Rajneesh claims that 'meditation is medicine. It is the only medicine'.

Meditation as medicine

Rajneesh's claims are not unfounded. Since the 1930s there has been abundant evidence that meditation as practised by yogins or adepts of zen confers a variety of beneficial effects.

In 1935 the French cardiologist Thérèse Brosse recorded measures of heart rate control in Indian yogins which indicated an advanced voluntary capacity to regulate autonomic functions including metabolic rate. Subsequently Sugi and Akatsu found that during meditation the oxygen consumption of zen monks decreased by 20 per cent and their output of carbon dioxide also decreased indicating a slowing of metabolism. In New Delhi Anand et al. (1961) made a similar finding when examining a yogin confined in a sealed metal box. These studies strongly indicate that meditation produced these effects through control of the autonomic nervous system, which is normally considered to be outside voluntary control.

Research during the 1950s and 60s was assisted by the development of the electro-encephalograph or EEG, an apparatus which detects the electrical rhythms generated by the brain. These occur in four principal groups, each of which can be approximately correlated with a particular brain activity or state of awareness.

beta: frequency 13-30 Hz (cycles per second) - the normal waking rhythm of the brain;

alpha: 8-13 Hz - which have very little meaning taken on their own, but which in conjunction with other rhythms appear to be a building block of other levels of awareness.

theta: 4-7 Hz - which occur with physiological relaxation and indicate a calming down or emptying of the mind;

delta: 0.5-4 Hz - which is the rhythm of sleep but is found in many persons in response to new ideas and in some people engaged in paranormal activities.

Explorations with the EEG showed that meditation produces changes in the electrical activity of the brain. Anand, China and Singh (1961) monitored the EEG traces of four yogins during samahdi and found that they demonstrated an abundance of alpha wave activity, and also theta which predominates when a person is deeply relaxed with eyes closed. These subjects were found not to be distracted by external stimuli such as strong light, loud noises, being burned with hot glass tubing, or vibrations from a tuning fork, suggesting an association between alpha regulation and ability to establish autonomic control. Anand et al (1961) also found that yogins practising meditation and showing prominent alpha activity had an increased pain threshold to cold water, being able to keep a hand submerged in water at $4^{o}C$ for 45-55 minutes without experiencing discomfort. Rose (1970) demonstrated that yogins were able to change the temperature of two patches of skin, making one hotter and the other simultaneously colder, and although only two inches apart, produce a temperature difference of 10 degrees.

Kasamatsu and Hirai (1966) undertook intensive investigation of four adepts of Soto zen and found that during seated meditation with eyes half open there was a predomin-ance of alpha waves which persisted when the eyes were open. The waves increased in amplitude and regularity, especially in the frontal and central regions of the brain, and experienced meditators showed other changes in that the alpha waves slowed from their normal frequency to 7-8 cycles per second and rhythmical theta at 6-7 cps appeared. Benson and Wallace (1972) report that in a further examination of yogins Das and Gastand found that alpha waves gave way to fast wave activity at the rate of 40-45 cps as meditation progressed and these waves in turn subsided with a return to the slow alpha and theta waves. Hirai (1975) has also shown that in *kinhin* or walking meditation where alpha might be expected to cease owing to activity and more rapid breathing zen priests show remarkably reduced breathing rates and high emission of alpha waves, and their physiological and mental states remained unaltered from zazen.

Another physiological response tested by early investigators was of skin resistance to a electric current. This measure is thought to reflect the level of anxiety, with a decrease in skin resistance representing greater anxiety and a rise indicating greater relaxation. It was found that in yogins skin resistance increases during meditation.

Bagchi and Wenger (1959) demonstrated that over 98 meditation sessions the pattern of physiological alteration that occurred was characterised by

- an extreme slowing of respiration to 4-6 breaths per minute
- more than 70 per cent increase in electrical resistance of the skin
- a predominance of alpha wave activity
- a slowing of heart rate to 24 beats per minute from he normal rate of 72 beats per minute

all of which is suggestive of a state of deep relaxation. Indeed, numerous studies have indicated that meditation is psychologically more refreshing and energising than deep sleep (Wallace 1970), and that after commencing regular meditation subjects require less sleep than prior to their commencing meditation (Bloomfield et al. 1975)

Various psychological effects are also claimed for meditators, including greater psychological stability (Schwartz and Goleman 1976), greater autonomic stability (Ormé-Johnson 1973), lower anxiety (Linden 1973; Nidich, Seeman et al. 1973; Ferguson and Gowan 1973); internal locus of control ie, a sense of being effective in the world rather than passive victim of circumstance (Schwartz and Goleman 1976) - all of which are essential goals of psychotherapy and psychosomatic medicine. Schwartz (1973) found a substantial drop in headaches, colds and insomnia among meditators and lower incidence of somatic complaints. He also found a reduced usage of alcohol, cigarettes, coffee, and dietary changes such as eating less meat and sweets. Meditators were also found to report more positive mood states and regular daily routines. Indeed meditation has been used successfully in the treatment of asthma (Honsberger and Wilson 1973), hypertension (Wallace and Benson 1972; Cooper and Aygen 1978) and phobias (Boudreau 1972).

Yoga has also been shown to have positive therapeutic benefits in the treatment of both psychosomatic and organic disorders. Patel (1973) and Patel and Datey (1975) have demonstrated its effectiveness in the management of hypertension, and Dostalek (1987) reports that the corpse pose or sarasana has proved to be suitable tool in managing hypertension, even in cases which have proved unresponsive to drugs. It has been shown to have similar effects to the tranquilliser Diazepam and that it is thus a valid replacement for synthetic drugs which have harmful side effects. Yoga postures have also been demonstrated to have significant effects on respiratory rate, heart rate, and EEG (Udupa 1978). Thus, Monjo (1987) claims that yoga has positive therapeutic benefits, and has been successful in the treatment of venous and lymphatic insufficiency, peripheral artery disease, chronic bronchitis, asthma, emphysema, sinusitis.

Research into Transcendental Meditation

However Wallace and Benson recognised that the variety of meditative practice led to a wide variety of response and so they chose TM, which, because it is so well standardised, enabled them to conduct large scale studies under reasonably well-controlled conditions. Other researchers followed their example, with the result that TM has been subjected to more scientific investigation than any other form of meditation, with results reported in several hundred published research papers.

Wallace and Benson found that the reduction in metabolic rate (and hence the need for oxygen) during meditation was reflected in a decrease, essentially involuntary, in the rate of respiration and in the volume of air breathed, oxygen consumption falling sharply from pre-meditation levels, rising again in the post-meditation period. Similarly they found that the elimination of carbon dioxide decreased during meditation.

They also found that subjects' arterial blood pressure remained at a rather low level throughout, and that there was a slight increase in the acidity of the blood. Blood lactate level (an indication of metabolism in the absence of free oxygen) declined sharply, nearly four times faster than in people resting normally in a supine position or in subjects during the premeditation period.

The reason for the fall in blood lactate remains uncertain but it is clear that this may have a beneficial psychological effect. Patients with anxiety neurosis show a large rise in the blood lactate level when placed under stress. Pitts and McClure (1967) found that experimental infusions of lactate would bring on anxiety attacks in such persons and even produce anxiety symptoms in normal subjects. Hypertensive persons also typically show higher blood pressure, and low lactate in meditators is associated with low blood pressure. Wallace and Benson (1972, p.129) thus suggest that 'all in all, it is reasonable to hypothesise that the low level of lactate found in subjects during and after TM may be responsible in part for the meditators thoroughly relaxed state'.

Other measures confirm the picture of meditation as a highly relaxed but wakeful condition. Skin resistance to electric current increases markedly, in some cases more than fourfold, and heart rate slows by an average of about three beats per minute, while EEG recordings reveal a marked intensification of alpha waves in all subjects. These wave records, when analysed by computer, typically show an increased intensity of slow alpha waves at 8-9 cps in the frontal and central regions of the brain during meditation, and in several subjects this change is also accompanied by prominent theta waves in the frontal area. These changes bear little resemblance to those which occur during sleep or hypnosis.

Hypnosis produces no noticeable changes in metabolic index, and during sleep oxygen level decreases appreciably only after several hours. During sleep concentration of carbon dioxide in the blood increases significantly, indicating a reduction in respiration, and while skin resistance commonly increases during sleep the rate and amount of the increase are on a much smaller scale than in TM.

EEG patterns of sleep are also different from those of TM, consisting predominantly of high voltage activity of slow waves at 12-14 cps and a mixture of low voltage waves at various frequencies - a pattern which does not occur in meditation, and the EEG patterns of hypnosis have no resemblance to those of the meditative state.

Wallace and Benson (1972) conclude that the pattern of changes observed suggest that meditation generates an integrated response, hypometabolic state or reflex mediated by the central nervous system apparently opposite to the 'fight or flight' arousal response identified by Cannon, which mobilised a set of physiological responses marked by increased blood pressure, heart rate, blood flow, oxygen consumption and muscle tension. This hypometabolic state is characterised by quiescence rather than hyperactivation.

Awareness of the possible therapeutic benefits has led to the application of TM in the treatment of stress, and stress-related conditions. There is evidence to suggest that meditation may confer long-term benefits on health (Wallace and Benson 1972; Fenwick et al. 1977); and that it is possible to develop a habitual low arousal state (Stoyva and Budzinski 1973).

The volume of evidence leaves little doubt that meditation is relaxing and is an effective antidote to anxiety. However, it is not unique in this respect and many studies have shown no difference between meditation and other forms of relaxation (Benson 1972; West 1979, 80). The matter remains controversial however, with a study by Throll (1981) suggesting that meditation is more effective than relaxation techniques in effecting changes in anxiety states.

Otis (1974) has speculated on some of the factors involved in the role of TM as a therapeutic agent, namely that certain selection variables may play a vital role in its efficacy . He suggests that certain psychological and personal characteristics are associated with those disposed to TM and it is people with these characteristics who get involved in scientific studies on TM. He claims that they are usually reasonably well integrated but bothered by neurotic guilts, anxieties and phobias, and, as young people tend to drop out (up to 50 per cent in the first few months), it is older persons who tend to keep meditating and the benefits experienced may be due to their high expectations.

Pelletier (1978) indicates that these factors need to be explored before any definite statements can be made about the effects of TM as such, but based on research using highly motivated persons, it seems that psychological and physical benefits accrue.

Clinically standardised Meditation

Although TM offers several advantages over other methods of meditation, as a subject for research its clinical applications are limited by its very nature. Although the International Meditation Society asserts that the practice is non-religious, in the opinion of Blows (1987) several incongruities remain. He claims that there is ambiguity and distinct cognitive dissonance in the way the TM method is presented.

Although the TM movement claims it does not involve any kind of philosophical belief, membership of any group, or religious commitment, being a completely mechanical technique which has the effect of producing a settled state of consciousness and concommitant physiological changes, the TM organisation acts to recruit members with the aim of establishing an 'enlightened' international community which favours peace and other objectives. Therefore to tell initiates that TM does not involve 'any kind of philosophical belief' is controversial. Other objections can be leveled at TM regarding its applicability to clinical practice and research, notably that its induction and details of practice are secret, and that no research findings involving TM may be published without permission from the International Meditation Society. Thus a basic ethical principle of science is violated under which knowledge is public and available for testing.

Patricia Carrington, a psychologist at Princeton, USA has therefore developed a modified and secularised TM technique, Clinically Standardised Meditation or CSM, which she claims is a centring technique, abstracted from traditional meditational practice and this method and variants of it, are widely and increasingly used in clinical practice. Like TM it involves the mental repetition of a mantra, and shares an emphasis on 'letting go' - or detachment from striving, and temporary dissolution of structural thought.

Biofeedback

Research over the past 25 years has established that bodily functions previously thought to be involuntary or autonomic are influenced during yoga, zen and other forms of meditation. These findings raised the question of whether individuals could learn to control these functions at will.

Studies by Pavlov in the early years of the century had shown that dogs could be conditioned not only to salivate on cue, but also to change their body temperature to the extent of controlling blood flow to one leg at a time. Neal Miller (1969) went further, demonstrating that by rewarding desired performance rats could salivate, accelerate or slow heart rate, alter blood pressure, control circulation in the stomach wall, and direct heat to one or other ear. One celebrated rat even learned to fire an individual nerve cell.

In subsequent research using human subjects it became clear that if an individual could become aware of some bodily function of which they were normally unaware they could learn to control it, and that such awareness could be achieved by providing some feedback of information about that function. Thus the concept of biofeedback came into existence, although the principle has been employed for many thousands of years in that most basic feedback device, the mirror. Bathroom scales are also a biofeedback instrument, providing information about body weight. Like all such instruments they are merely an aid to achieving control and do not in themselves produce effects. They cannot cure over or under weight, or maintain weight at a certain level, only indicate the success or otherwise of one's attempts to do so. As such they highlight an important principle of biofeedback, which is that to be effective it requires more than a simple reading of an instrument; it requires a response.

Biofeedback may be provided by electromyography which, when muscles contract or relax, records and displays, usually as a pen tracing, information transmitted through electrodes on the skin. More subtle biofeedback is provided by the Electrical Skin Resistance Meter (ESRM), a simple device, which when attached to the palm of the hand indicates the degree of a individual's arousal or relaxation by measuring changes in the polarisation of sweat gland membranes resulting from change in the rate of blood flow which varies with body tone. The ESRM therefore indicates the activity of the autonomic nervous system and can be used as an aid in modifying tension.

During the 1960s Kamiya pioneered the use of the electroencephalograph as a biofeedback device. This measures electrical activity of the brain and it revealed that every physiological state is accompanied by an apparent change in emotional and mental state, conscious or unconscious, and conversely that every conscious or unconscious emotional or mental state is accompanied by apparent change in physiology. By producing a pleasant sound which ceased when alpha waves fell below a certain level Kamiya found that most subjects could learn to produce or suppress alpha waves at will, and that alpha seemed to be associated with a feeling of well-being.

Gradually it emerged that any neurophysiological or other biological function that can be monitored or amplified and fed back can be regulated. It was established that over a period of weeks subjects could acquire control of their heartbeat (Lang et al. 1967); overcome rhythmic disabilities of atrial fibrillation and premature ventricular contraction (Engel 1972); control high blood pressure without the use of drugs (Elder 1977); vary the temperature of their hands (Green 1969), and regulate stomach acidity (Gorman and Kamiya 1972).

Research into these functions was greatly assisted by development of the polygraph, an instrument for simultaneous electrical or mechanical recording of several involuntary physiological activities including blood pressure, pulse rate, respiration and perspiration. Using this equipment it became possible for a subject to see the volatility of heart rates and appreciate that physical changes in breathing and posture can have profound effects on the heart. Simply sitting upright slows heart rate, whereas slouching or shallow breathing increases it. Such an awareness enables individuals to recognise links in their behaviour and makes regulation possible.

Therapeutic applications of biofeedback

Biofeedback has numerous therapeutic applications. It has been employed successfully in the treatment of migraine, tension headaches, where it has been demonstrated to be more effective that Diazepam (Paiva et al. 1982), ulcerative colitis, spastic colon, and in regaining control after periods of dysporesis (Pelletier 1978). It has been used to teach individuals to recognise bronchial tube diameter, which has implications for the control of asthma and other respiratory disease (Vachon 1973); to assist in the regulation of chronic diarrhoea and constipation (Stroebel 1972, cited in Pelletier 1978); and to retrain patients with faecal incontinence resulting form organic impairment (Miller 1974).

Encouraging results have also been reported in treating hemiphlegic patients paralysed for over a year (Johnson and Garton 1973), and partial paralysis resulting from stroke, in cases of Bell's palsy and other muscular problems (Marinacci 1968). Booker et al (1969) have successfully retrained severed facial nerves, and various cardiovascular disorders are reported as responding well to biofeedback (Brener and Klienman 1970). Peavey (1982) has also reported improvement in immune function following biofeedback assisted relaxation.

However, while many effects have been demonstrated in the laboratory these are not necessarily or readily achieved outside of it. Thus Schwartz (1973) was only able to demonstrate reduction of blood pressure within a clinical setting. This is a major drawback of biofeedback which, involving as it does a good deal of bulky and expensive equipment capable of monitoring precisely subtle biological changes, is essentially laboratory based. However, for biofeedback to be of lasting benefit the individual has to be able to transfer what is learned in the clinic to the outside world, therefore, as Pelletier indicates, therapists are increasingly supplementing it with meditation and other forms of relaxation.

A further drawback, identified by Benson (1975), is that usually no more than one physiological function can be fed back upon and changed at any one time. This is disputed by Pelletier who indicates that Schwartz at Harvard has taught individuals to regulate several functions simultaneously and found that when they were taught to reduce both heart rate and blood pressure together they spontaneously and consistently reported feelings of relaxation and calmness. Pelletier insists that biofeedback has clear advantages over meditation and other forms of relaxation in which stress reduction is achieved through an overall response.

> This is certainly beneficial but there is no conclusive evidence to indicate that an overall relaxation response has any effect upon the particular organ system in which that individual expresses his stress. There is a general tendency for all neurophysiological functions to move towards a state of deep relaxation during the meditation periods. However, the particular area of affliction, such as the high blood pressure of the hypertensive patient, may not necessarily drop during this overall relaxation period, therefore one major advantage of biofeedback is that the specific physiological function which needs to be corrected can be monitored, feeding information back to the patient to help him assess his progress in alleviating that dysfunction. This instantaneous feedback is a major asset in stress reduction therapy' (p.268).

The disadvantage is that self-regulation of a particular function such as heart rate does not necessarily mean that the person can generalise this. Pelletier therefore (p.269-70) argues that as individuals differ in patterns of response to stress and these manifest in a different organic system for each individual, a comprehensive approach to clinical intervention is needed which can be applied for relaxation in specific situations; and, monitoring of the specific systems in which the person is manifesting stress in order to help the individual self-regulate that system as unequivocally as possible.

Psychological applications of biofeedback

It has been demonstrated that just as people can learn to control physiological functions for medical purposes they can also do so in order to achieve altered states of consciousness, and thus biofeedback may be used as an aid in the development of meditational skills and self-development. Wise (in Cade and Coxhead 1979) observes that biofeedback 'offers a bridge that can lead people from the ordinary waking state to the development of higher states of consciousness'.

Blundell (1979, p.191) has observed a difficulty with biofeedback in that production of alpha waves in a laboratory does not necessarily help a subject in any way: 'The alpha wave can only be related to new understanding if there is something new to understand'. Training a person to produce alpha by means of biofeedback will not produce new insights, whereas if a person is taught to gain insight he may show high levels of alpha; the process is not reversible.

C. Maxwell Cade produced with Geoffrey Blundell a special type of EEG which enabled a clearer understanding of what occurs in the brain during meditation. This device, known as the 'Mind Mirror', differs from standard hospital encephalographs because the latter show only pathological responses of the brain and not responses to mood, thought and so on. For medical purposes the latter is considered a nuisance since it interferes with readings for pathological purposes. However for psychological purposes such knowledge is an essential guide to the subjects's development on the path of self-regulation.

The Mind Mirror measures rhythms from both hemispheres of the brain simultaneously and displays them in the form of a frequency analysis which allows the relationship between them to be seen as a pattern. Using this measure it has been found that meditation produces a combination of theta and alpha waves in both hemispheres, whereas normally a person produces primarily beta in one or other hemisphere. Thus meditation integrates the two hemispheres effecting a balance, or psychosynthesis, between rational and intuitive functions, a utilisation of the full mind; - a state which Cade calls 'The awakened mind'.

Moreover it has been demonstrated that yogins and swamis produce the awakened mind pattern of brainwaves throughout their everyday lives, thus supporting the claim that the effects of meditation generalise into all aspects of living.

Chapter 7

Hypnosis, Auto Suggestion and Autogenic Training

If a man could pass through Paradise in a dream, and have a flower presented to him as a pledge that his soul had really been there, and if he found that flower in his hand when he awoke - Ay! and what then?

Samuel Taylor Coleridge.

Misconceptions about Hypnosis

Most people think of hypnosis as a trance-like state in which the subject, at least partially, loses awareness of reality, and under the control of the hypnotist becomes able to perform a variety of feats that would be impossible in the normal state. This view is reinforced by popular writers, the media, stage performers and professional hypnotists anxious to maintain the mystique of their methods, and by dictionaries, which typically define hypnosis as a special state of mind resembling sleep, characterised by extreme suggestibility.

Such a view is highly misleading. There is abundant evidence that so-called hypnotic behaviour is not so remarkable as is commonly supposed, the feats performed under hypnosis being achievable under normal conditions (Spanos, 1986), and the notion of a special state unnecessary since well-established psychological processes can account for the effects very adequately. Nevertheless, the widespread belief in hypnosis as an altered state of consciousness 'by means of which the hypnotist can induce distortions in the areas of volition, memory and sensory perception' (Chertok 1981, p.23) persists in spite of contrary evidence and argument.

Accordingly hypnosis is still regarded by a large section of the general public more with fear than scepticism. Blythe (1979) identifies these fears as:

- being unconscious while under hypnosis and unaware afterwards of what occurred during the session
- being hypnotized against one's will, or without even being aware of it

- having the mind dominated by another person
- losing verbal control and revealing secrets when hypnotized
- not returning to normal afterwards.

Contemporary theories of hypnosis

The reality is that consciousness is not lost during hypnosis. The traditional view of hypnosis as a trance-like state, that is, of a condition of unawareness of external things in which visions and hallucinations are experienced and acts performed unconsciously, has been undermined over the past thirty years in numerous experimental studies (Barber 1961, 1969; Barber et al. 1974, Spanos 1982, 1986; Wagstaff 1977, 1981, 1986). Hypnosis is not a trance in which one even partially loses awareness, nor is it sleep. Spiegel, (cited by Hariman 1981) indicates that on a scale of human awareness hypnosis is at the very opposite end from coma, with ordinary consciousness in the middle. During hypnosis a person is fully aware of what is happening, and if anything, their awareness is enhanced.

Moreover, despite Chertok's claim (1969) that hypnosis is a fourth organismic state distinct from waking, sleeping and dreaming, there would appear to be nothing particularly unique about hypnosis which justifies it being termed a state. There is no difference in the EEG readings of subjects when normally awake or hypnotised (Casilneck and Hall 1959), and no difference in cortical potential, pulse rate, skin resistance or palmar electrical potentials, peripheral blood flow, or blood clotting (Langen 1969, Edmonston et al 1966). There is a slight rise in body temperature brought about by vasodilation of blood vessels, and small changes in the voltage of the life field, but these are very subtle and can be recorded in response to normal emotional reactions (Ravitz 1958), and are a characteristic feature of relaxation (Schultz 1959).

Nevertheless, the ability of subjects to endure severe pain when under hypnosis is often taken as evidence for the existence of a special hypnotic trance state. However, the issue is not quite as straightforward as this. Psychologists recognise that pain is not a simple sensation but a complex psychological response which involves expectation, anxiety, interpretation and suffering and that if any of these is modified so also are the perception and sensation of pain. Barber (1978) has demonstrated that task motivated instructions such as imagining a pleasant situation are as effective as hypnosis in reducing subjective and physiological responses to painful stimuli.

In fact the only way to tell if a person is hypnotised is if he responds to test suggestions, or declares afterwards that he has been hypnotised. Hariman (1981) suggests that hypnosis is merely an extension and more systematic use of the spontaneously occurring everyday phenomenon of deep absorption, which most people have experienced when 'carried away' by a task or situation. Indeed Spanos (1982) has established that when given a choice - an alternative scheme for classifying their experience - most subjects prefer to describe themselves as 'absorbed' rather than hypnotised. However, Naish (1986) observes that because the hypnotic condition does not involve the wonderful aspects the uninitiated tend to expect, it is not uncommon for those undergoing a hypnotic induction procedure to express doubts as to whether or not they are actually hypnotised. As he indicates, (p.10) 'subjects such as these have to learn to apply the label 'hypnotised' to a set of experiences different from the one's expected'. Furthermore, those who, when hypnotised, find it to be nothing exceptional, often conclude, incorrectly, that they have not been hypnotised successfully, and that it cannot be effective. Thus a person's declaration as to whether or not they have been hypnotised is not a very satisfactory criterion.

In this sense it is possible to be hypnotised without knowing it. Similarly it can be argued that if a person does not know he is hypnotised because the experience has not been explicitly defined as such, it is possible to be hypnotised against one's will. Even so, this would not affect the subject's awareness of what is going on. Therefore it is generally accepted by hypnotists of all theoretical persuasions that a person cannot be hypnotised against their will, and that hypnosis is a condition of consent.

As to the mind being dominated by another person, it is clear that the effects attributed to hypnosis are in fact produced and determined by the person themself. The work of Sheehan and McConkey (1982) shows that subjects employ a number of strategies in order to achieve these effects. Thus 'the traditional picture of the hypnotised person as being in a zombie-like state of complete subjection and unawareness is certainly wide of the mark. Hypnotic subjects cannot be simply conceptualised as passive recipients of hypnotic suggestions'. Accordingly hypnosis is not being in someone's power, the experimental evidence being very clearly in opposition to the long-cherished notion that once hypnotised the person cannot resist the hypnotist's suggestions (Orne 1972).

Claims, such as those made by two women in Australia that they had been sexually assaulted by a hypnotist, and although aware of what was happening, were unable to offer any resistance because hypnotised, have to be regarded with some caution; as does the counter-claim of the hypnotist that hypnotic coercion is impossible since a hypnotised person would immediately resist suggestions of an unwanted nature. Perry (1979) indicates that neither explanation is adequate and other factors need to be taken into consideration. For example, the patient's belief in their inability to resist hypnotic suggestion might be sufficient to create a self-fulfilling hypothesis.

Alternatively, the women's behaviour might be seen as constituting motivated helplessness in which their subsequent testimony was a retrospective rationalisation. Fellows (1986 p.46) suggests that 'Like alcohol, it is possible that hypnosis might be used by some people as a way of disowning responsibility for their own behaviour, which is otherwise perceived by them as being taboo'. Certainly this might be a factor in the often uncharacteristic behaviour of those volunteering as subjects for stage hypnosis. However, the question of whether hypnotised persons can be made to perform acts against their will remains controversial. Although it is argued that people cannot be made to do anything they don't want to, it remains a possibility that within the hypnotic situation what one 'really wants' might be changed. Naish therefore concludes that if the hypnotist seems to the client to be in control, then even if this control is illusory, it is clearly wise for them to choose a trustworthy therapist.

Given that there are no indications that the hypnotised person is ever in a different state, it follows that the fear of not returning to normal after hypnosis is unfounded. Similarly the evidence suggests that the fear of post-hypnotic phenomena is unjustified. Fisher (1954) found that subjects trained to scratch their ear post-hypnotically to a cue word did so, but failed to respond to a staged conversation in which the word was employed several times. He concluded that post-hypnotic suggestion works only because subjects do what they think is expected of them.

Fears that hypnosis may precipitate psychiatric illness are also unsupported by the evidence. Indeed, controlled experimental studies have found that subjects undergoing hypnosis are less likely to experience disturbance in everyday life than those in control groups, and that they report more relaxation, less anxiety, more pleasure and feelings of enhanced well-being after hypnosis (Coe and Ryken 1979). The idea that hypnotisa-bility may be a sign of mental weakness is also confounded by the understanding that hypnosis is actually concentration or absorption, and as such fostered by many scientists and artists (Krippner 1969).

Nevertheless, stereotypical and misleading views about hypnosis are still evident in the scientific community. Fellows (1986) argues that these have seriously impeded research and teaching on the subject. Negative attitudes have led to instruction in hypnosis being opposed in principle, with the result that as recently as 1985 only four out of fifty university and polytechnic departments of psychology in Britain introduced their students to theories and methods of hypnosis. Such attitudes are part of a legacy of mistrust and scepticism which originates in the discrediting of Franz Anton Mesmer (1734-1815), the modern pioneer of hypnotism.

Mesmerism

Mesmer did not discover the phenomenon which came to be named after him. There is evidence that it was used in ancient Egyptian, Greek and Roman civilisations. Indeed, it was largely as a result of Greek influence on European medicine during the eighteenth century that Mesmer came to re-discover it.

During this period the views of the sixth century physician Galen were still influential. He held that some invisible fluid filled the universe, planets and all living creatures, and that health could be maintained by achieving a balance of this fluid between mind, body, soul and the environment. Accordingly the universe was a living organism of balancing forces, and health lay in each part so adjusting to every other part that it reserved to the fullest of its capacity the directing, controlling and sustaining life of the whole (Butler 1982). Such a view, as Butler observes, was and still is fundamental to the Western esoteric tradition of magic, and is currently revived in Lovelock's 'Gaia' hypothesis (Lovelock 1979). Also current in Mesmer's time was the notion, evident since the time of Paracelsus, that magnets possessed special healing properties, and with their powers of polar attraction and repulsion could be used to influence this ethereal fluid. Healing by touch and stroking was also used during this period.

Mesmer simply combined all three features, teaching that this formative life force could be transmitted from one being to another. He viewed the body as a magnet and illness as the faulty distribution of magnetic fluid, which he attempted to redistribute by passing his hands over the body in much the way that a metal is magnetised. He believed that in this way he could realign the magnetic field associated with a sick person and effect a cure. Consistent with this view he saw the therapist or magnetist as an active agent in the process, and by implication, the patient as largely passive.

His concepts of animal magnetism and magnetic treatment, known as 'Mesmerism', became very popular, especially among the poor who could not afford orthodox medical treatment, and this led to its investigation by a Royal Commission led by the US Commissioner to France, Benjamin Franklin. Mesmer's claims for magnetic effects were systematically tested using magnetometers, which failed to detect any magnetism. The Franklin Report of 1785 thus concluded that there was no substance to Mesmer's claims, and that the imagination produces all the effects attributed to magnetism. By dismissing animal magnetism as imagination the commissioners implied that the Mesmeric procedures had no validity. What they failed to do was to distinguish between the procedures, which clearly did have therapeutic value, and Mesmer's explanation of how they worked. Reinterpreting hypnotic behaviour in terms of imagination does not imply that it should be invalidated or dismissed, but rather, that closer attention should be paid to this phenomenon. However, instead of highlighting the therapeutic value of imagination the Franklin Report resulted in it being dismissed along with hypnosis, and it is only now, some 200 years later that the implications of the commission's conclusions are beginning to be recognised and imagination given more serious consideration.

The Franklin Report discredited Mesmer, obliging him to leave Paris where he had been practising, and to live thereafter in obscurity. Nevertheless, interest in, and practice of Mesmerism continued. In 1841 a Scottish physician, James Braid (1795-1860), witnessed a demonstration of Mesmerism by Charles Lafontaine, and he commenced a series of experiments which led him to reject Mesmer's theories and to develop new concepts and methods. In a book of 1843 he proposed that the combined state of physical relaxation and altered awareness entered into by persons who were mesmerised should be called hypnotism, from the Greek *hypnos*, meaning sleep.

Subsequently hypnosis has been induced in a number of ways, but because the concept of hypnosis as sleep lingers on, most clinical methods are based on the concept of relaxation, with the result that hypnotic induction procedures 'may have a good deal in common with an antenatal relaxation class' (Naish 1986, p.6).

Hypnotic induction

Hypnotic induction usually commences with the subject sitting or lying comfortably, and the hypnotist addressing them in a slow, controlled and confident manner. The

subject's visual concentration may be trapped and held by their being asked to focus on an object positioned at the upper limit of vision, which strains the eye muscles and quickly induces the sensation of heaviness, resulting in more frequent blinking and the tendency to close the eyes.

The hypnotist then encourages feelings of heaviness and closing of the eyes, in so doing following rather than anticipating the subject's responses. When the subject closes their eyes relaxation is induced by instructing them to take deep breaths and to relax progressively various parts of their body. Deeper relaxation is induced by the hypnotist asking the subject to count backwards, or imagine descending steps. The subject is then encouraged to visualise as vividly as possible a relaxing scene, such as lying on a beach on a warm sunny day. The hypnotist may draw attention to certain sensory aspects of the scene by encouraging the subject to imagine sounds, sights and smells. During this procedure many people experience a sensation of profound relaxation and may also describe curious sensations in response to the hypnotist's instructions. The subjects suggestibility can then be assessed by observing their response to certain kinds of test suggestion which may involve motor effects such as immobility, or the inability to separate the hands. The most common is the arm levitation test in which the subject is instructed that one hand or arm will begin to rise higher and higher. Frequently these suggestions are augmented by appropriate visual imagery such as balloons or strings being attached to the subject's fingers, tugging upwards and drawing the fingers with them. Other sensory effects may involve asking the subject to brush away an imaginary fly, or to suck a lemon. Under these conditions memory manipulation may also be demonstrated, along with a great many other effects, including amnesia, regression, physical strength, relief from clinical symptoms and pain, improved memory, and the ability to effect organic tissue, for instance, by creating skin blisters (Chertok 1981).

Therapeutic applications of hypnosis

The most widely reported effects of hypnosis include anaesthesia and analgesia. The surgeon James Esdaile (1808-1859) carried out hundreds of painless operations during the last century using hypnosis as the sole anaesthetic, and hypnosis has since been widely used in obstetrics and operations such as appendectomy, caesarean section, breast surgery, skin grafting, heart surgery, removal of cataract, prostrate resection, haemorroidectomy, nerve restoration and the ligation and stripping of veins (Chertok 1981). Jameson (1963) reports that 90 per cent of all minor fractures in a casualty department can be treated without anaesthesia if hypnosis is employed. However, ether and chloroform subsequently proved to be simpler and less time consuming methods for the surgeon and hypnosis was largely abandoned as an anaesthetic, although many dental treatments and minor operations are still performed under hypnosis.

Hypnosis has also proved to be a potent analgesic, of value in terminal illness, and childbirth (Moon and Moon 1984), although its pain-killing effect is not yet fully understood. Certainly relaxation reduces anxiety, which by increasing muscle tension, increases pain. Thus relaxation may be effective in reducing pain, with suggestions of warmth and comfort possibly playing an important role in augmenting relief; or, as Taugher (1958) has suggested, hypnosis may work by getting the brain to ignore painful influences, or to dissociate from them (Hilgard 1973).

Studies have found that hypnosis is better than acupuncture, Valium, aspirin and placebos in the relief of experimentally induced pain, and its effects more or less equivalent with those of morphine (Stern, Brown et al. 1977). It could be, therefore, that hypnosis enables the person to produce endorphins, natural opiate-like substances, which have analgesic effects similar to morphine. This is suggested by the fact that Naloxone which blocks the effect of all opiate-like substances including endorphin, was found by Stephenson (1978) to reverse analgesia artificially induced by hypnosis, although this result has yet to be replicated, and other studies have suggested that hypnosis does not release endorphins (Finer 1982). Understanding of the role of endorphins has developed in recent years, and it is now clear that while not all endorphins are involved in pain control, some have a role in pain modulation as part of the body's general response to stress. The effects of hypnosis may therefore be due to chemical factors.

Hypnosis has been used to control pain (Erickson 1959), and also anxiety and insomnia associated with cancer (Hilgard 1959, Hilgard and Hilgard 1983, Sacerdote 1982). It has also been found to help restore the sense of self-control that is often lost during the course of invasive cancer treatment (Zeltzer 1980), and to overcome antici-patory emesis and nausea associated with cancer chemotherapy, which is commonly resistant to anti-emetic drugs (Redd et al. 1982). Hall (1983) has also demonstrated the role of hypnosis in improving immune functions in studies which found an increase in the number of lymphocytes after hypnotic sessions. However, although hypnosis has a wide range of application to clinical problems, it is thought to be more effective when the aetiology of the pain is known and the pain chronic in nature.

Hypnosis also has a wide range of application in psychotherapy. Freud recognised its value and promoted it as a means of accessing repressed unconscious material. However, he observed that much of the material produced under hypnosis was fanciful, fantasy or confabulation, and eventually abandoned its use in favour of free association.

Nevertheless it has proved effective in the treatment of anxiety and phobic reactions, psychosomatic disorders such as asthma, migraine, headache, psoriasis, eczema, warts, high blood pressure, peptic ulcer, bedwetting, backache and insomnia; in the treatment of repetitive and engrossing behaviours such as addictions, smoking, overeating and obsessive-compulsive reactions (Roet 1987); and depression (Dempster et al. 1976).

Research into hypnosis

Despite a wealth of research worldwide which has supported the claims made for hypnosis, and the British Medical Association's report of 1893 which stated that 'as a therapeutic agent hypnosis is frequently effective in relieving pain, procuring sleep and alleviating many functional ailments', orthodox medicine still regards it with open scepticism and hostility. Sacerdote (1966) suggests that a major reason for the lack of wider acceptance of hypnosis in medicine is related to the deep-seated reluctance of most physicians to undertake the development of meaningful relationships with their patients, and that the personality type of most successful surgeons makes it difficult for them to give time and attention to the interpersonal features of hypnosis.

However, medical practitioners who are opposed to hypnosis usually reject it as unscientific and mysterious, because research has failed to find a single explanation for its effects.

Wagstaff (1986) suggests that this is because the various phenomena may require different explanations, a range of processes interacting to give rise to hypnotic effects, which may vary from situation to situation and from person to person. On the basis of extensive research he has identified two processes that may be of central importance in understanding hypnosis: compliance and belief.

The power of the former was highlighted by Milgram (1974) in his controversial and alarming study of compliance and supported in research by Zimbardo (1969). Milgram's study aimed to establish the extent to which a person would comply with authority in a situation demanding the deliberate implication of an aversive, and potentially fatal stimulus to another human being. People were deceived into believing that in administering electric shocks of increasingly high voltage to a subject with an alleged heart condition they were participating in a study of learning. In actual fact the 'subject' was a 'stooge' or collaborator who received no such shocks, a recording of his voice being used to relay his painful shouts, protests and appeals for help to the true subject of the experiment - the person applying the supposed shocks.

The study demonstrated very clearly that having committed themselves to the experiment the majority of people obeyed the 'scientist' directing the experiment, carrying out his instructions even to the point of being prepared to administer lethal shocks to the subject.

Hunt (1979) has related the hypnotic situation directly to Milgram's analysis of obedience, arguing that the motivation to comply with the hypnotist's suggestions might come partly from a desire to 'have to go', which results in a social commitment. From this perspective hypnosis is a form of role play, which serves to highlight the possible power of the latter rather than dismiss the former.

Support for this view comes from a study by Wagstaff (1970) which demonstrates that reports of post-hypnotic amnesia could be eliminated by providing instructions that allowed subjects to admit role playing rather than being in a hypnotic state or trance. The most important finding of the study was that amnesia was removed when compliance was eliminated, which may be seen as suggesting that compliance could play a significant role in the hypnotic response.

Nevertheless some subjects genuinely believed themselves to have been hypnotised. According to the traditional view of hypnosis this is because they have fallen into a unique 'state'. However, there is evidence to show that in the face of ambiguous information subjects tend to rely on external factors to label their experience (Schacter and Singer 1962, Bem 1972), and that ambiguous inner states can be manipulated by giving people cues to their situation (Valins 1966, Valins and Ray 1967). Wagstaff suggests that a number of features of the hypnotic situation may evoke ambiguous sensations in subjects that they then interpret as evidence for their being hypnotised. These may include feelings of giddiness, changes in temperature, floating and detachment, sleepiness and reduced attention to external stimuli, all of which are readily experienced by individuals who have been trained to relax.

However, Wagstaff observes that although relaxation may form a major source of the sensations that the subject labels as hypnosis, the two are not to be equated because 'even when relaxation is not present, then as long as a situation is defined as hypnosis subjects may continue to show a high level of responsiveness to suggestions' (1986, p.66) He therefore proposes that these findings support his contention that subjects will report their experience as evidence for hypnosis if it accords with their beliefs about it.

Thus, although it would seem that compliance and belief interact in the hypnotic situation, there are grounds to suggest that the latter explanation would be more acceptable to most subjects, as Wagstaff indicates (1986, pp.87):

> Although compliance may be a major motivating force in hypnotic responding, it has obvious disadvantages to its perpetrator; the compliant subject may feel deceitful, the self-image may be threatened, and even intense personal disappointment may be experienced. If given the choice, therefore, between *believing* something has happened and experiencing the *pretence* that something has happened there will be strong internal pressures to accept the former. It can be argued that the motivation to believe something has happened or is happening will be particularly strong in the clinical context where 'pretence' would offer little relief from medical problems. There is evidence from social-psychological studies of cognitive dissonance theory, indicating that people can be strongly motivated to reduce discrepancies between private attitudes or beliefs. There is no obvious reason why such a mechanism should not operate in the hypnosis situation. In this way hypnosis subjects would be motivated to make hypnotic suggestions 'work' within the limitations of the hypnotic context. If possible the subject will attempt to carry out suggestions so that the resulting responses are both publicly and privately acceptable. The interaction between compliance and belief may therefore be seen as a three-stage process by which, when confronted by a suggestion or set of suggestions, subjects 1) decide what the hypnotist 'really' wants; 2) attempt to employ cognitive strategies to produce congruent actions and experienced; 3) if 2 fails, resort to behavioural compliance.

If Wagstaff's analysis is correct then hypnotic behaviour is first and foremost social behaviour. This is certainly the view held by Spanos (1986) who argues that 'like other complex social enactments, hypnotic responding is strategic rather than automatic. Hypnotic subjects retain rather than lose conscious control over their behaviour. These subjects guide their enactments in terms of their understanding concerning the requirements of the test situation and the social impressions they wish their enactments to convey. From this perspective individual differences in hypnotic susceptibility reflect individual differences in attitudes, motivations and interpretations concerning hypnosis and the hypnotic situation, and individual differences in imaginal abilities required to experience suggested effects' (1986, pp. 111-2).

Nevertheless, irrespective of these factors it is the person who 'hypnotises' themself and brings about the various effects. Thus, as Hariman (1981) observes - hypnosis can be more properly thought of as guided self-hypnosis, which, being the case, means that people should be able to hypnotise themselves.

Auto-suggestion

Alexandre Bertrand (1823) took the view that hypnosis and its effects were bought about by the person's imagination acting upon themself, and A. A. Liebault concurred with this view, claiming that hypnosis was entirely due to autosuggestion, that is, self-administered suggestions meant to bring about either psychological or physical change without subsequent effort or involvement.

Subsequently Emile Coué (1857-1926) claimed that if this were the case then it should be possible to devise a method which dispensed with the hypnotist altogether. He therefore experimented with auto-suggestion, and developed it into a psychotherapy which became known as Couéism and for which he claimed a 97 per cent success rate in overcoming client's presenting problems. This method became extremely popular, Blythe (1979) reporting estimates of some 40,000 people per annum being treated by Coué before World War One.

Initially each person was put through a series of hypnotic suggestibility tests to ensure they were amenable to suggestion. Then Coué would proceed to give a series of suggestions intended to promote psychological and physical well-being. He considered it necessary that these be repeated periodically until there was a marked improvement in the client's condition. After this, the length of time between sessions could be extended and finally discontinued. He also insisted that the person repeat fifteen to twenty times a day while in bed the phrase 'every day and in every way I'm getting better and better', which is often associated with Mary Baker Eddy the founder of the Christian Science, who was greatly influenced by Couéism.

However, the simplicity of the process eventually led to its falling into disrepute, as practitioners of Couéism simply repeated relevant formulae, ignoring to a large extent Coué's preparatory work with the client. Furthermore, as Blythe indicates, where a person has unresolved unconscious conflicts then hours of autosuggestion will not ameliorate the condition but rather activate the psychological Law of Reversed Effect, which Coué is credited with discovering, according to which the more one tries the harder the goal is to achieve.

Clearly, Couéism did not dispense with the therapist and was in most respects indistinguishable from hypnosis, so in no sense did it serve to demystify hypnosis and the power of the hypnotist. It did, however, highlight the power of suggestion.

It has since been demonstrated that the heart can be speeded up or slowed down by suggestion (Schultze and Luthe 1959); that near-sighted people can change the shape of their eyeballs and improve distance vision in response to it (Kelly 1961), and that stomach contractions resulting from great hunger can be eliminated by the suggestion of eating a large meal (Lewis and Sarbin 1943).

More recently research by Richardson, lecturer in psychology at St. Thomas' Hospital London (reported in *Medicine Now*, BBC Radio 4, 14th October 1988) has demonstrated that women receiving positive affirmations or suggestions via headphones during surgery for hysterectomy were found to be significantly better in terms of post-operative recovery time, pain, relaxation and post-operative temperature than controls, and that they were discharged from hospital on average 1.3 days or 16 per cent sooner. Recognition of the power of suggestion has led many therapists to encourage auto-suggestion - more commonly referred to as positive affirmation or positive thinking - in their patients (Manning 1989; Roet 1987; Jampolsky 1979) and books on the subject have become best-sellers (Koran 1964). Furthermore, the role of auto-suggestion in illness and premature death is being increasingly addressed as it is recognised that 'taken to its limit, auto-suggestion can even kill, and that every year thousands of people die simply because they believe it is inevitable' (Watson 1973, p.227).

Autogenic training

The principle of auto-suggestion is taken further in Autogenic Training, a 'psychophysiologic form of psychotherapy which the patient carries out on himself by using passive concentration upon certain combinations of psychophysiologically adapted stimuli' (Luthe 1969, p.309), and which, in contrast to other forms of psychotherapy, is directed to mental and bodily functions simultaneously.

Autogenic Training or AT was developed during the 1930s as a self-help medical therapy by the German neurologist and psychiatrist Johannes Schultz, who described it as a 'method of rational physiological exercises designed to produce a general psycho-biologic reorganisation in the subject which enables him to manifest all the phenomena otherwise obtainable through hypnosis'. As such it was one of the first self-help strategies which incorporated scientific discoveries on the physiology of arousal and relaxation.

Schultz based his system on the work of the distinguished brain physiologist Oskar Vogt who, in his research into sleep and hypnosis between 1890 and 1900, found that some people were able to hypnotise themselves for predetermined periods. He observed that those persons who achieved what he termed 'auto-hypnosis' had a substantial reduction of fatigue and tension, and a decrease in the incidence and severity of psychosomatic disorders such as headache.

Drawing on these observations Schultz combined the concept of autohypnosis with a number of specific exercises designed to improve and integrate mental and physical functions and eliminate maladjusted behaviour and its manifestations in neurotic and psychosomatic symptoms. He noted that hypnotised subjects generally reported two characteristic sensations - a pleasurable feeling of warmth in the limbs and torso, and heaviness. Both are in fact psychological correlates of relaxation, the subjective sensation of warmth being the psychological perception of vasodilation in the peripheral arteries, and the sensation of heaviness being the perception of muscular relaxation.

Schultz concluded that if he could design exercises which would enable subjects to induce these sensations in themselves he might be able to teach them to achieve the 'passive concentration' characteristic of hypnosis, and that once they were able to achieve this easily and rapidly it might be possible for them to progress to subtle psychological effects and to achieve a marked degree of autonomy over bodily functions. Luthe (1969) has described passive concentration as a casual attitude toward the intended outcome of concentrated activity, and distinguished it from active concentration which is characterised by concern, interest, attention and goal-directed active efforts in respect of its outcome and functional result. Pelletier (1978, p.231) suggests that during passive concentration subjects 'abandon themselves to an ongoing organismic process', and in so doing achieve a state of body and mind similar to the low arousal state of meditation.

Indeed, in Schultz' system, as in meditation, it is necessary to minimise external stimulation and turn attention inwards. To this end there must be monotonous input to various sensory receptors, and concentrated attention towards somatic processes which is achieved primarily by mental repetition of psychophysiologically adapted suggestions, while focusing attention on the parts of the body mentioned in these formulae. This is very similar to mantra yoga and meditation which as Day (1953, p.25) indicates has an affinity with Couéism in as much that it deals with positive affirmations that help strengthen will power. Furthermore, Schultz claims that given these conditions there occurs an overpowering reflexive-like psychic re-organisation followed by 'dissociative and autonomous mental processes leading to an alteration of ego functioning and dissolution of ego boundaries' (Pelletier, p.232). Thus a dream-like state of consciousness and plasticity of imagery occurs. Like yoga, it commences with physiologically oriented exercises progressing to exercises which focus primarily on mental functions, to special exercises developed for normalisation of certain patho-functional deviations, and with regular practice leads ultimately to the self-regulation of numerous mental and physical functions. There is thus stepwise progression through physical relaxation, unconscious symbolism and fantasy, to self-healing. However, Autogenic Training has the advantage over yoga and other forms of meditation in that it begins at a level easily understood and learned and progresses only slowly to more esoteric levels, and its emphasis on physical sensations frequently has more appeal to Westerners than more contemplative approaches.

Autogenic procedure

Schultz believed that any 'normal' person could achieve this progression but he insisted that there are several essential requirements if the training is to be successful: the individual must be highly motivated and co-operative, capable of a reasonable degree of self-direction and control, and able to maintain a suitable body posture. External stimulation should be reduced to the minimum, and restrictive clothing, jewelry and spectacles should be removed. Three basic postures are recommended: horizontal, reclined in an armchair, and simple sitting.

The horizontal posture requires the person to lie on a bed, couch or floor, legs slightly apart, feet inclined outwards in a V-shaped angle, and where possible with support under the knees to provide maximum relaxation of leg muscles. Heels should not be touching and the trunk and shoulders aligned symmetrically. The head must be positioned carefully and comfortably, without stiffness of the neck or cramped shoulders. Arms should lie relaxed and slightly bent, with fingers spread and relaxed, not touching the main part of the body. In the final position the body should be corpse-like with muscle tension absent. The posture is virtually identical with the sarasana or corpse posture of hatha yoga, which is known to have a significant effect in relaxing the body (Dostalek 1987, Singh and Udupa 1978).

Sitting postures help to guard against sleep and are useful for those who wish to practice the exercises in more public settings such as the office. Where an armchair is employed, ideally it needs a high back and a seat length equal to that of the thighs so that the small of the back rests easily against the back of the chair. Hands and fingers are relaxed with arms clear of the body or hanging loosely.

In a straight-backed chair the person should sit on the edge of the chair so that only the buttocks are on the seat and the thighs touching it only slightly. The feet are then positioned one in front of the other, so that the heel of one foot is in direct alignment with the toes of another. This serves to support the lower trunk.

Once these basic postures are achieved a standard procedure follows in which the individual is instructed to imagine a string from the top of his head to the ceiling which is pulling him into an upright position with both arms still hanging at his side. The person is then instructed to imagine that the string is cut so that his head flops forward like a rag doll. Pelletier (p.237) observes that generally this results in a vertical collapse of the trunk, shoulders and neck into a relaxed posture, but it is very important that the person doesn't collapse into such a concave posture that breathing becomes difficult. Following this the arms are allowed to swing upwards so that the hands and fingers hang loosely between the knees without touching. In this relaxed mode the first series of exercises, termed by Schultz the Autogenic Standard Series, commences.

Stage one:

Attention is first directed to whichever arm is most active, and while attending to this arm the person repeats silently to themselves the instruction 'My right/left arm is heavy' three to six times for 30-60 seconds. This period is terminated by applying a three step procedure, flexing arms energetically, breathing deeply and opening the eyes, while repeating the 'cancellation' formula 'arms firm, breathe deeply, open eyes'. This is then followed by vigorous movements of the arms, legs, feet, fingers, toes, shoulders and neck, during which the person is instructed to note any residual feelings of heaviness and relaxation that remain in the arm. The exercise is then repeated four times, allowing approximately one minute between each period for the effects to be noted.

Luthe (1969) observes that during this first exercise some 40 per cent of people will experience a feeling of heaviness in their forearm, which during subsequent training will spread to the entire arm. He claims that only about 10 per cent of trainees fail to experience this sensation of heaviness and that it is important for them to be assured that the exercises are still effective even if they feel nothing. Frequently people report a spreading or generalization of this sensation to other parts of the body, which is an important feature of Autogenic Training.

Attention is then focused on the less active arm and the process repeated, and when distinct sensations of heaviness are experienced in both arms the instruction is changed to 'both arms are heavy' and repeated several times with a 'cancellation' instruction between each. Pelletier (p.238) observes that, as with any meditative practice, it is as important to enter into a state of activation after a period of deep relaxation as it is to enter into a passive state, because 'deep relaxation is a precursor for more efficient activity and not necessarily an end in itself'.

Once both arms are reasonably relaxed the generalised relaxation should become more apparent in other parts of the body. However, there is considerable individual variation, with some people being able to induce feelings of heaviness immediately and others achieving this sensation only after several weeks of practice. Once achieved attention is directed to the legs, again with the more active leg being the initial focus, and the same procedure followed.

Stage two:

This focuses on the induction of feelings of warmth in the limbs. Frequently during the first stage people will notice the sensation of warmth spreading through their bodies along with that of heaviness. Luthe maintains that if the heaviness exercises have been successful then some degree of passive concentration has already been mastered and this is further enhanced by the second stage exercises. These are performed in the same sequence and using the same cancellation technique between each series as in the previous exercise. On average it takes between four and six weeks for people to master the establishment of warmth in all their extremities.

Stage three:

This is directed to cardiac regulation and is an amplification of the previous exercise. The instruction 'heart beat calm and regular' is repeated for four periods of 90-180 seconds with the cancellation instruction 'eyes open, breath deeply' and vigorous activity inserted between each.

Stage four:

While practising the first three stages most people notice a decrease in respiratory frequency and an increase in depth of respiration. In order to enhance this effect the individual focuses on his breathing and repeats the phrase 'it breaths me' four times for periods of 100-150 seconds with a cancellation period between each.

Stage five:

This exercise is designed to induce an experience of warmth in the abdominal region, which induces a calming of central nervous system activity and enhances muscular relaxation and drowsiness. The instruction employed is 'my solar plexus is warm', repeated as in the previous stages, and with the individual instructed to place a hand over the area and imagine heat radiating from it.

Stage six:

This involves cooling the forehead and uses the formula 'my forehead is cool'.

It is recommended that the entire series is practised three time daily, after lunch, before dinner and before sleep, and it is claimed that after training this can be performed very quickly, in a matter of 2-4 minutes. Pelletier indicates that this is usually achieved anywhere between two months and a year of practice.

Occasionally spontaneous muscular discharges or tremors occur, much like those experienced when sleep is approaching, and some people find these alarming. Luthe suggests that these motor discharges are sometimes attempts at self-regulation. Pelletier observes that sometimes these motor discharges are associated with violent crying in persons with a history of traumatised birth or dental surgery, abortion or suppressed emotions over significant events such as the death of a close relative. When these distressing events occur he suggests that a trained therapist is needed to help the individual work through these matters. Therefore as Wilson observes, on the whole AT is taught by doctors who insist medical supervision is essential.

However, these experiences are not confined to Autogenic Training, occurring frequently in other meditative disciplines, in biofeedback and under hypnosis, and although it is necessary for the individual to confront the previously suppressed or denied psychological or physiological trauma in order to fully alleviate the disorder rather than its overt symptoms, Lindemann (cited by Wilson) pleads for delegation of AT to a wider circle of people.

After a variable period of training the person should be able to proceed through the entire series in a few minutes, and maintain stability in the autogenic state for prolonged periods, during which they exhibit a marked increase in alpha activity in the brain consistent with deep relaxation, and are capable of regulating a wide range of other physiological functions through autosuggestion; including self-anaesthetisation against third-degree burns (Gorton 1959).

Research on Autogenic Training

Autogenic Training has been subjected to considerable experimental research and the impressive claims made for it by Schultz and Luthe have found much support.

During passive concentration on heaviness Siebenthal (1952), Schultz (1952), Wittstock (1956), Eiff and Jorgens (1961) recorded a significant decrease of muscle potentials, and Schultz (1932, 1961) found a significant reduction in patella response during passive concentration on heaviness in both legs.

Changes in peripheral circulation during passive concentration on heaviness and warmth have been verified by a number of independent researchers including Schultz (1959), Binswanger (1929), Stovkis, Renes and Landman (1961). Polzein (1955, 1959, 1961) carried out the most extensive studies and found that the rise of skin temperature was more pronounced in distal parts of extremities than in more proximal areas, the skin temperature of fingers varying between 0.2 and 3.5 degrees centigrade. Siebenthal (1952) and Muller-Hegemann (1956) (both cited by Pelletier 1978) independently recorded an increase in weight of both arms during passive concentration on heaviness, and Marchand (1956, 1961) demonstrated that during the standard exercises warmth in the liver area induced changes in blood sugar level. During stages one to three there was a slight increase in blood sugar, followed by a drop in stage four and slight rise in stage five. Numerous electronic studies have reported reductions (by as much as 10 per cent), in respiratory rate, blood pressure and heart rate, leading Polzein to conclude that the clinical and experimental observations gathered over the past 35 years have indicated that the physiological changes occurring during Autogenic Training are of a highly complex and differentiated nature, involving autonomic functions co-ordinated by brain mechanisms.

When the standard series has been mastered a series of special exercises enable the subject to modify pain threshold in different parts of the body and to train the individual to awaken at specific times. Subjects were reported by Schultz to be able to block the pain of dental drilling, others to warm their feet by raising skin temperatures by as much as three degrees Fahrenheit, and hypertensive patients to achieve decreases in blood pressure of between 10 and 20 per cent.

The meditative series of exercises which involve visualization is normally only started after some 6-12 months of standard training. The first stage of this series involves voluntary rotation of the eyeballs upwards and inwards towards the centre of the forehead, a movement which is known to induce alpha waves. Then various exercises in colour visualization are introduced, certain colours such as red, yellow and orange being chosen because they appear to reinforce sensations of warmth, and others such as green and blue to reinforce cooling of the forehead. The subject then proceeds to visualize clouds, geometrical shapes, and other persons, then abstract concepts such as justice and freedom, and selective states of feeling.

Schultz employed his system in treating conditions similar to those treatable by hypnosis, including peptic ulcers, indigestion, circulation problems, angina, heart arythmias, obsessive behaviours, sexual problems, diabetes, asthma, migraine and allergies. Wilson (1987) indicates that apart from Germany where it is used as a standard pre-operative procedure it is widely used throughout Europe, and although only translated into English in 1959, is now used in Canada, USA and Japan, and, according to Luthe, integrated into the medical training programmes of many universities.

Nevertheless Autogenic Training is not widely known or practiced in Britain, although this situation appears to be changing as more and more practitioners become aware of its benefits and advantages over other methods. Recent studies have found that 82 per cent of all patients referred for AT with a wide range of problems found it generally helpful, while 74 per cent found that it also helped specific symptoms and most reported feeling more relaxed and confident (Medik and Fursland 1984). Horn (1986) reports a study of 100 healthy persons aged between 25 and 60 tested on a number of physical and psychological measures designed to select stress variables and heart risk factors, half of whom were allocated to physical exercise training and half to AT. At the end of two months both groups had experienced considerable reductions in anxiety and depression, and improved their scores on general health questionnaires, reported an enhanced sense of well-being, improved sleep and reduced physical tension, and showed significant reductions in resting pulse rate, blood pressure and blood fatty acids. Indeed, in every respect AT proved to be as useful as exercise, which is an important finding given the results of studies by Prosser et al. (1985) which demonstrated that only 14 out of 215 patients having suffered a heart attack were prepared to continue exercise therapy. Almost half of the patients reported finding exercise inconvenient, 30 per cent found it boring, 25 per cent disliked exercise without medical supervision, while a further 25 per cent gave medical reasons for discontinuing the exercise programme. The advantage of AT over exercise is that it can be practised by anyone, whether in bed or confined to a wheelchair, as it is essentially sedentary, and can be successfully used in work and leisure contexts. Moreover, once mastered it is the fastest method of achieving passive concentration. It doesn't take much time, unlike yoga, and requires no apparatus as does biofeedback. Another advantage emphasised by Wilson (1987) is that the body is not expected to react in a stereotyped way. Apart from the increasing speed of reaction, subtle changes constantly take place as the intensity of the practice grows, and the suggestions can be changed to suit current needs as well as distant aims. Thus AT grows with practice and the practitioner.

Nevertheless Pelletier accepts that AT depends to a great extent on autosuggestion and that it is viewed by many people with suspicion. He indicates, however, that practitioners of AT insist there is a critical distinction between it and autosuggestion in as much that in the former people are trained over a long period of time into what constitutes a meditative state and the initial use of autosuggestion is only a means of instructing them and familiarising them with their ability to enter into that state of their own volition. Accordingly autosuggestion is used only as a means of training them in achieving low arousal.

Arguably, however, there are very much simpler means of achieving this end, which will be addressed in the following chapter.

Chapter 8

Relaxation

Take it easy, but take it

Woody Guthrie

The quieting down of the sympathetic nervous system, as manifested in altered skin resistance, brain wave and breathing patterns, and reduction in other measures of physiological arousal such as muscle activity, heart and pulse rate, blood pressure and blood hormone levels, is striking and similar in yoga, meditation, biofeedback, hypnosis and autogenic training. Indeed none of these self-control strategies is unique in eliciting these effects, which are now recognised as being consistent with a physiological state of deep relaxation.

However, the tendency to attribute these effects to altered states of consciousness, which has become fashionable since the 1960s, is not altogether unjustified because as Benson (1975, p.74-5) indicates, relaxation is an *altered* state inasmuch that it is not commonly experienced and does not occur spontaneously but must be consciously and purposefully evoked. Relaxation is not, as Pelletier (1978) indicates, merely a shift in physiological functions but an integrated combination of these which is not achieved simply by lounging in front of the television or chatting with friends. This was not fully appreciated until relatively recently when advances in technology facilitated precise recording of subtle physiological processes. Indeed it was not until the late 1920s that relaxation was first investigated systematically by the physician Edmund Jacobsen.

Yet relaxation or rest has long been recognised as the opposite of nervous hypertension which is a feature of many conditions and occurs in the guise of symptoms, causes or effects throughout almost the entire range of medical practice, surgery and specialities (Jacobsen 1938). Rest has therefore been seen as an antidote to nervous hypertension which increases general resistance to infection and other noxious agents, decreases blood pressure and strain on the heart, diminishes energy output, and movement of body parts, thereby averting strain or injury. Accordingly it has been prescribed in the treatment of numerous conditions including acute infections, ulcers, gastro-intestinal disorders, cardiac and renal conditions, high blood pressure, arthritis, systemic disease, neurotic conditions, after surgery and frequently, in preparation for it. Traditionally various means have been used to promote rest including tepid baths, massage and warm drinks, although the agents most frequently employed by physicians to promote nervous calm are sedative drugs. Nevertheless, patients often fail to derive the full benefits of rest, especially in hospitals where ward routines are typically put before the patients' need for peace and quiet (Cousins 1981).

Directing a person to 'rest' or to 'lie down and relax' is in itself quite futile as many people simply don't know how to, and their restlessness may be increased by distress, and vice versa. Normally people are unaware that their muscles are tense and cannot judge accurately whether or not relaxation has been achieved. Therefore what is customarily called rest or relaxation is in many instances inadequate, which accounts for the failure of many 'rest cures'.

Jacobsen (1938) observed that a person may lie on a couch apparently quiet for hours but remain sleepless and restless. He may show signs of mental activity, organic excitement, anxiety or other emotional disturbance, breathe irregularly, fidget, restlessly move his eyes or fingers, or start in response to sudden noise. Following such 'rest' the person frequently fails to feel refreshed and retains symptoms of fatigue and other ills. Moreover, even when the person feels fairly relaxed there are often clinical signs of residual tension such as irregular respiration, increased pulse rate, voluntary or local reflexes indicated in wrinkling of the forehead, frowning, movements of the eyeballs, tension in the muscles around the eyes, frequent or rapid winking, restless shifting or the head or limbs, swallowing, and a startle reflex following sudden noise.

However, in true relaxation residual tension is absent, respiration loses its irregularity, pulse rate drops to normal, the esophagus relaxes, the knee jerk reflex and nervous start diminish. The individual then lies quietly with flaccid limbs and no visible traces of stiffness, no reflex swallowing, and motionless, toneless eyelids.

Jacobsen recognised that residual tension disappears only gradually and that relaxation is slow and progressive rather than sudden and immediate. He therefore attempted to devise a method which eliminates residual tension by producing progressively an extreme degree of neuromuscular relaxation.

Progressive relaxation

Jacobsen took the view that it is only when a person knows what tension is that he can begin to relax. His system of progressive relaxation involves the individual learning to identify tension in muscle groups by contracting them and shortening their fibres. It is the cultivation of what Bell (1847) termed 'muscle sense', and can be thought of as a method of nervous re-education which helps the individual to become increasingly observant of muscle contractions in various parts of their body, and to recognise that subjectively relaxation is not a positive 'something' different from contraction, but simply a negative, non-doing. The aim is to show those who insist they cannot relax that if they can progressively contract muscles they can cease the same contraction, and that it is not necessary for them to move body parts or 'do' anything to achieve it.

In principle it can be taught to anyone in much the same way as golfing, skiing or driving a car, providing that they are willing, motivated to learn and practice, and able to follow instructions. Nevertheless some people are not successful in cultivating muscle sense and fail to gain fine control.

Jacobsen's method

Progressive relaxation has many forms depending on the condition to be treated, whether acute or chronic, and the ability of the person to follow directions. It may be brief and occasional, with 2-3 training periods being sufficient; or longer, extending over months or a year. Periods of instruction also vary, ranging from 30 minutes to an hour, and occurring daily or 3-4 times weekly. However, as repetition is the keynote of the method, daily practice by the individual is required.

In a quiet room the person either lies on their back with arms at their sides and legs uncrossed, or sits in a chair. He is then taught to recognise the presence of muscle contraction, however slight, and to relax it in all the noteworthy groups of the body in a certain order. Jacobsen adopted the sequence of left arm and hand, right arm and hand, left foot and leg, right foot and leg, abdomen, respiratory muscles, back, shoulders, chest, face and mouth.

The degree of relaxation is assessed by a number of methods: palpation of muscle groups and passive motion of the parts by the therapist; observation of the regularity and force of respiration; visual observation of the flaccidity of muscle groups; the absence of movement or contraction; the presence of sudden involuntary start or jerk of a local part (as sometimes occurs before sleep); increasingly slow responses to interruption or failure to respond; and sleepy eyed or vacuous, expressionless appearance.

Relaxation of mental activities is then achieved through the introduction of imagery. Visual, auditory and other sensory images are presented to enable the subject to recognise the subtle tensions of the small muscles or the sense organs which accompany imagery. Jacobsen describes this (1938, p.183) as a delicate matter that requires practice, but claims that when this is done mental imagery dwindles and ceases with the approach of general relaxation, and that without faint tension the image fails to appear.

Motor or kinesthetic imagery may likewise be relaxed away. Thus inner speech ceases with progressive relaxation of the muscles of the lips, tongue, larynx and throat. Furthermore, attention, recollection, thought processes and emotion gradually diminish, and Jacobsen claims that this is registered in the person's totally expressionless countenance.

> The thesis that progressive relaxation brings with it absence of thinking is apparent, literally, on the face of it.

> This thesis also harmonizes with the experience of all the subjects and patients who considered that it was impossible to be relaxed extremely and to have images at the

same time. With the advent of one condition, the other invariably ceased (1938, p.184)

Clearly, therefore, Jacobsen is suggesting that the end state of perfect or complete relaxation, achieved in a clinical manner without recourse to esotericism of any kind, is a state of inner silence, emptiness, or void which is the aim of meditation. Moreover, this state, as in meditation, is an ideal, which according to Jacobsen is not as a rule achieved, and then only for brief periods of time.

Regular and extensive practice is required to master progressive relaxation, but the method can be simplified or shortened in a number of ways, by restricting the training to a few muscle groups, for example. When the person recognises that relaxation can be effected as quickly as muscle contraction, he can be taught to scan the body for tension and to concentrate on relaxing only those muscles. It is possible to use everyday events such as traffic signals, hourly radio bulletins, or workshift bells as signals when to scan and relax muscles. A person may also achieve differential relaxation by learning to identify and relax the muscles not required in the execution of a task while achieving a minimum of tension in those that are.

Applications of Jacobsen's method

Jacobsen claimed the effectiveness of progressive relaxation in producing very marked improvement in the treatment of hypertension, insomnia, anxiety neuroses, cardiac conditions, compulsive neuroses, tics, hypochondria and stuttering, indicating that in many cases drugs and dietary restrictions could be abolished after relaxation.

He recommended its application as particularly suited to cases of acute neuromuscular hypertension such as nervousness or emotional disturbance, chronic neuromuscular hypertension; functional neuroses such as phobias, tics, habit spasm, insomnia, stuttering, stammering, anxiety, hypochondria, states of fatigue, exhaustion and debility; pre-operative and post-operative conditions; toxic goitre, disturbances of sleep; alimentary spasm, including mucus colitis, colonic spasm, cardiospasm and esophagospasm; peptic ulcer; chronic pulmonary tuberculosis; organic and functional heart disorders; and vascular hypertension.

Wolpe's Relaxation Method

Subsequently Wolpe (1977) developed a system of relaxation based on that of Jacobsen which he employed in conjunction with systematic desensitization in the treatment of phobias and anxiety states. His method is quite brief, comprising six periods of instruction with twice daily practice periods of fifteen minutes each.

Like Jacobsen he commenced the training by focusing on the muscle groups of the arms, largely because they are easy for demonstration purposes and easily checked upon by the therapist, progressing to the head where relaxation produces the most marked anxiety inhibiting effects.

The person is asked to grip the arm of a chair to see if he can distinguish any qualitative difference between sensations in the forearm and hand, and directed to take particular notice of the quality of sensation in the forearm, which is caused by muscle tension in contrast to the sensations in the hand which are caused by touch and pressure. The person is encouraged to note the exact location of forearm tensions. The therapist then grips the person's wrist and asks him to tense his arm against this resistance, thus making him aware of the tension in his biceps. Then, by instructing him to straighten his bent elbow against this resistance, he calls attention to the extensor muscles of the arm. The therapist shows the person how to achieve deep relaxation by asking him to resist the pull at the wrist by tightening the biceps and noting the sensations in that muscle, then instructing them to let go gradually as the force exerted against them is diminished. They are instructed to notice that the letting go is a non-activity - an uncontracting of muscle, and told to continue relaxing the muscle when their arm is resting on the chair. This is repeated until the person understands what is required of him, when he is asked to place both hands on the lap for a few minutes, relaxing all muscles and reporting any sensations experienced - usually warmth and heaviness. Initially, only limited success is likely, hence the need for regular practice.

In the second session training focuses on the facial muscles, sensations being demonstrated through contraction of the muscles of the forehead. Focus in the third session is upon tensing the muscles of the temple, jaw and neck by clenching the teeth, while the fourth session is concerned with the neck and shoulder muscles, which when contracted keep the head erect. The fifth session concentrates on the muscles of the back, abdomen and chest, through arching the body, and the feet; and finally, in the sixth session, all the previously trained muscle groups are worked on. Wolpe found this method effective in bringing about desired emotional changes and it has since been widely adopted in the psychological treatment of phobias and anxiety conditions.

Farmer and Blows' method of relaxation

Most of the methods of relaxation currently employed in therapy, whether psychological or medical, are a modification of those of either Jacobsen or Wolpe. A South African psychologist, Ron Farmer, has developed an even shorter method than that of Wolpe which incorporates principles of yoga practice, psychological learning theory and autosuggestion. This has been extended by Blows, who, influenced by TM, introduced passive observation, or the 'letting go' of cycles of thinking. This method entails lying in a supine position similar to the sarasana or corpse posture of yoga, awareness of breathing movements, passive observation of thought, and letting go of internally triggered cycles of mental activity.

Blows (1987) observes that in the methods of Jacobsen and Wolpe the state of relaxation is continually disrupted by the action of tensing the muscles, and for this reason progressive relaxation does not always yield the same neurophysiological indices as meditation. Farmer addressed this problem by using the principle of stimulus generalisation derived from learning theory.

Instead of tensing a series of muscles in the whole body, the client does the preliminary training with the dominant hand, tensing only that part of the body and allowing the experience of letting go to generalise to other parts in turn with no further tensing actions. Blows claims that once commenced the relaxed state is not disrupted but enhanced.

The exercise begins with the person focusing on their breathing and saying the word 'relax' softly on each breath. Relaxation is introduced in two simple steps so that without actually being told to do so the person concentrates on his breathing and prepares for the word 'relax' to become an affective signal within the brain, enabling the person to relax quickly in everyday situations. Blows suggests that saying the word 'relax' aloud helps to establish the habit, but also allows the therapist to monitor the coordination of breathing and relaxation. Tensing and release of the dominant hand is introduced coarsely at first in one cycle of breathing, then extended to gradual releasing over a number of breaths, becoming progressively finer. In the last stages of this preliminary procedure the client, while mentally rehearsing the word 'relax', is asked to imagine that after his hand feels fully relaxed a little more tension flows away each time he breathes out. Blows claims that gradual refinement of the contraction and release of the hand, commencing with coarse tensing which can be felt easily, prepares for generalised release of tension in other areas of the body which is enhanced by imagining further release of tension.

The instructions include the statement that effort is not required, only letting go, and a suggestion of heaviness of the limbs is also added. Each section of the body is then covered using common sense rather than strictly anatomical sections, consistent with people's ordinary body images. Normally two training sessions are required before the person can reproduce the experience reasonably well at home, where it is recommended that practice takes place twice daily at regular times.

Blows has included an additional phase of pleasant imagery of the person's own choice, and claims that with this modification the original Farmer method can be extended to produce a state similar to that attained during Transcendental Meditation. Thus it isn't restricted to muscular relaxation but can also be used to achieve mental calmness. Blows maintains that given a range of relaxation methods most people prefer the Farmer and Blows method, but as it has not yet been submitted to physiological tests or evaluative studies its efficacy has not been verified. Nevertheless it does have an advantage over other relaxation methods in that it avoids not only interruption of the relaxation process by muscle tensing but also a good deal of verbal instruction which is widely held to stimulate mental activity and logical thought. Recognition of this factor has led Meares (1977) to employ non-verbal quieting methods based on gentle touch and sound.

Relaxation tapes

In order to avoid the distractions of verbal instruction there is an increasing tendency to use music as an aid to relaxation and numerous audio-cassette tapes have been produced commercially. Matthew Manning, who has produced both verbal and musical tapes to assist relaxation has, more recently, tended to focus on the latter. He observes that the music generally thought to be relaxing tends to be light, airy and simple, and with repetition somewhat boring and ineffective. He has therefore produced a series of musical tapes of considerable complexity which he has found to promote more effective relaxation, and to withstand frequent repetition.

However, although a very popular means of promoting relaxation, audio-cassettes, whether verbal or not, lead to reliance on external devices and the failure of the person to develop their own internal cues to relaxation. They are thus antithetical to the principal aim of all forms of relaxation training which is to train the person in self-reliance and self-awareness. Furthermore they give the false impression that gaining muscle control can be acquired instantly, which frequently leads those who fail to do so to believe that they cannot relax. Certainly the promise of a speedy means of achieving relaxation is very attractive, especially when compared with those lengthy and time consuming methods which achieve relaxation by sequential contraction of muscle groups and focus on breathing. Hence the popularity of the relaxation method devised by Herbert Benson, Professor of Medicine at Harvard University Medical School, Director of the Hypertension Section of Boston's Beth Israel Hospital, and founder researcher in Transcendental Meditation.

The Relaxation response

Benson (1975) insists that the ability to relax is not a learned phenomenon or skill but an innate mechanism or universal human capacity, which he terms the Relaxation Response, and requires no special educational attainment or aptitude, no specific method, nor any lengthy period of training. Therefore 'it is not necessary to meditate or to be wired up to a machine to achieve it, nor is there any necessity to engage in any rites or esoteric practices to bring it forth and to reclaim its benefits' (p.123). The only requirement is time and conscious effort dedicated to it.

He developed a simple technique for eliciting the Relaxation Response derived from traditional forms of meditation. This involves the person adopting a comfortable posture in a quiet environment and a passive attitude, which is achieved by redirection of attention to a silently repeated sound, word or phrase, and to breathing.

Accordingly the person is directed to adopt a comfortable position, preferably seated as prone positions tend to promote sleep; to close the eyes, or focus the open eyes on a fixed point or object; and to become aware of breathing by inhaling through the nose and exhaling through the mouth. The person is directed to say 'one' silently to himself as he breathes out, thereby establishing a pattern of in-out-one which he then rehearses for 10-20 minutes, during which time he is told not to worry about success in achieving a deep level of relaxation, but merely to maintain a passive attitude and permit relaxation to occur at its own pace. Similarly the person is told not to dwell on distracting thoughts which may occur, but simply to turn their attention back to breathing and repeating 'one'.

Benson reports that subjective feelings accompanying the Relaxation Response vary among individuals. The majority experience a sense of calmness and relaxation, while some experience ecstatic feelings and others describe pleasurable sensations. Others note little subjective change. In this respect, therefore, their experiences are consistent with the response patterns to meditation, which Maupin (1969) found to include sensations of dizziness and foggy consciousness, calmness and tranquility, pleasant bodily sensations, vibrations and waves, feelings of the body being suspended or light, lucid consciousness with detachment from thoughts and feelings, and extensive loss of bodily sensation. However, regardless of the subjective feelings experienced, physiological changes occur during the Relaxation Response similar to those of TM (Benson 1975) and Benson reports its effectiveness in the treatment of hypertension, headache and other conditions.

Therapeutic applications of relaxation

The therapeutic effects of relaxation are increasingly being recognised. It has been demonstrated to be effective in the control of asthma (Erskine and Schonell 1981; Saxena and Saxena 1978), in the regression of cancer (Meares 1981), and the side effects of cancer chemotherapy (Burish and Lyles 1981; Bindemann, et al, (1986); in improvements in immune response (Kiecolt, Glaser et al. 1985); in reducing diabetics' need for insulin (Boryshenko, reported in Seigel 1986); in the treatment of anxiety conditions, where it has also been demonstrated to be effective in training patients to cope without the use of anxyolytic drugs (Skinner 1984); and in the control of chronic pain (Turner and Chapman 1981). Rowden (1984) comparing relaxation and hypnosis, found a greater reduction in physical arousal and subjective distress with relaxation.

Relaxation and pain control

The role of relaxation training in the control of pain is increasingly being recognised. Horn (1986) indicates that relaxation may alleviate pain associated with involuntary muscle tone, which may be confined to an area immediately around the primary pain, more generalised, or even at a site far distant from its source. Hence clenching the jaw may accompany abdominal pain, and low back pain often involves an increase in tension of back, buttock and leg muscles, whereas some chest and abdominal pain results in increased muscle tone all over the body. While the primitive function of the increased muscle tone might be to protect the primary pain site and prevent damaging movement, it is not useful in pain which is not associated with acute inflammation or injury. Indeed in non-acute pain the increased muscle tension often causes secondary pain which exacerbates the original problem. Moreover, increased pain interferes with relaxation and sleep and leads to a spiral of increasing tension and pain.

Severe pain is also accompanied by subjective feelings of distress and physiological arousal which can be brought under control by successful relaxation training. Horn indicates that emphasis on breathing can inhibit stress attacks. Moreover, relaxation has long-term effects. Libo and Arnold (1983) found in a study of patients undergoing relaxation training with biofeedback for a variety of conditions that, when followed up one to five years after therapy, 86 per cent of those who continued to practice relaxation had improved compared to only 5 per cent of those who had discontinued relaxation.

The application of relaxation methods in the treatment of cancer was pioneered by Achterberg et al. (1978) who recognised that relaxation served a variety of functions. They observed that 'for some it appears to be a way of recharging batteries' (p.126), whereas for others it help to break the cycle of fear and tension which often builds up and overwhelms people suffering serious illness. They claim that with fear reduced it is easier for people to develop a more positive expectancy, which results in a further reduction of fear and may be a significant feature in cancer regression.

Widespread recognition of the therapeutic value of relaxation has led to the mass-marketing of training courses in relaxation and audio or video cassette recordings of relaxation methods applied to every conceivable disorder, psychological and physical. These are avidly sought by a general public to whom stress has been depicted as an unavoidable by-product of rapid cultural change, urbanisation, socio-economic mobility, technological expansion and environmental uncertainty, and as the epidemic killer disease of the late twentieth century. However, it is doubtful whether modern life is more stressful than formerly, when plague, pestilence, famines, poverty and war were rife, and more likely that people are simply conditioned to be aware of it.

Stress - the killer disease?

There is nothing new in the idea that stress is linked with serious illness, this connection having been established in antiquity. In 1759 the surgeon Richard Guy highlighted the possible role of adverse life events in the development of cancer, and since then others have cited loss as an antecedent condition in the development of cancer (Snow 1893, and Evans 1926, both cited in Greer 1983; Miller and Jones 1948; Muslin et al. 1966; LeShan 1966, Priestman et al. 1985). A number of recent studies claim to have demonstrated a link between stressful events and cancer (Blumberg et al. 1954; Greer and Morris 1975; Schonfield 1975; Stoll 1979, Shekelle et al. 1981), and in the recurrence of cancer (Alvarez 1989), with the result that such a view is now widely accepted and promoted (Cooper 1988; Cooper et al. 1988; Editorial 1987).

Increasing concern about the stress of modern life led Holmes and Rahe (1967) to score the stress impact of life events on a scale from 0-100, with death of a spouse being assigned the maximum stress rating, and subsequently many 'experts' have drawn up tables of stressful events and jobs as a guide to the amount of stress a person can withstand.

However, it is now recognised that the interaction between life events and the individual is considerably more complex than was first recognised. Ornstein and Sobel (1988) observe that an unhappy marriage or poor working conditions, while not events *per se*, may nevertheless be highly stressful. Moreover, not only life events but ordinary mundane occurrences and irritations need to be taken into account because major life events are frequently accompanied by minor concerns, and in the short term these minor annoyances are better predictors of both psychosomatic and physical symptoms than are major life events (Kanner et al. 1981, Lazarus 1981 1984).

Awareness of these factors would appear to justify growing concern with stress. However the stress impact of an event, whether major or minor, may be very different when viewed objectively from the way it is subjectively experienced by an individual. Hence for some people the death of a budgerigar may be more stressful than the death of a spouse. Furthermore the impact of the same event will vary, often dramatically, from person to person. As Gordon Allport has observed, 'the same fire which melts the butter hardens the egg'.

Assigning a fixed numerical stress rating to a given event can therefore be highly misleading, so Cooper et al. (1988) have produced a more sensitive stress index which scores individual events on a ten-point scale, and includes items such as buying, selling and moving house, increasing a mortgage, having a child commence school, and pet-related problems.

Nevertheless emphasis on stressful events implies that stress is beyond the control of the individual, and obscures their role in determining stress. However, as Harrison (1984, p.172) indicates 'people construct circumstances for themselves which they then react to with stress; that is, they are not being stressed by external events beyond their control, but are stressing themselves'. Accordingly, stress is an option rather than an inevitability, which arises mainly from the individual's attitude toward, and interpretation of events.

From this perspective the stress associated with an event depends to a great extent on whether the person appraises it as a threat or a challenge, as positive or negative. Those who view an event positively tend to see it as an opportunity to learn, grow and develop, whereas those who view it negatively tend to experience it aversively, as stressful. The former not only cope with a series of stressful events without becoming ill, but may actually thrive on stress (Ecker 1987). The tendency to accentuate the negative outcomes of stress thus obscures the fact that it frequently serves a positive stimulus function in spurring people on to achievements and satisfactions, and, if avoided entirely would lead to people becoming totally inert, which may ultimately prove more hazardous, and stressful. Studies of sensory deprivation have demonstrated that understimulation can cause the central nervous system to go awry and produce mental and physical disorders. Therefore, 'the bored brain may be as damaging as the blitzed one' (Ornstein and Sobel, p.213). Boredom may be experienced as pain, and bored people frequently resort to painkillers of one sort or another, whether legal or illegal. The connection between boredom and illicit drug use is well-established particularly use of heroin and other opiates, which as Burroughs (1977) indicates 'kill time', enabling the user to live in a timeless, painless state. Therefore, according to Ornstein and Sobel (p.236) the difference between hardy and non-hardy types 'is that the former transform problems into opportunities whereas softies distract themselves with TV, drugs or social interactions'.

The concept of stress thus needs to be modified so as to distinguish between stress and stressors, that is, between the subjectively experienced effects of an event, and the event itself; and to take into account not only the nature of the stressor - its type, frequency, duration and intensity, and the resources available for dealing with it, but also other variables including the person's need for stimulation and excitement, and other psychological factors such as their attitude toward, and interpretation of events.

Psychological factors in stress-related illness

It is now recognised that psychological factors are of considerable importance in determining whether an individual experiences stress and succumbs to stress-related disease. The role of psychological factors in the development of disease has long been recognised. Galen observed that cancer more commonly occurs in women of melancholic disposition than in those of more sanguine personality type, and this view has found support among physicians throughout history. Other psychological factors have been identified in cancer patients. Reich (1975) described cancer as a disease following emotional resignation and giving up hope, and Manning (1988) suggests that it is found in those who, in trying to gain approval from others, suppress anger and other negative emotions. The tendency of cancer patients to suppress emotion has been confirmed by Kissen and Eysenck (1962) and Kissen (1963, 1964, 1967, 1969).

More recently studies have supported earlier observations that certain personality traits are characteristically associated with cancer (LeShan 1966; Soloman 1969; Abse et al. 1974; Achterberg et al. 1977). These include repression and denial of emotions, inability to express hostile feelings, poor outlet for emotional discharge, a tendency to self-sacrifice and blame, rigidity, impaired self-awareness and introspection, and a predisposition to hopelessness and despair.

The evidence strongly suggests that the suppression of emotion relates to illness and that cancer patients seem to ignore negative feelings such as hostility, depression and guilt. The link between breast cancer in women and the need to 'get something off the chest' is tentative but well established. Greer, Morris et al. (1979) found differences between benign and malignant breast cancer patients in their expression of anger, and Derogatis et al. (1979) found that long-term survivors of breast cancers express much higher levels of hostility, anxiety, alienation and other negative emotions than short-term survivors. Similarly Meares (1979) found that patients who express emotion freely and show an active determination to fight their disease live longer than meek, passive, compliant or defeatist types.

Simonton and Matthews-Simonton (1975) also identify cancer patients as characterised by greater tendency to hold resentment and not forgive, self pity, poor ability to develop and maintain meaningful long-term relationships, and poor self image. They suggest that the belief systems of those who eventually succumb to cancer are essentially negative, whereas those of patients whose cancers show spontaneous remission are positive. Cancer patients also report more subjectively experienced stress than controls (Hughes 1987).

Recognition of these tendencies, together with those toward conformity and compliance, led Greer and Watson (1985) to propose a cancer prone or Type C personality. Evidence in support of the cancer prone personality has been provided by Shekelle et al. (1981), but not by Dattore et al. (1980); and Schmale and Iker (1971) have argued that cancer patients are no different from patients who develop other serious illnesses. Certainly a number of studies suggest a common pattern of helplessness and hopelessness in both psychological and physical disease. Women with rheumatoid arthritis have been found to be tense, moody, depressed, concerned with rejection they perceived from their mothers and the strictness of their fathers; to show denial and inhibition of the expression of anger, and to reflect these traits, compliance, subserviance, conservatism, shyness, introversion and the need for security on MMPI scales (Moos 1964; Moos and Solomon 1965a, 1965b).

Nevertheless there are numerous difficulties in studying possible psychological causes of cancer and other illnesses. Although spoken of as one illness,cancer takes many forms which may have quite different causes, and factors which may be responsible for the initial onset of the disease may be different from those involved in its subsequent development. Onset of cancer may occur many years before any signs of the disease are evident, and factors which are cited as antecedent conditions may in fact have occurred after the cancer became established. Retrospective studies of cancer thus have several pitfalls, including the likelihood that the presence of a cancer, whether recognised by the patient or not, may influence their psychological state by its physical effects on the brain and body chemistry. Therefore the problems involved in designing research studies which will produce valid information about psychological precursors of cancer or other disease are formidable. Currently there is no generally accepted means of exactly defining and measuring many of the psychological variables investigated, with the result that the findings of different studies vary with the different methods employed, and are not comparable.

Psychological factors and immunity

Nevertheless there is abundant evidence which demonstrates the influence of psychological factors on endocrine and immune functions (Mason 1968; Solomon 1969; Curtis 1979; Rose 1980; Ader and Cohen 1975; Rogers et al. 1979; Editorial 1985, 1987; McClelland et al. 1980a, 1980b.). Of particular interest is Bresnitz' finding that expectation influences blood levels of the hormones cortisol and prolactin which are important in activating the immune system. It would appear that positive and negative expectations have opposite effects, respectively enhancing or depressing the immune response. The importance of expectancy, or belief, is well recognised in orthodox medicine, to the extent that doctors frequently prescribe a placebo, or imitation medicine, in cases where reassurance for the patient is more useful than conventional medication. However, it is only relatively recently that the placebo has received serious attention from medical researchers.

Although it is not understood how, it is now recognised that the placebo can have more profound effects on organic illness - including 'incurable' malignancies - than drugs. As Cousins (1981) observes, 'the placebo, then, is not so much a pill as a process' which begins with the patient's confidence in the doctor and extends through to the full functioning of his own immunological and healing system.

Cousins suggests that the placebo effect offers proof that there is no separation between body and mind, and that illness is always an interaction between both. He concludes that 'attempts to treat most mental diseases as though they were completely free of physical causes and attempts to treat most bodily diseases as though the mind were in no way involved must be considered archaic in the light of new evidence about the way the human body functions' (p.56-7).

The placebo will not work under all circumstances. The chances of success are believed to be directly proportional to the quality of the patient's relationship with the doctor. The doctor's attitude to his patient; his ability to convince the patient he is not being taken lightly; and his success in gaining the patient's full confidence are all vital factors, not only in maximising the usefulness of the placebo, but in the treatment of disease in general.

However, it is doubtful whether the placebo or any other treatment would prove effective without the patient's will to live; that is, his attitude to life.

The importance of the protection afforded by a positive approach to life is only one important clinical implication of the role of psychological factors in immunity. Others are that psychological treatments might be used as adjuvant therapy to suppress the immune response in certain life threatening diseases and less serious disorders, or to enhance the immune system in vulnerable groups (Editorial 1987). Presently, however, attention has only been directed to the role of psychological attitude in illness.

Attitudinal healing

Studies of cancer patients (Achterberg et al. 1975) have suggested that the attitude of the patient is vitally important in determining the outcome of the illness. Those with spontaneous remission of cancer are found to be positive in attitude. In Britain, the Cancer Research Campaign's trial of adjuvant psychological therapy in the treatment of women with breast cancer, which builds on the research of Greer et al. (1979) shows a clear correlation between mental attitude and length of survival. Similarly, those cancer patients who outlived predicted life expectancies, refused to give up in the face of stress, were more non-conformist, had greater psychological insight and were more flexible (Achterberg et al. 1977). Flexibility, or the willingness to make changes, seems to be a particularly crucial factor in recovery, those responding poorly to treatment usually being characterised by rigidity and holding on to self image and the familiar. Clearly, therefore prevention of illness and the maintenance of health involves not only relaxation of the musculature, and letting go of bodily tensions, but also letting go of mental attitudes, beliefs, negative emotions and expectancies. Indeed, relaxation can only be fully effective when this is achieved, and is most effective when positive expectancy is instilled (Bradley and McCanne 1981). Cousins (1981) insists that positive emotions are lifegiving experiences. Therefore creating attitude change - sometimes termed attitudinal healing - focuses on trying to move the person in a more positive direction. It works on the principle that if a person can change themself, and their outlook, they change the world around them. Rigidity is viewed as a response to threat or fear, so the individual is encouraged to let go of the fear and to transform it into a positive emotion and acceptance (Jampolsky 1979).

Manning (1988) outlines the requirements for such attitude change as the ability to accept criticism, recognising it as the other person's problem, and often as a way of expressing jealousy; acceptance of the self, and affirming self worth; seeing the positive in all circumstances, and problems as situations from which one can learn; looking forward with joy rather than backwards in sorrow; focusing on what one has rather than what one has not; learning from mistakes and converting them into successes; letting go of what is no longer needed, and making the most of what one attracts.

Cousins (1981) emphasises the importance of humour and laughter in overcoming negative attitudes and emotions, and his own recovery from a terminal condition is a testimony to their power in redressing illness. It would seem, as Konrad Lorenz has observed, that 'we don't take humour seriously enough'. Yet the physiological benefits of humour have long been recognised. The Buddha personifies Eastern belief in the healing value of laughter and Cousins cites the Bible, which states that 'a merry heart works like a doctor'; Robert Burton 400 years ago described mirth as a 'sufficient cure in itself'; Hobbes, Kant and the famous physician Sir William Osler all recommended mirth as medicine. Similarly Lorenz cites the contemporary scientific researcher William Fry of Stanford University who has demonstrated that respiratory function is improved by laughter.

The Simontons and Jeanne Achterberg proposed that teaching cancer patients a variety of self-help methods which encourage these features could increase their chances of survival and improve its quality. Support for this claim has been provided by Simonton et al. (1978), Fiore (1974), Meares (1981), Bindemann, et al. (1986). Newton (1980) found that in patients using psychological methods survival time was two to three times longer than would have been predicted on the basis of national norms, and that after five years it was found that 51 per cent of patients were living compared with only 16 per cent of patients who had not received the same treatment.

However, as Hegarty (1989) indicates, medical opinion on the issue remains divided. On the one hand doctors agree that the patient's attitude is vitally important to their survival and that it is important to do everything possible to support those with serious illness. Yet on the other hand they tend not to agree on whether it is appropriate to offer specific psychological approaches and imply they may cure or influence the course of disease. Accordingly the medical establishment has been slow in implementing psychological approaches, or carrying out controlled trials of their effectiveness.

Feinstein (1983) observes that attempts to establish a scientific basis of psychological approaches has been hampered because accounting for psychological factors complicates medical investigation with multiple variables that exceed the capacity of current research paradigms. Findings concerning psychological interventions are thus still very limited, and both controlled clinical trials and carefully documented case studies are still needed.

In practice, therefore, doctors often ignore psychological factors totally, and as Pullar (1988) suggests, programme patients with negative rather than positive expectancies; a view supported by Cousins (1981), Brohn (1986), Siegel (1986).

Conventional medical approaches are therefore likely to increase the likelihood of stress rather than reduce it, and to prompt patients to seek out approaches which offer hope, and the prospect of recovery.

Chapter 9

Visualization

To accomplish great things we must not only act, but also dream.

Anatole France

Visualization is the ability to form mental images of something not at the moment visible or capable of being viewed. It is therefore synonymous with imagination or fantasy (from the Greek *phantazein*: to make visible). All the indications are that the effects of deep relaxation are enhanced by visualization, which in promoting passive concentration or absorption not only facilitates a letting go of physical tensions but also, by creating imaginary new experiences and introducing flexibility into mental functioning, relaxes mental attitudes. It is therefore employed at various stages in most types of meditation, in hypnosis, autohypnosis, autogenic training and biofeedback.

Indeed the effects of these approaches are largely attributable to the individual's ability to visualize. Achterberg (1985) identifies the ability to use the imagination as the basis of individual differences in learning biofeedback, and reports that subjects unable to fantasize, who seldom remember dreams, and who are not particularly creative have most difficulty in achieving the biofeedback response.

Similarly, Barber (1961) attributes the effects of hypnosis to the vividness of the imagery created by the subject in response to suggestion, and in so doing he reiterates the major finding of the Franklin Commission of 1785.

Conversely there are indications that difficulty in visualization may have adverse consequences. Just as physiological effects and possible cure may be enhanced by the ability to visualize, the opposite may also be true. Gordon (1962) drew attention to a possible relationship between rigidity of imagery and rigid mental attitudes such as racial stereotyping, and suggested that this may have important, and possibly even lethal implications - heretics and martyrs exemplifying the tendency to follow a certain image or vision rigorously.

Rigidity of imagery may also have lethal outcomes given the importance of flexibility in the maintenance of health. Mental rigidity is known to be a feature of a number of conditions such as cancer, rheumatoid arthritis, heart attack, and inability to cope with stress. Kemple (1945, reported in Rosenman, 1986) discovered that Type A persons, successful as they are on superficial scrutiny, are nevertheless handicapped in their ability to indulge in 'introversive experiences of creative thought', a defect which he believed might increase their dependence on achievement in the external mundane world and work. However, as Feldman and Rosenman have since observed, it may well be that their drive to achieve could have decreased their dependence on the satisfactions to be derived from introversive experience.

Arguably the externalistic standpoint of the West typically trains an impoverished imagination, but it is simply not the case, as Russell (1978, p.45) claims, that 'we in the West do not use visualization to any great extent in our daily lives'. Although individuals vary in the vividness of their imagery, and whether it is predominantly 'visile, audile, or motile' (Galton 1883), visualization is for most people a normal feature of cognitive functioning which is employed in the planning, coordination and execution of everyday activities. Accordingly mental imagery and its applications have long been the subject of study by psychologists.

Everyday applications of imagery

The application of mental imagery most commonly investigated is its use as a mnemonic or memory aid. One of the simplest ways of learning a list of items, whether a shopping list or the Kings and Queens of England, is to link the first and second items together as vividly as possible with a strong visual image and then produce a further image to link a third item, and so on. This method of 'chaining' can be generalised to items other than words so that a sequence of ideas or actions can be memorised.

Perhaps the most extensively reported visual image mnemonic is that known as the Method of Loci (from the Latin *locus*: place), whereby a list or succession of ideas is committed to memory by imagining a familiar place and assigning images to certain landmarks or features thereof.

Studies of those with exceptional memory skill suggest that visualization can be modified in order to increase efficiency in performance. Hunter (1986) reports the case of Shereshevskii, who was studied by the distinguished Russian psychologist Luria during the 1920s. It was found that his encoding of material to be remembered was characteristically perception-like, albeit not exclusively visual. Typically he would remember a given item by summoning an image of it in its entirety, complete in its visual, auditory, tactile and even gustatory features, but upon deciding to capitalise on his exceptional memory by becoming a professional mnemonist he simplified his use of imagery, taking one detail to signify what formerly would have been a whole scene. Simplified thus the image was less defined and vivid, but just as effective in aiding recall. In public performances he also began to employ the Method of Loci, typically imagining himself walking down a familiar Moscow street and visualizing each successively presented item in a list with successive landmarks, which he would then recall merely by mentally retracing his steps along the street.

Investigations of Shereshevskii failed to establish whether his ability for visualization was inborn or acquired, but clearly demonstrated that it could be brought under conscious control and put to intentional use.

This feature of visualization can be demonstrated in its applications to problem solving.

Visual representation of problems

Problems can be represented primarily in words or in images, and whichever is employed has important consequences. Gellatly (1986) illustrates this by reference to the following problem devised by de Bono:

> You are organising a singles knock-out tennis tournament for which there are 111 entrants. For each match there must be a new set of balls. How many sets of balls do you need to order?

A visual image of the draw for the tournament is difficult. It is much simpler to represent the problem verbally, as follows:

> The number of entrants is 111. All of them lose once, except the winner of the tournament, so there must be 110 matches, and that is the number of boxes of balls that is required.

However verbal representations of some problems are not at all helpful, as he illustrates with reference to a problem devised by Duncker (1945):

> One morning at sunrise, a Buddhist monk began to climb a mountain on a narrow path that wound around it. He climbed at a steady three miles per hour. After twelve hours he reached the top where there was a temple, and remained there to meditate for several days. Then, at sunrise, he started down the same path. He walked at a steady five miles per hour.

> Prove that there must be a spot along the same path which he occupied on both trips at exactly the same time of day.

Here a visual representation of the problem as follows proves more efficient:

> Imagine a monk climbing a mountain in the course of a day. Imagine also a second monk descending a mountain in the course of a day. Now superimpose the two images as if the two journeys were undertaken on the same day. Clearly at some point during the day the monks must meet and therefore be at the same point at the same time. This holds equally true for the case of the single monk making the two journeys on two separate days.

These two examples demonstrate the importance of trying different representations of a problem and assessing their relative potential for yielding a solution. Visualization provides an alternative means of representing issues, and in this mode novel and significant features of which one was formerly unaware or unconscious may become apparent. However, this is not an either/or issue. In some cases the most efficient strategy employs both kinds of representation. Flexibility of representation is therefore desirable in effective problem solving.

Unfortunately a number of factors combine to make flexible representation difficult to achieve in practice. Gellatly identifies these as a person's *mental set* - that is, those mental habits acquired over the years which result in them becoming set in their ways, or rigid in attitude; *functional fixedness*, or the tendency to represent objects in terms of their function, which may be limiting, as was demonstrated by Maier (1931), who found that the tendency to think of pliers in terms of their usual function makes it difficult for some people to perceive their potential as a pendulum bob; and *smuggled assumptions*, unnecessary delimiting assumptions or negative thoughts which greatly reduce the likelihood of a solution.

Individuals vary in the extent to which these factors influence their thinking, with the result that some are considerably more flexible in their representations than others. Nevertheless, a major limiting factor in attaining flexibility of representation is the predominance of the verbal mode within Western culture, which ensures that for most people in the West visual representation is relatively less well developed. The focus of Western psychology on verbal processes also accounts for its relatively undeveloped understanding of imaginative processes. Cognitive psychology is largely preoccupied with processes that are verbal, or at least verbalizable. Shepard (1977) attributes this to the former ascendancy of behaviourism with its preference for overt responses, or responses which, if not overtly verbal can be readily made so. Whereas thoughts embodied in words and propositions have this property, mental images often do not.

Despite a general weakening of behaviouristic strictures this preoccupation continues, 'reinforced now by the dazzling emergence from linguistics of the inherently discrete formalisms of generative grammar and semantics, by the almost total dependence of work in artificial intelligence on computers designed for sequential manipulation of discrete symbols, and perhaps by the antimentalistic writings of such philosophers as Wittgenstein (1953) and Ryle (1949).' Shepard acknowledges that if mental images are at most subjective epiphenomena that play little or no functional role in significant processes of human thought, as some commentators such as Pylyshyn (1973) suggest, then the scientific study of mental imagery ought to be judged of little consequence, but he admits to being uneasy about making this assumption since imagery seems to have played such a central role in the origin of the most creative ideas of many illustrious scientists, inventors and writers.

He points to two particular lines of scientific and technological development of far-reaching significance in which mental imagery appears to have played a prominent role; electromagnetic field theory, and the theory and application of molecular structures.

The role of imagery in the development of electro-magnetic field theory

The modern conception of electric and magnetic fields has its origin in the mind of Michael Faraday, who without the benefit of any mathematical education beyond 'the merest elements of arithmetic' (Tyndall, 1868) was able to find a large number of general results requiring of others, as Helmholtz later observed with great astonishment, 'the highest powers of mathematical analysis'. And he succeeded in doing this, according to Helmholtz, 'by a kind of intuition, with the security of instinct, without the help of a single mathematical formula' (quoted in Kendall, 1955) (Shepard 1977, p.193)

Faraday's description of invisible lines of force as narrow tubes curving through space which 'rose up before him like things' (Koestler, 1964) suggests that the kind of intuition he employed was that of visualization, and as Hadamard (1945) observes, it was this ability to see in his inner eye which guided him to the invention of the dynamo and electric motor.

His successor, James Clerk Maxwell, also reported having developed the habit of 'making a mental picture of every problem' (Beveridge, 1957, p.56). He arrived at his formal equations only at the end of a series of elaborately visualized models.

The present-day reformulation of electro-magnetic theory originated in Einstein's 'gedanken' or thought experiments in which, as a result of imagining travelling alongside a beam of light, he realised that the stationary spatial oscillation he 'saw' corresponded neither to anything that could be perceptually experienced as light, nor to anything described by Maxwell's equations.

Einstein later stated quite explicitly in a letter to Hadamard that words played no part in his thinking, but 'certain signs and more or less clear images' (Inglis, 1987). He explained that his particular ability didn't lie in mathematical calculation either, but rather in 'visualizing ... effects, consequences and possibilities' (Holton, 1972, p.110). He also told his biographer Reiser that the 'gift of fantasy has meant more to me than my talent for absorbing information'.

Jacques Hadamard, in his study of creativity among mathematicians (1945) found that they often relied on their ability to exploit imagery in this way, usually through visual imagery but often in kinetic or auditory images.

The Yugoslavian electrical engineer Nikola Tesla, who developed the transformer, generator and dynamo, also used visualization to experiment with his inventions, which enabled him to test the turbine in his mind and in the laboratory. In this way he 'saw' the alternating current, and the self-starting induction motor, and the polyphase electrical system upon which it depends came to him in the form of vivid imagery of a rotating magnetic field (Hunt and Draper, 1964).

Shepard (1977) observes that spatial visualizations seem to have figured heavily in the geometrical conceptions of the complex electric and magnetic fields underlying the invention of the cyclotron, for which E. O. Lawrence was awarded the Nobel Prize, and the alternating gradient synchrotron developed by Nicholas Christofilos.

Imagery in the development of the theory and application of molecular structures

The German chemist Fredrich Kekulé claimed that his insights into the nature of the chemical bond and molecular structure, which form the basis of molecular theory, arose from spontaneous kinetic visual images. His cultivation of visionary practice culminated in his celebrated dream in which a snakelike writhing molecule chain suddenly twist into a closed loop as if seizing its own tail prompted him to solve the problem of the structure of benzine, which is fundamental to modern organic chemistry.

Inglis (1987) reports that McClintock solved the problems of the cytology of Neurospora, which had baffled distinguished geneticists for years, in the same way; and Shepard observes that not only did visualization lead to the cracking of the genetic code (Watson 1968), but is also crucial to the everyday work of many chemists.

Visual imagery and literature

Hadamard (1945) suggests that the construction of verbal or symbolic outputs may also be guided by non-verbal images of schemata that capture what he termed 'the physiognomy of the problem', and there are clear indications that this is frequently the case in various forms of literary endeavour and creativity. Indeed, it is well established that imagery is important to much creative output (Inglis 1987). Charles Dickens (quoted in McKellar 1968) insisted 'I don't invent it, really do not, but "see" it and write it down', and Robert Louis Stevenson, Lewis Carroll and Wordsworth acknowledged a similar debt to visualization. Coleridge's poem *Kubla Khan* came to him effortlessly and involuntarily, and his statement that 'all of the images rose up before him as things' (Ghiselin 1952, p.85) bears a striking resemblance to that of Faraday. The poems of William Blake were produced in a similar way, and Shepard indicates that many contemporary novels are claimed by their authors to have been developed entirely out of 'pictures in the mind'.

Imagery, mental rehearsal and sport

Imagery is frequently employed in mental rehearsal of an activity and its effects are well documented among athletes (Kiesler 1984), and other sports persons, who mentally rehearse every part of a race or competition. As a result imagery and visualization are widely promoted by sports psychologists.

The benefits of imagery are also well-attested in overcoming competitors' anxieties and self-doubts, and in training themselves to perform automatically. Recently former athlete David Jenkins attributed his failure to add an Olympic gold medal to his other sporting achievements to his inability to 'see' it happen.

As Shepard (1977) indicates, these anecdotal reports from various fields do not establish that mental images actually played the crucial *functional* role attributed to them by scientists, authors and others, but they nevertheless suggest that 'until we possess a more complete and satisfactory theory of the creative process, we run the risk of missing something of potential importance if we take it for granted that visual imagery is of no significance' (p.194).

The fundamental question which remains to be answered is, 'what is a mental image?'

The nature of mental imagery

Current controversy regarding mental imagery focuses on two closely related issues; namely whether mental images play a significant functional role in human thinking, or whether they are merely epiphenomenal accompaniments of underlying processes of a very different, less pictorial character; and the nature of mental images and the physical processes which underlie them in the brain. The problem which makes these questions difficult to resolve empirically, or even to clarify conceptually, is that despite attempts to externalise them, mental images are inherently internal. Nevertheless, Shepard and his collaborators have, as a result of extensive research in this field, thrown significant light on these issues.

They have demonstrated that mental images can substitute for perceptual images and answer questions about objects just as well when those objects are merely imagined as when they are directly perceived. In studies using two-dimensional shapes (Shepard and Chapman 1970), spectral colours (Shepard and Cooper 1975), one-digit numbers, represented as Arabic numerals, printed English names and patterns of dots (Shepard et al. 1975), familiar faces, odours and musical sounds (Shepard 1975), no statistically significant difference has been found between conditions in which objects were physically presented or only imagined, and in both conditions the subjects based their judgments on identifiable physical properties of these objects.

These studies suggest that subjects perform very similar mental processes in the perceptual and imaginal conditions and that these processes operate on properties of the relevant objects even when those objects are not physically present.

Cooper and Shepard (1973) also found that subjects respond to a test character in a rotated orientation with the same speed and accuracy when they prepare for the test by merely imagining the character in the appropriate orientation as when an actual outline of the character, already appropriately rotated, is physically presented to them. The finding that a purely mental image that is internally generated and transformed is virtually as effective as an external comparison stimulus already provided in that orientation is, they suggest, perhaps the most direct evidence available for a functional equivalence between imagery and perception.

Dynamic visual imagery

Thus far research has only considered static images, yet scientists' self-reports suggest the possibility of performing dynamic operations with images, and that it is this which confers upon them most of their creative power. Tesla, Lawrence, Kekulé and Watson have all referred to rotations of visualizations in space. Helmholtz (cited in Warren and Warren, 1968, pp.252-4) is quite explicit that

> without it being necessary, or even possible to describe [an object] in words ... we can clearly imagine all the perspective images which we may expect upon viewing from this or that side.

Shepard and co-researchers found that under a broad range of conditions the time required to carry out an imagined operation in space increases - often in a remarkably linear manner - with the extent of the spatial transformation; for example, with angle in the case of rotation, and this is equally true whether the mental operation is performed in the presence of the transformed physical object or in the imagination only. They take this as supporting the notion that mental transformation is carried out over a path that is the internal analog of the corresponding physical transformation of the external object (Cooper 1975; Cooper and Shepard 1973; Metzler and Shepard 1974; Shepard and Metzler 1971).

Moreover, by measuring reaction times to variously oriented test stimuli presented during the course of mental rotation they have established more directly that the intermediate stages of the internal process do indeed have a one-to-one correspondence with intermediate orientations of the external object. Their results show there is actually something rotating during the course of a mental rotation, namely the orientation in which the corresponding external stimulus, if it were to be presented, would be most rapidly discriminated from other possible stimuli.

Shepard argues that the internal process that represents the transformation of an external object, just as much as the internal process that represents the object itself, is in large part the same, whether the transformation or the object is merely imagined or actually perceived.

Accordingly he proposes that imagery is an analogical or analog process in which the internal states have a one-to-one correspondence to appropriate intermediate states in the external world. Thus, to imagine an object such as a complex molecule rotated in a different orientation is to perform an analog process in that halfway through the process the internal state corresponds to the external object in an orientation halfway between the initial and final orientations.

These analog processes, he suggests, are particularly effective in dealing with complex structures and operations of such structures. As Galton (1883, p.113) observed, 'a visual image is the most perfect form of mental representation, wherever shape, position and relation of objects in space are concerned.' Thus by imagining various objects and their transformations in space one can explore many possibilities without taking the time, making the effort or running the risk of carrying out those operations in physical reality.

The implications of these findings are that images are now believed to generate similar, albeit not necessarily identical internal response states as the actual stimuli themselves. Thus, for instance, during visual imagery the visual cortex is normally activated, although the more peripheral visual pathways such as the pupil may or may not be involved.

Imagery and health

The sixteenth century French essayist Montaigne declared that 'a powerful imagination begets the thing itself', observing that 'every one is struck by it, and some knocked down', and admitted to being one of those who felt its 'strong arm'.

> The sight of another's anguish gives me physical anguish, and my senses often usurp the sensations of a third person. A perpetual cough in another irritates my lungs and throat ... I catch the malady which gives me concern, and it takes root in me. I do not wonder that imagination brings on fevers and death in those who give it a free hand and encourage it (*The Essays of Montaigne*, trans. Trechmann).

He was in no doubt as to the effects of the imagination on health:

> We sweat, we tremble, we turn pale and blush through the shock of our imagination, and lying back in our feather-bed we feel our body agitated by its power, sometimes to the point of expiring.

He tells of a woman who became ill and died as the result of a practical joker telling her she had eaten a 'cat-pasty', and observes that 'going through the motions' of a process is sufficient to produce exactly that effect physically by loosening of the bowels.

On the positive side, however, he recognised the role of the imagination in healing, indicating that mental rehearsal could cure impotence, and detailing the placebo effect. In so doing Montaigne anticipated understanding of the role of the imagination in health and illness by some four hundred years.

It is now widely accepted that people may experience full-blown physiological responses to intense imagery. The Russian mnemonist Shereshevskii, for example, could increase his heart rate by imagining himself running, and could alter the size of his pupils and his cochlear reflex by imagining sights and sounds. Jacobsen (1929) demonstrated that subtle tensions of small muscles or sense organs accompany imagery, and it has since been shown that appropriate motor neurons are activated by visualization of a particular body movement. Simply imagining eating a lemon has a direct effect on the production of the salivary glands (Barber et al. 1964); and intense sexual and phobic imagery is accompanied by dramatic physiological changes (Kazdin & Wilcoxin 1975). Imagining noxious stimuli has been associated with physiological arousal as measured by heart rate, muscle tension and skin resistance levels (Lichstein and Lipshitz 1982), and muscle tension has also been found to increase in those who imagine lifting progressively heavy weights (Shaw 1946).

Barber (1978) suggests that images can elicit changes in blood sugar levels, gastrointestinal activity and blister formation, and investigations by Schneider, Smith, Whitcher and Hall (cited in Achterberg 1985) have suggested that imagery is also capable of controlling aspects of immune functioning. Similarly Siegel (1986) indicates that regular visualization can improve white blood cell response and the efficiency of hormone responses to standard tests of physiological stress, increasing the number of white blood cells in circulation and levels of thymosin-alpha I, a hormone especially important to T-helper cells.

Achterberg (1985) indicates that imagining a pleasant non-threatening situation is commonly used for slowing a pounding heart, lowering blood pressure and achieving homeostatic balance. Conversely, memory images of negative childhood experiences are accompanied by changes in heart rate, galvanic skin response, respiration and eye movements (Schwartz 1973); and images of sadness, anger and fear can also be differentiated by cardiovascular changes (Jordan and Lenington 1979).

Summarising, the research findings on imagery and physiology Achterberg (1985) states that

- images relate to physiological states
- they may precede or follow physiological changes, indicating both a causative and reactive role
- they can be induced by conscious deliberate behaviours as well as by subconscious acts (such as electrical stimulation of the brain, reverie and dreaming)
- they can be considered as a hypothetical bridge between conscious processing or imagination and physiological change
- they can exhibit influence over the voluntary (peripheral) nervous system, as well as the autonomic system.

She therefore concludes that imagery has both direct and indirect effects on the body, not only on the musculoskeletal system but also on the autonomic or involuntary nervous system, and is in turn affected by these reactions. According to Dossey (1982, p.67) these effects associated with visualization are 'as real as those produced by any drug'. He therefore argues that the processes of the imagination are potent therapeutic agents, as real as drugs or surgical procedures, and thus 'medicine' in the truest sense of the word.

> If your teeth can be set on edge at the thought of a fingernail scraped on a blackboard, or your mouth can water at the thought of a Marmite sandwich, if you can become sexually aroused by erotic fantasies, that mental power can be harnessed. And if you accept ... that the mind plays a very creative part in the formation of disease, so it follows that the mind can play an equally creative part in its eradication (Taylor 1987, p.36).

Possible explanations for the therapeutic function of visualization

Visualization and time sense

How visualization achieves physiological effects remains unclear. It may be supposed that the content of visualization is crucial to changes occurring in the body. So, for example, the experience of warmth may be promoted by imagining a warm sun or blanket. Dossey (1982) insists, however, that the actual image formed in the mind is much less important than might by supposed.

He observes that many people develop the ability to increase the temperature of their hands quite skilfully irrespective of what image they create, even if it is a visualization of frozen hands submerged in snow. He suggests this is possibly because regardless of differences in image content all subjects do one thing similarly which is that they exchange their usual time perception for one in which time ceases to flow. Although they are seeing events unfold in their imagination they have ceased to place them in flowing time. Thus despite changing sequentially these events are not occurring in the normal linear sense; they simply are. Therefore the psychological experience of inner time is annulled. The subject is physiologically calm as well as psychologically serene and in most cases the physiological response accompanying this is an increased temperature in the hands owing to the vasodilation of blood vessels, regardless of imagery.

Dossey observes that most people learn these skills quite easily and come to enjoy the experience of suspended time sense, and when practised regularly these visualization techniques are extremely effective in helping people adapt to a new way of being in which time is judged in ordinary waking consciousness as less urgent, less hectic and anxiety provoking. Thus they go some way to eliminate or reduce features associated with 'hurry sickness' and stress-related disease.

Visualization and lateralization of brain function

Research on lateralization of brain function (Sperry 1962; Gazzaniga 1967; Dimond 1977) suggests that the left hemisphere of the brain has executive function for language and verbal skills and logical sequential processes, whereas the right hemisphere has responsibility for non-verbal imagery, specifically body image, and is predominant in processing emotional information.

Research evidence suggests the pre-frontal lobes or most anterior aspects of the frontal lobes as possible storage areas for images (Nauta 1964). Although the function of these areas remains uncertain they do appear to be involved in memory storage and emotion and to have connections with the limbic system, that area of the brain which processes emotion. Indeed Achterberg (1985) indicates that the fibre pathways are so numerous that the anterior and frontal lobes appear to be an extension of the emotional system itself.

Other studies have suggested that this area is necessary for immediate memory or use by symbolic memory images (Jacobsen 1936). Patients with frontal lobotomy or leucotomy have been found not only to lack emotion but also to be unable to hold symbolic imagery (Meyer and Beck 1954). Further evidence for involvement of other right hemispheric lobes in imagery is provided by Humphrey and Zangwill (1951) who found little or no dreaming, dim waking imagery, and inability to function on tasks requiring visual, olfactory and auditory phenomena in patients with damage to posterior parietal areas of the right brain, and by Critchley (1953), Milner (1968), DeRenzi (1968), Penfield and Perot (1963) and Jackson (1980).

Achterberg points out that these notions of the way in which information is distributed in the brain are in no way inconsistent with holographic theory, which is essentially concerned with the method of transmitting, storing and receiving information. Pribram (1971) insists that neither behaviour nor language function can be adequately explained without a cognitive map or image of some sort, and viewed holographically the image, the behaviour and physiological concommittants are unified aspects of the same phenomenon. Thus belief systems and imagery become critical matters in health.

Achterberg (1985) indicates that by virtue of linguistic communication with others the left hemisphere may be conceptualised as an interface with the external world, while the imagery of the right hemisphere is the medium of communication between consciousness and the inner world of the body. Accordingly 'visualization has been aptly described as a bridge between the different levels of self' (Pelletier 1978, p.51). Nevertheless both systems are integral to health and well-being. Achterberg suggests that because of its implication in emotion the right hemisphere must have direct relationship with the autonomic nervous system. This supposition is supported by the existence of a vast network of neural connections between the right hemisphere and the limbic system. Achterberg also suggests that as the verbal functions of the left hemisphere are one step removed from the autonomic processes, both in evolution and function, messages have to undergo transformation by the right hemisphere into non-verbal or imagerial terminology before they can be understood by the involuntary or autonomic system.

Similarly, before the imagery characteristic of right brain functions can be processed into meaningful logical thought it must be translated by the left hemisphere. The images so intimately connected with physiology, health and disease are preverbal, without a language base except what is available through connections with the left brain. If these connections were to be severed and the left hemisphere thereby destroyed or rendered inaccessible, untranslated images would continue to affect emotions and alter physiology, but without intellectual interpretation. That this does occur is suggested by the disorder *alexithymia* (literally meaning without words for feelings) which has been suggested as a possible source of so-called psychosomatic disorders (Lesser 1981). In this condition emotions and images which remain untranslated are expressed physically in various body systems and may eventually be diagnosed as rheumatoid arthritis, ulcerative colitis, asthma, hives and migraine. Although its aetiology is as yet little understood functional or structural lesions of the cortical connective pathways or disruptions between the limbic system and regions of the cortex, and deficits in basal ganglia have been proposed.

Imaginative medicine: Shamanism

Irrespective of explanations for it, imagery has always played a key role in medicine. Levi-Strauss observed that folk medicine throughout the world is based on vivid imagery, and Achterberg (1985) describes shamanism - the oldest and most widely used system of healing in the world - as the medicine of the imagination.

For shamans, who have no direct knowledge of anatomy and physiology, images are as much a physiological reality as any other body function, capable of both producing symptoms and disease and curing them. Shamanic healing works directly on the body by creating powerful imagery in the patient. That orthodox medicine does likewise is indicated by Montaigne:

> Why do the physicians begin by playing on the credulity of their patients with so many false promises of cure, if not to the end that the power of imagination may assist the imposture of their decoction? (*The Essays of Montaigne*, trans. Trechmann, p.98).

Moreover, such a phenomenon is not confined to people of the early and middle ages. Dossey (1982) describes a contemporary American doctor 'pitting his medicine against that of an adversary' by conducting a 'de-hexing' ceremony, and thereby successfully curing a patient who was dying in response to a shaman's spell. Achterberg (1985, p.3) also points to those who travel to Lourdes in search of miracle cures, or cross from the USA into Mexico to obtain unproven remedies, and those who respond positively to placebos. She suggests that:

> the common features of these events - the mental rehearsals, the voodoo curses, visits to religious and medical shrines and response to placebos - is that they all serve to alter the *images* or the expectancy that the persons hold regarding their state of health. And in doing so, the images cause profound physiological change, a fact that must not be obscured by the glamour of modern medicine. Regardless of technological advancement, we will always have to contend with this vast complex of expectancies, beliefs, motivations, and the sometimes belligerent, sometimes miraculous, role of the imagination.

Although throughout the history of medicine imagination has been used to diagnose and treat disease the role of the imagination is all too frequently ignored or overlooked in conventional Western medicine. However, as Achterberg indicates, imagery plays a tacit role in even the most orthodox medical practice. It is an ever-present variable in matters of health, which although maybe not acknowledged, manipulated or used in any systematic way in treatment and diagnosis is nonetheless a critical determinant of health. It is not only a natural concomitant of healing, but is also involved in every interaction health care professionals have with their patients.

Bodily sensations summon images of internal landscapes, and as Achterberg observes, everyone forms mental images through a cognitive assessment of symptoms, and often an avalanche of symptoms follow. Hence a sore throat is easily imagined as cancer, and as the image takes over the throat tightens further as a result of anxiety and becomes more painful.

Diagnosis also sets the imagination in motion. Not uncommonly people die through the power of the imagination, (as in voodoo) or fail to do so because they have not recognised their condition as deadly. Indeed studies show that those who cannot comprehend the messages conveyed by society and its medicine die of different causes from those who can. Achterberg, Collerain and Craig (1978) demonstrated that death rates from cancer in mental retardates are consistently significantly low, only 4 per cent compared with 15-18 per cent in the population at large. Similar results in other studies suggest that the natural course of disease may be different when there is no expectancy of outcome.

Achterberg also points to the omnipotence of the medical profession in creating imagery, which can determine life or death independent of any medical intervention.

Images are also created by statistics such as those provided by government and medical bodies, and the media.

Increasingly however, techniques which rely on use of the imagination are being considered within medicine, as their potential of psychological and physical well-being are recognised. Achterberg describes the pioneers of visualization in modern practice as 'shaman-scientists', trying to bridge the gulf between worlds; not only the inner and outer worlds of the patient, but also the different realms of magic and modern medicine.

Imagery and psychotherapy

Visualization provides an alternative means of representing issues, and when various aspects or the self are represented in this way it may become a means of accessing the unconscious, and is therefore an important tool of self-discovery and creative change.

Long before lateralization of brain function and relevant physiology were understood, shamans, and the healers of ancient Egypt and Greece recognised that visualization offers a means of discovering the dynamics of mind, the symbolic discourse between mental events, and between mind and body.

Like others before him, Freud perceived this, describing dreams, which are a rich source of visual imagery, as the 'royal road to the unconscious'. Jung also saw the importance of dreams and everyday fantasy, but he disagreed with Freud that the dream is a facade behind which its meaning lies hidden, 'a meaning already known but maliciously, so to speak, withheld from consciousness' (1972, p.185). For Jung the dream harbours no intent to deceive, but expresses something as best it can, although the person may fail to recognise this through self-deception or lack or perception. Jung therefore avoided all theoretical points of view and helped people to understand their dream images without the application of rules and theory. He claimed that he knew of no technique that might fathom these inner processes other than paying close attention to fantasies, amplifying them and committing them to memory through sculpture and art.

Guided imagery

Carl Happich (1932), like Jung, saw symbolic consciousness as the point of departure for all creative production, and therefore all healing. Indeed, this connection between the processes of artistic creation and psychotherapy has been apparent throughout the history of psychology. Happich therefore explored the therapeutic possibilities of symbolic expression through guided imagery and meditation. Guided imagery, which can be likened to a waking dream, is a process in which a person guided by another creates in the imagination a new experience for themself. Its purpose is to create an experience for the client which, at least in part if not in its entirety, has not been previously represented in his model or cognitive 'map'. Thus guided imagery is most appropriately used when the person's representation is too impoverished to offer an adequate number of choices for coping in a given area. Bandler and Grinder (1975) indicate that it serves as a therapeutic tool in two ways: by presenting the client with an experience which is the basis for representation in his model where previously there had been none, or inadequate representation, it provides a guide for future behaviour and coping in this area; and it provides the therapist with an experience which he can use to challenge the client's presently impoverished model.

A similar technique was used by Desoille (1945). He held that when journeying through the landscapes of the imagination a person can relate to his own symbolism and can discover in it ways of dealing with the problems of life. He claimed that the person can learn to control and overcome fear of the archetypal imagery within himself, and in so doing can comprehend and resolve his personal conflicts within the larger context of man's inherent problems.

The goal of his technique was to direct the patient towards fulfillment of his potentialities through the creative development of basic biological impulses into a larger harmonic order.

Walter Frederking (1948) used a technique of deep relaxation and symbolism in which he stimulated the unconscious to spontaneous production of various kinds. He directed patients in progressive physical relaxation and fantasy, during the course of which they progressed from unclear visions to increasingly clear productions of a kind of 'symbolic strip thought' (Kretschmer 1969), which were followed scene by scene with the patient as both playwright and actors. In this way Frederking believed the person could directly confront the contents of his personal unconscious and relate them directly and dramatically to his psychic problems. He claimed this meeting with generally unrecognised aspects of oneself brings about a healing through various transforming symbols:

> In dreams and symbols man is led through every sphere of the psyche, during which
> the forms of the psychic force are unable to restore themselves without the use of
> other means and deep-going transformations are effected.

Friedrich Mauz (1948) used a related technique with psychotic patients. By way of monologue, he depicted the patient in representative pictures from childhood, the aim being to unlock and enliven suppressed emotions so that a meaningful conversation could later emerge. He also led patients to an imaginary meadow infused with symbols which he believed would awaken positive feelings and meanings in the person, and enable them to connect with their feelings and the world around them. He claimed that the creative power which flows from these feelings and symbols aids in closing the breach in the patient's personality thereby effecting healing.

Mauz identified several important principles of his approach. Essentially he regarded the symbolic scene as the effector of therapy, but 'only if it is experienced as real and actual', and if 'the therapist mixes himself into a common solution with the patient'. The latter is achieved by the therapist meditating on the patient, allowing himself to be 'caught up by formulations of their psychic power'. This, he claimed, 'is the mystical unity between the therapist and the sick.'

For Mauz, therefore, the 'simple human relationship' was the highest principle for therapy; an idea, which as Kretschmer (1969) observes, is still far removed from contemporary scientific medicine.

Common to all these approaches is an active provocation of the unconscious, the person being directed to make its creative possibilities available in the healing process. The patient takes an active conscious or oriented part in the healing process, which has the advantage of being quicker and more immediate, and with the patient not ordinarily transferring his problem onto the therapist.

Kretschmer observes, however, that the effectiveness of this approach depends very much on the competence of the therapist. With one a person may experience only the most banal contents of his unconscious, and with another may have a decisive experience of psychic depths. Such skill, he suggests, is not learned as a craft nor in medical or psychological training but develops through relations between therapist and patient.

> Great psychotherapy is unique, and cannot be copied any more than a work of art.
> It is because the work of a master cannot be copied that one can learn from him
> (Kretschmer 1969, p.228)

Imagery in Gestalt Therapy

One such 'master' was undoubtedly Fritz Perls who, like Jung, saw the importance of exploring everyday fantasy as well as dreams, recognising that within them there is a hidden reality which can be discovered and understood. As Stevens (1971, p.6) indicates more can be discovered about this reality if individuals invest themself in their fantasy, becoming aware of their physical feelings, perceptions and responses as they do so. Perls therefore eschewed the interpretation for which Freud is famous and encouraged the individual to reenact or live in the present their dreams and fantasies and so recognise that their every detail is an aspect of themselves, a personal creation for which they are responsible. Perls also made use of guided fantasy or imagery, encouraging the person to imagine a symbol or situation and inviting them to explore it as fully as possible. He recognised that in so doing they project aspects of themself into the material, and within this different representational mode may access features which cannot gain expression in other ways, and of which they may be largely unaware. Even resistance to particular imagery can therefore be highly significant in revealing aspects of the self.

Visualization is a rich source of information about the self, there being no limit on the kinds of imagery that can be created and used. Stevens (1971) provides a fascinating collection of guided imagery which can be employed by individuals, pairs or groups and for a variety of purposes. Similar exercises are provided by Gunther (1979), Schwartz (1980), Gawain (1985), Gallegos (1983), Siegel (1986), Taylor (1987), Achterberg (1985) and Manning (1989).

The richness and variety of imagery which can be used in visualization is complemented by a great range of methods by which these images may be accessed and explored. Perls (1976, p.86) elucidates:

> We can make use in therapy of fantasising and all its increasing states of intensity towards actuality - a verbalised fantasy, or one which is written down, or one which is acted out as psychodrama.

Perls' Gestalt Therapy utilises a variety of approaches, perhaps the best known of which is the empty chair technique whereby an individual visualizes an aspect of himself, another person, object or symbol in an empty chair and conducts an imaginary conversation with it, alternating chairs as it progresses and effectively acting out both sides of the dialogue. Dreams and fantasies are frequently explored in the same way, as well as intrapsychic and interpersonal conflicts.

A related technique requires the person to 'shuttle' or alternate between the manifest content of a fantasy or dream and its associations, which may help them understand its symbolic significance and sharpen their awareness by providing them with a clearer sense of the relationships in their behaviour.

Gestalt Therapy also makes use of monotherapy, a form of dramatization in which a person acts out every aspect of a dream or fantasy enabling them to identify with and take responsibility for it.

By requiring the person to create and enact his own stage, characters and props, and to direct and orchestrate every performance 'monotherapy thus avoids the contamination of the precepts of others, which are usually present in ordinary psychodrama' (Perls 1976, p.86).

Psychodrama

Psychodrama, developed by the Viennese psychiatrist Jacob Moreno, is a widely used psychotherapeutic method in which a principal actor or protagonist dramatizes his problems and conflicts in the company of several auxiliaries under the direction of a therapist, who assumes overall responsibility for the drama, and employs a number of techniques in facilitating the dramatic process.

One such technique is soliloquy whereby the protagonist verbalizes aloud his feelings to the audience. In another technique known as mirroring members of the group mimic or exaggerate the protagonist's behaviour as a means of providing him with effective feedback. Role playing, play acting and play in general have been developed into various forms of therapy, and methods utilising imagination are widely used in group therapy, bodywork and individual counselling.

Art therapies

Other approaches which employ imagery include the arts in their various forms, which being concerned with the expression of consciousness were recognised as having therapeutic significance by the ancients of Greece, Egypt and Rome. Art therapies may involve free drawing, painting, sculpture and other forms. They

> are concerned with art as subjective experience, as a tool of consciousness, as part of personal life and growth. In many cases they use art in a curative way to release blocked and stunted capacities for experience and feeling, but this is more than an act of healing: it is also an act or liberation (Anderson 1977, p.xv).

These therapies have advantages over conventional psychotherapies in being applicable to relatively inarticulate, non-verbal subjects such as very young children, the mentally ill and handicapped. They may also be employed in broaching subjects that are sometimes difficult to talk about such as death, dying and bereavement, guilt and blame. Kubler-Ross (1982) has made extensive use of spontaneous drawings in working with the terminally ill, especially children, and the bereaved.

Recognition of the power of these visualization techniques in the externalization of feelings has led to their application in the commercial field, notably advertising. Here what is termed 'psychodrawing', in which feelings are drawn using shapes, colour or symbols, modelled in clay, or mimed, is increasingly being used to explore unconscious associations to advertised products including medicines (Branthwaite and Cooper 1989).

Criticism of imagery

That visualization can be highly effective in the development of insight and resolution of inner conflicts and problems is beyond doubt, but it is not without its critics. One objection is that the energy expended in fantasy would be better utilised in coming to terms with reality. However, this fails to acknowledge that for many people their problems arise from our inability to distinguish reality from fantasy, from fantastical ideas of self, others and the world; and imagined threats and fears. Indeed most stressors reside in the imagination, anger often being a response to an imagined insult, and fear to anticipated rather than actual danger.

Ernst and Goodison (1981) suggest that visualization enables individuals to confront and accept the reality of who and what they are, rather than their fantasy ideals, and by exposing and exploring rather than ignoring fantasies prevents people being bound by them. Fantasy can thus be used to contact qualities within the self, to express personal power and potentials, and to enable action in the real world. Accordingly through visualization

> we can move from a situation where dreams frighten us, fantasies dominate our waking lives, and anxieties cut us off from the world, to a situation where we have more of our inner power available to lives creatively in the present.

Inasmuch as visualization facilitates exploration of a person's inner world it may also assist in the development of empathy between client and therapist. McKellar (1989) thus describes images as 'empathy bridges', and considers them of value in the treatment of both neurosis and psychosis.

Visualization and orthodox Western medicine

Insofar as visualization is concerned with integration and therefore wholeness, its applications are not confined to psychotherapy, for as Pelletier (1978, p.252) observes 'where the mind tends to focus the emotions and physiology are likely to follow'. Psychophysiological integration can therefore have a profound effect on the disease process.

Visualization thus has a direct application to health and healing in the broader sense. However, as Achterberg (1985) observes, techniques which rely on the power of the imagination are rarely credited as being essential to the practice of technological medicine, but they are at least considered to be useful to the patient's well-being. This has come about largely as a result of the pioneering work of Carl Simonton, a radiation oncologist, and his wife, psychotherapist Stephanie Matthews-Simonton, who applied the uses of visualization in the treatment of cancer.

Their approach attempts to use visualization as a means of dealing with both the patient's stress and their belief system. Their theory is that both can be modified to good effect by a combination of relaxation and visualization. They argue that since stress has been shown to depress the immune system, stress reduction through relaxation may be one way of restoring the body's ability to overcome invasive viruses and mutant cells. Furthermore, the belief system of the patient, which they regard as a major factor in the causation of health and illness, can also be explored through a combination of relaxation and imagery. They propose that the first step in getting well is to understand how beliefs and emotional responses contribute to illness. The next is to find ways of influencing those responses in support of treatment (1978, p.128). They insist that relaxation and mental imagery are among the most valuable tools for helping patients learn to believe in their ability to recover from cancer. Therefore not only is visualization an effective motivational tool for recovering health but an important tool for self-discovery and creative change.

In addition to decreasing tension and effecting physiological changes, enhancing the immune system and altering the course of malignancy, they regard visualization as important in confronting hopelessness and helplessness by decreasing a patient's fear, especially that of being out of control; and by enabling them to gain a sense of control, to recognise their role in regaining health; in bringing about attitude changes and strengthening the will to live; and in communicating with the unconscious where beliefs antithetical to health may be buried.

Their method involves instructing patients to relax three times daily while mentally picturing their cancer being destroyed and disposed of by their body's immune system.

Patients are first taught a simple form of relaxation which focuses on breathing. Each person is instructed to repeat silently the word 'relax' and to let go of tensions in various muscle complexes which are typically responsive to stress by focusing on them in turn. Once this is achieved the patient visualizes a pleasant scene and is encouraged to hold this in mind. Then they are asked to visualize their illness in any way it appears to them, and to visualize the form of treatment they are receiving. The cancer is then visualized as shrinking or otherwise responding in a positive way to treatment. The patient is also encouraged to visualize pain in the same way rather than trying to suppress it.

Of 159 patients initially treated by the Simontons with a diagnosis of medically incurable malignancy, none of whom were expected to live more than a year, twenty made a full recovery, the disease regressed in a further 22 per cent, and the average survival time was increased by a factor of 1.5-2. In addition, those who eventually succumbed to the malignancy maintained higher than usual levels of activity and achieved a significant improvement in their quality of life.

There has since been abundant anecdotal evidence which appears to confirm the Simontons' claim that, as adjuncts to orthodox therapy, relaxation and visualization have an important role to play in the treatment of cancer, and in improving the quality of life of patients suffering terminal illness. Empirical support has been provided by Fiore (1974); and Meares (1981) who has demonstrated that visualization has effects including cancer regression. Bradley and McCann (1981) found that guided imagery and visualization provided cancer patients with considerable pain reduction and relief from nausea, and Donovan (1980) has found visualization effective in reducing the side effects of chemotherapy. Compared with a control group those using visualization had a significant reduction in nausea, vomiting and anxiety, and improved function in everyday living. Lyles et al (1982) also found visualization effective in reducing the aversiveness of cancer chemotherapy, and in a study of eighteen patients with different forms of cancer and varying chemotherapy treatment, Walker (reported by Harley 1989) found 'nausea management training' employing visualization had good results. Similar successes have been reported by Brohn at the Bristol Cancer Help Centre (Harley 1989).

Nevertheless there is a need for further carefully controlled studies. Although the results of ongoing evaluative studies are not yet available, the Simontons' methods have been widely adopted in the USA and Europe, and promoted enthusiastically by orthodox practitioners such as Dossey (1982) and Siegel (1986), and more cautiously by Sikora (reported by Harley 1989).

Achterberg and Lawlis (1978) have researched and practised imagery in a variety of health care settings for over a decade 'in the belief that the shamanic techniques that served the world so well in medicine since the beginning of recorded history should not be discarded but improved on' (Achterberg 1985, p.101-2). They claim it has been validated on patients suffering chronic pain, severe orthopaedic trauma, rheumatoid arthritis, cancer, diabetes, burn injury, alcoholism, stress related disorders, and in childbirth. They point to many direct applications of imagery to health, including biofeedback, autogenic training and natural childbirth, and also to its use in general medical practice.

Visualization: practice and problems

Achterberg (1985) claims it is necessary to relax deeply before visualization so that motor responses, thoughts and external stimuli don't compete with the production of imagery. She observes that for this reason Jacobsen's method of progressive relaxation is notably inefficient for imagery production. She claims that almost any kind of relaxation is adequate, providing that it is not too wordy and not longer than twenty minutes. She also claims that the setting is important and should not generate or increase anxiety and that for this reason hospital settings are generally unsuitable. The author's experience does not altogether agree with Achterberg other than in the latter respect, inasmuch as deep relaxation is not found to be necessary prior to visualization. In most subjects absorption in imagery is found to promote relaxation and this, it is suggested, is a significant factor for those in whom pain prevents progressive physical relaxation. Moreover, the wordiness' of relaxation methods would appear to be irrelevant, given that in progressive relaxation most subjects spontaneously 'turn off' these external stimuli.

Nevertheless some people are, as Galton first noted in 1883, more 'visile' than others and those whose visual imagery is not strong often find difficulty in generating images or holding them in detail. Generally these difficulties can be overcome with practice, but those whose visualization remains weak should not be obliged to use visual imagery and encouraged to use the representational mode with which they feel most comfortable.

For some mind-wandering is a problem and can be aggravated by certain medical conditions and pain. The Simontons insist that the most effective way of dealing with the problem, is for the individual to confront it directly and to explore the reasons behind it. For some it may reflect a strong fear of the disease and lack of the body's ability to overcome it naturally and normally.

Others may feel that visualization which involves their cancer shrinking when they have been told it is actually growing constitutes lying. The Simontons indicate that it is important to emphasise that what is being visualised is the desired outcome rather than what is happening at the time. Therefore 'mental imagery is not a method of self-deception; it is a means of self-direction' (1978, p.139).

Some people feel reluctant to engage in the process of visualization because they feel that it is wrong for them to relax and 'indulge' themselves in this way; and, as Siegel (1986) points out 'many people do not actually want to get well', illness being for them a socially acceptable form of suicide.

Fricker (1977, p.59) makes a similar observation

> In some cases a patient has taken refuge in illness because it gives him a good reason for being able to avoid the responsibility and difficulty of living. Sometimes life has treated a person so cruelly that he cannot face any further pain, and the only solution is to escape into illness (1977 p.59).

Resistance of this kind, together with negative attitudes and strong negative expectancies, need to be identified at the onset of treatment to avoid them generating negative outcomes. In this regard it is also of considerable importance to establish the nature of the imagery employed by an individual.

Criteria for mental imagery

Achterberg and Lawlis (1978), in association with the Simontons, have drawn up a list of tentative criteria that can be used to evaluate the content of a person's mental imagery. They observe that representing cancer cells as ants, or as eggs in an incubator, is generally negative, suggesting as it does the likely proliferation of the disease. Similarly, crabs and other crustaceans which are tenacious and have hard impregnable shells generally symbolise the potency of the disease.

Negative expectancies may also underlie images of treatment. For example, chemotherapy may be conceived as yellow pills being greedily consumed by a large black rat, the cancer being imagined as strong and invasive and the treatment as weak and impotent.

The Simontons recognise that mental imagery involves a highly personal, symbolic language, and that the emotional meaning of any one symbol will vary greatly from one individual to another. One person's image of strength and power may be another's image of weakness. Given such variation it is important to explore a person's imagery with them, rather than impose meaning on it. The meaning of their imagery may not be readily apparent to the individual, and the Simontons observe that in order to translate the beliefs inherent in it, one must 'try on' the image to discover its meaning. Free drawing and other means of exploring imagery may be valuable in facilitating discussion and understanding.

Notwithstanding individual differences in imagery, the Simontons claim that positive images usually have certain qualitative features: the cancer cells being depicted as weak and confused, something soft which can be broken down, and the treatment strong and powerful; the healthy cells having no difficulty in repairing any slight damage treatment may do; the 'army' of white blood cells vast and overwhelming cancer cells. The white cells are aggressive, eager to 'do battle', quick to seek out cancer cells and destroy them. Dead cancer cells are flushed away from the body normally and naturally. By the end of the imagery the person sees themself healthy and free of cancer, reaching their goals in life and fulfilling their life's purpose.

They point out that those who succeed in overcoming their cancer have imagery which matches these criteria. However, they indicate that no person's imagery starts out containing all these elements. Their fantasy needs to be guided so as to enable them to discover strong enough images to capture a new positive expectancy. It is especially important in overcoming malignancy that the most powerful imagery is that relating to the white blood cells - the person's own natural defence system - rather than chemotherapy. The white cell imagery must be at least as vivid as that of the cancer cells but more numerous and powerful. The imagery of the cancer cells being flushed from the body must also be very vivid. Additionally, treatment must be visualized as a friend or ally. Patients are therefore encouraged to personalise it, giving chemotherapy or machinery used in radiotherapy a name. The Simontons suggest that this helps to reduce the side-effects of treatment, and a similar claim is also made by Siegel (1986), and Brohm (as reported by Harley 1989).

Given the need for vivid imagery the Simontons recommend that of white dogs (white cells) voraciously eating mincemeat (the cancer), and licking the area clean. However, it would seem that the Simontons don't apply their own dictum here, as their suggested imagery is somewhat ambiguous, particularly to non-dog lovers or those who might have received a dog bite and fear that animals with such voracious appetites might then 'turn on' them.

Indeed, much of the imagery recommended by the Simontons may provoke ambivalent responses. Current thinking is that the early work on imagination in cancer treatment placed too much emphasis on anger, killing and hating, and that some people 'got disgusted with the gore' (Achterberg 1985, p.191). Siegel (1986) is one of those who regards 'the gore' and the absence of the spiritual aspects of healing as shortcomings of the Simontons' approach. He observes that because their initial patient group were servicemen they assumed that everyone would be happy 'attacking' and 'killing' cancer, whereas in his experience many people are profoundly disturbed by the idea of attacking and killing anything, even an invading disease organism. Therefore, the prevailing imagery of warfare is upsetting to such people, even if they are not consciously aware of it. He suggests that words such as 'assault', 'kill', 'insult', 'blast', 'poison', and 'destroy', create conscious and unconscious rejection in some patients, and he relates the case of one, a Quaker, who resolved this by imagining the white blood cells carrying away cancerous cells and gently removing them from the body. Siegel points out that in the case of cancer this latter kind of imagery is perhaps more appropriate because it is the body's own cells gone awry, and therefore, in a sense, a direct aggressive attack on them constitutes an attack on the self.

Manning (1988, 1989) however, emphasises the importance of 'fighting' imagery. He claims that anger is a neutral rather than a negative emotion, and depending on how it is used, positive or negative. He suggests that many people who resist aggressive imagery often confuse anger and assertiveness, and argues that if there is anger within a person and the imagery used is passive than the anger has no release. In his considerable experience those who initially commence with aggressive imagery gradually dilute it as the anger is released, after which it changes spontaneously. He also observes that if the patient is angry they are far more powerful than if passive and this strength may be used for healing.

Visualization and the healing principle

In addition to using visualization directly in the treatment of cancer the Simontons also use visualization to access the healing principle which they believe resides within each person. This they refer to as the centre of the psyche, which they see as influencing, directing and regulating life, and equate with the Freudian notion of the unconscious, or Jung's 'essence' or inner self. They believe that it communicates with the conscious self through feelings, dreams, intuitions and imagery, but that in Western culture, with its emphasis on external events and objects, these messages are undervalued or ignored, with the result that little importance is attached to them. A number of cancer researchers have hypothesised that cancer patients may have become cut off from these unconscious processes, and from their inner resources. Their experience supports such a claim, many of their recovered patients having come to see their illness as, in part, a message to value and pay more attention to their unconscious self and its needs, rather than the demands of others. In addition, many of their patients have described specific insights, dreams or images which have provided valuable guidance in their attempts to overcome illness and regain health. The Simontons therefore teach a process - the 'Inner Guide Visualization' - which is essentially a guided fantasy for tapping these rich resources of strength and healing, and they provide numerous anecdotal accounts of those who have overcome cancer by following the advice of their inner guide.

However, as Siegel (1986) points out, getting well is not the only goal in the employment of visualization methods. He suggests that even more important is their role in helping people to live without fear and to be at peace with life, and ultimately, death. In this regard they can be of great assistance in improving the quality of life of the terminally ill and dying, helping them to complete their unfinished business, and to live their remaining life to the full, without fear or guilt. He provides accounts of his work in this field, but perhaps the most thorough account of the application of these methods to chronic and terminal illness is provided by Kubler-Ross (1982), who is internationally famous for her research in this area and for her practical healing workshops on life, death and transition.

Visualization and pain

Oscar Wilde observed that 'Nothing in the world is meaningless, suffering least of all'. Nevertheless 'medical civilisation tends to turn pain into a technical problem and thereby to deprive suffering of its inherent personal meaning' (Illich 1975, p.93). Accordingly pain is stripped of its subjective dimensions and objectified. It is controlled by the physician rather than approached in a way that might enable the person in pain to take responsibility for their experience, or to recognise its significance. Yet as Schwartz (1980) observes,

> Pain is a marvelous alarm system. It is not something to avoid but in fact a short-circuit designed to know when something is out of harmony - something to recognize and deal with.

He points out that the Tibetans take the view that pain will diminish of its own accord if heeded.

However, until recently most Western neurosurgeons took the view that the only way to prevent pain was to cut something. They regarded a pain pathway as like a telephone system in which the wires have to be cut if a message is to be prevented. Accordingly they frequently treated chronic pain by severing nerves, the nerve root or spinal cord, and even - when all else failed - by amputating limbs, so convinced were they that pain was really 'out there'. These views were overturned by the psychologist Ronald Melzack, who with physiologist Patrick Wall proposed a new theory of pain in 1965, and provided a new neuroscientific model which bridged psychology and biology. On the basis of his doctoral research Melzack recognised that the simple 'connect-the-dot' theory of pain transmission was inadequate, and that something more existed between the dots. He found that dogs could have injuries and not feel pain, and this led him to conclude that pain is multi-dimensional, being at once emotional and cognitive, involving attention, memories, emotions, expectations, indoctrination by training, and not merely a purely sensory experience.

Perceiving a stimulus as painful therefore depends on a number of factors, some of which, like stress, anxiety and depression, can make the pain more perceptible, while others like relaxation and distraction, work in reverse to make it less so. Through contact with pain sufferers Melzack also found that pain often has little survival value, and untreated can often take on a life of its own. Some pains are entirely out of proportion to the degree of tissue damage, and persist long after injured tissues have healed: 'Like a broken car horn, they may not be blaring any useful warning' (Warga 1987, p.53).

He speculated that a very rapidly conducting pathway exists that does not itself produce conscious experience but activates memories of past experience that interact with other pathways. These effectively tell the other components which incoming signals are important and which are not. Thus signals coming down from the brain can stop signals coming from other peripheral pathways at very early junctures or synapses in the spinal cord so that sensory information does not get through to the brain and is not felt. Melzack suggests that this is why footballers can sometimes play for hours with a broken leg; their attention and their implicit criteria for what is important and what isn't in a given situation 'close the gate' on incoming signals and do not let the pain pass through major transmission centres in the spinal cord. This also explains paradoxes such as the fact that some 65 per cent of men wounded in battle feel no pain whatever, yet complain of painful injections (Warga 1987), and victims of stabbing invariably feel no pain at the time of their injury. Ironically therefore a 'shot' can hurt more than actually being shot, and a 'stabbing' pain produce greater anguish than being knifed.

The central tenets of Melzack and Wall's Gate Theory of pain concern pain modulation, or the inhibition of incoming pain, and they are now widely supported by research evidence. The theory led both directly and indirectly to the discovery of the body's own natural opiate receptors and pain suppression centres, and to new treatments based on these, which are being exploited by health and sports psychologists who are training patients in a variety of cognitive techniques to control pain.

As a result a great deal is now known about the nature of pain, but much of this has not reached those who routinely deal with people in pain. Melzack (cited by Warga 1987) indicates that medical students and dentists are taught practically nothing about pain and receive no information on chronic pain syndromes, and that as a result many patients, especially children and cancer patients, suffer unnecessary pain because of outmoded medical training and information.

The Simontons' methods of dealing with pain in cancer patients are adapted from those developed by modern pain researchers. They use three imaginal processes specifically for managing persistent pain which include visualizing the body's healing forces, visualizing pain, and communicating with it.

Empirical evidence for the role of visualization in pain control is provided by Kenner and Achterberg (1983). They studied the effect of imagery on patients with major burn injuries, and found that a combination of relaxation and imagery was more successful than other methods in reducing muscle tension and patients' need for pain medication and sedatives, which suggests they had learned mental techniques for pain control.

Imagery has also been used systematically in childbirth for a number of purposes including relaxation, fear reduction and pain control. Grantley Dick-Read, who developed methods of natural childbirth, devoted a chapter of his *Childbirth Without Fear* (1942) to the discussion of imagery. He emphasised that if attitudes and imagery are changed, then body processes are dramatically affected, and thus the experience of childbirth.

Lamaze, a French gynaecologist, subsequently developed a method of 'painless childbirth', claiming that pain can be eliminated through a combination of positive attitude and imagery, but according to Melzack the promise is not fulfilled and there is no dramatic reduction of pain even if the woman feels positive about the method. However, research reveals that pain levels are lowered consistently by about 30 per cent (Warga 1987), which is not inconsiderable, and possibly comparable with other methods of pain control.

Imagery: its current status in orthodox medicine

Imagery has found a warm reception among nurses, especially in the USA where it is increasing taught as part of nurse training, largely as a result of the work of Krieger (1975,81), and Johnson, who has used modifications of guided imagery in order to help people cope with hospital techniques. The number of doctors using these methods in general practice would appear to be increasing (Achterberg 1985), and in Britain there are indications, such as the number of relevant papers in medical journals, that they are being given more serious consideration. Visualization techniques have been introduced in numerous cancer treatment programmes. Most recently it has been announced that Hammersmith Hospital, London is to introduce visualization in the treatment of cancer, following its successful application at the Bristol Cancer Help Centre. Harley (1989) cites a senior oncologist from the hospital as declaring:

'We are very interested in this new method. What has impressed us so much ... is that it works and is perfectly compatible with traditional methods.'

Timely Interventions as Methods
of Energy Conservation

In the West time is often spoken of as the great healer, but its significance in the creation and treatment of illness and in the maintenance of health has largely gone unrecognised and remains little understood, as are those apparently diverse techniques common to which is the modification of the individual's relationship with time.

Although in recent years there has been a grudging acceptance in some quarters that these may be effective and have a place in modern orthodox medicine, these 'timely interventions' - which are essentially methods of energy conservation - are nonetheless insufficiently understood for their full ramifications to be appreciated. As a result, tolerance - such as it is - is not extended to various unorthodox therapies, which although manifestly different from the former and from each other, are inherently sufficiently similar to justify their collective description as 'energy medicine'.

Part III

Energetic Treatments

Chapter 10

On the Nature of Energy

The time will come when you see we're all one
and life flows on within you and without you.

George Harrison

Asked to explain the apparent convergence of ideas in modern physics and ancient mysticism Maria von Franz (1985, p.135) asserted that Western physicists, extroverts looking outwards towards the cosmos, and introverted mystics looking inwards into their own unconscious, had discovered the same truth: that the universe is one great unity; that the process of this whole is an energy dance; and that everything is an energy phenomenon.

Both conceive this energy not as some underlying substance or 'stuff' but as dynamic patterns of activity, movement or change (hence the Greek *energeia*: activity) to be understood in terms of vibrations, pulsation, flow, rhythm, synchrony, resonance, and as relative to time.

The understanding that time and energy are relative and reciprocal, being interdependent aspects of one and the same phenomenon, found expression throughout the ancient world in mythologies where various gods representing movement were at once personifications of time and world-creating energy. In the Hindu tradition the god Krishna reveals his divine role as creator and destroyer of the world with the words 'Know that I am Time which causes the world to perish when the time is right for it,' and the god Shiva bears the titles *Maha Kala* (great time) or *Kala Rudra* (all consuming time), and is depicted as the cosmic dancer, who symbolises the energy of the universe.

The gods of ancient Iranian, Greek, Roman and Mayan civilisations were also equated with time:

> The archetypal image of a god in his world-creating energy is behind most personifications of time. Psychologically speaking this god personifies psychic energy in its multivalent instinctual image- generating spiritual creative power which embraces all psychic processes (Von Franz 1974, p.259)

In these cultures time is energy, or change in nature.

Within contemporary physics the same 'truth' is encountered, expressed in the symbols of mathematics rather than those of myth. The modern statement of this relationship is Einstein's celebrated formula $E=mc^2$, where energy is equivalent with matter (or nature as we know it), changing over time; transformations of which uphold in the psychological domain no less than in the physical world. According to Piaget (1965, p.25) the psychological concept of time

> seems to express a relationship of (1) its (time's) content ie: what happens in it (travelled space, achieved work etc), with (2) the speed of its flow in the form of speed - motion being either a speed frequency or a power (force);

and the psychological experience of time, as Ornstein (1969) has demonstrated, is determined largely by the amount of energy - physical or mental - expended in a given activity.

It follows therefore that modification of one feature will result in change in the other. This is demonstrable in time therapies, the most common claim of those who experience them being feelings of greater energy. It is also evident in the time/energy images used to describe personal experience. Those who claim never to 'have time' are invariably not using their energies effectively, while those who claim to have no energy are rarely using their time effectively. Indeed, Jacobsen (1977) indicates that most stress conditions, or 'time sicknesses', are manifestations of energy extravagance. He observes that 'tense people spend too much energy' (p.13), and therefore excessive adenosine triphosphate or cyclic TCP, the basic chemical utilised in nerve and muscle cells. This relationship is consistently overlooked in orthodox Western medical practice, despite the fact that 'lack of energy' is one of the most common presenting problems. Yet it is fundamental to all effective healing practices, which are essentially energetic treatments, concerned with the conservation and regulation of vital energy processes.

Energy medicine

Traditional approaches to healing throughout the world since antiquity share a belief in the existence of subtle energies, the mobilisation and balancing of which are fundamental to health; illness being viewed as the result of stagnation or disruption of energy patterns. In the West most concepts of energy, such as Mesmer's magnetic energy, Bergson's Élan Vital, Reich's orgone or bio-energy, von Reichenbach's odic force and the Theosophists' ether, were developed when Western science was formulated in exclusively objective, mechanistic terms. Accordingly life energy is frequently conceived as some kind of substance which flows through the organism, as is reflected in Freud's use of the term 'libido', which derives from the Latin *libare*: to pour.

However, in the East concepts of energy, variously referred to as chi, ki, prana, Kundalini, or Shakti, are markedly different, being akin to those of pre-scientific Western civilisations, notably Ancient Greece and Egypt. Here energy is conceived not as 'anything' but as continuous movement, or change. It is relative, resting on an inner polarity, or regulative function of opposites which flow into one another. This view was revived in more recent times by the German embryologist Driesch, who adopted Aristotle's concept of *entelekhia* or *entelechy* - the vital force which directs the life of an individual - to describe the impetus which urges the organism to self-fulfilment, a concept similar to the vital force described by Hahnemann, and to the self-actualising tendency of Maslow, Rogers and Perls. However, the most striking similarities with ancient and Eastern concepts of energy are found in the ideas of Jung, who indicated that psychic energy and physical energy may be but two aspects of one and the same reality, the world of matter appearing as a mirror image of the world of the psyche, and vice versa. He designated energy as physical when it is physically measurable, or psychic when it becomes psychically or introspectively perceptible. Accordingly, 'the psyche should be capable of appearing in the form of mass in motion, and insofar as psychological interaction takes place, matter should possess a latent psychic aspect' (von Franz 1974, p.157).

The fundamental concept common to these views is that all matter, including the human body, the psyche, and all phenomena, comprise energy in a particular state of vibration, and have both physical and psychic aspects - a view fully consistent with that of present-day physics. Accordingly wave motion, light, heat, colour and sound are merely different forms of vibration, as are thoughts and emotions, and healing approaches based on such a view utilise the various states of vibration to restore energy imbalances within the mind and body. Energy medicine, therefore, involves a number of techniques which are believed to influence the organism at a more fundamental level than the physical or psychological symptoms of illness.

> When we realise that the final analysis our bodies are in fact made up of nothing but energy in constant transformation it is easier to understand how subtle non-physical energetic influences such as emotions and thoughts can have a direct influence on our physical functioning, just as our physical functioning can have a direct influence on our emotional and mental experiences (Schwartz 1980, p.21)

Unfortunately insufficient people do realise this, and even within the scientific community many find it difficult to accept the implications of scientific discovery, much less accept that these have been mapped out with striking similarity throughout the world since antiquity. Yet this clearly is the case.

The Chakra system

The Hopi Indians, who according to Waters (cited by Wilson and Bek 1987), believe themselves to be the oldest inhabitants of the earth, view the human body and that of the earth as isomorphic. Both have an axis, in man the spine, along which, they maintain, there are several vibrating centres or vortices which distribute energy through the body.

The first centre at the top of the head receives life energy at birth and is the seat of communication with the creator; the second is situated at the brain; the third at the throat; the fourth at the heart; and the fifth at the solar plexus. Similar beliefs are common among Northern and Central American Indians, the Eskimo, and are a feature of early

Egyptian, Tibetan and Indian thought - hence the similarities in Hindu symbols and those of North American totem poles noted by Gallegos (1983). However, in addition to the centres described by the Hopi, the Hindu system includes a centre situated below the navel and another located over the sacral bone. These are described as three-dimensional pulsating wheels, known in Sanskrit as chakras, which rotate rhythmically from the centre outwards, rather like Catherine wheels, in a way which appears to seers like a cone, trumpet, or the convolvulus flower; and, according to the direction of spin, either draws energy in, or directs it out of the body, enervating or depleting its vitality.

Leadbetter (1927) indicates that most of what is written about these centres is in Sanskrit or Indian Vernaculars, the minor Upanishads and Puranas, and Tantric works. They were first described in English early this century by Leadbetter (1910, 1927) and in Sir John Woodroffe's *The Serpent Power*, but become more widely known through the writings of the Theosophists. Nevertheless, evidence that early European mystics were familiar with them comes from the *Theosophica Practica*, issued in 1696 and written by Gichtel, who was probably a Rosicrucian. Other evidence of early knowledge of the chakras in the West comes from Egyptian monuments and the ancient rituals of freemasonry.

Leadbetter describes the location and Sanskrit name of each chakra as follows:

1.	Base of spine	Muladhara
2.	Gonads	Svaddhisthana
3.	Solar plexus	Manipura
4.	Heart	Anahata
5.	Throat	Vishuddha
6.	Between eyebrows	Ajna
7.	Top of head	Sahasrava

He points out that in the Indian system these were traditionally stimulated or 'awakened' by (1) Raja, (2) Karma, (3) Jnana, (4) Hatha, (5) Laya, (6) Bhakti and (7) Mantra yogas respectively.

However, the position of the chakras was described differently by the Theosophists, the second centre being located not in the area of the generative organs, but the spleen. As Leadbetter (1927, p.4) explains: 'From our point of view the arousing of such a centre would be regarded as a misfortune, as there are serious dangers connected with it'. While this may be interpreted as Theosophical bias against tantric sexual practices, he insists that it was not merely a Victorian prudery, as the Egyptians had also taken elaborate precautions to prevent such an awakening. In addition to these major chakras, a number of minor chakras are variously described in different traditions.

Organisms are seen as drawing vital energies for use in the living economy of their body cells from the atmosphere and the earth by way of a finer body on whose surface they are situated. Known as the vital body in certain Rosicrucian schools, the astral, etheric body or double in other Western occult traditions, as ka in Ancient Egypt, the doppelganger in medieval Europe, linga sharirah in the East, and in French spiritism as the perispirit, (Butler 1982) it is generally seen as synonymous with spirit and as surviving physical death. Leadbetter indicates that in the Theosophical tradition man is viewed as a soul who possesses a body - several bodies in fact - rather than vice versa. In addition to the visible vehicle by means of which he transacts his business in the physical world, he has others not visible to ordinary sight, by means of which he deals with emotional and mental worlds. This is also the centuries-old claim of numerous seers and philosophers, and St Paul, who states (Corinthians 15 v.44) 'There is a natural body and there is a physical body'.

Energy, in the form of light, is drawn into the latter through its immaterial counterpart, which acts like a prism, breaking down the light into seven streams corresponding with the frequency bands of the electromagnetic spectrum, each of which is drawn to a different chakra whose vibrations are of the same frequency. Thus although the colours of the chakras are continually changing, the base colours of the chakras rarely change, if at all (Schwartz 1980). These vibrations become progressively more dense, heavy and lower in frequency along the length of the spine to its base where they merge with earth energies, represented in Indian thought as the coiled serpent, Kundalini, and in Chinese thought as a dragon. Each chakra, which as Beatty (1972) observes is equivalent to a transmitter or transformer of energy, is therefore believed to vibrate at a characteristic frequency as it distributes this energy throughout the body, the energy pattern around each being predominantly of a certain colour and associated with a musical note and a symbolic form whose vibrations also correspond with its basic frequency. In the Indian tradition each chakra is also associated with certain elements and forms represented by symbolic animals. Gichtel assigned planets to each chakra, suggesting that each is sensitive to certain planetary influences, and more recently these centres have been identified with the location and functioning of the glands of the endocrine system, namely the pineal, pituitary, thyroid, thymus, adrenals, liver and gonads respectively. The slightest imbalance of energy in any of the chakras is believed to influence the corresponding endocrine gland, giving rise to fluctuations in hormones, which are secreted directly into the bloodstream, creating immediate changes in mood, appearance, tension, respiration, digestion, intuition and intelligence, thereby affecting the entire organism.

Accordingly, the various traditions hold that by understanding its character, function, associated colour, sound and symbolic form, each chakra can be cleansed, opened and balanced, and it is this belief which forms the basis of most ancient forms of healing, including colour and sound therapies of ancient Egypt and Greece, the various practices of yoga, the use of 'power' objects such as crystals and stones by shamans and witch doctors, and systems of exercise such as T'ai Chi and Akido which promote the flow of energy through these centres.

The following schema, based on that of Gunther (1979), summarises the principal features of chakra theory common to most traditions;

1. *The first, root or base chakra* located at the base of the spine is concerned with basic existence and survival, influencing sexual and other activity and regulating creativity.

It affects the sex glands, ovaries and testes and is responsible for sex drive, reproduction and secondary sex characteristics. The transmutation of this procreative energy can be used to enhance all forms of creative activity, personal growth, health and healing. It is influenced by Saturn, and associated with the element earth, the symbolic form of the square, the metal lead (base metal), the colour red, the sense of smell, and the sound vibration LA.

2. *The second chakra*, located midway between the pubis and the navel, is considered the centre of sexual activity in traditional systems but is associated with the spleen in those of the West. It is known as the hara in Japanese systems, and is the centre of 'gut feelings', cleansing, purification and health, being associated with the liver, pancreas and spleen, glands which influence metabolism, digestion, detoxification, immunity to disease and the body's sugar balance. It is influenced by Jupiter and associated with water, tin, the sense of taste, the symbolic form of a pyramid with the capstone removed, the colour orange, and the sound BA.

3. *The third or solar plexus chakra*, located just above the navel, is the centre of emotion and power, influencing the adrenals which profoundly affect the sympathetic nervous system, and thereby muscular energy, heartbeat, digestion, circulation and mood. This centre is believed to be implicated in stress disorders characterised by excessive use of adrenalin, ulcers, nervous disorders and chronic fatigue. It is influenced by the planet Mars, and associated with fire, iron, sight, the symbolic form of a circle, the colour yellow/gold and the sound RA.

4. *The heart chakra*, located in the centre of the chest, is the source of love and compassion and expresses unconditional love for spirit, consciousness and every level of creation. It influences the thymus gland which is situated just behind the breast bone, the main function of which in adults is the proper utilization of the amino-competence factor, that aspect of the body which helps create immunity to disease. It is influenced by Venus, and associated with air, copper, touch, the symbol of the equilateral cross, the colour green, and the two syllable sound YM (Ya Mm).

5. *The throat chakra* is concerned with creativity and self-expression. It influences the thyroid gland which affects balance of the entire system, metabolism, musculature and control of body heat production. It is influenced by Mercury, and associated with ether, hearing, the symbolic form of the chalice, the colour sky blue, and the sound HA.

6. *The brow chakra* is located just above and between the eyebrows in the centre of the forehead and is traditionally known as the 'third eye'. It is regarded as the source of ecstasy, clairvoyance, heightened intuition and paranormal powers. It is associated with the pineal gland (now thought to have a significant role in processing of mental imagery and unconscious processes) and is regarded as being beyond the senses. It is influenced by the moon, and associated with both gold and silver, the form of the six-pointed star, the colour midnight blue or indigo, and the sound AH.

7. *The crown chakra* is located in the centre of the upper skull. It is regarded as the seat of cosmic consciousness or enlightenment and held to be beyond thought, name, form

or rational experience. Ancients saw it as the seat of the soul. It is associated with pure being, the colour purple, and symbolised by the thousand petalled lotus with its roots in the mud - the dense energies at the base of the spine, its stem in water, the emotional energies of the torso, but with its blossom untouched by water and fully open to the energy of the sun. It is associated with the sacred sound OM (ooh aa um), which is considered to be the total amalgam of all sound.

Leadbetter indicates that according to this system man is a septenary being, having a seven-fold nature. The first and second chakras are principally concerned with receiving physical energies from the earth, which are variously characterised as dragon or serpent energies, - and vitality from the sun; chakras three, four and five are concerned with forces which reach man via the personality; and six and seven by spiritual energies. Therefore the chakras, rather than regulating purely physical well-being, are also concerned with psychological and spiritual well-being and thus with the totality of body, mind and spirit. Accordingly the chakra system provides the impetus for the regulated, balanced flow of energy throughout whole organism, which is equivalent with health.

Aura theory

According to various traditions there is a radiant energy emitted from the body which bears a specific relation to the location and intensity of energy activity within it, and therefore reveals something of its state of functioning. This hazy emanation, which extends around the body for some distance beyond its surface, is normally invisible, but ancient and contemporary seers (Castaneda 1973, Schwartz 1980) describe it as large, shimmering, oval, comprising a mass of fine luminescent fibres or rays. Although widely referred to as the 'aura', in the early Christian tradition it was termed the 'halo' and frequently depicted as confined to the head region of the body.

However, what can be thought of as 'aura theory' postulates that every object, animate and inanimate, is completely enveloped by an individual aura, a field of electromagnetic energy - the forcefield of the etheric body - which acts as a medium for the interplay of other energies present in the immediate environment; and that collectively these create a common auric realm plane of untapped energy.

The appearance, shape and size of the individual aura is considered to reveal the overall state of functioning of the form it envelopes. In the human being the aura is the sum total of the energy given off by the chakras. Well-being depends on the proper reception and distribution of energies by these centres, and therefore on their harmony and balance. When the chakras are operating in a balanced and harmonious manner the colour emanating from each should be very pale and clear, indicating that their energy transmission is pure and subtle. The presence of darker, denser colour emanations manifesting in the aura as patches or blotches is an indication that a chakra is not functioning properly and that energy is therefore not being transmitted effectively. Since the etheric body controls and effects the physical body, energy imbalance is indicated in the aura before its effects are manifested in the physical body. Accordingly the aura can be used for diagnosis:

The subtle energy fields that surround the human body can convey advance warning of problems that may not yet have manifested themselves on the physical plane, and in any case, an understanding of these energy fields can aid in a clearer perception of what really is amiss in a case of mental, emotional or physical illness (Schwartz 1980, p.21)

Furthermore, since the etheric body controls the energies within the physical body, it is here that remedial action can commence to restore energy imbalances. This requires a clear understanding of the nature of both the aura and subtle energies.

The aura

The aura is mapped out in seven bands or layers, each of which corresponds with the functioning of a chakra and its characteristics base colour, as follows:

The ovum: This is blank space, between the physical body and the first colour emanation of the aura described by Schwartz as being of a dirty golden or ivory colour (1980, p.45) Many people who claim to see auras in fact only see the ovum which, because it is part of the densest of energy fields, is more readily visible.

The first layer or health band emanates from the base of the sacrum and reflects the overall vitality of the physical body. According to Ouseley (1981) it is reddish in colour but it is frequently described as blue.

The second layer or emotional band, sometimes known as the astral band, emanates from the second chakra and reflects 'gut feelings'. It is pinkish in colour.

Third layer or mental band emanates from the solar plexus and reflects lower mental functions based on the intellect and objective knowledge. In a well-balanced person who is mentally alive it is resplendent and very shiny or brilliant.

The fourth layer or heart band emanates from the heart chakra and corresponds with what Gunther (1979) terms the paraconscious, and Ouseley (1981) the soul principle. It reflects higher mental abilities such as intuition, inspiration and creativity in all forms, and is green in colour.

The fifth layer or casual band emanates from the throat chakra and reflects the progress of the soul through successive incarnations, its karma. It is blue in colour.

The sixth layer or spiritual band emanates from the sixth chakra and reflects the spiritual development of the individual. Its colour is indigo.

The seventh layer or cosmic band reflects cosmic awareness. It has no colour but is described by Schwartz (1980) as sometimes appearing gold-speckled in highly spiritually aware individuals.

Each band radiates different colours of varying intensity which reveal the individual's state of health, character, emotional disposition and tendencies, abilities, attitudes, past problems and spiritual development. Throughout history seers or sensitives have reported seeing or sensing these bands, often representing them in sketches or paintings known as aurographs, and using them as a basis for diagnosis and treatment, or counselling on personal, interpersonal and transpersonal development. Contemporarily the Dutch clairvoyant Jack Schwartz, whose abilities have been subject to extensive scientific investigation, uses auric diagnosis in counselling. However, Karagulla (1967) found that many orthodox physicians also have the ability to diagnose illness through the energy field they perceive around the patient, or energy vortices connected with the endocrine system.

One doctor who admits to using auric diagnosis is John Pierrakos (1971) who claims that the number of pulsations per minute that the energy field emits is an indication of the internal state of the human body. He maintains that against a homogeneous background of either very pale or very dark blue one can see with the naked eye or with the aid of colour filters, a cloud-like blue-grey envelope extending some 2-4 feet from the body where it loses its distinctiveness and merges with the surrounding atmosphere. This envelope is brilliant and swells slowly for 1-2 seconds away from the body until it forms an almost perfect oval shape with fringed edges, then abruptly disappears completely, reappearing again after an interval of 2-3 seconds before repeating the process. His claim that in an average resting person this process is repeated 15-25 times a minute is currently being investigated by a research team at the Institute of Bioenergetic Analysis in the USA, which is seeking to objectify his observations by developing a means of detecting auras with a sensitive photomultiplier tube which measures the electromagnetic field around the body.

It is claimed that sensitivity to auras may be trained in many people and exercises for developing auric sight are provided by Gunther, (1979) Laurie and Tucker, (1982), Schwartz, (1980), Taylor, (1987) and Butler, (1982). Arguably, however, everyone has a certain degree of sensitivity to auras - typically describing others in energy or colour images, as brilliant, shining, sparkling, radiant, dim or dull, green, blue, or in the pink. It is easy to dismiss this as merely a tendency to ornate and colourful speech, and the entire phenomena with it, but there is objective evidence for the existence of the aura.

In 1911 Dr Walter J. Kilner of St. Thomas' Hospital, London published a dissertation on the human aura, *The Human Atmosphere* in which he claimed that a force field exists around the human body which can be charted and analysed. He subsequently developed a special kind of glass, the Kilner screen, which enabled the aura to be seen objectively by sensitizing vision, but his prediction that in the future it would be possible to photograph this aura and use it for more accurate diagnosis of all types of illness and mental disturbance was dismissed as fanciful. Similarly the views of Dr. F.S.C. Northrup of Yale, who postulated the existence of dynamic life fields around the living things, which he termed L-fields, was not given serious attention. Then in 1935 Harold Sexton Burr, Professor of Anatomy at Yale announced the discovery of a second body possessed by all human beings - an energy body which provides a blueprint for the physical body, controlling and determining cellular and organic function, shape, colour and size of the physical body, and in turn being affected by emotional and psychological states in the individual. He concluded that these electric fields are the organisers of life systems and anticipate the physical events within them.

Also during the late 1930s developments occurred in high voltage photography which appeared to fulfil Kilner's predictions about objective perception of the aura. Kirlian photography, named after its pioneers Semyon and Valentina Kirlian, revealed streams of apparent energy flowing from the fingertips in a manner suggested by Aura Theory. Over a period of ten years these scientists became convinced that this reflected the well-being or otherwise of the organism, and this subsequently appeared to be supported in research on plants.

The Kirlians' research was further developed by Professor Vladimir Inyushin. While the Kirlians had maintained that the strange energy captured in their pictures was caused by changing the non-electrical properties of bodies into electrical properties which are transferred onto film, Inyushin declared that the phenomenon was not caused by the electrical state of the organism but by a biological plasma body, which Tomkins and Bird, (1973) suggest, seems to be but a new term for the etheric or astral body of the ancients. Inyushin maintained that inside the bioplasmic body processes have their own labyrinthine but non-chaotic motion different from the energy pattern of the physical body; a whole unified organism which acts as a unit emitting its own electromagnetic fields which are the basis of all biological fields.

Another researcher Viktor Adamenko subsequently claimed to have found that the bioplasma concentrates at hundreds of points on the human body which correspond with the acupuncture points of the Ancient Chinese system, and that these 'blobs' of energy on the skin differ with different illnesses. Although this discovery appears to lend support to traditional Aura Theory Adamenko prefers to define this phenomena not as a bioplasmic body or aura but the 'cold emission of electrons from the live object into the atmosphere'. When the study of this phenomenon spread to America researchers there also avoided esoteric terminology, preferring to refer to it as 'corona discharge'.

Indeed as the Russian research became more widely known in Europe and the USA it initially met with scepticism. It was suggested that the observed phenomenon is simply the result of physiological variations at the surface of the skin. However, this was rebutted by Professor Thelma Moss of the Neuropsychiatric Institute of the University of California School of Medicine, who was the first serious researcher of the phenomenon in the USA. She demonstrated that while there is no correlation between the observed corona and variations in skin temperature, peripheral changes or perspiration there are apparent correlations with psychological states. Relaxation produced by meditation, hypnosis and acupuncture is characterised by more brilliant coronas, while states of tension and emotional excitement result in a contracted corona with red blotches at the fingertips; a finding which reflects the relationship between time therapies and energy. Further evidence that the phenomenon is not a physical variation of the photographed surface comes from the discovery that when a leaf has pieces removed or human fingers are amputated the corona discharge in each case shows as a whole William Tiller of Stanford University has therefore suggested that the energy apparently emitted from the fingertips is present prior to the formation of solid matter. This, he claims, may be another level of substance producing a hologram; a coherent energy pattern which is a forcefield for organising matter to building itself into this kind of physical network. Thus if part of the network is cut away the forming hologram still remains. Various devices such as the verograph have been developed to produce Kirlian effects, and during the 1960s Leonidov, a Russian researcher, developed a lightless microphoto which provided further objective evidence for the aura by capturing the fading life of a dying plant.

Taken together the chakra and aura theories provide a comprehensive and consistent account of the distribution and functioning of subtle energies within and around the body, and an integrative framework for what can be thought of as subtle energy therapies, which are many and various.

Subtle energy therapies

Acupuncture, acupressure or shiatsu, and the related system of reflexology, (also known as zone therapy, or metamorphic technique) represent the more obvious of the subtle energy therapies, and are among the most intricately detailed.

The efficacy of acupuncture in the treatment of many conditions is now recognised in the West. Whereas twenty years ago it was unacceptable to orthodox medicine it is now available in most district general hospitals, even though it is not yet fully understood (Lewith 1989). Pain relief - one of the major effects claimed for acupuncture - is to some extent the result of the deep relaxation it induces when applied to certain points.

However, Downey (1988) reports that the application of needles into the acupuncture points of rats has been found to produce endorphins, natural opiate-like substances in the body which yield analgesic effects; and studies conducted at St Bartholomew's Hospital, London (reported by Hodgkinson 1989) indicate that in addition to releasing these substances into the body, acupuncture also modifies the body's perception of pain by releasing beta-endorphin together with the neuro-transmitter serotonin.

Currently no anaesthetist in the UK routinely uses acupuncture as the sole method of pain relief during operations but its protagonists argue that it is cheaper and causes fewer side effects such as vomiting and headaches than conventional anaesthetics. This claim finds support in a recent study, also reported by Hodgkinson, which compared 1000 births by caesarean section with 237 by epidural anaesthesia, and showed that acupuncture gave rise to on average 112 ml. less blood loss than epidurals, and faster post-operative recovery with fewer complications. Of the mothers who received acupuncture only 5.2 per cent needed the powerful painkiller pethidine, compared with 29.9 per cent of those who received epidurals. More widespread use of acupuncture has led to various technological developments in its application. In Russia Viktor Adamenko has substituted the traditional needles with a tobioscope, an instrument containing photoelectric cells which records the skin resistance over acupuncture points and meridians, registering any imbalances which are then treated by various means including stimulation by lasers.

Elsewhere instrumental measurement of acupuncture points is also being developed. In the USA an acuometer has been developed which detects points on the skin which seem to be consistent with those of traditional Chinese acupuncture, and most recently sonoacupuncture has been developed which applies high frequency sound to these points. At the Institute of Religious Psychology in Tokyo, Motoyama has developed a computer know as AMI which diagnoses chi energy, but this has met with opposition among traditionalists who insist that diagnosis by electronic instruments is insufficiently sensitive to the whole process involved, which incorporates the practitioner's ability to blend his chi energy with that of the patient.

Homeopathy

Also widely known, and with a similar conceptual basis to acupuncture and its variants, although not generally recognised as such, is homeopathy, which was developed during the last century by the physician Samuel Hahnemann (1755-1843). In Britain it has been available through the National Health Service since 1977. In addition to six homeopathic hospitals, there are numerous homeopathic physicians within orthodox medical practice, whose most distinguished patrons include the Royal Family. Homeopathy is also widely and increasingly practised within the field of veterinary medicine.

Hahnemann considered there to be certain basic vibrational patterns of disease, or miasms, which originate in the aura, setting up patterns in the individual's life and body which spread their subtle influence through all the energies of the person. These miasms may be inherited genetically, or acquired by resonance, the principle whereby energies vibrating with a certain frequency and amplitude reverberate with similar energies in the environment. The former, in the genetic code, and the latter in the form of bacteria or viral attack, toxic pollution in food or the environment, can lie dormant for years flaring up at times of weakness. Then the organism reacts to this disease or imbalance of its energies by attempting to restore balance, in so doing producing the symptoms and signs the patient feels and the doctor observes. The homeopath, unlike the ordinary physician, does not consider these to be the illness *per se*, but rather the body's reaction to the original state of imbalance. They are thus an indicator of the extent of imbalance and of how profoundly the organism is affected by it, and can be used to determine treatments appropriate to restoring balance, and hence health. Homeopathic treatments restore the balance of subtle energy fields of the body by matching various natural remedies of different vibrational characters with the disharmonies of the body, thereby restoring harmony to its energy patterns and inducing health. They therefore utilise the principle of resonance, applying remedies which subject the organism to a periodic disturbance of the same frequency as that of the body, at which frequency the body displays an enhanced oscillation or vibration. Given the importance of the therapeutic relationship in homeopathy Capra (1982 p.377), suggests that the crucial resonance in omeopathic therapy is that between the patient and the homeopath, with the remedy merely a crutch. Clearly, however, the therapeutic relationship and the remedies in homeopathy are mutually reinforcing.

In stimulating energy levels and moving them towards more harmonious arrangement, homeopathic treatments operate on similar principles to dissipative structures, enabling the system to escape to a level of greater organisation by shaking up existing patterns of energies within the body. Similar transformations are effected by a number of psychological therapies, whose 'shake up' of existing energy forms is more clearly perceptible but none the less subtle.

Chapter 11

Psychosomatic Treatments

With this body, mortal as it is, and only six feet in length, I do declare to you, are the world, and the origin of the world, and the ceasing of the world, and the path that leads to cessation.

Buddha

The psychological treatments which more obviously fit within the framework of 'energy medicine' are those which derive from the work of Wilhelm Reich who devised a number of devices for concentrating energy, and techniques for removing obstacles to its natural flow, which have become known as bioenergetics.

Bioenergetic therapies

For Reich

life energy is the vitality of our being; when we are moved, this is what moves. Emotions are e-motions; movements out; but they are not just in our minds but in our bodies, in the charge of energy which builds up and with luck discharges; in the flooding of hormones, the surge of bodily fluids and electrical potential, expanding from deep within us towards the surface, or retreating into the caves of the abdomen or flowing through and out via head and hands and legs and pelvis, shifting form easily between muscular or electrical tension, fluid, sound, movement, sensation, emotion (Totton and Edmondson 1988, p.7)

He recognised that when this energy cannot flow freely in the body this sets up over time a chronic imbalance in tissues or organs which allows infection or functional disorder to become established, and neurotic responses, which are indicated behaviourally in 'character patterns' of muscular expressions and postures, or muscle armouring

Accordingly emotional and psychological ways of relating to the world are reflected physically in the body, and vice versa, the organism being viewed as united in its response to various influences rather than separable into mind and body. In attacking neurotic symptoms in their psychic and somatic manifestations at the same time, and thus linking treatment of the body with psychotherapy, Reich laid the foundations of a somatic psychology, and for psychosomatic treatments, which in a quite literal sense address the psyche - the mind or soul - by way of the body.

His therapy was directed towards identifying and eliminating the muscle armouring physically, thereby releasing blocked bio-energy at both physical and psychological levels, re-establishing its natural flow and normalising physical and psychological functioning.

Reich used his hands to effect emotional release by pressing on tight muscles which hold back its expression, particularly the breathing muscles which for Reich were essential in maintaining an even flow of energy (for him synonymous with breath) throughout the body. He also pressed, poked, tickled and stretched muscles in a process which was invariably painful for the recipient, pain being regarded as a powerful tool in catharsis.

Subsequently many different forms of 'bodywork' or bio-energetic therapy have grown up on the Reichian tradition with the common aim of relaxing the body and releasing the energy held in by various tensions, and Reich's insight have informed many other humanistic psychotherapies, notably Fritz Perls' Gestalt Therapy.

The basis of Reich's approach was

> a tremendous vision of the streaming of energy in the cosmos, the galaxies, the oceans, the weather - and in our own bodies. He saw it as the same energy, following the same patterns, the same dance. Although Reich condemned 'mysticism - by which he meant flight from bodily reality - his own vision is in the best sense a truly mystical one (Totton and Edmondson 1988, p.138)

Indeed, as David Boadella (1987) observes, the system he built upon it bears a striking similarity to the chakra system.

Reich describes seven rings of tension or character structure resulting from muscle armouring which are at right angles to the main axis of the body and divided it into sections as follows:

Armour segments	*Character structure*
1. eyes, forehead, scalp	ocular
2. mouth, chin, jaw	oral
3. neck, shoulders	cervical
4. thorax, heart, lungs, arms	thoracic
5. diaphragm	diaphragmatic
6. abdomen, lower back	abdominal
7. pelvis, sex organs, legs	pelvic

Boadella therefore suggests that an alternative way of looking at the principal character structures and problems of Reichian theory is to regard them as primary functional disturbances of the chakras. This, and other aspects of Reich's work, have been developed by Boadella, who terms his approach Biosynthesis.

Biosynthesis

The fundamental concept of Biosynthesis is that there are three major energetic currents or lifestreams in the body which express themselves as a flow of movement through muscular pathways; a flow of perceptions, thoughts and images through the neuro-sensory system; and a flow of emotional life in the core of the body through the deep organs of the trunk.

Stress before birth, during infancy and later life is seen as breaking up the integration of these three streams giving rise to dysfunctional character structure. Biosynthesis aims to reintegrate them through breath release and emotional centring, retoning of muscles and postural grounding, and with the facing and shaping of experience through eye contact and voice communication.

Boadella (1987) discusses character patterns in relation to dysfunction of the chakras as follows:

1. *The root chakra*, the primary function of which is grounding in the sense of commitment to the body and the will to survive. Where well developed there is a sense of independence and personal power. Where dysfunctional there are tendencies to over-groundedness and fear of dependence, or under-groundedness and fear of independence. It therefore expresses a polarity between rigidity and helplessness, control and collapse.

2. *The hara chakra*, the primary function of which is charge. Closely related to the navel and the sense of contact (via umbilical chord). In infancy the centre of well-being, later the sex centre. Dysfunction will show as over or under-charge; the former as hypersexuality, casual contact and difficulty in achieving satisfactory relationships, the latter as hyposexuality, impotence, frigidity and sexual anaesthesia through inability to make satisfactory contact.

3. *The solar plexus chakra*, which relates to power and mastery and is thus related to boundaries, to anger and anxiety. In anger there will be a tendency to invade others and in anxiety to be invaded. Basic conflicts will be expressed in identification with power and domination, or of submission, rather than blending and cooperation.

4. *The heart chakra*, whose core function is compassion, deep love and the formation of strong relationships is the centre of bonding. Dysfunctions can be distinguished as overbonded, addictive and stifling patterns in relationships, or alternatively underbonding expressed as superficial or transitory relations, perhaps with a degree of indifference, or as total withdrawal from relationships.

5. *The throat centre* relates to communication or sounding, how well the heart is expressed through the voice. Expressiveness is a sign of health, but dysfunctions show as distortions in language; introjection, or swallowing the views of others whole, without discrimination or reference to one's own feelings; and projection, believing others to have attributes one is unwilling to ascribe to oneself. Guilt and blame are strongly implicated when this centre is blocked.

6. *The brow chakra*, or third eye, concerned with vision and contemplation, looking out and seeing in, carries the ability to face oneself and others clearly. Related to imagination and insight. Dysfunctions show obsession, narrowing of vision to a single fixed beam, loss of imagination and insight; feelings of possession, being invaded by others, being too telepathically open.

7. *The crown chakra* concerned with openness to something greater than self which when dysfunctional can lead either to messianic inflation, feelings of omnipotence; or nihilistic deflation, existential depression and fear of death - ultimate meaninglessness. The function of the chakra is related to the contact between inner and outer space. Disorders therefore relate to spacing out and fear of extinction in a void.

These functions can be summarised as: Root chakra, grounding; Hara, centring; Solar plexus, bounding; Heart, bonding; Throat, sounding; Brow, facing; Crown, spacing.

In addition to this outer ground of the body, Biosynthesis also recognises an inner ground underlying that of action, feeling and thought which expresses the essence or spirit of the person which is integrated using imagery.

Bioenergetic analysis

Alexander Lowen, a pupil of Reich, developed Bioenergetic Analysis as a systematic methodology for dealing with the relationship between somatic functioning and psychological trauma. He established the Institute of Bioenergetic Analysis in the USA in 1956 and since then it has been developed throughout Europe and elsewhere.

The aim of Bioenergetic Analysis is the healthy integration of the body and mind through breathing, relaxing character structures, and grounding - a method which teaches a particular stance whereby, through making positive contact with the ground, bodily energies move in a harmonious flow, enabling the individual, literally and metaphorically, to make contact with reality and discover their sense of identity.

Defensive blocks in the body are thought to be revealed in patterns of breathing which are unconsciously established by chronic muscle tensions which result from emotional trauma in earlier years. Breathing is developed by placing the body under stress, typically through the use of a breathing stool over which the person's body is positioned.

Biodynamic therapy

Gerda Boyeson, a Norwegian psychotherapist derived Biodynamic Therapy from Reichian notions of bio-energy and armouring. It is an holistic approach in which psychological and physical processes are seen as interrelated aspects of one biodynamic entity.

In Boyeson's theory the primary personality is seen as becoming submerged during development in a secondary personality which corresponds with Reich's concept of the armouring by which the person protects themself from the onslaughts of the environment and their own socially unacceptable emotions. Thus a child punished for expressing fear may suppress it through muscular effort, which over time becomes part of their muscular armouring and body structure, and no longer feel that emotion. However, Boyeson takes Reich's concept of armouring further in terms of her concepts of visceral tissue armour, central to which is the principle of the emotional cycle, which is both a physical and a psychological process in the sense that emotional events cause physiological changes which cease when the emotional event has passed. This can only occur in conditions of relaxation when the organism is no longer tensed for action, because when people are under stress the self-regulating process is inhibited. It loses its capacity to clear itself with the result that the effects of the trauma are retained. Thus loss of homeostatic response constitutes visceral armouring and when this prevents bioenergy flowing freely in the body every cell is impaired resulting in tissue armouring. This is similar to Aura Theory according to which when ill or stressed the energy field of the body shrinks, losing its ability to absorb vitality and enervate the body.

Biodynamic therapy varies with each client but often involves special massage techniques to disperse the body armouring. In some persons this process achieves results at the organic level only, while in others it is accompanied by profound psychological change.

Structural integration

This therapy, which is also known as Rolfing after its originator Ida Rolf, was developed during the 1930s in America. Drawing heavily on the work of Reich it is essentially a method of deep - some would claim, brutal - massage in which the therapist manipulates the client's body in order to return it to a desired postural and structural position, and in so doing releases imbalances resulting from the armouring process and discharges emotional and psychic blockages. It is therefore not simply physical massage but a technique for freeing the body, mind and emotions from their conditioning. Energies locked up in physical armour and defence mechanisms are released, prompting insight into the fears and inhibitions which initially provoked these responses.

Rolfing involves loosening and lengthening of specific muscles and fascia of the body, repositioning of muscle fibres and returning them to their natural position. A course of therapy usually entails ten weekly sessions, the first seven of which attempt to remove ingrained stress patterns, postures and habitual responses. The initial session typically focuses on freeing the muscles of the chest area and rib cage to improve breathing, while the second focuses on the feet and ankles, which are seen as having an important bearing on an individual's standing in the world and the way in which the person maintains contact with reality. The focus of subsequent sessions is on the integration of newly loosened muscles into new patterns of movement by manipulation of the fascia in appropriate directions. As the therapy progresses deeper and deeper tensions and resistances become apparent, and the increasing self-awareness of the client assists the therapist's hands in their dissolution.

Psychomuscular relief therapy

Psychomuscular Relief Therapy, developed by Peter Blythe, is based on the premise that most chronic and persistent psychoneurotic conditions such as anxiety states, depression and phobias are the result of people being unable to relax certain muscles which are permanently in spasm. PMRT aims to release the feelings locked behind muscle tension which continually threaten to break through. It clearly owes a debt to Reich in both theory and practice, viewing muscles in spasm as initially tightened against intense internal emotional responses to specific incidents and situations. These spasms can thus be seen as a natural way of coping with life, but through continued usage the muscle tension becomes permanent and ceases to be an adaptive response, habitually transmitting via the afferent system of the central nervous system strong signals which the brain interprets as anxiety.

Somatography

Bryn-Jones and King jointly developed during the 1970s a bodywork system they call somatography which combines awareness of relationships between subtle energies in the body and muscular stresses and tensions. Patients are taught how to develop this awareness in a series of individual sessions each lasting 60-90 minutes. Awareness of tension and pain is used as the first step in retraining the body-mind complex to signal the approach of inner stress and conflict before it manifests itself too deeply and at a level far removed from conscious awareness.

The Alexander technique

Related to bioenergetic therapies is the technique developed by F. Matthias Alexander (1896-1955) for the improvement of postural and muscular activity. It shares with these approaches the holistic assumption of no separation between body and mind, to which Alexander added the observation (supported in the empirical work of Jacobsen) that every activity, whether physical, mental or spiritual is translated into muscular tension which becomes habitual and distorts thinking, feeling and doing. The technique is not a set of exercises as such, but the development of an individual's self-awareness as to how certain activities are performed. It is concerned not with what is done, but how it is accomplished, and as such demands the same kind of self-awareness as zen and other oriental disciplines such as Yoga, Akido, and T'ai Chi.

It presumes that by increased personal awareness of physical attitudes the individual will perceive choices in the way they act and will choose more natural and spontaneous expression. Thus, although not promoted as such, the principles of the Alexander Technique are fully consistent with those of humanistic psychotherapy, and its effects claimed as similar by supporters, such as Barlow (1975) who observes that it gives rise to profound psychological and emotional changes, and feelings of well being.

The Feldenkrais method

Moshe Feldenkrais (1980) has developed a technique for developing full efficiency and functioning of the body which incorporates elements of the Alexander Technique and martial arts discipline. It focuses on the gradual training of bodily awareness and sensitivity but differs from the Alexander Technique in its emphasis on body motion rather than posture. In this sense it can be likened to a Western form of T'ai Chi.

It is in many respects similar to *Curative Eurythmy*, the system of exercises and movements developed for the treatment of energy imbalance by Rudolph Steiner (1861-1925), the originator of Anthroposophical medicine, which is an holistic system based on occult science (Steiner 1969) and as such fully consistent with traditional energy medicine.

Polarity therapy

What distinguishes bioenergetic 'bodywork' from the Alexander Technique, and the methods of Feldenkrais and Steiner is that in the former, touch - in some cases of a particularly vigorous and forceful nature - is employed by a trained specialist to break up or otherwise shake-up energy blockages as they manifest in dysfunctional response patterns in the body. They generally require in the therapist, and promote in the client, awareness of and sensitivity to subtle energies. A specific awareness forms the basis of Polarity Therapy which was developed during the 1940s and 1950s by Dr Randolph Stone who for many years studied Hindu healing techniques. Underpinning his therapy is the belief that the body is a magnified cell with a natural polarity, an expansion of the neutral life force which has its seat in the brain and the cerebro-spinal fluid. Accordingly its central axis is neutral, the right hand side positive, holding positive electrical potential and radiating positive energy, and the left hand side negative.

Stone claims that with this knowledge it is possible to balance energies and so relieve pain and discomfort, all pain being the result of obstructions of the flow of vital energy at molecular, electromagnetic and more subtle levels. As Stone also considers thoughts and emotions to be energy forms, negative thoughts and feelings are also regarded as energy blocks which manifest ultimately in degenerative conditions. These can be relieved by removing blockages through hand movements and stroking, which according to Stone, have psychologically energising effects. Inflammation or pain caused by excessive energy is relieved by placing the cooling (negative) energies of the left hand over it, whereas spasm, congestion or stagnation are vitalised by application of the positive energies of the right hand. All polarity treatments take place from side to side, front to back, above and below. Davis and Rawls (1979) have charted the electrical potentials of the body and claim that in the healing techniques used by Dr. Stone there is a direct correspondence between the electrical polarities of the hands and the parts of the body where they are placed, and that this form of natural healing is used spontaneously, and to good effect by most people. A mother, for example, might soothe a child by placing the front of her left hand or the back of her right hand (both negative in energy) on the child's forehead (also negative). Similarly she may instinctively apply her right hand palm to the back of its head. In so doing, they suggest, she is using the natural polarity of her body to balance those within the child. Davidson (1987) suggests that this natural polarity forms the basis of all treatments involving touch.

Certainly practices can be found in ancient traditions, where energies of the body are balanced by placing the palms of the hands at the crown of the head and the base of the spine, and in present-day healing practices such as cranio-sacral therapy, a sophisticated form of osteopathy. It stems from an awareness of the cranial rhythm, (8-12 cycles per minute), whose functions are still being explored, modifications of which are known to exert profound effects on systemic functions, reducing blood pressure, changing respiratory and cardiac rhythms, gastro intestinal and neuroendocrine functions (Maslak 1987). Research in Australia, the USA and Europe shows craniosacral therapy to some extent parallels the effects of yoga and biofeedback (Upledger 1983).

Therapeutic touch

Dolores Krieger, former Professor of Nursing at New York University, spent thirteen years developing Therapeutic Touch and pioneering it as a nursing modality, which is now widely taught and practised in the USA and Canada, where it is regarded as a natural extension of professional nursing skills.

Therapeutic Touch is based on the principle that healing is the rebalancing of energies within the body, and the belief that this can be achieved through the direction of a healer's own energy, or their redirection of the energies within the body and energy field of a patient. It has five stages, the first of which is that the healer must learn to centre themselves psychologically and physically; that is, to relax and focus their attention inwards, so that they effectively maintain a meditative state during healing. Accordingly Therapeutic Touch can be more properly regarded as a healing meditation. Indeed healers' brainwave patterns during meditation have been found to resemble those of meditators (Krieger 1979).

Having achieved this, the healer then makes an assessment of the patient's energy balance by passing their hands through the energy field surrounding the body, some two to three inches above its surface. Differences in energy flow resulting from imbalance and disease are detected through sensations in the healer's hand such as variations in temperature, 'pins and needles', tingling, pulsing, pressure or electric shock.

The healer then 'unruffles the field', relieving congestion and freeing bound energy by stroking or sweeping gestures away from the affected part, which is often sufficient to relieve symptoms and mobilise the patient's own healing resources. After this the healer washes their hands or shakes them to remove the charge picked up from the patient. The healer then places both hands on either side or over the affected area of the patient and imagines directing energy to it. However it is not sufficient merely to channel energy to the patient because, it is claimed, in an ill person whose energies are depleted this may do more harm than good. The energy must be modulated through use of colour imagery. The healer therefore mentally pictures sending blue energy to cool or sedate, red to warm or stimulate, yellow to energise, and this continues until such time 'when there are no longer any cues; that is, relative to the body's symmetry there are now no perceivable differences bilaterally, between one side of the field and the other as one scans the healee's field' (Krieger 1979, p.69). In other words, until the patient's body all 'feels the same' to the healer.

What distinguishes Therapeutic Touch from most other bio-energetic therapies is that it has been subjected to quite extensive empirical investigation and has been demonstrated to be effective. Heidt (1981) found that subjects experienced a significant reduction in state anxiety according to pre- and post-test comparisons, and a markedly greater reduction in post-test anxiety scores than subjects who received intervention by casual touch or no touch at all. Quinn (1984) testing the hypothesis that movements or passes could be hypnotic and so produce their effect, found that reduction in post-test anxiety was far greater in subjects receiving actual Therapeutic Touch than in those who received imitation procedures.

Therapeutic Touch has been successfully employed in a number of settings including prisons, and in the operating theatre, where it is found to greatly assist the induction of general anaesthesia. It has also been found to be of benefit to dying patients as an adjunct to pain relief and emotional support; in the reduction of clinical symptoms of fever and intestinal inflammation; and in assisting bone healing in children (Turton 1988). As a result it is now being more widely employed in healing approaches such as physiotherapy and osteopathy.

Krieger's achievement has been considerable. Not only has she pioneered and effectively promoted Therapeutic Touch within orthodox Western medicine, but in so doing she has also revived the ages-old natural healing tradition of laying on hands, which is the basis of her approach, and established a means by which it can be systematically trained.

Laying on hands or Contact Healing

Contact healing by laying on hands, most commonly referred to simply as 'healing', is almost certainly the most widespread therapy in the world, the most ancient, and possibly the most misunderstood. There is documentary and pictorial evidence for its use in Western civilisations since those of Ancient Egypt and Greece but nowhere is it more evident than in the scriptures of the early Christian Church.

Christ appeared to teach of a spiritual realm in which healing energies work more powerfully than man ever dreamed; a view consistent with that of ancient traditions of both the East and West; and he directed his disciples to heal with this knowledge. As Weatherhead (1951, p.50) indicates, there can be no doubt whatever that Christ's original mission was to establish a healing ministry. The healing of the body therefore played an enormous role in the early Christian period, as the Gospels and Acts of the Apostles reveal. Numerous acts of healing by Christ are documented, as are those of his followers: 'Many that were palsied and lame were healed' (Acts 8 v.7), by Peter and John (Acts 3 v.10), and Peter (Acts 9 v.32-4). Ananais (Acts 9 v.17) and Paul (Acts 14 v.8-10; 28 v.7-8) also healed the sick, as subsequently did Saints Bernard of Clairvaux, Francis of Assisi, Catherine of Siena, and Francis Xavier, Martin Luther and John Wesley (Weatherhead 1951).

Laying on hands therefore became a recognised religious practice. Indeed, as a result of its purges on witches and other 'lay' healers whose practices were condemned as 'the work of the devil', the Church held a monopoly on healing from the Middle Ages onwards. In Britain until 1951 lay healers were under threat of the Witchcraft Act which carried a death penalty, and in the USA were subject to a legal prohibition on anyone without a recognised qualification manipulating another's body. The practice of healing in both countries has therefore tended to be confined within churches, outside of which it has flourished only since the relaxation of these laws.

Healers in Britain have been able to treat patients in hospital since 1959, but only in 1977 did the General Medical Council change its policy and allow doctors to suggest or agree to patients seeing healers. Negative attitudes towards healing no doubt owe much to the legacy of the Church and its opposition to witchcraft, but a good deal results from widespread misunderstanding of what it involves. Largely owing to its religious connotations laying on hands is widely thought to be synonymous with faith healing, and its effects the result of suggestion. Belief and suggestion have an undisputed role in all healing, including orthodox medical treatment and cure, as is amply demonstrated by the placebo effect, and they unquestionably play a similar role in unorthodox treatments, but they do not account adequately for the effects of laying on hands. Edwards (1987) indicates that faith, belief or suggestion are merely an auxiliary to actual healing, and that if this were not so the healing of children, the mentally sick, animals and those unaware of receiving this form of healing could not occur. That it does is beyond doubt; 'There is enough solid experimental work and enough careful evaluation of reported claims to make this clear' (LeShan 1982, p.102).

One of the most intensive investigations of the phenomenon, conducted by Dr. Bernard Grad of McGill University, Montreal (1967) demonstrated that the effects of healing are not attributable to the patient's beliefs. Indeed he eliminated this possibility by using plants and animals as his experimental subjects. In a series of double-blind experiments Grad demonstrated that injured mice healed much faster than controls when a noted healer, Oskar Estebany, held his hands over them. He also demonstrated the healer's ability to prevent the development of thyroid goitres in mice, and that plants and fungi can be significantly affected by healing. Barry (1968) also demonstrated the effects of healing on fungus cultures.

Further experiments by Justa Smith (1968, 72), a professor of biochemistry, revealed that Estebany was able to increase enzyme reactions over time, and that the longer he held a test-tube of enzymes the more rapid the reaction - effects similar to those noted with high intensity electromagnetic fields. Indeed she found that Estebany's hands, although not emanating any 'energy' that could be measured, affected the digestive enzyme Trypsin in a way comparable to the effects of an electromagnetic field measuring 8-13,000 gauss (normally human beings live in an electromagnetic field of O.5 gauss). She subsequently found that irrespective of the type of enzyme investigated the change noted after exposure to the healer's hands was always in a direction of greater health of the cells and greater energy balance. She also found that other noted healers such as

Olga and Ambrose Worrall could cause damaged enzymes to reintegrate and return to normal structure and function, and enhance plant growth; an effect confirmed by Miller (1972). Other studies of Olga Worrall (Holmes 1975) employed a cloud chamber - an electron detection device developed by nuclear physicists to make the path of high energy particles visible. The experimental procedure involved Mrs Worrall placing her hands around the apparatus in an attempt to determine whether they might exert an influence on its uniform vapour pattern. They were found to produce a wave pattern in the vapour which seemed to move vertically from her palms, and altered course when she changed the position of her hands, an effect not found with non-healer control subjects. Furthermore, Mrs. Worrall could affect the cloud chamber from a distance of 600 miles, when it was found that the aftermath of energy turbulence in the chamber took about eight minutes to subside.

Studies of healers have also shown that they can affect living tissue *in situ*. Krieger (1975) found that following treatment by Estebany, the haemoglobin levels of patients exceeded pre-treatment levels, and that other healers could also accelerate repair in living organisms (1981). Furthermore, after receiving training from Estebany thirty-two registered nurses could also produce statistically significant effects (Kreiger 1982).

Matthew Manning, perhaps Britain's most extensively investigated healer, was found in various studies to be able to prolong the life by up to four times of red blood cells in a weak salt solution in which they normally burst (the probability of this occurring by chance is 100,000 to 1); and to influence cancer cells in sealed containers. Manning's brain wave patterns during healing have been found to show a large increase in low theta and delta range frequencies, a pattern which because of its appearance on EEG records, has been termed a 'ramp function'. This pattern, suggestive of very deep sleep, has been found to originate in the limbic system of his brain, and Canadian studies have shown that it is transferred to people receiving healing from him. Moreover, when held by him, the hands of those receiving healing show a highly unusual Kirlian photographic image with a brilliant white corona. Other healers have also been found to produce greater corona emanations during healing (Krippner 1973).

Cade (Cade and Coxhead 1979) demonstrated that the EEG patterns of healers while using their abilities are similar to those of clairvoyants and yogins, and that the brain wave patterns of the recipients of healing alter simultaneously with those of the healer. Thus as Gerber (1988, p.306) indicates, 'the diverse range of experimental data on the biological effects of healing is supportive of the hypothesis that a real energetic influence is exerted by healers on sick organisms'. Furthermore, this would appear to be exerted while healers are in a highly relaxed state.

Most healers do in fact believe that they are originators or transmitters of energy, and that they obtain their best results when calm, relaxed and under as little pressure from outside events as possible (LeShan 1980, 87). Nevertheless, as Edwards (1987) indicates, there is no personal healing technique. Healers do not themselves heal and are not technically responsible for the healing result. They are merely an instrument, a channel for energy, which is variously attributed to God, other deities and entities, or spirits, and frequently invoked by prayer, chanting and other rituals. Some healers experience this energy physically as a pattern of activity within their hands and body, and heal by trying to transmit it to another person. Hall (1950, p.40) describes the feeling as a 'pulsing vibration that is not just mental, but is an actual physical sensation which may be felt pouring over the entire body. The portion of the anatomy which is more acutely conscious of the feeling ... is the hands, and it is through the hands that the actual transmission takes place'. Therefore, as he indicates, healers usually place their hands on the upturned hands of patients, or elsewhere on their body.

LeShan (1980) initially distinguished the attempt to heal by 'doing' something to or for the person as quite different from, and less important than healing where the healer does not attempt to do anything but simply experiences a feeling of being 'at one' with the person to be healed. However, the distinction is false, because as Edwards (1987) indicates and LeShan subsequently acknowledged, there are universal features common to all healing of this kind. Irrespective of idiosyncratic rituals, all healers do one thing similarly, which is to shift consciousness and become one with the person to be healed, albeit momentarily. This is not achieved by concentration but, on the contrary, by mental abandonment or relaxation. The resulting state of being united or in harmony with another is reminiscent of Rogers' concept of empathy in which the therapist, rather than doing anything, reaches out with his being to another, attending to them fully and without barrier. Accordingly 'True healing is a partnership between healer and patient. The removal of the personality barrier results in the condition known as contact and rapport' (Ouseley, p.84). It is this communication or relationship between them which sets up an interplay of energy which is frequently experienced physically by one, other or both parties and accelerates the patient's self-healing. In physical terms this may be thought of as a state of attunement or harmony in which the healer 'gets on the same wavelength' as the other person, enabling healing to occur through the principle of resonance.

As Edwards indicates this psychological harmony between healer and patient is the essential 'contact', and it is only after this is established that hands are laid on the body. However, as he points out, it is difficult for many novice healers to accept that healing is so simple, and no effort is required. Misunderstanding of the process frequently leads them to engage in various rituals which are unnecessary, and often an impediment. Edwards observes that 'if a healer feels that he can give expression to his desire to heal the patient by the use of his hands then no harm is done. The patient may feel comforted. There is, however, no curative value in the passes themselves, and all exaggerations should be strictly avoided as being useless and unnecessary'. He thus discounts the healing value of passes, pointing out that no physical movement, as such, can produce the healing result.

It would follow therefore that laying on hands is not necessary either, other than in reinforcing the psychic contact already established between the healer and patient, and that healing can be achieved without physical intervention of any kind. That this is in fact the case is suggested by the phenomenon of absent healing in which the healer makes psychic contact with a person at a distance, without even being in their presence.

Accordingly, despite appearances to the contrary, all 'healing' involving laying on hands achieves its effects psychologically and can properly be described as psychic.

Chapter 12

Psychoenergetic Treatments

All of the body is in the mind,
but not all of the mind is in the body.

Swami Rama

Psychic healing

In a seminal work LeShan (1982) found that in the basic state of consciousness associated with healing the healer does not 'act' as one does in the ordinary world of sensory reality, but simply and literally perceives themself and the healee as one entity, (each with their uniqueness maintained) within a metaphysical system, which he terms the Clairvoyant Reality. Within this frame of reference, which he claims is common to mystics, mediums and modern physicists, reality is clearly perceived as a timeless and unified whole, in which there are no boundaries and nothing is separated from anything else; all things flow into each other, and are part of a larger whole where neither time nor space can prevent exchange of information and energy. He suggests that when healers alter their consciousness to this clairvoyant mode with the person to be healed as its focus, they are able to mobilise the self-repair system of that person, even at a distance, simply by bringing them to mind.

In this mode the healer does not attempt to 'do' anything to the other person but simply 'is' at one with them, and

> When the healer - for a moment - absolutely knows this to be true, that he and the healee are one, the healee sometimes responds with a mobilization of his self-repair and self-recuperative abilities (LeShan 1982, p.148)

LeShan proposes that when the healer attends with love, this is in some way transmitted to the healee so that he knows it also. He is then in a different existential position, part of a unity or whole, and more complete. This, LeShan observes, constitutes healing, and under these conditions positive biological changes may occur. Accordingly it is the interaction between the healer and healee which is itself healthy in the sense that it is integrative. Nevertheless, LeShan considers that the energy changes which occur in the healee's body as a result of this union are confined to the kinds of results the body can achieve on its own naturally under optimal conditions, and that the healer cannot influence these energies in any way. He is therefore constrained simply to 'be' rather than to 'do'. LeShan considers that everyone has the ability to heal in this way, and that it can be trained. In 1970 he established a five day training programme and found that of some 400 people who have taken this course over a ten year period 80-90 per cent have learned to alter consciousness to the clairvoyant mode and achieve positive biological changes in others. Nevertheless, although having trained himself and others to heal in this way, LeShan admits having 'not the faintest idea as to why it gets results or what is happening'.

Despite numerous reference to healing 'forces', 'energies' and 'abilities', he claims that the concept of energy is not especially helpful in a consideration of psychic healing, as opposed to Transpsychic Healing in which he considers the concept of energy to be of central importance.

Transpsychic healing

LeShan distinguishes transpsychic healing as that in which the healer, rather than merely arousing and strengthening the patient's own healing resources through a partnership of harmony and cooperation, mentally attempts to use his knowledge of unity to direct the immense resources of the cosmos on behalf of the healee. Here, according to LeShan, there is a conscious attempt to influence the greater 'one', of which the healer is part, to move to the aid of another part. He observes that this 'One' may be conceptualised as God, and the healer's influence exerted through prayer, but that this state of consciousness can be attained and used just as effectively for healing with other constructs.

LeShan acknowledges that for many individuals, including himself, the concept of energy is particularly useful:

> Knowing for the moment that you are part of the total One of the cosmos, and that there are vast energies which maintain the universe on its course (so to speak, the cosmic 'homeostatic' forces), you attempt by total concentration and 'will' to bend these energies to increase the harmony of the healee, another part of the cosmos. Knowing yourself a part of an all-encompassing energy system, you will the total system to direct additional energies to the repair and harmonization of a part that needs it (p.150).

However, as he indicates, willful determination is not necessary to direct these energies. It is sufficient for the healer to become so attuned to these forces that he becomes a channel for them. As LeShan explains,

> If I can perfectly align myself with the harmonies of the universe then their energies can flow through me to the healee whom I hold in consciousness.

This requires a complete surrender of will other than the desire for what is best for the healee, and a complete identification with the All. LeShan describes it as reaching towards a state 'where you wear the universe like a glove, and it wears you'.

This state where the healer reaches out beyond mind to Unity - which LeShan terms the Transpsychic Reality - is superconscious or transcendent rather than conscious or psychic, and he claims that the results of this mental action can be remarkable, even miraculous, giving rise to physical change beyond the body's ability for self-repair. He suggests that it may account for the dramatic effects of healers such as Harry Edwards; the so-called 'psychic surgeons', whose controversial miracle cures' are well-documented (Puharich 1962; Watson 1974; Playfair 1977; Coxhead 1979; Dooley 1973; Chapman and Stemman 1978; Taylor, 1987); and the perception of the flow of energies by some healers and their patients. LeShan believes that this Transpsychic Healing can also be trained, but only in those with a serious background in meditation and contemplation. Although admitting to not understanding how it 'works', he believes it to be 'the mobilization and focusing of some as yet undefined type of energy' (p.165). His own enquiries into its nature led him 'against all [my] expectations and preferences into fields hitherto left to religion' (p.166), and to conclusions similar to those of Reich and Jung before him, and various Eastern and Western traditions:

> The recurring theme 'God is love' appears to mean exactly what it says; that there is a force, an energy, that binds the cosmos together, and moves always in the direction of its harmonious action and the fruition of the separate connected parts. In man, this force emerges and expresses itself as love, and this is the 'spark of the divine' in each of us. When this force is acknowledged and reinforced by the culture it is possible for human beings to relate harmoniously to themselves, to others, to the rest of the cosmos, and to move toward the most unique and awesome self-fulfilment.

> When this force is ignored or discouraged, the energy becomes blocked and distorted, and in all human history has been expressed in self-hatred, a hunger for power, materialistic greed and ultimately, as the dehumanisation of our time makes clear, the real possibility of man's so disrupting the expression of this energy as to end his part of the cosmic design.

> It seems to me that the challenge to science, to man, to the human experiment, is finally and irrevocably, whether or not man can accept that he is a part of the energy of the universe and can only function harmoniously within it through his capacity to love - infinitely (1982, p.166-7).

Thus, although not explicitly stated as such, LeShan's Transpsychic Healing may be regarded as spiritual in nature.

Spiritual healing

The term 'spiritual' lends itself to a good deal of confusion and misunderstanding, especially in materialistic cultures which are markedly 'aspiritual'. It may be taken as referring to the spirit or soul, and interpreted as relating to Churches and religions. Accordingly Spiritual Healing is attributed to God or gods, and typically invoked by prayer and other rituals. Healing flourishes in all the religions and movements including the Christian Church, and in less orthodox movements such as Christian Science, which was developed in the last century with the aim of reinstating the healing ministry of early Christianity. Hall (1950) deplores the tendency of some Christian communions to regard healing as only possible for those who are members of a particular branch of the Christian faith. As Edwards (1987, p.4) indicates:

> Spirit healing is not the prerogative of any religion or race; it is a common heritage for the whole of the human family. It is extensively practised in the lamaserys of Tibet, and every Mohammedan priest invokes the healing aid for his supplicants. The gift of healing is no more a perquisite of Christianity then any other religion.

Moreover,

> There is not one set of healing laws for the Spiritualist and another for the Methodist or Christian Science practitioner. There are general laws that govern healing, as there are laws that govern every other effect produced in the universe.

Hall observes that church membership and theological terminology may be unacceptable to the vast numbers of people who have a deep belief in the power of God as the ruling force of the universe, but do not subscribe to any particular religious beliefs, and to the very great number who are members of faiths other than the Christian. He therefore proposes the term Primal Healing which, he argues, meets the needs of all these people while in no way detracting from the basic essence of healing as taught within Christianity, describing it as a form of healing that arises from complete attunement of the human mind and body with the first cause of the universe, whether described as God, Spirit, Universal Force, or otherwise.

Nevertheless the term spiritual healing persists, and is often further confused by the common belief that it pertains to 'spirits', discarnate beings surviving in another realm and communicating with those on earth through mediums. This widespread belief is fostered by the emphasis on healing within the Spiritualist Church.

The National Spiritualists' Association recognizes several different ways by which healing is effected; by spiritual influences working through a medium and infusing curative, stimulating and vitalising energies into the diseased body of another; by the spiritual forces illuminating the brain of the healing medium thereby intensifying perception of the cause of disease and its remedy; and through absent treatments where spiritual energies blending with those of the medium are directed to a person distant from them. It therefore covers all aspects of spiritual healing, including psychic diagnosis and absent treatment.

Confusion undoubtedly arises as a result of failure to distinguish between 'spirits' and Spirit. The former may be regarded as non-physical entities which function to transmit information or energies through the medium of one person's body or mind to that of another, whereas the latter may be thought of as the source of these energies, a great cosmic power which pervades the entire universe. The latter concept, which forms the basis of Spiritualist philosophy, owes much to the influence of ancient and Eastern traditions and Theosophy where 'poor spirits' - mental or physical - are thought to arise rom the person's inability to mentally attune themselves to the great forces of the niverse which are essential to life. As Carrington (1920, p.158) explains:

> This vital energy which is imparted by means of spiritual healing is a great cosmic power, which pervades the whole universe. It is everywhere; it is back of every phenomenon: 'in it we live and move and have our being'. It is illimitable in extent and in power; we simply have to draw upon it to the extent we can; and the more we can 'draw', the more rapidly do we become well; the speedier the cure. There is no reason to suppose that, if we could 'tap' this great Reservoir in the right way, we should not become well instantly - and indeed there are many cases of this character, where, apparently, this has been done - instances of so-called 'miraculous cures' being of this nature. We must learn to tap the source of spiritual energy, and when we have reached this inexhaustible fountain, then health and strength will be ours.

rom this perspective man is a spiritual being within a spiritual universe: everything is pirit. Irrespective of what they choose to call it, most spiritual healers believe in this piritual reality and are concerned to channel this Absolute Energy, while only a ninority subscribe to a belief in 'spirits' and claim to channel these energies. Therefore, piritual healing has for the most part little to do with spirits. Nevertheless, all spiritual ealers are mediums in the sense that they mediate between an energy source and its ventual recipient.

Spiritual healing depends largely on an understanding of universal energies and the neans of attunement with them. Central to it is the principle that the physical body can e acted on and influenced from higher spheres or planes of activity through, or by neans of the vital or etheric body which acts as a vehicle through which cosmic energy lows. The problem for the healer, according to Carrington, is to connect the etheric ody with the physical body on the one hand, and with the great reservoir of spiritual nergy on the other. It may well be that these are two different processes. What has been lescribed as psychic healing, involves the creation of what Hall (1950) terms a 'mind ridge' between healer and the patient which establishes the channel or wave band over vhich the cosmic or primal force then travels directly into the mind or body of the patient, whether they are in contact with or distant from the healer.

This mental connection is considered possible because both parties are immersed in common etheric field through which energy and information can be transmitted. Accordingly the patient need not be present for the purposes of diagnosis and treatment. Such a view is consistent with holographic theory, according to which, information bout the whole is available at once in each of its parts. It is therefore sufficient to 'bring he patient to mind' - in order to effect, and be effected by them.

Hall suggests that the healer establishes this mind bridge or channel by means akin o radio waves, albeit of a very much higher vibration. Edwards also views the healing orces operated by healers as states or vibration, claiming that when a healing takes lace a set of correcting vibratory forces is applied to a given condition thus bringing bout the change necessary to restore true balance and harmony. This, he suggests, 'may vell be the ABC of spirit healing'.

Hall claims that these vibrations can be directed by the healer timed to a split second and that those to whom they are attuned actually receive an influx of energy. This finds support in studies by Cade (Cade and Coxhead 1979), which have demonstrated that the EEG patterns of the recipients of healing alter simultaneously with those of the healer, even during absent healing; and by Holmes (1975) who found that when using her absent healing technique Olga Worrall could influence patterns in a cloud chamber 600 miles distant; and in studies of Matthew Manning. The same principle is the basis for the related healing approaches of radionics, medical radiestheia and psionic medicine, which diagnose and treat illness from an energetic frequency perspective.

Radionics, medical radiethesia and psionic medicine

Radionics originated in the work of Dr Albert Abrams (1863-1923), teacher of pathology and later Director of Studies at Stanford University Medical School. He pioneered within orthodox medicine diagnosis by percussion or tapping various parts of the body to produce resonating sounds, and developed a box containing resistors to measure disease reactions in ohms. This met with hostility among the medical orthodoxy, despite the fact that the practice of percussion has a very long history in traditional medicine and is demonstrably effective as a diagnostic technique.

The basis of radionics theory and practice (Abrams 1916) were subsequently developed and refined by a number of pioneers, most notably Dr Ruth Drown and George de La Warr (Day and de La Warr, 1956; 1966), and more recently by David Tansley, Malcolm Rae and Aubrey Westlake (Tansley 1972; Tansley, Rae and Westlake 1977).

Radionics is similar to Eastern, Theosophical and Spiritualist schools of thought in viewing man as an integrated whole of body, mind and spirit. In addition to the physical body there are held to be etheric, emotional and mental 'bodies' in which illness first manifests, and it is to these more subtle bodies that the practitioner directs healing energy via specific instruments.

Basic to radionics theory is the realisation that all matter, whether alive or dead, has magnetic polarity and emanates energy of different frequencies, which is measurable. All material forms therefore have their own electromagnetic field which merge into common ground.

Disease is thought to result from distortion of the energy field around life forms and, like body organs and remedies, to have characteristic frequencies or vibrations which can be expressed in numerical values known as 'rates' and calculated on radionic instruments. Ruth Drown identified a series of rates which in effect constitutes the vibrational patterns of known diseases.

Diagnosis employs the principle of dowsing, which is the detection of subtle energies by means of various instruments. It is an ancient art which has been used down the ages to locate water, minerals and lines of force deep within the earth, and more recently in Japan to sex newly born chicks, and to detect submarines (Davidson 1987). Although depicted on Mayan and Egyptian reliefs and practised throughout medieval Europe, the earliest written references to dowsing in English were by Robert Fludd in 1638. The term radiesthesia was first applied to the practice at the turn of this century by the Abbé Elexis Bouley in the belief that the phenomena observed in the act of dowsing are the result of some kind of radiation, (Bell 1965).

Medical radiesthesia became popular in England during the 1930s. It is used in detecting hidden causes of disease which do not lend themselves to identification by means of standard clinical tests, and to find treatments which will eliminate the disease. Psionic Medicine developed by Dr George Lawrence represents a modern development on the application of radiesthesia to health (Westlake 1977).

Although ostensibly a physical method, dowsing or radiesthesia ultimately depends on the psychic abilities of the practitioner and their sensitivity to subtle radiations of varying vibrational frequencies. The dowsing instrument, whether a rod, stick, pendulum or more complex device, merely serves to indicate what the human 'instrument' initially detects. Radionics systems which indicate this sensitivity more accurately have been developed and tested in the USA and Europe for several decades. Gerber (1988) terms these 'psychotronic technologies' because of the central role of the operator's consciousness in obtaining information from the device. He claims that the operator achieves a psychoenergetic link with various subtle energies through a process of attunement, which he explains as follows:

> This psychic process of tuning in ... occurs at the level of our higher frequency vehicles of expression. In most individuals this energetic linkup takes place at an unconscious level. The unconscious mind acts as a passageway through which higher frequency levels of consciousness may interact with the physical body. Higher psychic impressions are translated into various forms of the body's neurological circuitry. If the psychic information reaches conscious awareness, it does so through the expressive mechanism of the cerebral cortex. Unconscious intuitive information may filter through the right cerebral hemisphere and then be transferred to the left hemisphere where it is analyzed and expressed verbally. While psychic information may not always reach conscious awareness, it is still processed by the nervous system and expressed through unconscious pathways of neurological and motor activity (p.227).

> The mechanical output of the pendulum, like the radionic device, is dependent upon the unconscious nervous output induced by psychic perceptual functioning. In the instance of the radionics device, the unconscious output is conveyed through the autonomic nervous system. In the case of the pendulum, the medium of expression is tiny unconscious skeletal muscle movements. Both systems of the physical body as a means of translating unconscious psychic data into conscious diagnostic energetic information (p.233).

At its most simple the radionics procedure involves a biological specimen - usually a spot of blood or a lock of hair - referred to as the 'witness' - which is placed in the well of the radionics instrument, a device consisting of a black box with a number of tuneable dials on the front, each numerically calibrated, and usually attached to variable resistors or potentiometers inside the box which are also connected by wires to the circular metallic well and to a rubber pad which forms the interface between the operator and the device.

Then

> while mentally tuning in to the patient in question, the radionics operator lightly strokes a finger across the rubber pad. As the practitioner does this, he or she slowly turns one of the dials on the front. The operator will register a positive response when he/she feels a sticking sensation in the finger as he/she strokes the pad. This might be viewed as a type of sympathetic resonance reaction. The resonance occurs between the energetic frequency of the patient and the subtle energy system of the radionics operator's nervous system. The dial is left tuned to the setting which induced a resonance response. The operator then moves on to a second dial, repeating the same procedure with the finger stroking until he/she has tuned all the dials to their appropriate test settings. Each dial represents a digit in sequence which, when combined, produces a multidigit number referred to as a 'rate'. The rate reflects the energetic frequency characteristics of the patient being remotely tested by the radionics device.

> Based on a comparison of the patient's rate with a type of 'rate reference table', the radionics practitioner is able to make a presumptive diagnosis of the patient's pathologic condition. Comparison of patient rates with the standard rate reference tables allows matching of the patient's frequency with known vibrational frequencies associated with particular illnesses (Gerber 1988, p.224).

Gerber suggests that this frequency matching procedure is similar to that in homeopathy except that radionics directly measures the patient's primary energetic frequency disturbance rather than depending upon empirical frequency matching of remedy to symptom complex. He acknowledges that to most orthodox physicians this process may seem nonsensical, but indicates that it is based on the scientific principles of biological resonance and holography.

According to the latter the witness reflects the total energetic structure of the entire organism and continues to do so because of resonance with the person from which it came, remaining in energetic equilibrium with its source regardless of its distance from them.

Having thus divined the energetic frequency imbalances within the patient, radionics devices allow the practitioner to transmit vibrational energy of the needed frequency characteristics back to the patient. Therefore, as in spiritual healing, treatment involves the application of corrective vibratory forces.

These forms of healing are all claimed by their exponents to exert their influence at the etheric level by attempting to restore energy imbalances in the etheric body which controls the physical body. They are considered to achieve their effect by attunement to and amplification of the higher vibrations of man, which results in the stimulation of the body's self-healing processes. The process can be likened to that of applying 'jump leads' to a car battery, the depleted energies of which are 'boosted' by those of another, after which it is able to 'charge' itself.

Psychic surgery

This process may well be different, in degree if not in kind, from that effected by psychic surgeons and healers such as George Chapman, the results of which are dramatic:

> The phenomena which occur are at times incredible, sometimes amusing, but always remarkable. For instance, tissue anywhere on the body is parted using only the bare hands of the healer; tissue or strange objects may be removed from the opening - egg shells, broken glass, old plastic bags, pieces of seaweed, a live shrimp. Cotton wool, dipped in oil, may be dematerialized into the chest of the patient and a few minutes later rematerialized in one ear and later removed from another.
>
> A healer may point his own forefinger or that of a bystander from a distance of about eight inches at the spot on the body where he wishes to make an incision, whereupon a clean cut, oozing a few drops of blood appears almost instantaneously. Some healers have been seen to remove an eyeball, remove connective tissue from the rear and then replace it. A healer may also use a knife, sharp or blunt, which he wipes on his sleeve before manipulating around the eye of a patient whilst he removes a small growth without causing any pain or damage (McCausland 1979, p.181).

These phenomena are not necessary for the actual healing, but as McCausland indicates, they frequently satisfy the 'seeing is believing' principle. Whether believed or not, extraordinary numbers of people are treated by these healers, and psychic surgery takes place throughout the Philippines and Brazil, in Britain, and has been reported in North Africa, the Himalayas and the Andes.

McCausland suggests that it utilizes the etheric body to obtain its remarkable results, the psychic surgeons working with the energy body to alter its blueprint, whereupon changes take place in the physical body, often with startling suddenness.

The process may be likened to 'charging' the battery of the body by joining it to the main supply, a far greater power source than merely another battery. This being the case it could be argued that the healer, through applying vibration (from the Latin *vibrare*: to shake or move) is creating a perturbation in the system which enables it to escape to a higher order of organisation; and thus creating new forms through dramatic 'shake-up' of the old.

Nevertheless an external agency may not be necessary to effect healing. This is suggested by the Indonesian practice of Subud, the central feature of which is latihan, a collective exercise in which people submit themselves to 'an energy which activates the inner nature, and through its purifying process tends to move and vibrate even those parts of us which we cannot see, which are "out of mind"' (Blair 1975, p.11). This force is received through complete non-doing and according to Blair, may be 'sufficient to disrupt and to traumatise the patterns of the psyche and the nervous system'. During the exercise, therefore, healings often occur as a result of individuals being brought into new harmony. Nevertheless, the exercise also carries with it the danger of spiritual crisis, and a 'Subud Syndrome' or 'Psychosis' similar to, but differing from, schizophrenia has been identified in a number of medical journals (Blair 1975).

Indeed, this phenomenon serves as a reminder of Prigogine's observation that reintegration or disintegration may follow shake-up of energies. Therefore the intensification of energy through healing is not necessarily curative, and this important distinction between healing and curing cannot be overstressed.

Energy transformation

In all these apparently different methods of healing it is the psyche which mediates between spiritual, or higher mental energy and physical energy. Mind is thus the medium whereby energy is transmitted and transformed. The notion of the mind as an energy transformer is misleading however, suggesting as it does different energy factors. Yet as Jung and others have observed, the striking similarity between the concept of energy in present-day physics and that underlying numerous psycho-spiritual traditions, both ancient and modern, suggests that 'they may well designate one and the same factor viewed from two complementary angles' (von Franz 1974, p.155). Accordingly, mind might more appropriately be thought of as a refractor which imposes a different 'angle' on this energy, transforming only in the sense of redirecting it. The healer's belief that they are mentally 'channeling' energy seems consistent with this notion, but how this is achieved remains open to question.

Eddington (1939) observes that efforts to represent a comprehensible picture of what is known about energy - which, since it is conserved might be viewed as the modern successor of substance - require a conception of 'form'. This is no less true of relativity and quantum theories, in the former energy being pictured as the curvature of space-time and in the latter as a periodicity of waves.

Number and rhythm

Von Franz suggests that amorphous energy probably does not exist at all, inasmuch as when it manifests in either psychic or physical dimensions it is always 'numerically' structured, as 'waves' for example, or as (psychic) rhythm. Jung (1967) observed the tendency of all emotional or energy laden psychic processes to become rhythmical; 'Any kind of excitement ... displays a tendency to rhythmical expression, perseveration, and repetition' (p.219-10). This, von Franz suggests, may explain the basis of various rhythmic and ritual activities practised by primitive peoples, and the dependence of work-achievement on music, dancing, singing, drumming and rhythm in general; 'Through them, psychic energy and the ideas and activities bound up with it are imprinted and firmly organised in consciousness' (p.974, p.157). Therefore, she suggests that the application of rhythm to psychic energy 'was probably the first step towards its cultural formation, and hence its spiritualization'.

According to Jung (1967) the Chinese concept of number is based on association with this type of rhythmic activity in man, and, as von Franz indicates, the Chinese from the very earliest times used number to assess feeling-intensities of all things that had a psychic effect on man. Number, she suggests, remains the common ordering factor of both physical and psychic manifestations of energy, and is consequently the element that draws psyche and matter together.

> Natural numbers appear to represent the typical, universally recurring, common motion patterns of both psychic *and physical energy*. Because these motion patterns (numbers) are identical for both forms of energy, the human mind can, on the whole, grasp the phenomena of the outer world. This means that the motion patterns engender 'thought and structure' models in man's psyche, which can be applied to physical phenomena and achieve relative congruence. The existence of such numerical constants in the outer world, on the one hand, and in the preconscious psyche, on the other ... is probably what finally makes all conscious knowledge of nature possible.

Number can therefore be regarded as a mediator between psychic or 'inner' situations and physical or 'outer' ones. Thus when trying to understand these latter patterns consciously one makes use of the abstractions of higher mathematics for the observation of quantitative manifestations of energy. Accordingly mathematics is the language of physics, and through its use physicists attempt to provide accurate descriptions of physical reality.

Symbolism and imagery in healing.

However, there is, as Whyte (1954) points out, no branch of mathematics for the observation and description of qualitative manifestations of energy. Von Franz therefore suggests that to render these structures comprehensible one must first develop a qualitative view of number, such as she attempted in her discussion of rhythm.

Arguably, however, 'comprehensive pictures' of the qualitative aspects of energy are provided, quite literally, by the symbols of visual imagery, which is why imagery is traditionally the language of the mystic, the 'medium' and the poet, and why in recent times striking parallels have been noted between their descriptions of reality and the mathematical descriptions of the physicist. As Blair (1975,p.106) observes: 'The hidden order which surrounds us cannot be perceived by "logic" alone and we must pass over to the ships of symbolism to ride through the waters of the soul'.

Symbolism, (from *sumballein*: to throw together) is that which brings together. Symbols are therefore the supreme mediators between different worlds of experience, and thus, as Jung (1967) indicates transformers of energy. That they are employed as such by healers can be gleaned from their accounts (Edwards 1987; Manning 1988,9; Schwartz 1980; Worrall, in Miller 1975); those of healer-trainers (LeShan 1982); and in Reiki the Japanese tradition of healing by laying on hands. Common to all of these is an emphasis on the use of imagery combined with relaxation.

Mrs Worrall described to Miller (1975) imagining energy in the form of light flowing from her hands into the patient during healing. LeShan also describes his use of symbols in training himself and others to attain the clairvoyant mode in which he believes healing is achieved:

For example, I might use the symbol of two trees on opposite sides of a hill with the tops visible to each other. From one viewpoint they looked like two separate trees, but inside the hill the two root masses met and were one. The two trees were really one and inseparable. Further, their roots affected the earth and the rocks until I could know that in the whole planet and cosmos there was nothing that was not affected by them and affecting them. This sort of symbolization, different in each case, as the healer and I are different in each healing encounter, would often be useful in helping reach the Clairvoyant Reality with the healee and myself centred in it. (1980 pp.199-20)

According to tradition Usui, a Japanese academic searching for an explanation of how Buddha and Christ healed by laying hands, had a vision following meditation in which he saw symbols which later enabled him to channel the energy of Reiki or Universal Life for himself and others. He evolved the use of these symbols in association with laying on hands, and his system was subsequently developed by Dr Hayashi and Haiwayo Takata.

Gawain (1985) employs the principle of resonance, whereby vibrational forms tend to attract to energy of a similar quality and vibration, to explain the role of thought and imagery in mobilising energy:

> The idea is like a blueprint; it creates an image of the form, which then magnetises and guides the physical energy to flow into that form and eventually manifests it on a physical plane (p.6).

Art therapy

Externalisation of these images, as in artwork, may, according to Jacobi (1962), be even more potent in mobilising energy:

> Symbols are transformers of energy. They have expressive and impressive features. On the one hand they express the intrapsychic process in images, but on the other, when they become 'incarnated' in pictorial material they make an impression: ie their meaning content influences the intrapsychic process and furthers the flow of psychic energy.

The expressive features of symbols have been used in the diagnosis and treatment of disease from the earliest of times, while their impressive features have been used to good effect in all shamanic traditions of medicine throughout the world, both ancient and modern; in the healing traditions of the East, notably the Hindu, and those of ancient Western civilisations such as Egypt and Greece; by Jung and his followers; and more recently in various forms of art therapy.

Sound therapies

Visual images and thoughts are not the only psychic mediators of energy, as Needleman (1972, p.139) observes:

Sound, when understood generally as matter in a state of vibration, obviously encompasses much more than we can ordinarily hear with our ears. We can readily acknowledge that sound, even in the ordinary sense, has effects beyond bringing pleasant or unpleasant associations to mind. It can directly affect our body, just as certain sounds can break glass. Theoretically it is thus obvious that all sound has some effect on us, even though we may not recognize what it is.

This understanding forms the basis of the traditional use of sound in healing. Needleman indicates that variations in energy may be regarded as different qualities of vibration and associated with different levels of reality, which correspond with a hierarchy of sound. It is therefore possible to equate divine energy with divine vibration or sound. This 'mantra theory', dates far back in the history of religion.

'Sacred language' may from one point of view be defined as a system of sounds based on knowledge which we, in present times, do not have. Thus speaking very abstractly, a sacred language is a reflection of the entire spectrum of creative energies in the universe. The use of music and chanting, the arrangement of words in a song or myth, probably have to be understood in this context. Theoretically we would have to recognise the distinction between that aspect of language which provokes certain images and ideas which in turn affect our organism, and another aspect of language which directly affects our organism by vibration in a carefully controlled way. Surely scripture, if it is 'sacred' does both. 'Secular' or ordinary language may be understood simply as language in which these elements are poorly recognised and uncontrolled (Needleman 1972, p.139).

It is said that Sanskrit is such a sacred language and that the Vedic hymns, which are the root of all Hindu scripture, were composed and sung as reflections of the divine play of creative energy. Many mantras used in traditional forms of meditation are short phrases or words from the Vedas and even those from other sources are all Sanskrit. Needleman indicates that even when Indian disciples spread to foreign lands the mantras used tended to remain in Sanskrit because of what is understood to be the cosmic and psychological properties of the language.

Although certain mantras such as 'Om' are supposed to produce the same effect for anyone who intones them correctly, the practical use of mantras is also based on the idea that individuals vary in regard to which special sound is helpful to them. The dispensation of mantras is therefore regarded as demanding an extraordinary psychological knowledge, 'not only of men as they are, but of men as they can become', (Needleman, p.139), because repetition of any sound or mantra over months or even years will produce certain effects. Therefore it is generally considered to require the understanding of great masters.

Among North American Indians religious words have a special potency integral to their special sounds (Epes Brown 1985). What is named is therefore understood as present in the name rather than merely symbolised by it. Moreover, just as words bear power, a statement or thought is also understood to have a potency of its own.

In the religious traditions of Central and South America each individual is considered to have a particular note and pitch, knowledge of which can be used to effect their purification and healing, or their death. Similarly, throughout Africa and the East the human voice is widely used in healing and in influencing emotional states. Watson (1973, p.105) observes that the 'kiai', the fighting cry of the Japanese Samurai, is said when uttered in a minor key, to produce 'partial paralysis by a reaction that suddenly lowers the arterial blood pressure'. It is tempting to suggest that the famous 'blood curdling' cry uttered to devastating effect by Laurence Olivier in his performance as Coriolanus was achieved similarly, albeit unwittingly.

Modern science utilises the same principles, harnessing very high frequency sound waves in the form of the ultrasonic scanner within medicine, and at the other extreme very low frequency sound waves are being explored as a military weapon (Stanway 1987).

Other physical effects of sound are claimed in the legends of Mexico and Peru according to which ancient peoples had such 'sound knowledge' that by this means alone they could split massive stone slabs along precise harmonic lines and then move them into position by resonance. The temples of Uxmal and Machu Pichu are therefore thought to have been raised and patterned in symphonies of sound (Blair 1975). Navajo Indian legend tells of shamans who could produce pictures in sand merely by speaking to it, and that this may indeed be possible was demonstrated by the 18th century German physicist Ernst Chladni who discovered a way of making vibration patterns visible.

Chladni observed the changing patterns of sand scattered on steel discs in response to violin notes. He noted that the disc resonates to the violin only in certain places shifting sand only to those areas which are inert. The resulting patterns, known as Chladni figures, have been extensively used in physics to demonstrate wave functions but can also be used to show that different frequencies produce patterns with different forms. Watson (1973, p.101) observes that using powders of different densities and a wide range of frequencies it is possible to induce a pattern of almost any form, and that commonly they adopt familiar organic forms.

> Concentric circles, such as the annual rings in a tree trunk; alternating lines, such as the stripes on a zebra's back; hexagonal grids, such as the cells in a honeycomb; radiating wheel spokes such as the canals in a jellyfish; vanishing spirals, such as the turrets of shellfish.

Sound therapies attempt to harness sound waves in the diagnosis and treatment of disease. Their exponents maintain that disease, which manifests in a change of fundamental frequency of the vibrational or energy output of the body, can be treated by application of vibrations of a similar frequency. The electrocardiogram, which records the vibrations of electrical frequencies of the heart, and the electrocephalogram which measures brain waves, are extensively used in orthodox medical diagnosis, as is the ultrasonic scanner. However, sonic and ultrasonic treatments are less well developed their experimental use being largely confined to osteoplasty.

Cymatics

The study of the effects or waves or vibrations on matter was termed cymatics by Hans Jenny, who has recently expanded and refined Chladni's research, in so doing producing further evidence that form is a function of frequency (Jenny 1966, 68). In his film *Cymatics* Jenny demonstrates that raising the pitch of sound causes a pattern to invert itself into a moving one; and by raising it again, a static but different pattern is produced once more, and so on. Thus the formalized expression of the ascending musical scale alternates between static and fluid, which Blair (1975 p.114) suggests is a visual expression of the yin/yang concept of duality.

As he explains, there are always patterns on the disc, the one formed by sand, and the background which is free of sand.

> The runnels of sand which we see are simply where it has collected at the 'dead' areas of the disc, whereas the 'life' of the pattern is vibrating in the background behind, or between the runnels, where invisible energy is causing chaos to coalesce into form. The paradox is that the *visible* expression of energy is the inverse of the actual vibrationary pattern, which is invisible.

He therefore concludes that

> After centuries of concentrating only on what it can see and touch, science is now beginning to look *between* these runnels, into the background of metaphysical order. We are reminded again of the Gnostics' assertions that the physical world is but a pale shadow - the mirror image or outermost shell, of a supreme ordering energy which exists in another dimension.

Jenny further developed his experiments, devising a 'tonoscope' which transforms sound uttered into a microphone into a three-dimensional visual representation on a screen. When correctly intoned into it the sacred Sanskrit syllable 'Om' can be seen to produce a perfect circle, which then fills with concentric squares and triangles, and finally a 'yantra' - the formal geometric expression of sacred vibration which is found in many world religions. The would seem to suggest that 'liturgical language and music supplied not only a special vocabulary through which the ancient priest classes could speak of different realities, but a vocabulary which itself resonated to the vibrations it described' (Blair, p.115).

Music therapy

In this regard the significance of music cannot be overlooked. Blair points to Ethiopian legends according to which language developed from song, early man only being able to sing, until gradually he forgot the tune and had to rely simply on speaking the words. He suggests that 'the vibrations of music, such a primal part of primitive expression, hints at a forgotten awareness of the rhythms and tones which actually keep us alive' (p.116), and that 'the central place occupied by music in the education of the Greeks was due to the recognition that the harmonics of sound unlocked in the student an awareness of the interplay of invisible relationships' (pp.106-7).

Healing has long recognised and exploited music as a mediator between physical and metaphysical realities, and a means of achieving psychic reintegration. Accordingly music had a widely acknowledged therapeutic significance in the ancient world, and music therapy is a longstanding member of various traditions of both East and West.

Contemporary music therapy involves the controlled use of music in the treatment rehabilitation, education and training of those suffering physical, mental and emotional disorder, and it has been found to be especially useful in the treatment of educationally sub-normal and mentally deficient children (Dickinson 1976; Alvin 1959), and spastics (Lubran 1961; Ward 1976) and in remedial education (Hedderly 1983).

Chromatics

Cymatics has demonstrated that sound and form are simply a matter of vibrational frequency, and it is now recognised that this is also true of light and colour. Chromatics the science of colour, is the study of this relationship.

Colour is light of different wavelengths or vibrational rates. Red has the longest wavelength and the slowest vibrational rate, while violet has the shortest wavelength and the fastest vibrational rate. Red is commonly associated with heat, both in the human mind and in nature, fire, cloves, capsicum and musk all being of this colour. It is also associated with 'heated' emotions such as passion and anger, and expressed in disease by inflammation and fever. Blue, of which violet is a shade, is typically associated with lack of warmth, as is reflected in the phrase 'blue with cold', and snow and ice which have a blue tinge, as do astringents used to relieve inflammation. Red is therefore generally thought to be vital and stimulating, while shades of blue are believed to have a more sedative effect.

Experiments have lent support to these notions, demonstrating that plants grown under red glass shoot up four times more quickly than in ordinary sunlight, and that growth is much slower in plants grown under blue or green glass (Wood 1987). Gimbel (1978,87) has also found that red filtered lights initially overstimulate plants, whose growth eventually becomes stunted, whereas blue light produces slower growth but taller, thicker plants. Structural changes have been found in amoeba subjected to different coloured light, blue producing a loose, open molecular structure and red a tighter, more dense formation (Wilson and Bek 1987). Birren (1963,1969) reports similar results in studies of both plants and animals. Rodents kept under blue plastic grow normally, but when kept under pink or red plastic increase their appetite and growth rate, and chinchillas kept under blue light grow denser coats.

Colour has also been found to effect various physical conditions in human subjects. Exposure to red light is known to 'stimulate', raising blood pressure, increasing respiration rate and heartbeat, while exposure to blue light has the opposite effect. During the last century red light was found to prevent scar formation in cases of smallpox, and startling cures were later reported among TB patients exposed to sunlight and ultra-violet rays. Indeed in the USA ultraviolet is now the standard treatment for soriasis and other skin conditions, white light being widely used in conjunction with photosensitive drugs in the treatment of herpes sores; and in the last 15 years baths of blue light have also replaced blood transfusions for babies born with potentially fatal neonatal jaundice. In both the USA and the USSR the use of colour is being explored for the treatment of cancers, tumours and lung conditions, (Wood 1987).

Studies have also confirmed the effects of colour on emotions, a connection reflected in phrases such as 'seeing red', 'feeling blue', 'being in the pink', and experiencing golden moments'. Schauss, Director of Washington's Institute for Biosocial Research is cited by Wilson and Bek, (1987) as claiming that this is because the electromagnetic energy of colour affects the endocrine system, notably the pituitary and pineal glands and the hypothalamus, thereby influencing mood at all times, usually subtly but sometimes quite dramatically.

Various studies have suggested that the colour pink has a soporific or tranquillising effect and suppresses hostile, aggressive and anxious behaviour (Rosetti 1983; Wilson and Bek 1987), which is of interest given its traditional association with females in Western culture. It would appear that when subjected to pink surroundings people cannot be aggressive or angry even if they want to be because the colour saps their energy. Its sedative and muscle-relaxing effects are now being used in geriatric and adolescent units, family therapy clinics, prisons and reformatories, and in business settings. Even colour blind persons are tranquillised by pink rooms.

Indeed it is well established that colour need not be visually perceived for it to have definite psychological and physiological effects. Moreover it can be distinguished by blind, colour blind and blindfolded subjects. This phenomenon, variously referred to as eyeless sight', dermo-optic vision or bio-introscopy has been researched since the 1920s when Jules Romains established that hypnotised blind-folded persons could recognise colours and shapes with their forehead. In further studies he found that non-hypnotised blind-folded subjects could precisely describe colours and shapes presented under glass. Research in Russia during the 1960s was stimulated by studies of Roza Kulesheva (Ivanov 1964) who, when blind-folded, could distinguish colour and shapes with her fingertips, and could even read in this way.

Further experiments by Novomeiskii (1965) found that she was not as exceptional as had first been thought and that one in six experimental subjects could recognise colour with their fingertips after only 20-30 minutes training, and that blind people developed this sensitivity even more quickly. Some subjects who could distinguish colours correctly by holding their fingers 20-80 centimeters above colour cards, described experiencing sensations varying from needle pricks to faint breezes depending on the colour.

Initial explanations of the phenomenon focused on structural differences in dyeing substances but this failed to explain how colour could be distinguished under glass or tracing paper, or how Kuleshova could distinguish coloured light beams. Thermal differences were eliminated by systematically heating and cooling cards, even though the subjects did not report temperature differences as the basis of their discrimination.

Novomeiskii suggested that dermo-optic vision was in some way electrical, becaus when colour cards were placed on good conductors and subjects stood on rubber mat their response improved. However, this failed to explain how some subjects were sti able to detect colours under aluminium foil, brass or copper plates. Despite considerabl research (Reported by Novomeiskii, Mashkova, Shevalev, Konstantinov et al; Baskk rova and Romains in the *The Int. Journal of Parapsychology* VII, 4 Autumn 196! Ostrander and Schroeder 1973, and Vilenskaya 1982) the phenomenon remains a enigma. Clearly, however, colour is experienced subjectively or qualitatively as well a objectively.

Therefore

> Since our body is interlinked with the mental activities, emotional reactions and the metabolic system, we must remember that colours not only stir the psychological side of our being but also influence chemical changes by programming our physical system. These chemical changes may be so fine that by the normal standards of present day recording procedures such changes can only rarely be substantiated and proven (Gimbel, cited by Branson 1988, p.4).

Chromotherapy

Recognition of these subtle effects has formed the basis of the use of colour in healin since ancient times. The Egyptians and Greeks both used colour sanctuaries in healing and in the first century AD Aurelius Cornelius Celsus wrote several treatises on medicin which included the use of coloured ointments, plasters and flowers. Galen and Paracel sus also described the use of colour in healing, and Avicenna (980-1027), an Arabia philosopher and physician pointed to its importance in his Canon of Medicine. Colou is a significant feature of Indian and Tibetan healing traditions, and in India th traditional practice of drinking water which has been exposed to sunlight throug various coloured glasses is still prescribed in the treatment of specific conditions.

A similar practice was developed by Edwin Babbitt, a colour therapist and the autho of *Principles of Light and Colour* (1878), who claimed to cure various ailments b passing sunlight through coloured glass. He developed a number of devices such a chromodiscs and flasks and the chromolume for use in colour therapy, and establishe a chain of correspondence between colour and minerals.

Rudolph Steiner also advocated the use of colour in the treatment of variou conditions and conducted considerable research on colour therapy. However, the mo! extensive research into colour and its applications to healing has been conducted by former pupil of Steiner, Theo Gimbel, who has established the Hygeia Studios an College of Colour Therapy in England.

Among the principles being tested by Gimbel are the claims of Dr Max Lüsche former Professor of Psychology at Basle University, that colour preferences are indic; tive of states of mind, glandular imbalance or both, and can be used as the basis c physical and psychological diagnosis. Lüscher's theory, which forms the basis of th Lüscher Colour Test, is that the significance of colour for man originates in his earl history when his behaviour was governed by night and day. The colours associated with these two environments, dark blue and yellow, are claimed to be associated with differences in metabolic rate and glandular secretion appropriate to the energies required for night-time sleep and rest and daytime foraging and hunting. Other autonomic responses are thought to be associated with other colours.

Gimbel, like Steiner, relates colour to form, shape and sound and to various organic forms. He indicated that the vibrational quality of certain shades is amplified by certain forms, certain combinations of colour and shape having either destructive or regenerative effects on living organisms. Accordingly Gimbel has been commissioned to design various hospitals, sanatoria and classrooms which incorporate combinations of shape and colour known to benefit certain ailments. At the Sunfield Children's Home, Stourbridge, England, disturbed children are treated by colour in this way, and at the Steiner-inspired Bristol Waldorf school classrooms are painted and textured to correspond with the 'mood' of children at various stages of development.

Colour therapy is consistent with the principles of energy medicine, disease being viewed as depletion of energies within the physical and etheric bodies which can be built up by applying appropriate colour vibrations to the relevant chakra. Treatment may be through direct contact with the patient or by absent healing methods. In the former the colour therapist works with the aura, sensing imbalance clairvoyantly or by passing their hands over the body and noting changes in vibration associated with various parts of the body. Coloured light is then projected to the relevant chakra by means of various lamps and filters.

In absent healing the healer meditates on 'sending' a particular colour ray to the individual being treated, and Gimbel notes that in either case visualization improves the power of the therapy.

As pigments in clothing and furnishings are believed to exert an effect on those exposed to them there is a growing trend towards colour counselling, not only in the health field but in the design of business, leisure and residential settings.

Flower therapies

Flowering plants are an important feature in human environments, whether placed there by the design of nature or of man himself. Flowers are valued for their form, colour and fragrance as well as their medicinal properties which have been recognised since the earliest times. Herbal medicine is well established throughout the world. Indeed it is the basis of the modern pharmaceutical industry, most effective drugs being plant derivatives or synthetics thereof. However, various forms of healing employ the non-chemical features of plants in treatment, being based on similar principles of energy medicine as colour and sound therapies.

Bach flower remedies

One of the more widely known therapeutic approaches is that developed by the distinguished British bacteriologist and physician, Edward Bach, who in the 1930s gave up a thriving Harley Street medical practice in order to develop his Flower Remedies.

Bach distinguished between plants that relieve symptoms and those that contain genuine healing powers. The latter he regarded to be of a higher order inasmuch that they established a direct contact with the spiritual aspects of man, his Higher Self, activating all parts of his nature and all the planes of his aura, thereby treating incipient illness before it manifests in the physical body. These flowers, according to Scheffer, (1986, p.25), 'act as divine energy impulses, across all energy levels'.

Such a view was not new. In various esoteric traditions of the world the flower has been used as a symbol of the development of man's higher faculties; the rose being adopted as such by the Rosicrucians and the Sufi, and the lotus flower by the Hindu. The Tibetans also teach of a direct link between man's unconscious and the plant kingdom, man being regarded as able to contact his own essential nature or soul at an unconscious level through plant nature and so restore harmony within himself.

In developing his flower remedies as a system of treatment, which he outlines in two brief works (1931; 1986), Bach was greatly influenced by Hippocrates and by Hahnemann, as is clear from the following.

> Disease will never be cured or eradicated by present materialistic methods, for the simple reason that disease in its origin is not material. What we know as disease is an ultimate result produced in the body, the end product of deep and long acting forces, and even if material treatment alone is apparently successful this is nothing more than a temporary relief unless the real cause has been removed (1931 p.6).

For Bach the 'real' cause of disease is conflict between Soul and Mind, or personality, which he considered could never be eradicated except by spiritual or mental effort. This conflict manifested in a distortion of wavelength in the energy field of the body, which then slows down, having a negative effect on the whole psyche and resulting in negative 'soul states'. These soul states were held to correspond with certain flower remedies, thirty eight in all, each empirically tested by Bach and believed by him to have the same harmonious frequency as the soul quality concerned but without distortion and at the normal rhythm. Each remedy therefore has an affinity with the soul quality and is able to establish contact with it and through its own harmonious frequency waves or vibration re-establish harmony in the soul. The remedies, operating at subtle energy levels through the principle of resonance, thus act as a catalyst for reintegration.

> The action of these Remedies is to raise our vibrations and open up our channels for the reception of our Spiritual Self; to flood our natures with the particular virtue we need, and wash out from us the fault which is causing harm. They are able, like beautiful music or any glorious thing which gives us inspiration, to raise our very natures and bring us nearer to our souls, and by that very act bring us peace and relieve our sufferings. They cure, not by attacking disease, but by flooding our bodies with the beautiful vibrations of our Higher Nature, in the presence of whom

disease melts away as snow in sunshine (Bach 1934, quoted in Ramsell and Murray 1987, p.12).

In each case the mental outlook of the person is chosen as the guide to the necessary remedies, because Bach believed that the mind shows the onset and cause of disease more definitely than the body.

Aromatherapy

The origins of aromatherapy can be traced back to ancient Egypt, the effect of odours on the emotions having been recognised for centuries. Recently, however, Dr Paolo Rovesti has been investigating the effects of plant essences on the mind, using those which are essentially nerve stimulants or sedatives to treat depression and anxiety.

A more recent approach to aromatherapy, however, is concerned with essences, not as chemical mixtures, but as 'liquid vibrations' each having a certain resonance which corresponds with a certain colour and sound and with different bodily organs. Hence cinnamon, which corresponds with the colour orange, is basically warming, stimulating the heart and the circulation and slightly elevating body temperature.

Accordingly odours can be used like colour to treat disease on a level which corresponds to the subtle energy body of the individual and which is fully consistent with the principles of what is termed here 'energy medicine'.

Healing, Time and Energy

The premise developed in the foregoing chapters is that all forms of healing are ultimately modifications of time and energy, factors which are inextricably linked. Time therapies modify the individual's relationship to time and facilitate greater mobilization or utilization of energy, whereas energy therapies work directly with bodily energies and indirectly influence the individual's experience of time. In all cases the medium by which this is achieved is psychological - in the sense that the psyche of the individual is directed to their own healing or that of another. Accordingly, healing of the self or others is possible given time and energy.

However, time, energy and the relationship between them are not 'given' inasmuch that, as expounded here, they are premises neither generally accepted nor properly understood in the West, even though they are implicit in contemporary scientific formulations about the nature of the universe.

Prigogine and Stengers (1985 p.xxviii) point out that:

> if one asked a physicist a few years ago what physics permits us to explain and which problems remain open, he would have answered that we obviously do not have an adequate understanding of elementary particles or cosmological evolution but that knowledge of things in between was pretty satisfactory. Today a growing minority, to which we belong, would not share this optimism: we have only begun to understand the level of nature on which we live.

Indeed the scientific vision of nature is undergoing a radical change which is proceeding on all levels and resulting in an understanding of the world which is totally new to the West.

However, such a radical reformulation of reality is profoundly unsettling to those who are attached to the old scientific paradigm. This term, derived from the Greek *paradigma* meaning pattern, was coined by Thomas Kuhn (1962) to refer to the pattern of the universe perceived by scientists. As such it is a kind of super-theory about the nature of reality, of such wide scope that it accounts for all, or most, of the major known phenomena in its field. The paradigm therefore becomes an implicit framework or perspective for most scientists.

Tart (1985) indicates that it also inevitably becomes a set of blinkers inasmuch as it defines certain kinds of endeavours and issues as trivial, impossible, or meaningless. However, when the impossible becomes possible, or the apparently trivial yields results inconsistent with the dominant paradigm, a state of crisis arises in the fields so affected. Then, suggests Ferguson (1982), most problems can be likened to zen koans, which cannot be solved at the level on which they are being addressed but have to be reframed in a wider context.

This change of context represents a new paradigm, and such crises are therefore a precondition for the emergence of a new perspective. Kuhn introduced the concept of paradigm shift' to explain this change in the perceived pattern, and indicated that the history of science is characterised by such shifts, because it is only as a result of these changes in perspective that scientific understanding develops.

He suggests that a paradigm shift commences with the blurring of the existing pattern, and consequent loosening of the rules for normal research. This is ushered in by a proliferation of competing views, a willingness to experiment, the expression of explicit discontent and argument over fundamentals.

Nevertheless, although scientists begin to lose faith in the existing paradigm, they do not renounce it. Part of the difficulty is that it is not possible to embrace a new paradigm until the old one has been relinquished. The perceptual shift involved is, as Kuhn points out, rather like the gestalt switch which operates in the perception of visual illusions, and must occur all at once. Accordingly, all important advances are sudden intuitions, or new ways of seeing.

The 'old order' is threatened in other senses also. Established scientists, who are emotionally and habitually attached to the old paradigm, are rarely able to make the switch, and tend to react towards proponents of the new paradigm with scorn, scepticism, derision and hostility. Thus, where such paradigm clashes occur, so also does profound antagonism.

Science did not win its now dominant cultural position easily, and the scientific establishment (henceforth called Science, to distinguish it from science in practice) had reason to guard against non-scientific ideas, that were opposed to Science. Yet while it proved less vicious than the formerly dominant Church in suppressing competitive ideas, it has been equally self-righteous in professing the 'one true science' and equally thorough in expunging 'non-scientific' ideas and practices within its ranks and in denigrating them throughout its own and other cultures - non-scientific ideas being defined as everything identified as inner knowledge, and all outer knowledge gained within world views, theories or tests other than those officially recognised by Science as science because it has not separated itself from sacred or inner knowledge (Sathouris 1990, p.12).

Nevertheless, as Sathouris observes, among the greatest scientific advances of the twentieth century is the understanding of science itself as an evolving human endeavour within an historical context.

In particular, philosophers of science have shown us that scientific world views - views of so-called 'reality' - are historically changing constructs - that the prevailing scientific paradigm of one era can be invalid in the next; that scientific theories can be judged only by their usefulness, not by their truth; that science is the endeavour to create maps to reality and differs from religion by constructing these maps rationally and refining them through experimental tests rather than accepting without question maps acquired by revelation (1990, p.13).

Discoveries therefore do not dictate a single world view or approach to science. On the contrary they suggest the possibility of alternative world views, theories and experimental tests all within the realm of science.

Nevertheless these advances in scientific understanding have not been easily implemented in scientific practice because, as Sathouris observes, it remains difficult to accept the implied uncertainty of scientific knowledge after taking such stock in its certainty. Thus she claims, much scientific pronouncement and practice suggests that most scientists still hold science to be the ultimate arbiter of truth in the world. Schrödinger (1957) claims that this resistance towards accepting a new perspective ensures that at least fifty years elapses before any major scientific discovery penetrates public consciousness.

The implications of this time-lag are considerable, however, because in the meantime adherence to the old order results in attempts to solve problems with outmoded concepts and methods, rather than those appropriate to the task, and, therefore, to escalation of the crisis.

There are clear indications that the world is currently facing such a crisis, and that it is existential rather than merely intellectual. This is manifested in, among other things, high unemployment, inflation, escalating drug and alcohol abuse, pollution, environmental hazards, global warming, overpopulation, famine, rising crime, violence and terrorism. Numerous commentators have suggested that these problems are different facets of what is essentially a crisis in perception which derives from leading thinkers, academics, and politicians subscribing to a narrow world view and trying to apply the concepts and methods of an outdated paradigm to a reality that can no longer be understood in these terms.

As was stated in the introduction, the crisis in orthodox Western medicine is only too clear. The incidence of cancers would appear to be rising, with one person in three in the industrialized world likely to develop one form or another. Chronic degenerative conditions are also on the increase and recent years have witnessed the incidence of what appear to be new diseases such as myeloencephalopathy, Total Allergy syndrome, and of course AIDS, which in San Francisco alone has claimed more lives than the combined totals of World War I and II, and those in Korea and Vietnam. That people have 'lost heart' in orthodox medicine is suggested by the fact that one person in five falls victim to coronary heart disease, and in Britain approximately 180,000 people die annually from heart-related illness (Holden, 1988).

The optimistic hope is that with time, effort and increased financial resources devoted to the task, a cure will be found for all these conditions. Accordingly the last fifty years have witnessed a vast expansion of, and investment in, the biomedical model of medicine, which places a very high value on the use of drugs and sophisticated surgery. This trend continues despite a number of recent research programmes which clearly suggest that these approaches are not fruitful. This is particularly evident in relation to coronary heart disease, the major 'killer' disease of the Western world. Holden indicates that the three major 'causes' of coronary heart disease claimed by biomedical theorists have been disproved several times in recent years; that investigations into the effects of drugs have found that in many cases they actually increase the risk of coronary heart disease, and may also worsen the quality of life; and that similar reservations exist in relation to coronary artery by-pass surgery, the most common type of heart operation.

The expression of discontent is not confined merely to learned medical and research journals. It is evident in the growing disillusionment of health care workers and members of the general public. The growing hostility of the public to medical orthodoxy was perhaps most clearly evidenced in the violent demonstrations witnessed at the International Congress on AIDS held in San Francisco in 1990.

The proliferation of 'alternative' medical practices is also testimony to the dissatisfaction with orthodox approaches. The willingness of the public to experiment with these has led to a broadening of research as some of these methods are subjected to empirical test. As a result of the former, traditionally excluded practices such as acupuncture, osteopathy, chiropractic and homeopathy are becoming acceptable within orthodox medicine, and other more psychological approaches are being given more serious consideration. Inevitably these developments - all of which are consistent with Kuhn's concept of a paradigm shift - have led to argument about the fundamentals of medicine.

Holden (1988, p.6) suggests that HRH The Prince of Wales summed up the views of many when, in his address to the British Medical Association on 14th December 1982, he observed that 'the whole imposing edifice of medicine, for all its breathtaking successes, is, like the celebrated Tower of Pisa, slightly off-balance.'

He claimed that one of the most unfortunate consequences of this unhealthy imbalance - which he attributed to the move away from traditional methods of psychological healing and towards bio-medical therapeutics - is that the patient's individuality and their emotional, mental and spiritual needs are lost sight of. Another undesirable consequence, he suggests, is that in placing control of health care and rehabilitation in the hands of doctors and surgeons insufficient emphasis is given to the role of patients 'who could learn much about the possibility of preventing their own illnesses through a different attitude to existence'.

Like the Prince of Wales, Norman Cousins (1988) argues that in order to create a balanced perspective in medicine it is necessary to recognise that a strong will to live, higher purpose, a capacity for festivity, and a reasonable degree of confidence are not 'alternative' to competent medical treatment but ways of enhancing it:

> The wise physician favours a spirit of responsible participation by the patients in a total strategy of medical care. It is a truism that compliance is strengthened in an atmosphere of patient understanding and involvement.

> Most of all the wise physician understands that there is no contradiction between compassion and competence, between the arts of reassurance where reassurance is possible, and cautionary notes where required, between personal observation and

technological data; in short, between respect for the intangibles of medical care and respect for scientific quantification. (1988, p.1610)

In this light he reviews the considerable recent research on the connection between psychological and physiological factors, pointing to the now emerging picture of the specific ways in which emotions, experiences and attitudes can create physiological change, and how complex psychological factors govern the functioning of the immune system. He admits that not all new research in this area is flawless and that additional research is needed, but concludes nevertheless that 'there has been enough replication involving controlled studies to point to a presiding fact, namely, the physician has a prime resource at his disposal in the form of the patient's own apothecary' (1988, p.1612).

He also points to the growing body of research which highlights the importance of the doctor-patient relationship. These research findings, which are increasingly featured in respected orthodox medical journals have led to a more widespread recognition of the need for what has been termed a 'biopsychosocial' approach to health. This holistic model is described by its champion, Dr Peter Nixon of Charing Cross Hospital, London, as a programme of treatment and prevention which provides for both the full utilization of medical science and the full development of the human healing system. Like many others who support this model, he believes that medicine must combine the high technology and symptom-suppression techniques of the bio-medical health care model with those which are concerned with an understanding of the psychological and social origins of illness.

There is, of course, nothing new in this model. It is precisely that established some 2000 years ago by Hippocrates and originating in the traditional magical practices of the ancients. What is new is that for the first time within Western scientific medicine there is acknowledgement of the need to examine, understand, and restore to their proper place in health care, the principles and practices of the psychology of healing. Such an endeavour will involve, in every sense, both time and energy.

Bibliography

Abrams, A., (1916), *New Concepts in Diagnosis and Treatment*. The Philopolis Press. San Francisco, California.

Abse, D. W., van der Castle, R. L., Buxton, R. L., Demars, W. D., Brown, J. P. and Kirschner, L. G., (1974), Personality and behavioural characteristics of lung cancer patients. *Journal of Psychosomatic Research*, 18, 101-113.

Achterberg, J., Simonton, S. M. and Simonton, O. C., (1977), Psychology of the exceptional cancer patient: A description of patients who outlive predicted life expectancies. *Psychotherapy: Theory, Research and Practice*, 14, 4 Winter, 416-422.

Achterberg, J., Collerain, I. and Craig, P., (1978), A possible relationship between cancer, mental retardation and mental disorders. *Journal of Social Science and Medicine*, 12th May, 135-9.

Achterberg, J. and Lawlis, G. F., (1978), *Imagery of Cancer*. Champaign, Illinois: Institute for Personality and Ability Testing.

Achterberg, J., (1985), *Imagery in Healing: Shamanism and Modern Medicine*. London: New Science Library, Routledge and Kegan Paul.

Adamenko, V., (1970), Living detectors (on the experiments of K. Bakster). *Tekhnika Molodezhi* 8, 60-62.

Ader, R., (Ed.), (1981), *Psychoneuroimmunology*. New York: Academic Press.

Ader, R. and Cohen, N., (1975), Behaviourally conditioned immunosuppression. *Psychosomatic Medicine* 37, 333-340.

Alvarez, A., (1989), Stressful life events and the recurrence of breast cancer in women. Reported in *Medicine Now*, BBC Radio 4, 15th February, 1989.

Alvin, J., (1959), Music in a school for mentally deficient children. *Special Education*, 48, 2.

Anand, B. K., Chhina, G. S. and Singh, B., (1961, reprinted 1969), Some aspects of electroencephalographic studies in Yogis. *Electroencephalography and Clinical Neurophysiology*, 13, 452-456.

Anand, B. K., Chhina, G. S. and Singh, B., (1961, reprinted 1969), Studies on Shri Ramananda Yogi during his stay in an airtight box. *Indian Journal of Medical Research*, 49, 82-89.

Anderson, N., (1982), *Open Secrets: A Western Guide to Tibetan Buddhism*. Harmondsworth: Penguin.

Anderson, W. (Ed.) (1977), *Therapy and the Arts: Tools of Consciousness.* New York and London: Harper Colophon Books.

Ashe, G., (1977), *The Ancient Wisdom.* London: Macmillan.

Babbitt, E., (1978 reprint, orig. pub. 1976), *Principles of Light and Color: The Healing Power of Color.* Secancus, NJ: Citadel Press.

Bach, E., (1931), *Heal Thyself: An Explanation of the Real Cause and Cure of Disease.* Saffron Walden: C. W. Daniel and Co. Ltd.

Bach, E., (1986), *The Twelve Healers and Other Remedies* (19th Imprint). Frome, Somerset: Hillman Ltd.

Baer, R. N. and Baer, V. V., (1984), *Windows of Light: Quartz Crystals and Self-Transformation.* San Francisco: Harper and Row.

Bagchi, B. K. and Wenger, M. A., (1959), Electrophysiological correlates of some Yoga exercises. In L. van Bagaert and J. Radermecker (Eds.) *Electroencephalography, Clinical Neurophysiology and Epilepsy,* Vol. 3 of First Int. Congress of Neurological Sciences. London: Pergamon.

Bandler, R. and Grinder, J., (1975), *The Structure of Magic, Vol. I.* Science and Behaviour Books. Palo Alto: California Press.

Barber, T. X., (1961), Psychological Aspects of Hypnosis. *Psychological Bulletin,* 58, 390-419.

Barber, T. X., (1969), *Hypnosis: A Scientific Approach.* New York: Van Nostrand.

Barber, T. X., (1978), Hypnosis, suggestions and psychosomatic phenomena: A new look from the standpoint of recent experimental studies. *American Journal of Clinical Hypnosis,* 21, 13-27.

Barber, T. X., Chauncey, H. H. and Winer, R. A., (1964), Effects of hypnotic and non-hypnotic suggestion on parotid gland response to gustatory stimuli. *Psychosomatic Medicine,* 26, 374-380.

Barber, T. X., Spanos, N. P. and Chaves, J. F., (1974), *Hypnotism, Imagination and Human Potentialities.* New York and Oxford: Pergamon.

Barlow, W., (1975), *The Alexander Principle: How to use your body.* London: Arrow.

Barry, J., (1968), General and comparative study of the psychokinetic effect on a fungus culture. *Journal of Parapsychology,* 32, 237-243.

Baskkirova, G., (1965), Little girl sensation. *Int. Journal of Parapsychology,* vii, 4, Autumn, 379-394.

Beatty, C., (1972), *Gate of Dreams.* London and Ireland: Geoffrey Chapman.

Bek, A., (1987), Yoga and Healing, Chapter 43, 151-156 in Gharote, M. I. and Lockhart, M., *op. cit.*.

Bell, A. H. (Ed.) (1965), *Practical Dowsing: A Symposium.* London: G. Bell and Sons.

Bell, C., (1947), *The Anatomy and Philosophy of Expression as connected with the fine arts.* 4th edition. London: John Murray.

Bem, D. J., (1965), An experimental analysis of self-persuasion. *Journal of Experimental Social Psychology,* 1, 199-218.

Bem, D. J., (1972), Self perception theory. In L. Berkowitz (Ed.) *Advances in Experimental Social Psychology,* Vol. 6. New York: Academic Press.

Bennett, J. G., (1985), Foreword in *The International Manual of Homeopathy and Natural Medicine.* C. H. Sharma, 2nd edition. Wellingborough, Northants.: Thorsons Publishing Co.

Benson, H,. and Wallace, R. K., (1972), Decreased drug use with Transcendental Meditation - a study of 1,862 subjects in drug abuse, in Zarafonetis, C. J. D., (Ed), *Proceedings of the Internal Conference*. Philadelphia: Lea and Febiger.

Benson, H., Rosner, B. A., Marzetts and Klemchuk, H., (1974), Decreased blood pressure in pharmacologically treated hypertensive patients who regularly elicited the relaxation response. *Lancet*, 289, 23rd March.

Benson, H. D. with Zlipper, M. Z., (1975), *The Relaxation Response*. London: Collins.

Bergman, R. L., (1973), A school for medicine men. *American Journal of Psychiatry*, 130, 6th June, 663-666.

Berry, M., (1987), Quantum physics on the edge of chaos. *New Scientist*, Vol. 116, No. 1587, November 19th, 44-47.

Bertrand, A., (1823), *Traite du Somnambulism*. Paris.

Besant, A. (1899), *The Ancient Wisdom: An Outline of Theosophical Teachings*. 2nd edition. London: Theosophical Publishing Society. Aberdeen University Press.

Beveridge, W. I. B., (1957), *The Art of Scientific Investigation*, 3rd edition. New York: Vintage.

Bindemann, S., Milstead, R. A. V., Kaye, S. B., Welsh, J., Babeshaw, T., and Calman, K. C., (1986), Enhancement of quality of life with relaxation training in cancer patients attending a chemotherapy unit. In M. Watson and S. Greer (Eds.) *Psychosocial Issues in Malignant Disease*. Oxford: Pergamon.

Binswanger, H., (1929), Beobachtungen an entspannten und versenkten Versuchspersonen: Ein Beitrag zu möglichen Mechanismen der Konversionhysterie, *Nervenarzt*, 4, 193.

Birren, F., (1963), *Color: A Survey in Words and Pictures*. New York: University Books.

Birren, F., (1969), *Light, Color and Environment*. New York: Van Nostrand Co.

Birren, F., (1978), *Color and Human Response*. New York: Van Nostrand.

Blair, L., (1975), *Rhythms of Vision*. London: Croom Helm.

Blavatsky, H. (1888), *The Secret Doctrine: The Synthesis of Science, Religion and Philosophy*. Vols. 1-3. London: The Theosophical Publishing House.

Blofield, J., (1979), *Taoism: The Quest for Immortality*. London: Allen and Unwin.

Bloomfield, H., Cain, M. and Jaffe, R., (1975), TM: *Discovering Inner Energy and Overcoming Stress*. New York: Delacorte Press.

Blows, M., (1987), Relaxation and Meditation: Borrowing and Returning. In Gharote, M. I. and Lockhart, M., *op. cit.*

Blumberg, E. M., West, P. M. and Ellis, F. W., (1954), A possible relationship between psychological factors and human cancer. *Psychosomatic Medicine*, Vol. 16, Part 4, 277-286.

Blundell, G., (1979), Biofeedback. In A. Hill, *op. cit.*

Blythe, P., (1979), Hypnosis, 188-189, in Blundell, *op. cit.*

Boadella, d., (1987), *Lifestreams: An Introduction to Biosynthesis*. London: Routledge and Kegan Paul.

Bohm, D., (1980), *Wholeness and the Implicate Order*. London: Routledge and Kegan Paul.

Booker, H. E., Rubow, R. T. and Coleman, P. J., (1969), Simplified feedback in neuromuscular training: An automated approach using electromyographic signals. *Archives of Physical Medicine and Rehabilitation*. 615-21.

Boudreau, L., (1972), Transcendental meditation and yoga as reciprocal inhibitors. *Journal of Behaviour Therapy and Experimental Psychiatry*, 3, 97-98.

Bradley, B. and McCanne, T., (1981), Autonomic responses to stress; the effects of progressive relaxation; the relaxation response and the expectancy of relief. *Biofeedback and Self-Regulation*, 6, 235-251.

Braid, J. (1843), *Neurypnology: Or the Rationale of Nervous Sleep considered in relation with Animal Magnetism.* London: Churchill (Rep. ed. 1976), New York: Anne Press.

Branson, L., (1988), Chromotherapy: Nature's healing rainbow (part 3), in *Attitudes*, Matthew Manning Centre, No. 9, Spring, 4-7.

Branthwaite, J. A. and Cooper, P., (1989), Psychology and Market Research. In Hartley, J. and Branthwaite, J. A., *op. cit.*

Brener, J. and Kleinman, R. A., (1970), Learned control of decreases in systolic blood pressure. *Nature*, 26, 1063.

Bresnitz, S. (Ed.) (1983), *The Denial of Stress.* New York: International Universities Press.

Brohn, P., (1986), *Gentle Giants.* London: Century Publishing.

Brome, V., (1978), *Jung: Man and Myth.* Frogmore, St. Albans: Paladin, Granada.

Brosse, T., (1946), A Psychophysiological Study. *Main Currents of Modern Thought*, 4, 77-84

Brown, R. I. F., and Kissen, D. M., (1969), A further report on personality and psychsocial factors in lung cancer. *Annals of New York Academy of Science*, 164, 5-44.

Bryn-Jones, H., (1979), *Somatography.* In Hill, A., *op. cit.*

Burish, T. G. and Lyles, J. N., (1981), Effectiveness and relaxation training in reducing adverse reactions to cancer chemotherapy. *Journal of Behavioural Medicine*, 4, 65-78.

Burroughs, W. S., (1977), *Junky.* Harmondsworth: Penguin.

Butler, W. E., (1982), *Magic: Its Ritual, Power and Purpose.* Wellingborough, Northants: The Aquarian Press.

Butler, W. E., (1987), *How to read the Aura.* Wellingborough, Northants: Aquarian Press.

Cade, C. M. and N. Coxhead., (1979), *The Awakened Mind: Biofeedback and the Development of Higher States of Awareness.* Dorset: Wildwood House.

Cannon, W. B., (1914), The emergency function of the adrenal medulla in pain and the major emotions. *American Journal of Physiology*, 33, 356-372.

Capra, F., (1976), *The Tao of Physics.* England: Fontana/Collins.

Capra, F., (1982), *The Turning Point: Science, society and the rising culture.* London Wildwood House.

Carrington, H., (1920), *Your Psychic Powers and How to Develop Them.* London: Kegan, Paul Trench, Trubner and Co. Ltd.

Carrington, P., (1977), *Freedom in Meditation.* New York: Anchor.

Cassem, N. H., Hackett, T. P. and Wishnie, A., (1968), The coronary care unit: An appraisal of its psychological hazards. *New England Journal of Medicine* 279, 1365

Castaneda, C., (1973), *A Separate Reality.* Harmondsworth: Penguin.

Castaneda, C., (1975), *Journey to Ixtlan.* Harmondsworth: Penguin.

Castaneda, C., (1976), *Tales of Power.* Harmondsworth: Penguin.

Castaneda, C., (1978), *The Second Ring of Power.* Harmondsworth: Penguin.

Castaneda, C., (1982), *The Eagle's Gift.* Harmondsworth: Penguin.

Castaneda, C., (1984), *The Power Within.* London: Black Swan Books.

Chapman, G. and Stemman, R., (1978), *Surgeon from Another World.* London: W. H. Allen
. and Co.

Charlesworth, E. A. and Nathan, R. G., (1987), *Stress Management*. Transworld Publishers Ltd.

Chaudhuri, H., (1965), *Integral Yoga: The Concept of Harmonious and Creative Living*. London: Allen and Unwin.

Chertok, L., (1969), The Evolution of Research into Hypnosis. In *Psychophysiological Mechanisms of Hypnosis*. New York: Springer Verlag.

Chertok, L., (1981), *Sense and Nonsense in Psychotherapy: The Challenge of Hypnosis*. Oxford: Pergamon Press.

Chuang-Yuan, C., (1975), *Creativity and Taoism*. London: Wildwood House.

Coe, W. C.and Ryken, K., (1979), Hypnosis and risks to human subjects. *American Psychologist*, 34, 673-681.

Colegrave, S., (1979), *The Spirit of the Valley: Androgyny and Chinese Thought*. London: Virago.

Colt, E. W. D., Wardlaw, W. and Frantz, A. G., (1981), The effect of running on plasma beta - endorphin. *Life Science* 28, 1637.

Cooper C., Cooper, R. and Eaker, L., (1988), *Living with Stress*. Harmondsworth: Penguin.

Cooper, J. C., (1981), *Yin and Yang: The Taoist harmony of opposites*. Northampton: Aquarian Press.

Cooper, L. A., (1975), Mental transformation of random two-dimensional shapes. *Cognitive Psychology* 7, 2043.

Cooper, L. A. and Shepard, R. N., (1973), Chronometric studies of the rotation of mental images. In W. G. Chase (ed) *Visual information Processing*. New York: Academic Press.

Cooper, M. and Aygen, M., (1978), Effect of meditation on blood cholesterol and blood pressure. *Journal of The Israel Medical Association*, 95: 1 July, 2.

Cousins, N., (1981), *Anatomy of an Illness as perceived by the Patient: Reflections on Healing and Regeneration*. New York, London and Toronto: Bantam.

Cousins, N., (1988), Intangibles in medicine: an attempt at a balancing perspective. *Journal of the American Medical Association*, September 16th, 260, 11, 1610-12.

Cox, T., (1981), *Stress*. London: Macmillan.

Coxhead, N., (1979), *Mindpower*. Harmondsworth: Penguin.

Crasilneck, H. B. and Hall, J. A., (1959), Physiological changes associated with hypnosis. *J of Clinical and Experimental Hypnosis*, 7, 9.

Critchley, M., (1953), *The Parietal Lobes*. London: Edward Arnold.

Curtis, G. C., (1979), Psychoendocrine stress response: Steroid and peptide hormones. In B. A. Stoll (Ed.) *Mind and Cancer Prognosis*. Chichester: Wiley.

Dass, R., (1978), *Journey of Awakening: A Meditator's Guidebook*. Bantam.

Dattore, P. J., Schontz, F. C. and Coyne, L., (1980), Premorbid personality differentiation of cancer and non-cancer groups: A test of the hypothesis of cancer proneness. *J. Consult-Clinical Psychology* 48, 388-94.

Davidson, J., (1987), *Subtle Energy*. Saffron Walden: The C and W. Daniel Co.

Davies, P., (1984), *God and the New Physics*. Harmondsworth: Penguin.

Davis and Rawls (1979), *The Magnetic Blueprint of Life*. Exposition Press, cited in Davidson, (1987), *op. cit.*.

Day, H., (1951), *About Yoga*. London: Thorsons Publishing Ltd.

Day, H., (1953), *The Study and Practice of Yoga*. London: Thorsons Publishing.

Day, L. and de LaWarr, G., (1956), *New Worlds Beyond The Atom*. London: Vincent Stuart Lt(

Day, L. and de LaWarr, G., (1966), *Matter in the Making*. London: Vincent Stuart Ltd.

Deikman, A. J., (1969), Experimental meditation. Ch. 13 199-218 in C. T. Tart, *op. cit.*.

Dempster C. R. and Batson, P. and Whalen, B. Y., (1976), Supportive hypnotherapy during th radical treatment of malignancies. *J. of Clinical Experimental Hypnosis*, 21, 1-9.

DeRenzi, E., (1968), Non verbal memory and hemisphere side lesions. *Neuropsychologia*, (181-9.

Derogatis, L., Abeloff, M. and Melisaratos, N., (1979), Psychological coping mechanisms ar survival time in metastatic breast cancer. *J. of the American Medical Association*, 24: 1504-8.

Desoille, R., (1945), *The Waking Dream in Psychotherapy: An Essay on the Regulator Function of the Collective Unconscious. (LeReveille en psychotherapie)* Paris: Universitair(

Dhonden, Y. and Tschering, G., (1976), What is Tibetan Medicine?. In Darva Norbu (Ed.) A *Introduction to Tibetan Medicine*. New Delhi: Tibetan Review.

Dick-Read, G., (1953), *Childbirth without Fear*, New York: Harper and Row.

Dickinson, P. I., (1976), *Music With ESN Children*. NFER.

Digiusto, E. L. and Bond, N., (1979), Imagery and the Autonomic Nervous System. *Perceptu(and Motor Skills*, 48, 427-438.

Dimond, S., (1977), Evolution and Laterilization of the Brain: concluding remarks. *Annals (the New York Academy of Science*, 299, 477-499.

Donovan, M., (1980), Relaxation with Guided Imagery: A Useful Technique. *Cancer Nursin(3, 27-32.

Dooley, A., (1973), *Every Wall A Door: Exploring Psychic Surgery and Healing*. Londo(Transworld.

Dossey, L., (1982), *Space, Time and Medicine*. Boulder and London: Shambala.

Dostalek, C., (1987), The Empirical and Experimental Foundation of Yoga Therapy. Ch.(26-33 in Gharote, D. M., and Lockhart, M., *op. cit.*

Downey, S., (1988), Acupuncture, in Rankin-Box, *op. cit.*

Drury, N., (1978), *Don Juan: Mescalito and Modern Magic: A Mythology of Inner Spac(London: Routledge and Kegan Paul.

Drury, N., (1979), *Inner Visions: Explorations in Magical Consciousness*. London and Henle(Routledge and Kegan Paul.

Drury, N., (1987), *The Occult Experience*. London: Robert Hale.

Duncker, K., (1945), On Problem Solving. *Psychological Monographs* 58, 5. Whole No. 27(

Duquesne, M. and Reeves, J., (1982), *A Handbook of Psychoactive Medicines*. London: Quarte

Ecker, R., (1989), *The Stress Myth*. Tring: Lion Publishing.

Eddington, A. E., (1939), *The Philosophy of Physical Science*. Cambridge University Press.

Eddy, M. B., (1906), *Science and Health*. Published by the Trustees under the will of M. Bak(Eddy. Boston, USA.

Editorial (1977), The Psychology of Mysticism. *The Practitioner*. No. 1306. April, Vol. 21(p477.

Editorial (1985), Emotion and Immunity. *Lancet* ii, 133-134.

Editorial (1987), Depression, Stress and Immunity. *Lancet* 27th June, 1467-1468.

Editorial (1988), Holding Back the Tide of Consciousness. *British Medical Journal*. Septembe

Edmonston, W. E. and Pessin, M., (1966), Hypnosis as related to learning and electrodermal measures. *American Journal of Clinical Hypnosis*, 9, 31.

Edwards, H., (1987), A *Guide to Spirit Healing*. Tenth Impression. G. B. The Harry Edwards Spiritual Healing Sanctuary Trust.

Eiff, A. and Jorgens, H., (1961), Die Spindelerregbarkeit beim autogenem Training. In *Proc. Third. Int. Congress Psychiat. Montreal*.

Elder, S. T., (1977), Apparatus and procedure for training subjects to control blood pressure. *Psychophysiology*, 14, 68.

Eliade, M., (1959), *The Sacred and The Profane: The Nature of Religion*. New York: Harcourt, Brace and World Inc.

Eliade, M., (1964), *Shamanism: Archaic Techniques of Ecstasy*. New York: Pantheon Bollingen Foundation.

Eliade, M., (1970), *Yoga: Immortality and Freedom*. Princeton, New Jersey: Princeton University Press.

Engel, B. J., (1972), Operant conditioning of cardiac functioning. *Psychophysiology*, 9, 161.

Engel, B. J., (1977), The need for a new medical model: A challenge for biomedical science. *Science*. April 8. 196, 129.

Epes Brown, J., (1985), North American Indian Religions. Pp.392-411 in J. R. Hinnells (Ed.) *A Handbook of Living Religions*. Harmondsworth: Penguin.

Erickson, M. H., (1959), Hypnosis in painful terminal illness. *American Journal of Clinical Hypnosis*. 2, 117-122, 95-101.

Ernst, S. and Goodison, L., (1981), *In Our Own Hands: A Book of Self-help Therapy*. London: Womens Press Ltd.

Erskine, M. J. and Schonell, M., (1981), Relaxation therapy in asthma: a critical review. *Psychosomatic Medicine* 43, 365-372.

St Exupéry, de. A., (1974), *The Little Prince*. London: Pan.

Feinstein, A. D., (1983), Psychological interventions in treatment of cancer. *Clinical Psychology Review*. Vol. 3 1-14.

Feldenkrais, M., (1980), *Awareness Through Movement: Health Exercises for Personal Growth*. Harmondsworth: Penguin.

Fellows, B. J., (1985), Hypnosis teaching and research in British Psychology Departments: current practice, attitude and concerns. *British Journal of Experimental and Clinical Hypnosis*, 2, 151-155.

Fellows, B. J., (1986), The concept of trance. Pp. 37-58 in Naish, P. L. N. (Ed.) *What is Hypnosis: current theories and research*. Milton Keynes: Open University Press.

Fenwick, P. B., (1983), Can we still recommend meditation? *British Medical Journal*. Vol. 287 12 Nov. p1401.

Fenwick, P. B., Donaldson, S. and Gillis, L., (1977), Metabolic and EEG changes during TM: an explanation. *Biological Psychology*, 5, 101-118.

Ferguson, M., (1982), *The Aquarian Conspiracy: personal and social transformation in the 1980s*. London: Paladin Granada.

Ferguson, P. C. and Gowan, C., (1973), The influence of Transcendental Meditation on aggression, anxiety, depression, neuroticism, and self-actualization. Unpublished manuscript cited in Pelletier, *op. cit.*

Ferguson, J., (1982), *The Religions of the Roman Empire*. London: Thames and Hudson.

Ferguson, M., (1983), *The Aquarian Conspiracy: Personal and Social Transformation in the 1980s*. London: Paladin.

Ferrucci, P., (1982), *What We May Be*. Turnstone Press.

Finer, B., (1982), Endorphins Under Hypnosis in Chronic Pain Patients: some experimental findings. Paper given at Ninth Congress of Hypnosis and Psychosomatic Medicine, Glasgow.

Fiore, N., (1974), Fighting Cancer: one patient's perspective. *New England Journal of Medicine* 300, 284.

Fisher, S., (1954), The role of expectancy in the performance of posthypnotic behaviour. *Journal of Abnormal and Sociological Psychology*, 49, 503.

Fitzsimons, C., (1988), Addicts to sue over 'happy pill' misery. *The Observer*. Sunday 1 February.

Forbes, A., (1979), Cymatics. p.160 in Hill, A., *op. cit.*

Francis, K., (1979), The Aura, in Hill, A., *op. cit.*, 46-47.

Frankl, V. E., (1969), *The Doctor and the Soul*. London: Souvenir Press.

Franz, von. M. L., (1974), *Number and Time: reflections leading towards a unification of Psychology and Physics*. London: Rider and Co.

Franz, von M. L., (1975), *C. G. Jung; His Myth in Our Time*. London: Hodder and Stoughton.

Franz, von M. L., (1985), Synchronicity and the I Ching. In Rawlence, C. (Ed) *About Time* London: Jonathan Cape.

Frederking, W., (1948), *Deep Relaxation and Symbolism*. Psyche 2.

Freedom Long, M., (1954), *The Secret Science Behind Miracles*. USA Huna Research Publications.

Fricker, E. F., (1977), *God is My Witness*. London: Arthur Barker Ltd.

Friedman, M. and Rosenman, R. H., (1971), Type A Behaviour Pattern: its association with coronary heart disease. *Annals of Clinical Research*. 3, 300-312.

Friedman, M. and Rosenman, R. H., (1974), *Type A Behaviour and Your Heart*. New York Alfred A. Knopf.

Friedman, M. and Rosenman, R. H., (1986), Type A Behaviour pattern: Its Association with coronary heart disease. *Holistic Medicine*, Vol. 1, 1, 57-73.

Fromm, E., (1951), *Psychoanalysis and Religion*. London: Gollancz.

Fromm, E., (1980), *The Greatness and Limitations of Freud's Thought*. London: Cape.

Fromm, E., Suzuki, D. and De Martino, R., (1960), *Zen Buddhism and Psychoanalysis*. London Allen and Unwin.

Fulder, S., (1987), *How to Survive Medical Treatment: an holistic approach to the risks and side effects of orthodox medicine*. London: Hodder and Stoughton.

Gallegos, E. S., (1983), Animal Imagery: the chakra system and psychotherapy. *Journal of Transpersonal Psychology*. Vol. 15 no.2 125. T 136.

Galton, F. (1883), *Inquiries into Human Faculty and its Development*. London: Macmillan.

Gawain Shakti (1985), *Creative Visualization*. New York: Bantam.

Gazzaniga, M. S., (1967), The split brain in man. *Brain and Consciousness*. August 118-123.

Gellatly, A., (1986), How can Memory Skills be Improved. In *The Skilful Mind: An Introduction to Cognitive Psychology*. Milton Keynes: Open University Press.

Gerber, R., (1988), *Vibrational Medicine: new choices for healing ourselves*. Santa Fe, New Mexico: Bear and Co.

Gharote, M. I. and Lockhart, M. (Eds.) (1987), *The Art of Survival: A guide to Yoga therapy*. Unwin Hyman Ltd.

Ghiselin, B., (1952), *The Creative Process*. New York: New American Library.

Gibran, K., (1978), *The Prophet*: London: Book Club Associates.

Gibson, S. and Gibson, R., (1987), *Homeopathy for Everyone*. Harmondsworth: Penguin.

Gillie, O., (1989), Treatment of Pain. *Health Independent*. Tuesday January 3rd.

Gimbel, T., (1978), *Healing Through Colour*. Saffron Walden: C. W. Daniels and Co.

Gimbel, T., (1987), *Form, Sound, Colour and Healing*. Saffron Walden: C. W. Daniels and Co. Ltd.

Goldfield, M. and Trier, C., (1974), Effectiveness of relaxation as an active coping skill. *Journal of Abnormal Psychology*, 83, 4, 338-342.

Goldstein, A., (1980), Thrills in response to music and other stimuli. *Physiological Psychology*, 4, 8, 126-9.

Goleman, D., (1978), *The Varieties of the Meditative Experience*. London: Rider and Co.

Gordon, R., (1962), Stereotyping of imaging and belief. British *Journal of Psychology Monograph Supplements*. Cambridge University Press.

Gorman, P. and Kamiya, J., (1972), Voluntary Control of Stomach pH. Research note presented at Biofeedback Research Society Meeting, Boston, November.

Gorton, B. Autogenic Training. *American Journal of Clinical Hypnosis*, 2, 34-41.

Gottleib, C., (1959), pp. 157-88 in Feifel, H., (Ed.) *The Meaning of Death*. New York: McGraw Hill.

Grad, B., (1963), A telekinetic effect on plant growth. *International Journal of Parapsychology*, 5, 117-134.

Grad, B., (1965), Some biological effects of the 'laying on of hands': A review of experiments with animals and plants. *J. of American Society for Psychical Research*, 59, 95-129

Grad, B., (1967), The 'laying on of hands': implications for psychotherapy, gentling and the placebo effect, *J. American Soc. Psych. Research* 61, 286-305.

Grad, B., Cadoret, R. J. and Paul, G. J., (1961), The influence of an unorthodox method of treatment on wound healing of mice. *International Journal of Parapsychology*, 3, 5.

Graham, H., (1986), *The Human Face of Psychology*, Milton Keynes: Open University Press.

Green, E. E., (1969), Voluntary control of inner states. *Psychophysiology*, 6, 371.

Greer, S., (1983), Cancer and the mind. *British Journal of Psychiatry*, 143, 535-543

Greer, S. Morris, T. and Pettingdale, K. W., (1979), Psychological Response to Breast Cancer: effect and outcome. *Lancet*, 2, 785-787

Greer, S. and Morris, T., (1975), Psychological attributes of women who develop breast cancer: a controlled study. *J. of Psychosomatic Research*, 19, 147-153.

Greer, S. and M. Watson (1985), Towards a psychological model of cancer: psychological considerations. *Social Science Medicine*, Vol. 20. No. 8, 773-77.

Grof, S., (1979), *Realms of the Unconscious*. London: Souvenir Press.

Gulliver, N., (1988), Shiatsu. Ch3, pp 27-41 in Rankin-Box, *op. cit.*

Gunther, B., (1979), *Energy Ecstasy and your Seven Vital Chakras*. 2nd edition. Los Angeles, California: Guild of Tutors Press.

Gurdjieff, G., (1978), *Meetings with Remarkable Men*. London: Pan.

Hackett, T. P. and Cassem, N. H., (1975), Psychological management of the myocardia infarction patient. *J of Human Stress*, 1, 25-38.

Hadamarad, J., (1945), *The Psychology of Invention in the Mathematical Field.* Princeton New Jersey: Princeton University Press.

Hall, A. G., (1950), *Primal Healing: a discussion of the newest approach to Scientific Spiritua Healing.* London: Pearson Foundation.

Hall, H. R., (1985), Hypnosis and the Immune System: A review with implications for cance and the psychology of healing. *American Journal of Clinical Hypnosis,* 25, 92-103.

Hamlyn, E., (1979), *The Healing Art of Homeopathy: the organon of Samuel Hahnemann* Beaconsfield, Bucks: Beaconsfield Publishers Ltd.

Happich, C., (1932), Das Bildbewusstseinals Ansatzstelle Psychischer Behandlung. *Lbe psychother.* 5. 663-667.

Happich, C., (1948), *Anteitung zur Meditation (Introduction to Meditation)* 3rd Edition Darmstadt: E. Rother.

Harding, J., (1988), Hello, John, Got a New Mantra?. *Sunday Times* Magazine, December 11 p101.

Hariman. J., (1981), *How to use the Power of Self-Hypnosis.* Wellingborough, Northants Thorsons.

Harley, G., (1989), Mind over body in cancer care. *Sunday Times* 30 April.

Harman, W., Willis, R. H., McKim, R. E. Mogar, J. Fadiman, M. J. Stolaroff (1969), Psychedeli Agents in Creative Problem Solving: A Pilot Study. Ch. 30, 445ff. In C. T. Tart, *op. cit.*

Harrison, J., (1984), *Love Your Disease: it's keeping you healthy.* London and Australia: Angu and Robertson.

Hartley, J. and Branthwaite, J. A. (Eds.), (1989), *The Applied Psychologist.* Milton Keynes Open University Press.

Hawking, S. W., (1988), *A Brief History of Time: From the Big Bang to Black Holes.* London Bantam.

Heather, N., (1976), *Radical Perspectives in Psychology.* London: Methuen.

Hedderly, R., (1983), The role of pop music in remedial education. *Remedial Education.* 18,2

Hegarty, J. R., (1989), Psychologists, doctors and cancer patients. In Hartley, J., an Branthwaite, J. A., *op. cit.*

Heidt, P., (1981), Effect of Therapeutic Touch on anxiety level of hospitalised patients. *Nursin, Research,* 30(1), 32-7.

Hewitt, J., (1982), *The Complete Relaxation Book: A manual of Eastern and Wester Techniques.* London: Rider.

Heywood, R., (1978), *The Infinite Hive: a personal record of extra-sensory experience.* Harmondsworth: Penguin.

Hilgard, E., (1965), *Hypnotic Suggestibility.* New York: Harcourt, Brace and World.

Hilgard, E. R., (1973), A Neodissociation theory of pain reduction in hypnosis. *Psychologica Review. 80: 396-411.*

Hilgard, E. R. and Hilgard, J. R., (1975), *Hypnosis in the Relief of Pain.* Los Altos, Californi W. Kaufman.

Hill, A. (Ed.) *A Visual Encyclopedia of Unconventional Medicine.* London: New Englis Library.

Hillman, J., (1971), commentary in *Kundalini: the evolutionary energy in man.* Gopi Krishna: Boulder and London Shambhala

Hinnells, J. R. (Ed) (1985), A Handbook of Living Religions. Harmondsworth: Penguin.

Hirai, T., (1975), *Zen Meditation Therapy.* Japan Publications Inc.

Hodgkinson, N., (1987), Doctors go to class for bedside manner. *Sunday Times* 4th October, 13.

Hodgkinson, N., (1988), Surge in 'needless' births by Caesarian. *Sunday Times* 9th October, 9.

Hodgkinson, N., (1989), Doctors see the point in pins. *Sunday Times* 8th January.

Holbrook, B., (1981), *The Stone Money: An Alternative Chinese-Scientific Reality.* New York: William Morrow and Co.

Holden, R., (1988), Modern cardiology: the biophysical approach to heart disease. *Caduceus,* 4, 6-9.

Holmes, E., (1975), Thought as energy. *Science of Mind Annual,* California.

Holmes, T. H. and Rahe, R. H., (1967), The social readjustment rating scale. *Journal of Psychosomatic Research,* 11, 213-18.

Holton, G., (1972), On trying to understand scientific genius. *American Scholar,* 41, 95-110.

Honsberger, R. and Wilson, A. F., (1973), Transcendental Meditation in treating asthma: Respiration Therapy. *Journal of Inhalation Technology,* 3, 79-81

Hopson, B., (1982), Transition; understanding and managing personal change. In A. J. Chapman and A. Gale (Eds.) *Psychology and People: A tutorial text.* London: Macmillan.

Horn, S., (1986), *Relaxation: modern techniques for stress management.* Wellingboro, Northants: Thorsons.

Hostie, R., (1957), *Religion and the Psychology of Jung.* London: Sheed and Ward.

Hughes, J., (1987), *Cancer and Emotion: psychological preludes and reactions to cancer.* Chichester: J. Wiley.

Humphreys, C., (1962), *Zen.* London: Hodder and Stoughton Ltd.

Humphrey, M. E. and Zangwill, O., (1951), Cessation of dreaming after brain injury. *J. of Neurology Neurosurgery and Psychiatry,* 14, 322-325.

Hunt, I. and Draper, W. W., (1964), *Lightning in his hand: the life story of Nicola Tesla.* Denver, Colorado: Sage Books.

Hunt, S. M., (1979), Hypnosis as obedience behaviour. *British Journal of Social and Clinical Psychology.* 18, 21-7.

Hunter, I. M. L., (1986), Exceptional memory skill, Ch. 7, 76-86 in Gellatly, A. (Ed) *The Skilful Mind.* Milton Keynes: Open University Press.

Huxley, A., (1954), *The Doors of Perception.* London: Chatto and Windus.

Illich, I., (1975), *Medical Nemesis: The Expropriation of Health.* London: Marion Boyars.

Illiffe, S., (1988), *Strong Medicine.* London: Lawrence and Wishart.

Inglis, B., (1986), *The Hidden Power.* London: Jonathan Cape, Ltd.

Inglis, B., (1987), *The Unknown Guest.* London: Chatto and Windus.

Inyushin, V. M. and Chckurov, P. R., (1977), *Biostimulation through Laser Radiation and Bioplasma.* Copenhagen: Danish Soc. for Psychical Research. (Trans. Scott Hill and G. Hoshal).

Inyushin, V. M. and Fedorova, N. N., (1969), On the Question of the Biological Plasma of Green Plants. Unpub. Diss. Alma Ata., USSR.

Isherwood, C. (Ed.) (1972), Vedanta for Modern Man. New York: Signet Books.

Ivanov, A., (1965), Soviet experiments in Eyeless Vision. *International Journal of Parapsychology,* VI, 1, 5-22.

Jackson, J. H., (1980), On right or left-handed spasm at the onset of epileptic paroxysms and on crude sensation warnings and elaborate mental states. *Brain,* 3, 192-206.

Jacobi, J., (1962), *The Psychology of Jung.* London: Routledge and Kegan Paul.

Jacobs, J. S., (1987), Yoga and Ayurveda. Ch. 11, p.121-131 in Gharote, M. I., and Lockhart M., *op. cit.*

Jacobs, T. J. and Charles, E., (1980), Life events and the occurrence of cancer in children *Psychosomatic Medicine, 42, 1-24.*

Jacobsen, C. F., (1936), Studies of cerebral function in primates, I. Functions of the frontal association areas in monkeys. *Comparative Psychology Monographs,* 3, 3-60.

Jacobsen, C. F., (1929), Electrical measurements of neuromuscular states during mental activities: imagination of movement involving skeletal muscle. *Am. Journal Physiology,* 91 597-608.

Jacobsen, E., (1938), *Progressive Relaxation.* Chicago: University of Chicago Press.

Jacobsen, E., (1977), *You Must Relax.* London: Souvenir Press.

Jacq, C., (1985), *Egyptian Magic.* Warminster: Avis and Phillips Ltd.

Jampolsky, G. G., (1979), *Love is Letting Go of Fear.* Berkeley, California: Celestial Arts.

Jenny, H., (1966), *Cymatics.* Basel: Basilius Press.

Jenny, H., (1968), Visualising Sound. *Science Journal,* June.

Johnson, J. E., (1978), Sensory information: instruction in a coping strategy and recovery from surgery. *Research in Nursing and Health,* 1 (1), 1, 4-17.

Johnson, H. E. and Garton, W. H., (1973), A practical method of muscle reeducation in hemiplegia: electromyographic facilitation. Unpublished manuscript. Casa Colina Hospital for Rehabitative Medicine, Paloma, California.

Jones, I., (1986), Cancer following bereavement: results from the OPCS longitudinal study Paper presented BPOC meeting University of Leicester.

Jordan, C. S. and Lenington, K. T., (1979), Physiological correlates of eidetic imagery and induced anxiety. *Journal of Mental Imagery,* 3, 31-42.

Jourard, S. M., (1971), *The Transparent Self.* London: D. Van Nostrand and Co.

Jung, C. G., (1946), *Psychology and Religion.* London and Oxford: New Haven, Yale University Press.

Jung, C. G., (1959), *Face to Face with C. G. Jung.* First Broadcast, Oct. 1959, repeated BBC2 16.10.88.

Jung, C. G., (1966), *Modern Man in Search of A Soul.* London: Routledge and Kegan Paul.

Jung, C. G., (1967), Symbols of Transformation. In *Collected Works : Vol. 2.* (2nd edition) London: Routledge.

Jung, C. G., (1972), *Memories, Dreams, Reflections.* London: Collins Fontana.

Jung, C. G., (1978), *Psychology and the East.* London: Routledge and Kegan Paul.

Kakar, S., (1982), *Shamans, Mystics and Doctors: A psychological inquiry into India and its healing.* London: Unwin.

Kamiya, J., (1968), Conscious control of brain waves. *Psychology Today,* 1, 57-60.

Kamiya, J., (1969), Operant control of the EEG alpha rhythm and some of its reported effects on consciousness. Chapter 35, p.507-518 in C. T. Tart, *op. cit.*

Kanner, A. D., Coyne, J. C., Shaefer, C. and Lazarus, R. S., (1981), Comparison of two modes of stress measurement. Daily hassles and uplifts versus major life events. *J. of Behavioural Medicine*, 1-39.

Kaptehuk, T. and Croucher, M., (1986), *The Healing Arts: A journey through the faces of medicine.* London: BBC Publications.

Karagulla, S., (1967), *Breakthrough to Creativity.* Santa Monica, Los Angeles, California: C. A. De Vorss.

Kasamatsu, A. and Hirai, T., (1966), Studies of EEGs of Expert Zen Meditators, *Folia Psychiatria Neurologica Japonica* 28: 315.

Kasamatsu, A. and Hirai, T., (1969), An electroencephalographic study on Zen Meditation (Zazen). ch.33 pp. 489-502 in C. T. Tart, *op. cit.*

Kazdin, A. E. and L. A. Wilcoxin (1975), Systematic Desensitization and Non-Specific Treatment Effects: a methodological evaluation. *Psychological Bulletin* 83 p5.

Kelly, C. R., (1961), Psychological factors in myopia, *Proceedings of the American Psychological Association*, 31 August.

Kendall, J., (1955), *Michael Faraday, man of simplicity* London: Faber and Faber.

Kennedy, J. Tellegea, A. Kennedy, S. Havernick, N., (1976), Psychological response of patients cured of advanced cancer. *Psychosomatic Medicine*, 38 2184-2191.

Kenner, C. and Achterberg, J., (1983), Non-pharmacologic pain relief for patients. Paper presented to American Burn Association Annual Meeting, New Orleans April 1983 reported Achterberg, J., (1985), *op. cit.*

Kiecolt, J., Glaser, J. and Glaser, R., (1985), Psychosocial Enhancement of Immuno Competence in a geriatric population. *Health Psychology* 4 pp24-41.

Kiesler, E., (1984), The Playing fields of the Mind. *Psychology Today* July 18. pp18-24.

Kilner, W. J., (1911), *The Human Atmosphere*, republished 1984 as *The Aura.* New York: Weiser.

Kirlian, S. D. and V. H. Kirlian (1968), *Investigation of Biological Objects in High-Frequency Electrical fields. Bioenergetic Questions - and Some Answers* USSR Alma Ata.

Kissen, D. and H. J. Eysenck (1962), Personality in male lung cancer patients. *British Journal of Medical Psychology* 36 pp123-7.

Kissen, D. M. and H. J. Eysenck (1967), Psychosocial factors, personality and lung cancer in men aged 55-64. *British Journal of Medical Psychology* 40 pp 29-43.

Kissen, D. M. and H. J. Eysenck (1963), Personality characteristics in males conducive to lung cancer. *British Journal of Medical Psychology* 36, 27-36.

Kissen, D. M. and H. J. Eysenck (1964), Relationship between lung cancer, cigarette smoking, inhalation and personality. *British Journal of Medical Psychology* 37, pp 203-16.

Koestler, A., (1964), *The Art of Creation.* New York: Macmillan.

Koestler, A., (1975), *The Ghost in the Machine.* London: Pan Books.

Koestler, A., (1984), *The Sleepwalkers: A history of man's changing vision of the universe.* Harmondsworth: Penguin.

Koran, A., (1964), *Bring out the Magic in Your Mind.* Preston: A. Thomas and Co.

Kretschmer, W., (1969), Meditative techniques in psychotherapy. Chapter 14, p. 219-231 in C. T. Tart, *op. cit.*

Krieger, D., (1975), Therapeutic Touch: The imprimatur of nursing. *American Journal of Nursing.* May, 784-787.

Krieger, D., (1979), *The Therapeutic Touch: How to use your hands to help and heal.* Englewood Cliffs, New Jersey: Prentice Hall.

Krieger, D., (1981), *The Renaissance Nurse.* Philadelphia: J. B. Lippincott C.

Krieger, D., (1982), Therapeutic Touch Mediscope. *Manchester Medical Gazette,* 61(1), 10-12, Manchester University.

Krippner, S., (1969), Psychedelic State, Hypnotic Trance and the Creative Act. Chapter 18, p.271-290, in C. T. Tart, *op. cit.*

Krippner, S., (1973), *Galaxies of Life: Human aura in Acupuncture and Kirlian Photography.* New York: Gordon and Breach.

Krishna, Gopi (1971), *Kundalini: the evolutionary energy in man.* Boulder and London: Shambhala.

Krishna, Gopi (1988), The true aim of Yoga. In J. White (Ed.) *What is Enlightenment?* Wellingboro', Northants.: Aquarian Press.

Krishnamurti, J., (1966), *Discussions with Krishamurti in Europe.* Ojai: California.

Kubler-Ross, E., (1977), *On Death and Dying.* London: Tavistock.

Kubler-Ross, E., (1982), *Working it Through.* Cother, N. Y.: Macmillan.

Kuhn, T. S., (1962), The structure of scientific revolutions (2nd edition). *International Encyclopaedia of Unified Science* 2, 11. London and Chicago: University of Chicago Press. (Reprinted 1970).

Laing, R. D., (1959), *The Divided Self: An existential study of sanity and madness.* London: Tavistock.

Lang, P. J., (1967), Effects of feedback and instructional set. *Journal of Experimental Psychology,* 75, 425.

Langen, D., (1969), Peripheral changes in blood circulation during Autogenic Training hypnosis. In *Psychophysiological Mechanisms of Hypnosis.* New York: Springer Verlag.

Laurie, S. G. and Tucker, M. J., (1982), *Centering: the power of meditation.* Wellingborough, Northants: Excalibur Books.

Lazarus, R., (1979), Positive denial: the case for not facing reality. *Psychology Today,* November, 109-118.

Lazarus, R. S., (1981), Little hassles can be hazardous to health. *Psychology Today,* 15, 58-62.

Lazarus, R. S., (1984), Puzzles in the study of daily hassles. *Journal of Behavioural Medicine,* 7, 375-389.

Leadbetter, C. W., (1910), *The Inner Life.* London: Theosophical Publishing House.

Leadbetter, C. W., (1927), *The Chakras: a monologue.* Adyar Madras, India: Theosophical Publishing House.

LeShan, L., (1966), An emotional life-history pattern associated with neoplastic disease. *Annals of New York Academy of Science,* 125, 780-793.

LeShan, L., (1977), *You Can Fight for your Life.* New York: Evans and Co.

LeShan, L., (1978), *How to Meditate: A guide to self-discovery.* London: Sphere Books.

LeShan, L., (1982), *Clairvoyant Reality: Towards a general theory of the paranormal.* Wellingborough, Northants.: Turnstone Press.

LeShan, L., (1984), *Holistic Health: How to understand and use the Revolution in Medicine.* Wellingborough, Northants.: Turnstone Press.

LeShan, L., (1987), *The Science of Paranormal: The last frontier.* Wellingborough, Northants.: Aquarian Press.

Lesser, I. M., (1981), A review of the Alexithymia Concept. *Psychosomatic Medicine,* 32, 531-543.

Levine, S., (1987), *A Gradual Awakening: A practical introduction to meditation.* London: Century Hutchinson.

Lewis, J. H. and Sarbin, T. R., (1943), Studies in Psychosomatics. *Psychosomatic Medicine, 5, 125.*

Lewith, G., (1989), Acupuncture. *Medicine Now,* BBC Radio 4, 10.1.89.

Libo, L. M. and Arnold, G. E., (1983), Relaxation practice after biofeedback therapy: a long term follow-up study of utilization and effectiveness. *Biofeedback and Self-Regulation,* Vol. 8, No. 2.

Lichstein, K. L. and Lipshitz, E., (1982), Psychophysiological effects of noxious imagery. *Behaviour Research and Therapy,* 20, 339-345.

Lilly, J. C., (1977), *The Centre of the Cyclone: An autobiography of Inner Space.* St. Albans, Frogmore: Granada Publishing.

Linden, W., (1973), Practising of meditation by schoolchildren and their levels of field dependence-independence, test anxiety and reading achievement. *Journal of Consulting and Clinical Psychology,* 41, 139-143.

Lindop, E., (1987), Factors associated with student and pupil nurse wastage. *Journal of Advanced Nursing,* 751-756.

Lindop, E., (1988), Stress Intervention in Nurses. Talk given at University of Keele Centre for Occupational Studies, January 11th.

Lovelock, J. E., (1979), *Gaia.* London: Oxford University Press.

Lowen, A., (1981), *Fear of Life.* New York: Collier Macmillan.

Lubran, A., (1961), Music therapy and the spastic child. *Special Education, 50, 2.*

Luce, G. G., (1973), *Body Time: The Natural Rhythms of the Body.* St. Albans: Paladin.

Ludwig, A. M., (1969), Altered states of consciousness. In C. T. Tart, *op. cit.*

Luthe, N., (1969), Autogenic Training: method, research and application in medicine. Chapter 20, 309-320 in C. T. Tart, *op. cit.*

Lyles, J., Burish, T., Krozezy, M. Oldham, R., (1982), Efficacy of relaxation training and guided imagery in reducing the aversiveness of cancer chemotherapy. *Journal of Consulting and Clinical Psychology,* 50, 4, 509-524.

Maharishi M. Y., (1969), *Science of Creative Intelligence.* Maharishi International.

Maier, N. R. F., (1931), Reasoning in Humans II: The solution of a problem and its appearance in consciousness. *Journal of Comparative Psychology,* 12, 181-189.

Manning, M., (1988), Seminar on Self Healing. Holistic Health Workshop given at Farnham Holistic Health Centre, April 30th 1980.

Manning, M., (1989), *Matthew Manning's Guide to Self-Healing.* Wellingborough, Northants: Thorsons.

Marchand, H., (1956), Die Suggestion der Wärme im Oberbauch und ihr Einfluss auf Blutzucker und Tenkozytem. *Psychotherapy* 3, 154. Cited in Pelletier, *op. cit.*

Marchand, H., (1961), Das Verhalten von Blutzucker und Tenkozytem während des autogenen Trainings, in *Proc. Third Int. Congress of Psychiatry*, Montreal. Cited in Pelletier, *op. cit.*

Marinacci, A. A., (1968), *Applied Electromyography.* Philadelphia: Lea and Febinger.

Mason, J. W., (1968), Organisation of psychoendocrine mechanisms. *Psychomatic Medicine, 30, 565-608.*

Maslak, R. A., (1987), Yoga and Osteopathy: Health Care for the year 2000. Chapter 15, p.162-168, in Gharote, M. I. and Lockhart, M., *op. cit.*

Mathews, K. A. and Volkin, J., (1981), Effort to excell and the Type A behaviour pattern in children. *Child Development, 52,* 1283-1289.

Maupin, E. W., (1969), On Meditation. Chapter 11, pp.177-186, in C. T. Tart, *op. cit.*

Maupin, E. W., (1969), Individual differences in response to a Zen meditational exercise. Chapter 12, p.187-198, in C. T. Tart, *op. cit.*

Mauz, F., (1948), The psychotic man in psychotherapy. *Archiv. fur psychiatrie.*

Meares, A., (1977), Atavistic regression as a factor in the remission of cancer. *Medical Journal of Australia,* 2, 132-133.

Meares, A., (1979), Meditation: a psychological approach to cancer treatment. *Practitioner,* 222, 119-122.

Meares, A., (1980), What can the cancer patient expect from intensive meditation? *Australian Family Physician,* May, Vol. 9, 322-325.

Meares, A., (1981), Regression or recurrence of carcinoma of the breast at mastectomy site associated with intensive meditation, *Australian Family Physician,* 10, 218-219.

Medik, L. and Fursland, A., (1984), Maximising scarce resources: Autogenic Relaxation Classes at a Health Centre. *British Journal of Medical Psychology,* Vol. 57, 181-185.

Melzack, R. and Wall, P. D., (1975), Pain mechanisms: A new theory. *Science,* 150, 971-979.

Mettler, C. C. and Mettler, F. A., (1947), *History of Medicine.* Philadelphia: Blakiston.

Metzler, J. and Shepard, R. N., (1974), Transformational studies of the internal representation of 3-dimensional objects. In R. Solso (Ed.) *Theories in Cognitive Psychology.* The Loyola Symposium, Potomac, MD: Erlbaum.

Meyer, A. and Beck, E., (1954), *Prefrontal Leucotomy and Relation Operations: Anatomic aspects of success or failure.* Springfield, Illinois: Chas C. Thomas.

Milgram, S., (1974), *Obedience to Authority: An experimental view.* New York: Harper and Row.

Miller, F. R. and Jones, H. W., (1948), The possibility of precipitating the leukaemia state by emotional factors. *Blood,* 8, 880-885.

Miller, N. E., (1969), Learning of visceral and glandular responses. *Science,* 163, 434.

Miller, N. E., (1974), Biofeedback: Evaluation of a new technique. *New England Journal of Medicine,* March 21st, Vol. 290, No. 12, 684-685.

Miller, R. N., (1972), The positive effect of prayer on plants. *Psychic,* April,

Miller, R. N., (1975), Taped talk with Olga Worrall 'Scientific Methods for the Detection and Measurement of Healing Energies'. Science of Mind Symposium Thought as Energy. California.

Milner, B., (1968), Brain mechanisms suggested by studies of temporal lobes. p.122-145 in F. L. Darley (Ed.) *Brain Mechanisms underlying Speech and Language.* New York: Grune and Stratton.

Monjo, de V. P., (1987), The conditions of Yoga therapy. Chapter 6, p.66-78, in Gharote D. and Lockhart, M., *op. cit.*

Moon, T. and Moon, H., (1984), Hypnosis and childbirth: Self report and comment. *British Journal of Experimental and Clinical Hypnosis,* 1, 49-52.

Moos, R. H., (1964), Personality factors associated with Rheumatoid Arthritis: review. *Journal of Chronic Disorders,* 17, 41.

Moos, R. H. and Solomon, G. F., (1964), Minnesota Multiphasic Personal Inventory response patterns in patients with Rheumatoid Arthritis. *Journal of Psychosomatic Research,* 8, 17.

Moos, R. H. and Solomon, G. F., (1965), Psychological comparisons between women with Rheumatoid Arthritis and their non-arthritic sisters I: personality test and interview rating data. *Psychosomatic Medicine* 27, 135.

Moos, R. H. and Solomon, G. F., (1965), Psychological Comparisons between women with Rheumatoid Arthritis and their non-arthritic sisters II. Content Analysis of interviews. *Psychosomatic Medicine* 27, 150.

Morris, T. Greer, S, Pettingale K. W. and Watson, M., (1981), Patterns of expression of anger and their psychological correlates in women with breast cancer. *Journal of Psychosomatic Research* 25, 111-117.

Motoyama, M., (1987), Yoga and Acupuncture. Ch.9, pp 107-15 in Gharote, D. and Lockhart, M., *op. cit.*

Musante, L., MacDougall, J. M., Dembroski, T. M. and Van Horn, A. E., (1983), Component analysis of the Type A coronary-prone behaviour pattern in male and female college students. *Journal of Personality and Social Psychology, 45,* 1104-1117.

Muslin, H. L., Gyarfas, K. and Pieper, W. J., (1966), Separation experience and cancer of the breast. *Annals of the New York Academy of Science,* 125, 802-6.

McCausland, M., (1979), Psychic Surgery, in Hill, A., *op. cit.,* 180-182.

McClelland D. C., Floor, E., Davidson R. J., and Saron, C., (1980), Stressed power motivation, sympathetic activation, immune function and illness. *J of Human Stress,* 6, 11-19.

McClelland D. C. and Jemmott J. B., (1980), Power motivation stress and physical illness. *J. of Human Stress,* 6, 6-15.

McKellar, P., (1968), *Experience and Behaviour.* Harmondsworth: Penguin.

McKellar, P., (1989), Abnormal Psychology: Its Experience and Behaviour. Lecture given at University of Keele, May 8.

McKee, A., (1988), A fight to the Death: *The Times.* Thurs. Oct. 27th. p14.

McMahon, C. E., (1976), The role of imagination in the disease process: Precartesian History. *Psychological Medicine,* 6, 179-184.

Naish, P. L. N., (ed) (1986), *What is Hypnosis?: Current Theories and Research.* Milton Keynes: Open University Press.

Naranjo, C., (1974), *The One Quest. London:* Wildwood House.

Nauta, W. J. H., (1964), Some efferent connections in the prefrontal cortex of the monkey. In J. M. Warren and Akert K. (Eds.) *The Frontal Granular Cortex and Behaviour.* New York: McGraw Hill.

Needleman J., (1972), *The New Religions.* London: Allen Lane, Penguin.

Newton, B. W., (1980), The use of hypnosis in the treatment of cancer patients: A 5 year report. Presented at the Annual Science Progress of the American Society of Clinical Hypnosis, Minneapolis.

Nidich, S., Seeman W. and Dreskin T., (1973), Influence of Transcendental Meditation: A replication. *J. of Counselling Psychology,* 20, 565-66.

Nikhilananda, S., (1968), *Hinduism: Its meaning for the liberation of the spirit.* Myalore, Madras, India: Sri Ramakrishna Math.

Ollendorff-Reich, I., (1969), *Wilhelm Reich: a personal biography.* London: Elek Books.

Ormé-Johnston, D. W., (1973), Autonomic stability and Transcendental Meditation. *Psychosomatic Medicine,* 35, 341-49

Orne, M. T., (1966), Hypnosis, motivation and compliance. *American Journal of Psychiatry,* 122, 721-6.

Orne, M. T., (1972), On the simulating subject as a quasi-control in hypnosis research: What, Why and How? In Fromm, E. and Shor, R. (eds) *Hypnosis: Research Developments and Perspectives.* Chicago: Aldrine-Atherton 399-443.

Ornstein, R. E., (1969), *On the Experience of Time.* New York: Penguin.

Ornstein, R. E., (1973), The traditional esoteric psychologies. In R. E. Ornstein (Ed.) *The Nature of Human Consciousness.* San Francisco: W. H. Freeman.

Ornstein, R. E., (1975), *The Psychology of Consciousness.* Harmondsworth: Penguin.

Ornstein, R. E. and Sobel D., (1988), *The Healing Brain: A radical new approach to health care.* London: Macmillan.

Ostrander, S. and Shroeder L. S., (1973), *Psychic Discoveries Behind the Iron Curtain.* London: Sphere Books.

Otis, L. S., (1974), The facts of transcendental meditation: If well integrated but anxious, try TM. *Psychology Today* 7, 45-46.

Ouseley, S. G. J., (1981), *The Power of the Rays: The Science of Colour-Healing,* eleventh impression. London: L. N. Fowler and Co. Ltd.

Oyle, I., (1976), *Magic, Mysticism and Modern Medicine.* Millbrae, California: Celestial Arts.

Pagels, H. R., (1983), *The Cosmic Code: Quantum Physics as the Language of Nature.* London: Michael Joseph.

Paiva, T., Nunes, J. S., Moreira, A., Santos, J., Teixelra, and Barbosa, A., (1982), Effects of frontalis EMG Biofeedback and Diazepam in the treatment of tension headache. *Headache,* 22, 216-20.

Patel, A., (1980), *Man and Transformation in Ancient India Culture.* DASE dissertation (unpublished) University of Keele, July.

Patel, C. H., (1973), Yoga and biofeedback in the management of Hypertension. *Lancet,* Nov 10.

Patel, C. H. and Datey, K. K., (1975), Yoga and biofeedback in the management of hypertension: two control studies. *Proceedings of the Biofeedback Research Society.* Monterey, California.

Patel, M. S., (1987), Evaluation of Holistic Medicine. *Social Science Medicine,* Vol 24 No.2, 169-175.

Paul, G., (1969), Physiological effects of relaxation training and hypnotic suggestion. *Journal of Abnormal Psychology,* 74, 4, 425-437.

Peavey, (1982), Biofeedback assisted relaxation: Effects on phagocytic immune functions. Ph. D Dissert. North Texas State University. Cited in Achterberg J., (1985), *Imagery in Healing.* London: New Science Library, Routledge and Kegan Paul.

Pelletier, K. R., (1978), *Mind as Healer, Mind as Slayer.* London: George Allen.

Penfield, W. and Perot, P., (1963), The brain's record of auditory and visual experience. *Brain*, 86, 595-6.

Perls, F. S., (1969), *Gestalt Therapy Verbatim*. New York: Bantam reprint 1976.

Perls, F. S., (1976), *The Gestalt Approach and Eyewitness to Therapy*. New York: Bantam.

Perry, C., (1979), Hypnotic coercion and compliance to it: A review of evidence presented in a legal case. *International Journal of Clinical and Experimental Hypnosis*, 27, 187-218.

Peters, L. G. and Price Williams, D., (1980), Towards an experiential analysis of shamanism. *American Ethnologist 7, 398-418*.

Piaget, J., (1965), Psychologie et epistemologie de la notion du temps. In Verhandinngen der Schweizenschen naturforschenden gesellschaft (Bern) Gonera vol CXLV cited in M. von Franz *Number and Time*. London: Rider and Co. 1979.

Piaget, J., (1969), *The Child's Conception of Time*. London: Routledge and Kegan Paul.

Pierrakos, J. C., (1971), *The Energy Field in Man and Nature*. New York: The Institute of Bioenergetic Analysis.

Pirsig, R. M., (1974), *Zen and the Art of Motorcycle Maintenance: an inquiry into values*. London: The Bodley Head.

Pitts, F. N. Jr. and McClure, J. N. Jr., (1967), Lactate Metabolism in Anxiety Neurosis. *New England Journal of Medicine* 277, 1329-1336.

Playfair G. L., (1977), *The Unknown Power Research into Paranormal Phenomena in the World's Most Psychic Country*. Frogmore, St. Albans: Granada.

Poddar, H. P., (1965), *The Divine Name and its Practice*. Gorakhpur, India: Gita Press.

Pollak, K., (1968), *The Healers: The doctor, then and now*. London: Thomas Nelson and Sons Ltd.

Polster, I. and Polster, M., (1975), *Gestalt Therapy Integrated*. New York: Bruner Mazel.

Polzein, P., (1955), Die Anerdung der Temperaturregulation bei Gesamtumschaltung durch das autogene Training. *Ztschr. exp. med*. 125, 469. Cited in Pelletier, *op. cit*.

Polzein, P., (1961), Therapeutic possibilities of Autogenic training in hyperthyroid conditions. In *Proceedings of Third International Congress of Psychiatry*. Montreal.

Polzein, P., (1961), Electrocardiogram changes during the first standard exercise, and respiratory changes during passive concentration on heaviness. In *Proceedings of Third International Congress of Psychiatry*. Montreal.

Prabhupadha, S., (1973), *On the Way to Krsna*. Los Angeles: Bhaktevedanta Book Trust.

Pribram, K. H., (1971), *Language of the Brain*. Monterey: C. Brooks/Cole Publishing Co.

Pribram, K. H., (1976), *Consciousness and the Brain*. New York: Plenum.

Priestman, T. J., Priestman, S. G. and Bradshaw, C., (1985), Stress and Breast Cancer. *British Journal of Cancer*, 51, 493-498.

Prigogine, I. and Stengers, I., (1985), *Order out of Chaos: Man's new dialogue with Nature*. London: Fontana.

Prosser, G. V., (1989), Does exercise reduce heart disease? Chapter 10 in Hartley, J. and Branthwaite, J. A., *op. cit*.

Prosser, G. V., Carson, P. and Phillips, R., (1985), Exercise after myocardial infarction: Longterm rehabilitation effects. *Journal of Psychosomatic Research*, 29, 5, 535-540.

Puharich, A., (1962), *Beyond Telepathy*. London: Pan Books.

Pullar, P., (1988), *Spiritual and Lay Healing*. Harmondsworth: Penguin.

Purvis, A., (1987), Sage of the inner limits. *Weekend Guardian.* Sat/Sun. July 1-2nd.

Pylyshyn, Z., (1973), What the mind's eye tells the mind's brain: A critique of mental imagery. *Psychological Bulletin,* 80, 1-24.

Quinn, J., (1984), Therapeutic touch as energy exchange. *Advances in Nursing Science,* January 42-49.

Rajneesh, B. S., (1983), *The Orange Book: The Meditation Techniques of Bhagwhan Shree Rajneesh.* Rajneeshpuram, Oregon: Rajneesh Foundation International.

Ramsell, J. and Murray, N., (1987), *Questions and Answers: Clarifying the basic principle and standards of the Bach Flower Remedies.* England: The Bach Centre.

Rankin-Box, D. F. (Ed.) (1988), *Complementary Health Therapies: A Guide for Nurses and the Caring Professions.* London: Croom Helm.

Ravitz, L. J., (1958), How electricity measures hypnosis. *Tomorrow,* 6, 49.

Redd, W. H., Andresen, G. V. and Minagawa, R. Y., (1982), Hypnotic control of anticipatory emesis in patients receiving cancer chemotherapy. *Journal of Consulting and Clinical Psychology,* Vol. 50, No. 1, 14-19.

Reibel, L. 1984), A homeopathic model of psychotherapy. *Journal of Humanistic Psychology* Winter, Vol. 24, No. 1, 9-48.

Reich, W., (1942), *The Function of the Orgasm,* trans Theodore P. Wolfe. New York: Orgon Institute Press. Second edition 1961, New York: Ferraro, Strauss and Giroux.

Reich, W., (1975), *Reich Speaks of Freud.* Harmondsworth: Penguin.

Reid, D., (1985), Japanese Religions. pp344-364 in J. R. Hinnels (Ed.) *A Handbook of Living Religions. Harmondsworth: Penguin.*

Rime, B. and Bonami, M., (1979), Overt and covert personality traits associated with coronary heart disease. *British Journal of Medical Psychology,* 52, 1, 77-84.

Roet, B., (1987), *All in the Mind.* London: MacDonald Optima.

Rogers, C. R., (1959), Toward a theory of creativity. pp69-82 In H. Anderson (Ed.) *Creativity and its cultivation.* New York: Harper and Row.

Rogers, M. P., Dubey, D. and Reich, P., (1979), The influence of the psyche and the brain on immunity and disease susceptibility: a critical review. *Psychosomatic Medicine,* 41 147-164.

Rosch, P. J., (1984), Stress and cancer. In C. L. Cooper (Ed.) *Psychosocial Stress and Cancer* Chichester: Wiley.

Rose, J. (Ed) (1970), *Proceedings of the International Congress of Cybernetics.* New York Gordon and Breech.

Rose, R. M., (1980), Endocrine responses to stressful psychological events. *Psychiatric Clinic of N. America. 3, 251-276.*

Rosenman, R. H., (1974), The role of behaviour patterns and neurogenic factors in the pathogenesis of coronary heart disease. pp123-141 in R. S. Eliot (Ed.) *Stress and the Heart* New York: Futura.

Rose, S., Kamin, L. J., and Lewontin, R. C., (1984), *Not in our Genes: biology, ideology and human nature.* Harmondsworth: Penguin.

Rosnow, R. L., (1981), *Paradigms in Transition: The methodology of social inquiry.* Oxford University Press.

Rossetti, H., (1983), *Colour: Why the world isn't grey.* Pelican.

Roszack, T., (1970), *The Making of a Counter Culture: Reflections on the counter culture and its youthful opposition.* London: Faber and Faber.

Rowden, R., (1984), Relaxation and visualisation techniques in patients with breast cancer. *Nursing Times,* Sept. 12. pp42-44.

Russell, B., (1948), *History of Western Philosophy and its connection with political and social circumstances from the earliest times to the present day.* London: Allen and Unwin.

Russell, B., (1959), *Mysticism and Logic and Other Essays.* London: Allen and Unwin.

Russell, P., (1978), *Meditation: Paths to tranquility.* London: BBC Publications.

Rycroft, C., (1979), *Reich.* London: Fontana Collins.

Ryle, G., (1949), *The Concept of Mind.* New York: Barnes and Noble.

Sacerdote, P., (1966), The uses of hypnosis in cancer patients. In Bahnson, C. B. and Kissen, D. M. (Eds.) *Psychophysiological Aspects of Cancer. Annals of NY Academy of Sciences,* 125(3), 101-119.

Sacerdote, P., (1982), Techniques of hypnotic intervention with pain patients. In Barber, J. and Adrian, C. (Eds.) *Psychological Appproaches to the Management of Pain.* New York: Brunner Mazel.

Sahtouris, E., (1990), The Brink of Maturity: Towards a Scientific Myth of our Times. *Leading Edge.* England: New Age Publications Ltd 1, July, 12-22.

Samuels, A., (1984), *Beyond the relaxation response: Self regulation mechanisms and clinical strategies.* Los Angeles, California: UCLA Extension. Oct. 26-28.

Sandroff, R., (1980), The Sceptic's Guide to Therapeutic Touch. *Registered Nurse.* Jan. pp26-29.

Saso, M., (1985), Chinese Religions. pp344-369 in Hinnells, J. R. (Ed.) *A Handbook of Living Religions.* Harmondsworth: Penguin.

Santa Maria, J., (1978), *Anna Yoga: the Yoga of food.* London: Rider and Co.

Saxena, R. P. and Saxena, U., (1978), Psychotherapeutic approach in the treatment of asthma. *Journal of Chronic Disease and Therapeutic Research,* 1, 25.

Schacter, S. and Singer, J. E., (1962), Cognitive, social and physiological determinants of emotional state. *Psychological Review,* 69, 379.

Scheffer, M., (1986), *Bach Flower Remedies: Theory and Practice.* Wellingborough, Northants.: Thorsons.

Schmale, A. and Iker, S. H., (1966), The effect of hopelessness and the development of cancer, I. Identification of uterine cervical cancer in women with atypical cytology. *Psychosomatic Medicine,* 28, 714-721.

Schmale, A. and Iker, S. H., (1971), Hopelessness as a predictor of cervical cancer. *Social Science and Medicine,* 5, 95-100.

Schneider, J., Smith, C. W. and Whitcher, S., (1982), The relationship of mental imagery to white blood cell (Neutrophil function). UN Archive Monograph, Michigan. Cited in Achterberg, J. *Imagery in Healing: Shamanism and Modern Medicine.* London: New Science Library, Routledge and Kegan Paul.

Schonfield, J., (1975), Psychology and life experience differences between Israeli women with benign and cancerous breast lesions. *Journal of Psychosomatic Research,* 19, 229-234.

Schrödinger, E., (1957), *Science Theory and Man.* New York: Dover.

Schultz, J. H., (1932), *Das Autogene Training.* Stuttgart: Geergthieme Verlag. Cited in Pelletier, *op. cit.*

Schultze, J. H. and Luthe, W., (1959), *Autogenic Training: a psychophysiologic approach to psychotherapy.* New York: Grune and Stratton.

Schultz, J. H. and Luthe, W., (1961), Autogenic Training. *Proceedings of Third International Congress of Psychiatry, Montreal.*

Schwartz, G. E., (1973), *Pros and Cons of Meditation: Anxiety, self control, drug abuse and creativity.* Paper delivered at 81st Annual Convention of the American Psychological Association, Montreal.

Schwartz, G. E. and Goleman, D. J., (1974), Meditation as an alternative to drug use: accompanying personality changes. Unpublished paper.

Schwartz, G. E. and Goleman, D. J., (1976), Meditation as an alternative to drug use: accompanying personality changes. Unpublished paper cited in Pelletier, K., *op. cit.*

Schwartz, J., (1980), *Human Energy Systems.* Hillsdale, NJ: Erlbaum.

Scott, E., (1983), *The People of the Secret.* G. B.: Octagon Press.

Selye, H., (1956), *The Stress of Life.* New York: McGraw Hill.

Siegel, B. S., (1986), *Love, Medicine and Miracles.* London: Rider.

Serrano, M., (1966), *C. J. Jung and Hermann Hesse.* Liverpool, London and Prescot: C. Tinling and Co.

Shah, I., (1973), *The Exploits of the Incomparable Mulla Nasrudin.* London: Pan.

Shapiro, D. H., (1982), Overview: clinical and physiological comparison of meditation with other self-control strategies. *American Journal of Psychiatry,* 139, 267-274.

Sharma, C. H., (1979), Ayurvedic Medicine, in Hill, A., *op. cit.*

Sharma, C. H., (1985), *The International Manual of Homeopathy and Natural Medicine,* Second edition. Wellingborough, Northants: Thorsons.

Shaw, W. A., (1946), The relaxation of muscular action potentials to imaginal weightlifting. *Archives of Psychology,* 247, 250.

Sheehan, P. W. and McConkey, K. M., (1982), *Hypnosis and Experience: the exploration of phenomena and process.* Hillsdale, New Jersey: Lawrence Erlbaum.

Sheikh, A. A. (Ed.) (1983), *Imagery: Current theory, research and application.* New York and Chichester: Wiley.

Shekelle, R. B., Raynor, W. J., Ostfield, M. D., Garron, D. C., Bieliauskas, L. A., Lin, S. C., Maliza, C. and Paul, O., (1981), Psychological depression and 17 year risk of death from cancer. *Psychosomatic Medicine,* 43, 117-125.

Shepard, R. N., (1975), Form, formation and transformation of internal representations. In Solso, R. (Ed), *Information Processing and Cognition: The Loyola Symposium.* Hillsdale, NJ: Erlbaum.

Shepard, R. N. and Cermack, G. W., (1973), Perceptual-cognitive explorations of a toroidal set of free-form stimuli. *Cognitive Psychology,* 4, 351, 377.

Shepard, R. N. and Cooper, L. A., (1975), Representation of colours in normal, blind and colour blind subjects. Paper presented at annual meeting of American Psychological Association, Chicago, September 2nd 1975. Reported in Shepard, R. N. Chapter 11 in J. S. Seamon (Ed.) *Human Memory: Contemporary Readings.* 1980. Oxford University Press.

Shepard, R. N. and Metzler, J., (1971), Mental rotation of 3-dimensional objects. *Science,* 171, 701-703.

Shepard, R. N., (1977), The Mental Image. Paper presented at American Psychological Association, San Francisco, August 29th. Cited in Seamon, J. S. (Ed.) *Human Memory: Contemporary Readings.* 1980. Oxford University Press.

Shepard, R. N., (1978), Externalization of mental images and the act of creation. In B. S. Randhawa and W. E. Goffman (Eds.) *Visual Learning, Thinking and Communication.* New York: Academic Press.

Shepard, R. N. and Podgorny, P., (1978), Cognitive processes that resemble perceptual processes. In Estes, W. K. (Ed.) *Handbook of Learning and Cognitive Processes.* Hillsdale, New Jersey: Lawrence Erlbaum.

Shepard, R. N., Kilpatric, D. W., Cunningham, J. P., (1975), The internal representation of numbers. *Cognitive Psychology,* 7, 82-138.

Shepard, R. N. and Judd, S. A., (1976), Perceptual illusion of rotation of 3-dimensional objects. *Science,* 191, 952

Shepard, R. N. and Feng, C., (1972), A chronometric study of mental paper folding. *Cognitive Psychology,* 3, 228-243.

Shepard, R. N. and Chipman, S., (1970), Second-order isomorphism of internal representations: shapes of states. *Cognitive Psychology,* 1, 1-17.

Simonton, O. C. and Matthews-Simonton, S., (1975), Belief systems and management of the emotional aspects of malignancy. *Journal of Transpersonal Psychology,* Vol. 8, 29-47.

Simonton, O. C., Matthews-Simonton, S. and Creighton, J., (1978), *Getting Well Again.* New York: Bantam.

Singh, R. H. and Udupa, K. N., (1976), Role of certain yogic practices in the prevention and treatment of gastro-intestinal disorders. *Journal Res. Med. Yoga and Homeo.* 11, 2, June, 51-9.

Skinner, B. F., (1973), *Beyond Freedom and Dignity.* Harmondsworth: Penguin.

Skinner, P. T., (1984), Skills not pills: learning to cope with anxiety symptoms. *Journal of the Royal College of Practitioners,* May. 258-259.

Smith, M. J., (1968), Paranormal effects on enzyme activity. *International Journal of Parapsychology,* Vol. 32, 281.

Smith, M. J., (1972), Paranormal effects on enzyme activity. *Human Dimensions* 1, 15-19.

Smith, R., (1988), Good Health: Review of Strong Medicine. *Observer,* Sunday, 3rd July, p43.

Smith, T., (1987), *Understanding Homeopathy.* Worthing, Sussex: Insight Editions.

Solomon, G. F., (1969), Emotions, stress, the CNS and Immunity. Second Conference on Psychophysiological aspects of cancer. *Annals of New York Academy of Science,* 335-342.

Spanos, N. P. and Barber, T. X., (1974), Towards a convergence in hypnosis research. *American Psychology,* 29, 500-511.

Spanos, N. P., (1986), Hypnosis and the modification of hypnotic susceptibility: A social psychological perspective. pp85-120 in Naish, P. L. N. (Ed.) *What is Hypnosis? Current theories and research.* Milton Keynes: Open University Press.

Spanos, N. P., (1982), A social psychology approach to hypnotic behaviour. In Weary, G. and Mirels, H. L. (Eds.) *Integrations of Clinical and Social Psychology.* Open University Press.

Sperry, W., (1962), Some general aspects of interhemispheric integration. In J. Young (Ed.) *Interhemispheric Relations and Cerebral Dominance Conference.* Baltimore: Johns Hopkins University Press.

Spiro, H., (1989), *Medicine Now.* BBC Radio 4, 10.1.89.

Stanway, A., (1982), *Alternative Medicine: A guide to natural therapies.* Harmondsworth: Penguin.

Steiner, R., (1969), *Occult Science: an outline.* (Trans by George and Mary Adams). London: R. Steiner Press.

Stephenson, J. B. P., (1978), Reversal of hypnosis - induced analgesia by Naloxone. *Lancet,* 11, 991-992.

Steptoe, A., (1974), The learned control of differential temperature in the human earlobe. *Biological Psychology,* 1, 237.

Stern, J. A., Brown, M., Ulett, G. H. and Stellen, I., (1977), A comparison of hypnosis, acupuncture, morphine, valium, aspirin and placebo in the management of experimentally induced pain. *Annals of New York Academy of the Sciences,* 296, 175-193.

Stevens, J. O., (1971), *Awareness: exploring, experimenting, experiencing.* Utah: Real People Press.

St. Exupéry, de. A., (1974), *The Little Prince.* London: Pan Books.

Stoll, B. A., (1979), Restraint of growth and spontaneous regression of cancer. In B. A. Stoll (Ed.) *Mind and Cancer Prognosis.* Chichester: Wiley.

Storr, A., (1973), *Jung.* Glasgow: William Collins Fontana.

Stovkis, B., Renes, B. and Landmann, H., (1961), Skin temperature under experimental stress and during autogenic training, in *Proc. Third Int. Congress of Psychiat.* Cited in Pelletier, *op. cit.*

Stoyva, J. and Budzynski., (1973), Cultivated low arousal - an antistress response? In Dicara, L. V. (Ed.) *Recent Advances in Limbic and Autonomic Nervous System Research.* New York: Plenum.

Stutley, M., (1985), *Hinduism: the eternal law. An introduction to the literature, cosmology and cults of the Hindu religion.* Wellingborough, Northants: Aquarian Press.

Sullivan, J. W. N., (1949), *The Limitations of Science.* New York.

Suzuki, (1958), second series *Essays in Zen Buddhism.* London: Rider.

Szasz, T. S., (1979), *The Myth of Psychotherapy: mental healing as religion, rhetoric and repression.* Oxford: Oxford University Press.

Tansley, D., (1972), *Radionics and the Subtle Anatomy of Man.* Essex, England: Health Science Press.

Tansley, D., Rae, M. and Westlake, A., (1977), *Dimensions of Radionics: New Techniques of Instrumented Distant Healing.* Essex, England: C. W. Daniel and Co.

Tart, C. T. (Ed.) (1969), *Altered States of Consciousness.* London: John Wiley and Sons.

Tart, C., (1975), *Transpersonal Psychologies.* London: Routledge and Kegan Paul.

Taugher, V. T., (1958), Hypno-anaesthesia. *Wisconsin Medical Journal,* 57, 95.

Taylor, A., (1987), *I Fly out with Bright Feathers: The quest of a novice healer.* London: Fontana/Collins.

Thomas, D. and Abbas, K. A., (1978), Comparison of Transcendental Meditation and progressive relaxation in reducing anxiety. *British Medical Journal,* 4, 1749.

Throll, D. A., (1981), Transcendental Meditation and progressive relaxation: their psychological effects. *Journal of Clinical Psychology,* 37, 776-781.

Timbs, O., (1989), Treatment of pain. In Gillie, O. (Ed.) *Health Update.* Independent Times, 3rd January.

ˈoffler, A., (1985), Science and change. Foreword to Prigogine, I., and Stengers, I., *Order out of Chaos: Man's Dialogue with Nature*. London: Fontana.

ˈompkins, P. and Bird, C., (1973), *The Secret Life of Plants*. Penguin, Allen Lane.

ˈotton, N. and Edmondson, E., (1988), *Reichian Bodywork: Melting the blocks to life and love*. Dorset, England: Prism Press.

ˈrechmann, E. J. (translator - undated) *The Essays of Montaigne*. New York and London: Oxford University Press.

ˈurner, J. A. and Chapman, C. P., (1981), Psychological intervention in chronic pain: A critical review. I. Relaxation and Biofeedback. *Pain*, 12, 1, 21.

ˈurton, P., (1988), Healing: therapeutic touch. Chapter 10, 148-162 in D. F. Rankin-Box (Ed.) *Complementary Health Therapies: A guide for nurses and the caring professions*. London: Croom Helm.

ˈyndall, J. (1868), *Faraday as a Discoverer*. London: Longmans, Green and Co.

Jdupa, K. N., (1978), *Disorders of Stress and their Management*. Benares Hindu University press. Varanas.

Jpledger, J., (1983), *Craniosacral Therapy*. Chicago: Eastland.

ˈachon, L., (1973), cited in Pelletier, *op. cit.*

ˈalins, S., (1966), Cognitive effects of false heart-rate feedback. *J. of Personality and Social Psychology*, 4, 400-8.

ˈalins, S. and Ray, A. A., (1967), Effects of cognitive sensitization of avoidance behaviour. *J. of Personality and Social Psychology*, 7, 345-50.

ˈilenskaya, L., (1982), Studies in skin vision. *Applied psi Newsletter*.1. Issue 2 May/June.

ˈithoulkas, G., (1980), *The Science of Homeopathy*. New York: Grove.

ˈivekananda, S., (1972), Vedanta Philosophy. A lecture and discussion at Harvard University. Swarmi Niramoyananda: UD Bodhan Office, Calcutta, Seventh Edition. July.

ˈivekenanda, S., (1974), *Practical Vedanta*. Himalayas: Advaita Ashrama, October.

ˈivekenanda, S., (1975), *The East and the West Himalayas:* Advaita Ashrama, December.

ˈollmar, K., (1987), *Journey through the Chakras* Bath: Gateway Books.

ˈagstaff, G. F., (1977), An experimental study of compliance and post-hypnotic amnesia. *British Journal of Social and Clinical Psychology* 16, 225-8.

ˈagstaff, G. F., (1981), *Hypnosis, Compliance and Beliefs*. Brighton: Harvester Press.

ˈagstaff G. F., (1986), Hypnosis as compliance and belief: A socio-cognitive view. pp.59-84 in Naish. P. L. (ed) *What is Hypnosis?; current theories and research*. Milton Keynes: Open University Press.

ˈaley, A., (1934), reprinted 1942. *The Way and its Power: A study of the Tao-te Ching and its place in Chinese thought*. London: George Allen and Unwin.

ˈallace, R. K., (1970), Physiological effects of Transcendental Meditation. *Science*, 167, 1751-54.

ˈallace R. K. and Benson H., (1972), The Physiology of Meditation. ch.14 pp 125-131 in *Altered States of Awareness readings from Scientific American*. San Francisco: W. H. Freeman and Co.

ˈard, D., (1976), *Music as relaxation for spastic Children: heart and hands and voices*. Oxford University Press.

ˈarga, C., (1987), Pain's Gatekeeper. *Psychology Today,* August 51-6.

Warren, R. M. and Warren, R. P., (1968), *Helmholtz on perception: its physiology an development.* New York: Wiley.

Watson, J. D., (1968), *The Double Helix.* New York: The New American Library.

Watson, L., (1973), *Supernature: The Natural History of the Supernatural.* London: Hodd and Stoughton.

Watson, L., (1974), *The Romeo Error: A Matter of Life and Death.* London: Hodder an Stoughton.

Watson, L., (1976), *Gifts of Unknown Things.* London: Hodder and Stoughton.

Watson, L., (1985), *Dreams of Dragons.* London: Hodder and Stoughton.

Watts, A., (1961), *Psychotherapy East and West.* New York.

Watts, A., (1976), *Tao: The Watercourse Way.* London: Jonathan Cape.

Watts, A., (1978), *The Two Hands of God: The myths of polarity.* London: Rider and Co.

Waxman, D., (1986), The Development of Hypnosis as a therapeutic force. pp13-36 in Nais P. L. N. (Ed) *What is Hypnosis?: current theories and research.* Milton Keynes: Ope University Press.

Weatherhead, L. D., (1951), *Psychology, Religion and Healing.* London: Hodder and Stoughto

Weitz, M., (1980), *Health Shock: A guide to ineffective and hazardous medical treatmen* Newton Abbott and London: David and Charles.

Welch, A. T., (1985), Islam. pp123-170 in Hinnells J. R. (Ed.) *A Handbook of Living Religion* Harmondsworth: Pelican.

West, M., (1979), Meditation. *British Journal of Psychiatry,* 135. 457-67.

West, M., (1980), Meditation and the EEG. *Psychological Medicine.* 10, 369-75.

West, M., (1980), Physiological effects of meditation. *Journal of Psychosomatic Research,* 24 265-73.

Westlake, A. T., (1977), *The Origins and History of Psionic medicine.* London: Psionic Medica Society.

Whyte, L. L., (1954), *Accent on Form.* New York: World Perspectives.

Wilson, V. S., (1987), Autogenic training in the context of Yoga. Ch. 10 pp 116- in Gharote D. and Lockhart, M., *op. cit.*

Wilson, A. and Bek, L., (1987), *What Colour are you: the way to health through colou* Wellingborough, Northants.: Aquarian Press.

Wilson-Ross, N., (1973), *Hinduism, Buddhism, Zen.* London: Faber.

Wise, A. Biofeedback Meditation and the Awakened Mind: A new gateway to an ancient path Ch12, pp132-150 in Gharote, D. and Lockhart, M., *op. cit.*

Wittgenstein, L., (1953), *Philosophical Investigations.* (G. E. M. Anscombe, trans). New York Macmillan.

Wittgenstein, L., (1978), *Tractatus Logico-philosophicus.* London: Routledge, Kegan Paul.

Wittstock, W., (1956), Untersuchungen über cortikale Einflüsse auf korperienen Aktionsströme. *Psychiat. neurol. med. psychol.* 2/3, 85.

White, K. D., (1978), Salivation: the signifance of imagery in its voluntary control *Psychophysiology 15, 3, 196-203.*

White, L. L., (1954), *Accent on Form: World perspectives.* New York.

Wolpe, J., (1977), Systematic desensitization based on relaxation. In Morse, S. J. and Watson R. I. (eds). *Psychotherapies: a comparative case book*, 298-306. New York: Holt Rinehart Winston.

Wolpe, J., (1958), *Psychotherapy by Reciprocal Inhibition*. Stanford University Press.

Wood, B., (1987), *The Healing Power of Colour*. Wellingborough, Northants: Aquarian Press.

Zeltzer, L. K., (1980), The adolescent with cancer. In Kellerman, J. (Eds.) *Psychological Aspects of Childhood Cancer*. Springfield, Illinois: Chas C. Thomas.

Zimbardo, P. G., (1969), *The Cognitive Control of Motivation*. Scott Foresman.

Zukar, G., (1980), *The Dancing Wu-Li Masters: An overview of the new physics*. London: Fontana.

Index